THE CELLS OF THE BODY

A History of Somatic Cell Genetics

HENRY HARRIS

Sir William Dunn School of Pathology
University of Oxford

COLD SPRING HARBOR LABORATORY PRESS
1995

THE CELLS
OF THE BODY
*A History
of Somatic Cell
Genetics*

Cover: Autoradiograph showing a heterokaryon produced by fusing a labelled human cell with an unlabelled mouse cell. The human nucleus in the heterokaryon is labelled, but the mouse nucleus is not. (From the original series of experiments described by Harris and Watkins 1965.)

Library of Congress Cataloging-in-Publication Data

Harris, Henry, 1925–
    Cells of the body : a history of somatic cell genetics / Henry
    Harris.
        p.   cm.
    Includes bibliographical references and indexes.
    ISBN 0-87969-460-2 (alk. paper)
    1. Cytogenetics.   2. Somatic cells.   I. Title.
QH441.5.H37 1995   95-23314
574.87'322--dc20   CIP

All Cold Spring Harbor Laboratory Press publications may be ordered directly from Cold Spring Harbor Laboratory Press, 10 Skyline Drive, Plainview, New York 11803-2500. Phone: 1-800-843-4388 in Continental U.S. and Canada. All other locations: (516) 349-1930. FAX: (516) 349-1946.

For some old friends in a far-off country

Contents

Preface

There are now many scientists for whom last year's discoveries are already old hat. I am not one of them. How we have arrived at the beliefs we now hold, either about the cell or anything else, is, for me, only marginally less interesting than the beliefs themselves. So I make no apology for writing this history of my subject. But one of my colleagues at Oxford, a most eminent historian, once said to me that he thought the history of science too important to be left to ageing scientists. I did not have the wit then to ask him whether it was the age of the scientists that worried him or their quality as historians. It is difficult to see, nonetheless, how someone who is not intimately familiar with the ideas and the technology that underlie a scientific discipline can write perceptively about it; and I hope that what I have written does not display too prominently the failing of my powers. Another of my colleagues, now long gone, used to divide scientists into two groups: the discoverers and the colonisers. Throughout this book I have borne this distinction in mind and have found often enough in the 19th as well as the 20th century that the voice of the discoverer has been all but drowned by the clamour of powerful colonisers. I have enjoyed reading the works of the 19th century more than those of the 20th, and much more than those of the last decade or so. Virtually every paper that I consulted in the 19th century was written by a single author who described work that he himself had done. Nineteenth century papers inevitably reflect the characters of their authors: the argumentative pedantry of Flemming, the infinite patience of van Beneden, the experimental brilliance of Boveri. But what can a paper with 58 authors (the highest tally I came across) tell me of the character of any of them?

Twenty-five years ago I wrote a little book called *Nucleus and Cytoplasm* in which I presented one man's imperfect view of the cell as it then appeared to him. I now offer one man's imperfect view of how the structure of our present understanding of cell heredity came to be assembled. Writing this book has given me much pleasure; but, having finished it, I look forward with even greater pleasure to the prospect of spending more of my time with my experiments.

I wish to thank Valerie Boasten who, in addition to her many other duties, undertook the immense task of turning my barely legible manuscript into impeccable copy ready for press. I am also most grateful to Catriona Simpson and Joan Ebert of Cold Spring Harbor Laboratory Press for their meticulous attention to every detail in the editorial process.

H. H.

Oxford, Hilary 1994

THE CELLS
OF THE BODY

1
SOMATIC CELLS AS GENETIC UNITS

THE BEGINNINGS

Before it could be envisaged that genetic methods might be used to study the cells of the body, it had to be established that these cells were entities whose characteristic features were inherited in a predictable and systematic manner. It took the best part of 70 years of observation and argument before it was finally agreed, at about the beginning of the 20th century, that this was indeed the case. This protracted controversy revolved around two fundamental questions. Could body cells be formed *de novo* from less highly organised noncellular material? And if, like the organisms that they constituted, such cells were able to generate progeny, did they endow their progeny with a faithful copy of their own hereditary material? The first question was, of course, intimately connected with the concurrent debate about the possibility of 'spontaneous generation' of organisms (*generatio aequivoca*). As Redi, Spallanzani, Bassi, Schulze, Schönlein, Vogel and, finally, Pasteur drove their nails into the coffin of *generatio aequivoca*, so it became increasingly difficult, as the 19th century wore on, to defend the view that cells could be generated spontaneously. But the idea died hard.

As far as I can discover, the first systematic assault on the assumption that cells could arise *de novo* out of less highly organised material came, surprisingly enough to a modern eye, from a *Naturphilosoph*, Lorenz Oken (Fig. 1). *Naturphilosophie* gets short shrift in most contemporary histories of science, and justifiably so if one concentrates on its excesses. But it is easy to forget that much before the middle of the 19th century, the categorical distinction between observation and speculation that now dominates the biological sciences could hardly have been conceived. All those formidable 18th century figures whom we would now recognise as experimental scientists were at the same time philosophers and saw themselves as such. It is therefore not surprising that in Oken's writings we find an inextricable mixture of empirical observations that we accept and speculative arguments that appear to have no roots in the real world at all. Oken's *Die Zeugung* (perhaps best translated as Procreation) appeared in 1805. It is a rare book and although, after Singer (1931), it is often cited, it seems unlikely that it can often have been read. Oken took the view that the fundamental units of which living forms were composed were the 'infusoria', a name given at that time to a heterogeneous collection of organisms that included protozoa as well as bacteria. Here are the key

1

FIGURE 1 Lorenz Oken (1779–1851) appears to have been the first to propose that the body was an agglomerate of independently viable microscopic units that never arose *de novo* out of inanimate matter but were always formed by the division of pre-existing units. He argued that the growth and development of both plants and animals were driven by the multiplication and specialisation of these elementary components. (From B.J. Gottlieb and A. Berg 1942 in *Das Antlitz des Germanischen Artzes in vier Jahrhunderten* [*Courtesy of Rembrandt Verlag GMBH, Berlin*].)

passages from *Die Zeugung*: "The simplest living beings that the eye, and even the microscope, reveal to us are the infusoria, beings in which the chaos of creation is renewed and disappears each day. They arise whenever organic bodies decay, in all plant and animal infusions whether open to the air or covered, cold or warm". But this *generatio aequivoca* is not seen as creation *de novo*. It is "not the generation of an animal by coalescence of organic material, not the creation of animals that didn't previously exist, but the disaggregation of a composite form of organisation into its constituent parts; not creation by mating or by mere chance, indeed not creation at all, but, strictly speaking, simply the disaggregation of infusoria that had previously grown together into a mass". "If all flesh decomposes into infusoria, then the sentence can be inverted, and all higher animals must be composed of infusoria as their essential elements".

Basing his case on the work of Abraham Trembley (1744, 1747), who had observed that the multiplication of bell-polyps was produced by the division of the mature polyp longitudinally into two, Oken goes on to argue that the growth of higher organisms is similarly due to the multiplication of the infusoria of which they are composed: "The creation of a plant is a synthesis of infusoria, for this creation involves growth—an increase in size—and the only way that a family of infusoria can increase in size is by multiplication, by joining together of living elements which, moreover, must also be present in pollen. Thus all creation in the organic world is a synthesis of infusoria". In the light of this conclusion, Oken attacks a dictum that he attributes to Harvey: *omne vivum ex ovo*. Several of the principal contributors to the development of the cell doctrine in the 19th century rang the changes on this Latin tag, but, as quoted by Oken, it is not to be found in Harvey. In the section containing supplementary material at the end of the *De generatione animalium*, the first point that Harvey makes is indeed that an egg is the common origin of all animals. But he goes on to explain that by 'egg' he means any primordium that is capable of giving rise to a living form. He makes no distinction between the worm or scolex of Aristotle and an egg. However, in the allegorical drawing that forms the frontispiece of the *De generatione, Ex ovo omnia* is written across two halves of an egg that have been pulled apart. *Ex ovo omnia* is obviously absurd, and it is reassuring to find that these words were added after Harvey's death (Keele 1965). The version attacked by Oken came from von Siebold, and since the egg from Oken's point of view is not the ultimate origin of life, he ends *Die Zeugung* with the words: "*Nullum vivum ex ovo! Omne vivum e vivo*".

Omne vivum e vivo is as categorical a denial of spontaneous generation as you could want; and if, in *Die Zeugung*, the word 'cell' is substituted for 'infusorium' we have a view of the basic organisation of higher animal and plant forms that is not too far removed from our own. That Oken made no distinction between 'infusoria' and the cells of higher forms is not remarkable. In 1805, little enough was known about the properties of either category, and it must have seemed altogether plausible to suppose that, in principle, one was dealing with the same sort of thing in the two situations. In his later writings on the composition of higher organisms, no doubt because a good deal of information about infusoria had accrued in the interim, Oken substituted the word *Urbläschen* (primary vesicles) for infusoria. In the second edition of his *Lehrbuch der Naturphilosophie*, published in 1831 (the first edition of 1809 was not available to me), he concludes that the growth of a plant is caused by the multiplication of *Urbläschen* which elongate because of the polarity of the plant and eventually differentiate to form all the mature plant tissues. In the spaces between the *Urbläschen*, the process of differentiation produces vessels through which the sap runs. It is clear that Oken had a strikingly prescient view of the role of the cell in the formation of higher animals and plants, even if the words infusorium and primary vesicle that he used to describe the cell now have a hopelessly obsolete, if not misleading, connotation. Although now largely forgotten, Oken's work was very widely read in his day. The *Lehrbuch der Naturphilosophie* ran to three editions, the last appearing in 1843, and the second edition was translated into English. I found a copy of this translation not only in the Radcliffe Science Library at Oxford, but also in one of the college libraries that I have consulted.

CELL DIVISION

Cell division was observed in unicellular forms of life (infusoria) more than half a century before it was clearly seen in multicellular organisms. According to Baker (1951, 1953, 1955) who reviewed the early literature, the first observations on protozoa were made by Trembley (1744, 1747). Trembley described cell division in the diatom *Synedra* in 1766, and Müller described it in the desmid *Closterium* in 1786. Ehrenberg (1838) in his monograph, *Die Infusions-thierchen*, described division and segmentation in a whole range of unicellular organisms. However, these early observations, including those of Ehrenberg, were made at a time when it was generally held that the infusoria were generated *de novo* out of the fluid in which they found themselves, and none of these observers envisaged the possibility that cell division might be the only way in which such organisms could be formed. But who was it who first described cell division in multicellular organisms, and, more important, who was the first to propose that this was the *only* way in which cells could be generated?

In our quest for the answers to these questions, we are not helped by the classical review of the subject given by Julius Sachs (1875) in his famous history of botany. Indeed, in some ways Sachs is perhaps deliberately misleading. Unfortunately, historical accounts of the origins of the cell doctrine seem to have engaged patriotic emotions to an unusually high degree, and several of the best known versions show an unmistakably nationalistic bias. Sachs, for example, states that, in this connection, only the Germans are worth talking about (*...nur von Deutschen die Rede ist*). Since Grew, Sachs claims, the English have contributed nothing, and this is also true of the Italians since Malpighi. The French had indeed published a lot but, in Sachs's view, they did not resolve any fundamental questions. Sachs is clear that the honour of being the first to describe cell division must go to Mohl. Sachs sets out the case for Mohl in great detail and weighs it against the competing case that might be made for de Mirbel. Mohl appears to have first observed cell division in the confervae (filamentous algae, silkweeds). The initial record of his observations appeared in his doctoral thesis which was printed in 1835. In 1837, the work was published in *Flora* (Mohl 1837). In 1838, according to Sachs, Mohl accurately described the development of the septum in young epidermal cells and the subsequent splitting of the septum into two lamellae; and in 1839, Mohl reported the division of spore mother cells in the liverwort *Anthoceros*. de Mirbel saw cell division in the liverwort *Marchantia* and described the successive formation of septa in the regions where budding was about the take place. de Mirbel presented the first part of his treatise on *Marchantia* to the Académie des Sciences in Paris in 1831–1832, but it was not published until 1835 (de Mirbel 1835). However, in Sachs's judgement, de Mirbel misinterpreted his observations, whereas Mohl's descriptions were accurate and definitive. Nonetheless, both de Mirbel and Mohl claimed to have observed the formation of cells *de novo*. The reference to Dumortier in Sachs's book is especially interesting. Sachs gives him no more than a sentence in which he baldly states that Dumortier observed cell division in 1832 (three years earlier than the first of Mohl's publications on the subject). Sachs does not give the original reference to Dumortier's paper, but only a secondary source, Meyens's *Neues System, 11*: 344. This implies that Sachs had not read Dumortier's paper when he wrote that simple sentence about him. But this is rather surprising because Dumortier's paper, although written in French, was published in a well known German journal (Dumortier 1832); and one might have thought that Sachs, anxious to settle the question of priority, would have been eager to consult a paper that decisively antedated Mohl. In fact the paper, although published in 1832, was presented to the Académie des Sciences in Paris by Cuvier in 1829, and is, in my view, the first and decisive demonstration of cell division in a multicellular organism (Fig. 2).

FIGURE 2 Barthélemy Charles Dumortier (1797–1878) was the first to observe cell division in a multicellular organism and to conclude from direct experimental evidence that the growth of the organism as a whole was indeed determined by this mechanism alone. Dumortier was also a politician and eventually became a minister of state. The bust shown here was sculpted in the last year of his life and is to be found in the Jardin Botanique National de Belgique at Meise. *(Courtesy of the Service des Archives, Université Libre de Bruxelles.)*

Dumortier's paper has a rather generalised title—*Recherches sur la structure comparée et le développement des animaux et des végétaux*—but the detailed observations described in it were all made on silkweed, the same material as that subsequently used by Mohl. Dumortier was able to show with absolute clarity that new cells were formed by the division of pre-existing cells, that this process occurred only in the terminal cells of the filament, and that it was achieved by the formation of a partition that divided the new cell from the old. The key passages are worth quoting at length:

> The development of the confervae is as simple as their structure. It is brought about by the addition of new cells to old, and this addition always takes place at the tip [of the filament]. The terminal cell elongates to a greater extent that those below it, and halfway down the cell in the internal fluid an extension of the inner cell wall is produced in such a way that it divides the cell into two parts. The lower of these remains stationary whereas the upper, now terminal, again produces a new internal partition and so on. There is no way of determining whether this partition at the mid-point is, in principle, single or double, but it is certainly true that, later on, it appears to be double in conjugated filaments, and when two cells come apart of themselves, each of them is closed at its extremity. This can be easily demonstrated in the confervae when they have matured or when the cellular tissue has been frozen, for in that condition the individual cells still enclose the fluids that they previously contained, which would not be possible if they were not sealed by a membrane. The observed production of a mid-line partition in the confervae seems to us to provide a perfectly clear explanation of the origin and development of cells, which has hitherto remained unexplained...

Moreover, Dumortier takes an uncompromising stand against the notion that cells can be generated *de novo* by the coalescence of less highly organised particles in the surrounding fluid:

> M. Kieser's view is thus untenable. What's more, this view, as well as the one advanced by M. Tréviranus is based on a hypothesis that is anything but proved—the idea that granules or globular particles can be transformed into cells. We believe that we can be quite certain on the strength of our own observations that this transformation never takes place and that starch grains as well as globular particles are entirely different entities from cells. On the other hand, the production within the cell of a mid-line partition fits in so well with the organisation of the rest of the plant that it can hardly be denied.

Dumortier does not for a moment believe that the confervae are a special case. What he had observed in these simple filaments he believes to be true for plant growth generally:

> The study of infinitely simple creatures presents us with an anatomical structure that is already laid down, and this simplicity makes observation less uncertain because it openly displays what complex creatures display in their interior. We have seen that the formation of cells in the confervae is brought about by the production of a mid-line partition; but this occurs in a strictly linear fashion. The cells do not form lateral agglomerations or join together or organise themselves into organic centres. The new cells are laid down in a linear series, and since they develop only and always at the tip of the filament they follow the law of indefinite elongation. Here again the confervae display openly what higher plants hide within them. All production of vessels or of fibres, all series of cells follow the same law which seems to apply to the whole of the plant kingdom. The fronds of algae, the thalluses of fungi, the stalks of mosses and Jungermanniales display the same characteristics. It is only that in these cases the cells, instead of developing in a single series as in the confervae, often show substantial connections between series.

It is clear that Dumortier not only got it right, but got it as completely right as one could reasonably expect given the state of knowledge at that time and the instruments available to him. Even in the matter of the septum having two lamellae, a point stressed by Sachs, Dumortier anticipated Mohl by several years. And unlike Mohl, Dumortier decisively rejected the idea of cell formation *de novo*.

In his history of cytology, Hughes (1959) states that Vaucher also observed cell division in silkweeds, but at a much earlier date than Dumortier (Vaucher 1803). Vaucher's *Histoire des conferves d'eau douce* is a delightful book with splendid illustrations. It was written in the post-revolutionary republican era, so that experiments are described as having been done in the months of Pluviôse or Thermidor, and scientific colleagues are referred to as Citoyen X or Citoyen Y. Vaucher's main interest was in the taxonomy of silkweeds and he concentrates on the various modes and stages of sexual reproduction in these plants (conjugation, fertilization, sporulation, germination). Vegetative growth receives scant attention. Vaucher certainly saw filaments emerging from the germinating spores and noted that as the filament elongated the number of partitions in it increased. However, I doubt whether he actually saw the formation of a new cell by the division of a pre-existing one, and nothing in his work indicates that he had any idea of the general significance of cell division for the growth of the plant. Here are the relevant passages:

> At almost the same moment and on the same day, or at least in the same week, all the seeds of *conferva jugalis* (I had several thousands) opened up at one end just like the two cotyledons of a seed from which an embryo is being formed; and from the bottom of the opening a green sack emerged, very small at first, but which soon elongated to such an extent that it was several times as long as the globule itself. In the interior of the sack, spirals soon appeared. They were accompanied by their bright dots as in a fully developed plant. The tube itself showed partitions, first one, then two, then a larger number. Finally the offspring broke away from its seed and floated alone on the liquid. Then, apart from its size and its two ends which were still pointed, it completely resembled the plant that gave birth to it.

> As far as the internal partitions that divide the plant are concerned, they are, like the tube itself, formed by a very fine transparent membrane. Although they appear single, I have reason to believe that they are double; for I have often seen the tube separate into two, or into three, or even into as many pieces as the number of compartments that the tube originally contained. And since these separated compartments do not lose their contents but retain the green material and the spirals that they originally enclosed, it must be presumed that they were shut tight. Otherwise, the phenomenon that I observed could not have taken place.

In this Vaucher does anticipate Dumortier.

> The tubes of silkweed with which we are here concerned can therefore be considered not as single plants but rather as aggregates of a large number of plants. On this view, each compartment in the tube is itself a plant which does not communicate with the others contained in the same tube. One compartment can be apposed to another or separated from it. Each has its own envelope, its spirals, its particles, in a word, everything that constitutes a plant, and, as we shall soon see, it can also reproduce itself.

All this is admirable, but my reason for believing that Vaucher did not actually see cell division is that he does not note anywhere that the formation of the internal partitions (and hence of the new cell) takes place only in the terminal cell of the filament. It is difficult to believe that if he had seen cell division he would not have reported where in the filament he saw it. So, as far as I can judge, it is Dumortier who must be credited not only with the first description of cell division in a multicellular organism, but also with an accurate appreciation of its significance.

The second part of Dumortier's paper deals with animal cells. Unlike the first part, it does not contain any first-hand observations. This is not surprising, given the state of knowledge about animal tissue at that time and the histological techniques available. Apart from early observations on the formation of the cleavage furrow in the egg, which were not then equated with cell division, more than a decade elapsed between the presentation of Dumortier's paper to the Académie and the first descriptions of cell division in animal cells (Remak 1841a,b). Nonetheless, Dumortier takes it for granted that in animals just as in plants, growth is achieved by the multiplication of cells in a manner analogous to what he had observed in silkweeds. In this he adumbrates the principal thesis later advanced by Schwann (1839). He also makes an interesting generalisation of a rather 'naturphilosophical' kind. Conscious of the immense importance of his observation that cell division takes place only at the extremities of silkweed filaments, Dumortier proposes that all cell multiplication in plants is similarly 'centrifugal', that is, limited to the peripheral zones of the plant such as growing tips or buds. He suggests, on the other hand, that growth in the animal is 'centripetal' in the sense that cell multiplication takes place internally and generates peripheral cells that do not multiply. While this generalisation is, of course, totally inadequate to explain the complex patterns of cell multiplication that we now know to occur in animal development, there are several tissues, for example stratified epithelia, where it would not be misplaced to describe the distribution of multiplying cells as 'centripetal' in Dumortier's sense.

OMNIS CELLULA E CELLULA

With hindsight, it is difficult to see why Dumortier's ideas on the constitution of plants and the role of cell division in their development were not at once taken up and explored further. This can hardly have been because his work was unknown. I think it more likely that his conclusions were not thought to have general application and were soon displaced by the resonance of the views propounded by Schleiden and Schwann. The celebrated papers of these two authors (Schleiden 1838; Schwann 1839), commonly cited as the cornerstones of the cell doctrine, added nothing but confusion to the study of how new cells were generated. Schleiden believed that new cells were normally formed *de novo* out of a homogeneous viscid solution (*Gummilösung*). In this solution he purported to see the formation of granules that progressively enlarged to become nucleoli. The material that was to generate the cell (the *Cytoblastem*) then made its appearance and induced the formation of vesicles which became progressively more distended. These distended vesicles eventually developed into cells. Sachs (1875) expressed the view that it was difficult to find a single correct observation in Schleiden's paper, and I am inclined to agree with him apart from the fact that Schleiden did insist that plants were composed entirely of cells and their products. This was, as I have indicated, by no means a wholly new idea, but Schleiden's vigorous and often polemical advocacy of it was remarkably influential and might explain, although it does not justify, his prominent place in the history of biology. Schwann's view of how new cells were generated in the animal body was taken directly from Schleiden, with whom he had personal contacts. Schwann also believed that the nucleolus was the first structure to appear, and that the nucleus was organised around it out of the *Cytoblastem* by a process akin to crystallization. The rest of the cell was then assembled around the nucleus and finally partitioned off from its surroundings by the cell membrane. This, according to Schwann, was "the universal principle governing the development of all the elementary components of organisms".

The model proposed by Schleiden and endorsed by Schwann seems to have been very persuasive, for although there were reports of cell division in plant cells both before and after the publication of Schleiden's papers, several years had to elapse before Schleiden's views on cell formation were finally demolished; and in the case of animal cells the issue was not publicly decided until the appearance of Virchow's famous paper in 1855. The first frontal assault on Schleiden's position appears to have been made by Unger (1841), who concluded from observations on the position and size of daughter cells that they must have been generated by cell division. In a later paper, Unger (1844) took Schleiden to task again and concluded that the growth of all parts of the plant was normally driven by meristematic cell division. Nägeli (1844), in a paper that was widely read at the time, described cell division in a number of plant species and concluded that cell formation *de novo* was limited to a few exceptional situations. Nägeli's paper did much to undermine the model proposed by Schleiden.

With regard to animal cells, the key figure in the demolition of Schwann's 'universal principle' was Robert Remak, a scientist whose magnitude is only now beginning to be appreciated (Fig. 3). In a magisterial paper published in 1852, Remak states that, at the very first promulgation of the cell doctrine, the proposition that animal cells could be formed *de novo* seemed to him to be as improbable as the *generatio aequivoca* of unicellular organisms (Remak 1852). It was this scepticism that prompted him to initiate his studies of the formation of red blood cells in the chick embryo. The first published account of his observations appeared in 1841 (Remak 1841a,b), that is, only two years after Schwann's famous paper. Remak showed clearly that red cells were not generated *de novo* but arose by division of pre-existing cells. This was not a chance observation, but one that Remak demonstrated regularly to the classes he gave as a *Privatdozent* at the University of Berlin. In 1845, he described the formation of new muscle cells by division of pre-existing cells aligned in the primitive muscle bundles (Remak 1845). By the time he wrote his 1852 paper, he had seen cell division in other parts of the developing embryo and especially clearly in the primordium of the rudimentary vertebral column. (This region is of interest because it was in the *chorda dorsalis* that Johannes Müller first drew Schwann's attention to the similarity between the histological appearance of this animal tissue and the cellular structure of plants.) By 1852, Remak had also reached the conclusion that cell division followed by morphological mod-

FIGURE 3 Robert Remak (1815–1865) provided the decisive experimental evidence that in the animal body cells were produced only by the division of pre-existing cells. He argued that this was true not only for normal growth but also for pathological new growths. He also appears to have been the first to describe division of the cell nucleus and to observe the multiplication of vertebrate cells outside the body. Only two photographs of Remak are known to have survived. This is the better of the two. *(Courtesy of Prof. Heinz-Peter Schmiedebach and the Institut für Geschichte der Medizin, Freie Universität Berlin.)*

ification of the progeny was the general mechanism that determined the development of the whole embryo:

> At this point my aim is merely to draw attention, provisionally, to the fact that in the primordia of the most diverse tissues you can observe progressive division of existing cells, but nowhere do you find nuclei or cells being formed in the extracellular fluid.

Moreover, in the 1852 paper, Remak argued that the conclusions he had drawn from the developing embryo also applied to pathological processes:

> These findings are as relevant to pathology as they are to physiology. It can hardly be disputed that pathological tissue formations are simply variants of

normal embryological patterns of development, and it is not probable that it is their prerogative to generate cells in the extracellular fluid. The so-called 'organisation of plastic exudates' and the earliest stages of the development of tumours need investigation in this respect. On the strength of the conclusions that many years of critical experiments have generated, I make bold to assert that pathological tissues are not, any more than normal tissues, formed in an extracellular cytoblastema but are the derivatives or progeny of normal tissues in the organism.

Remak also appears to have been the first to use hardening agents to improve the definition of histological preparations. This enabled him to demonstrate the cell membrane in the frog's egg and to show that the segmentation of the egg to produce blastomeres was simply cell division in which the membrane acted as a ligature to cut the cell into two (*Abschnürung*) (Remak 1854a). In the same year, Remak extended his observations on malignant tumours and again argued that these arose from pre-existing cells and grew as a consequence of cell division (Remak 1854b). Remak's great book on the development of vertebrates appeared a year later (Remak 1855), and in the final chapter entitled *Die Zellentheorie* he spells out his definitive position on the central and indispensable role of cell division in physiological and pathological development.

Remak's conclusions were not easily or generally accepted. In a paper that appeared in 1858, he reviewed the reaction to his work in some detail. The observations on cell division that he had reported in 1841 were confirmed by Kölliker in 1845 and Gerlach in 1847, and his conclusions were supported by Leydig, Schultze and Virchow. However, there were others, including Reichert and Henle, who opposed them. Because of this opposition, Remak resumed his studies on embryonic erythrocytes in 1856 and was then able to demonstrate all stages of cell division and, in some detail, the division of the cell nucleus (Remak 1858). He also showed that cell division could be arrested by a drop in temperature or by perfusing the preparation with a dilute solution of potassium permanganate. In the latter case, the dividing cell sometimes rounded up again and thus gave rise to a binucleate cell. In the light of this observation, Remak concluded that if cell division was aborted, binucleate or multinucleate cells might arise, and this could give the false impression that new cell formation was taking place endogenously. The mode of formation and the biological significance of multinucleate cells was a matter on which Remak and Virchow disagreed. Although Remak's views on this question did subsequently vacillate (Remak 1862), it is now clear that the conclusion that he reached in his 1858 paper was essentially correct.

It is of more than passing interest that Remak, despite many years of meticulous work and the repeated exposition of his conclusions in widely read journals, failed to win the acquiescence, to say nothing of the acclaim, that he merited. The mass conversion of the disbelievers required an advocate of much greater skill. Virchow (Fig. 4) was fully familiar with Remak's work on the division of erythrocytes and did not have any reservations about it. He was also familiar with the observations that had been made on cell division in the plant world. What he was initially unsure about was whether, as Remak claimed, this was the only way in which cells were formed in the animal body. As pointed out by Kisch (1954), the last sentence of Virchow's review of Remak's 1854b paper on malignant tumours is decidedly cool: "In conclusion he [Remak] insists, as he has done before, that there are no free nuclei nor any

FIGURE 4 Rudolf Virchow (1821–1902) whose powerful advocacy, encapsulated in the persuasive catch-phrase *omnis cellula e cellula*, finally persuaded the medical world that all cells were derived from other cells and that they never arose spontaneously out of non-cellular material. (From B.J. Gottlieb and A. Berg 1942 in *Das Antlitz des German-ischen Artzes in vier Jahrhunderten* [*Courtesy of Rembrandt Verlag GMBH, Berlin*].)

formation of cells in the extracellular fluid". This critical reserve was character-istic of Virchow's reaction to any dramatic new claim and was not, in my view, specifically directed against Remak as Kisch suggests. Virchow was, for example, initially resistant to the idea that infectious diseases might have a mi-crobial origin and to Koch's demonstration of the causative agent of tuber-culosis. In the fields of epidemiology, anthropology and even archaeology, it is not difficult to find instances in which Virchow's reaction to an important discovery was initially very guarded (see Vasold 1988). What induced Vir-chow to commit himself in the time that elapsed between his review of

Remak's work in 1854 and his own famous paper in 1855 is not clear. This latter paper appeared as the leading article in the eighth volume of the *Archiv* that Virchow had himself founded (Virchow 1855). It is essentially a clarion call to pathologists to abandon speculative and philosophically based models of disease and to strive instead to explain all pathological processes in cellular (and experimental) terms. In this article, Virchow unreservedly adopts Remak's position and argues forcibly that free cell formation out of noncellular elements does not occur:

> For *generatio aequivoca*, even if it is conceived as some kind of self-excitation, is still either downright heresy or the work of the devil. And if, indeed, we defend not only the hereditary character of generations on a large scale but also legitimate succession in the formation of cells, then that is assuredly not suspect testimony. In accordance with the outlook of cellular pathology, I formulate the doctrine of the pathological generation of neoplasia simply thus: *Omnis cellula a cellula.*

And later:

> In a word, the irritability of the individual cellular elements of the tissues is in complete agreement with the assumption that they are autonomous living forms and, in particular, the processes that generate new elements out of pre-existing ones are no different from those that produce cleavage and division of the egg under the influence of the sperm.

This is pure Remak. But Virchow makes no mention of Remak in his article. For this he has been criticised by some modern historians, and he was certainly bitterly criticised by Remak himself in a letter that irretrievably damaged the relationship between the two men. Although there is no doubt that Virchow could have been more generous to Remak than he was, it must be borne in mind that Virchow's article was not a scientific paper in the strict sense, or even a review of the subject. It was an editorial that set out to proselytize, and it did not mention by name any of the investigators whose work had established the doctrine that Virchow was advocating.

Virchow's remarkable success as an advocate was due in part to his having used a memorable catchphrase—*omnis cellula a cellula*. This is an obvious elaboration of Oken's *omne vivum e vivo* with which Virchow must surely have been familiar. It is therefore surprising that he originally wrote *a cellula* and not *e cellula*. There is documentary evidence that Virchow, although reasonably proficient in translating out of the classical languages, had a rather insecure grasp of their grammar (see Vasold 1988). According to J.R. Baker (1953), it was Leydig (1857) who suggested the correction of *'a'* to *'e'*, and this was taken into the first edition of Virchow's *Cellularpathologie* which appeared in 1858. (I have been unable to obtain a first edition of the book to check this.) The *Cellularpathologie* (Virchow 1858) was based on a series of public lectures that Virchow gave in the University of Berlin two years after his appointment to the professorship of pathology there. Virchow's lectures were always well attended, and in this case the audience was drawn from a wide range of medical disciplines. The published version of the lectures, containing a preface dated 20 August 1858, sold out almost at once and a second edition, with a preface dated 7 June, appeared in the following year. A third edition appeared in 1861. The book was immensely popular in Europe and was soon translated into French and English. The first chapter introduces and elaborates the *leitmotif* of the new cellular pathology—that the mechanism of cell generation proposed by Schleiden and Schwann is decisively incorrect and that cells are never formed *de novo* out of non-cellular material:

> In pathology too, we can go so far as to lay it down as a general principle that no development at all originates *de novo* and that in the developmental history of the individual components of the body no less than in the development of the whole organism we reject *generatio aequivoca*. Just as we cannot now accept the idea that a roundworm might arise out of saburral mucus or that an infusorium or a mould or an alga might be formed from the residues of decomposed animals or plants, so, in the analysis of physiological or pathological processes that occur in the tissues, we cannot now entertain the notion that a new cell might have arisen out of some non-cellular material (*Omnis cellula e cellula*) any more than we can doubt that an animal can be generated only from another animal and a plant only from another plant.

Virchow ends this opening chapter with two demonstrations of cell division. One is a longitudinal section through a young lilac bud in which the leaf hairs in particular show dividing cells (an observation not too different from that made by Dumortier a quarter of a century earlier), and the other is a section through a piece of hypertrophied costal cartilage in which proliferation of the cartilage cells can be readily seen.

There are two matters on which Remak and Virchow disagreed. Virchow believed that multinucleate cells in tumours were centres of cell formation, and he appears to have prevailed upon Remak to admit this possibility (Remak 1862) although Remak's initial conclusion from his own observations was, as previously described, that the binucleation and multinucleation resulted from failure of the cell as a whole to complete division (Remak 1858). Nonetheless, by 1871, when the fourth, revised, edition of *Cellularpathologie* appeared, Virchow had apparently come round to Remak's initial position. The final sentences of the opening chapter read as follows: "Nowhere is there to be found any kind of new cell formation except that produced by fission. One element after another divides into two; each generation arises from the preceding generation". The other point of disagreement between the two men was that Virchow allowed a much greater degree of transformation of one cell type into another than did Remak. Remak believed that the cell type was laid down during embryological development and retained its essential character thereafter, even if later it became a tumour cell (a process that we would now call 'determination'). In this respect also, Remak's views were a good deal closer to the truth than Virchow's. It is difficult to see in Virchow's writings on the genesis of cells any original experimental contribution, but there is no doubt that it was his skilful advocacy and, above all, the continuing and widespread influence of successive editions of *Cellularpathologie* that eventually won universal acceptance for the doctrine encapsulated in *omnis cellula e cellula*. By the time the fourth edition of the book had percolated through the medical world, no one was in any doubt about how the cells of the body were formed. But whether the cell nucleus divided and, if so, what the significance of that division might be, remained an open question.

DIVISION OF THE CELL NUCLEUS

It appears that, once again, it was Remak (1841a) in his studies on the multiplication of embyronic chick erythroblasts who first observed division of the cell nucleus and concluded that there was continuity of nuclear material from one cell generation to the next. What Nägeli (1844) saw and did not see in plant material at about the same time, or a little later, is somewhat obscure. Nägeli described division of the nucleus into two equal halves in the terminal cells of the staminal hairs of *Tradescantia*, but he regarded the formation of new nuclei by this mechanism as unusual. He noted that there was a single nucleus in the spore mother cell in *Navicula* and that a similar nucleus arose in each of the daughter cells. In *Anthoceros* he observed two primary nuclei in the spore mother cell giving rise to four secondary nuclei. However, Nägeli also described the formation of a new nucleus while the primary nucleus was still intact and attached to the cell wall in a peripheral position. Whereas it is clear that Nägeli did see the formation of new nuclei in daughter cells and *inferred* that in some cases they arose by division of the nucleus of the mother cell, I do not believe that he actually saw a nuclear division. My reason for this view is that in the one case where he actually illustrates the process, he shows the nucleus being split into two by a partition which is shown as an inward extension of the nuclear membrane. Since such a process does not occur, Nägeli could not have seen it, and I conclude from this that, unlike Remak, he did not observe nuclear division but simply imposed on the nucleus a process that he knew to take place in the cell as a whole. Moreover, Nägeli did not believe at this stage that the nucleus was an essential component of all cells, although he noted that "objects resembling nuclei" (*kernähnliche Gebilde*) were seen in many plant cell types on closer examination. The confervae, he claimed, usually showed no trace of a nucleus. It is clear that Nägeli did not in 1844 have any idea of the importance of the nucleus in the life of the cell.

Reichert (1847) accurately observed in the fertilized egg of the nematode *Strongylus auriculatus* that when the cell prepared to divide the nuclear membrane dissolved. He also observed the formation of new nuclei within the daughter cells. These observations were the origin of the view that the nuclear material was not continuous from one cell generation to the next, but was formed *de novo* at each cell generation. In his 1852 paper, Remak states that he is unable to confirm Reichert's observations on the disappearance of the nucleus at cell division and argues strongly for the continuity of nuclear material from mother to daughter cell. He appears to have believed that the nucleus divided directly into two halves but, unlike Nägeli, he did not produce drawings of processes that he did not see. The illustrations accompanying his 1858 paper clearly show anaphase and telophase figures, but in the legends to these figures Remak describes them as "shrivelled nuclei" (*verschrumpfte Kerne*), from which I conclude that he probably regarded them as nuclei damaged by the experimental procedures used and not as mandatory stages in the processes of nuclear division. Indeed, in this same paper he proposes that the division of the nucleus is preceded by division of the nucleoli. This he infers from estimates that he made of the number of nucleoli present before and after division. Apparently he was able to convince himself that the number of nucleoli increased before cell division and decreased after, but this might well have been one of the few cases of Remak giving way to wishful thinking. He sums up his position as follows: "As a rule, the nucleolus undergoes fission into two parts and the nucleus likewise divides into two nuclei". In the 1858 paper, Remak also describes various forms of irregular cell division, such as the production of daughter cells of different size, daughter cells lacking a nucleus, and multinucleate cells arising as a consequence of incomplete division of the cell membrane.

MITOSIS

If Remak had been more familiar with the botanical literature, he would have taken the mitotic figures that he observed more seriously. For in 1848 Hofmeister (Fig. 5) produced a remarkable series of papers in which the whole sequence of mitosis was accurately described and illustrated. Initially in the pollen mother cells and staminal hair cells of *Tradescantia*, but later in a number of other species, Hofmeister discerned the following mitotic stages: (i) morphological changes in the cell nucleus; (ii) dissolution of the nuclear mem-

FIGURE 5 Wilhelm Hofmeister (1824–1877) provided the first accurate descriptions of all the stages of mitosis. (From K. von Goebel 1926 in *Wilhelm Hofmeister: The work and life of a 19th century botanist*, translated by H.M. Bower [*Courtesy of the Royal Society of London*].)

brane; (iii) assembly of the nuclear material, easily recognisable to a modern eye as chromosomes at the metaphase plate; (iv) anaphase; (v) reconstitution of the daughter nuclei, initially without a nuclear membrane; (vi) formation of a new membrane around the daughter nuclei; and (vii) the appearance of the partition that divides the cell into two. Hofmeister followed the whole process through again in the daughter cells and recorded the formation of multiple nuclei by the same mechanism. It could reasonably be argued that Hofmeister's work, which appeared in book form in 1849, was the starting point of the idea that division of the nucleus did not take place by 'direct' fission, but 'indirectly', as it came to be known, by a more complex mechanism.

Although, as I have described, mitotic figures containing recognisable chromosomes were observed in plant cells by Hofmeister in 1848 and in animal cells by Remak in 1858, it was Balbiani (1876) who first drew attention to the mechanical significance of this morphological transformation of the cell nucleus. In mitotic cells of the ovarian epithelium of the grasshopper *Stenobothrus*, Balbiani noted that the nuclear substance was first gathered into a bundle of *'bâtonnets étroits'* (narrow little sticks), each of which then divided into two halves. Balbiani thought, mistakenly, that this division took place transversely across the middle of each little stick, but he did correctly describe the separation of the division products into two secondary bundles which, when the cell had finally divided, became the nuclei of the two daughter cells. Schleicher (1878) observed a similar sequence of events in cartilage cells of toad tadpoles and in 1879 gave an accurate and detailed description of prophase, metaphase, anaphase, telophase and reconstitution of the nucleus in cartilage cells in the scapula of a young frog and of a newborn cat. It was Schleicher who coined the terms 'karyokinesis' to describe this sequence of nuclear changes. Strasburger (1879, 1880) also provided a detailed description of the whole process but in living cells, the staminal hair cells of *Tradescantia*. However, like Balbiani, Strasburger believed that the mitotic chromosomes divided transversely across their middle and maintained this view even after Flemming (1879) had demonstrated decisively that division occurred longitudinally along the length of the chromosomes. In the first edition of his book *Zellbildung und Zelltheilung*, which appeared in 1875, Strasburger still argued that in the embryo sac of higher plants the endosperm was formed by 'free cell formation' as postulated by Schleiden, but by the time the third edition appeared (1880) he had accepted that endosperm formation was simply a special case of karyokinesis in which many nuclei were generated rapidly and the cell walls were formed later.

Flemming's 1879 paper provided the definitive description of chromosome behaviour at mitosis, a word that he himself coined. Choosing as his material for study the epithelial cells of salamander larvae, which are large and translucent, he was able to discern that the chromosomes that arrived at the metaphase base plate consisted of two threads that separated from each other along their length. He then saw that the separated threads moved apart and that one set passed to each of the two daughter cells. The only completely novel contribution in Flemming's paper was his observation that the chromosomes divided longitudinally, but the text is burdened with extensive discussions of minute differences between his own observations and those of previous workers, differences that are needlessly magnified into major bones of contention. Flemming divided the process of mitosis into seven or possibly eight distinct phases, but these phases were patently an over-elaboration of the data and were not accepted either by his contemporaries or later. Although he took the view that the 'indirect' nuclear division that he described in such detail was a quite general phenomenon, Flemming still believed that 'direct' nuclear division by simple fission could occur in some cell types, for example, amoebae and 'colourless' blood cells. He did not, however, accept that nuclei might be formed *de novo* and, at a later date, taking a leaf out of Virchow's book, he coined the phrase *omnis nucleus e nucleo* (Flemming 1882). There is no evidence in Flemming's 1879 paper that he was at all conscious of the genetic consequences of the chromosome mechanics that he had observed. Indeed, he rather testily declined to discuss the many theoretical papers on the function of the nucleus that had appeared in the five years that preceded the publication of his paper. The other two papers in this series (Flemming 1880, 1881) extend the observations to other cell types. There is a good deal of polemical material in the 1881 paper directed especially against Strasburger's book *Zellbildung und Zelltheilung* (1880), but the essential conclusion was that the phenomena seen in the epithelial cells of salamander larvae also occurred in the fertilized ovum, in the eggs of three different species of sea urchin, in the embryo sac of the lily and other plants, and in the corneal epithelium of man.

Flemming's observations on the behaviour of mitotic chromosomes in fertilized eggs rested on previous work that had already established that one of the pronuclei in the egg was generated from the sperm. Warneck (1850), studying the process of fertilization in freshwater gastropods, appears to have been the first to observe two rounded bodies (pronuclei) in fertilized eggs, but his work, published in a Russian journal, passed unnoticed until it was resurrected by Fol more than a quarter of a century later. Bütschli (1873), unaware of Warneck's observations, observed the formation of two pronuclei in the fertilized eggs of nematodes. Auerbach, a year later (1874), also saw the two pronuclei in fertilized eggs and considered that their fusion into a single nucleus was an essential part of the process of conjugation. Hertwig (1875, 1877, 1878), working with fertilized eggs of the sea urchin *Paracentrotus lividus*, confirmed and extended the findings of Warneck, Bütschli, and Auerbach. Fol (1876, 1877a) actually observed the penetration of the sperm into the sea urchin's egg and concluded that, in general, only a single sperm penetrated each egg. He gave a clear and accurate description of the formation of the second pronucleus from the single sperm that had entered the egg. Fol (1877b) also recorded similar observations in starfish eggs and in the eggs of the arrow worm *Sagitta*. The description given by Selenka (1878) of the sequence of events in fertilized sea urchin eggs does not differ materially from that given by Fol. All these authors, including Flemming, considered that the two pronuclei simply fused together to make the single compound nucleus of the fertilized egg.

CHROMOSOMES

van Beneden's classic paper on the maturation and fertilization of the egg appeared in 1883 and is 375 pages long (Fig. 6). It is, both conceptually and technically, a major advance on the observations that I have so far described. His choice of material—the eggs of the horse roundworm *Ascaris megaloceph-*

FIGURE 6 Édouard van Beneden (1846–1910) showed that the chromosomes (*anses chromatiques*) derived from the male and the female parent did not merge in the fertilized egg, but retained their separate and stable identities through subsequent cell division. In collaboration with A. Neyt, van Beneden also elucidated the role of the centrosome in cell division and established the independent inheritance of this organelle. *(Courtesy of the Service des Archives, Université Libre de Bruxelles.)*

ala—was crucial. Not only are these eggs transparent, but they contain only four chromosomes which are large enough to be morphologically distinguishable. Moreover, along the length of the uterus, the stages of fertilization are synchronised so that at any one level one can see large numbers of cells at the same stage. The most important new observation made by van Beneden was that the two pronuclei do not ever fuse together. A specific 'cleavage-nucleus' as postulated by Hertwig did not, according to van Beneden, exist. Both the sperm pronucleus and the oocyte pronucleus, having shed the two polar bodies, underwent maturation and eventually became indistinguishable from normal nuclei. van Beneden realised, however, that they were 'half' nuclei, one carrying the female genetic load and the other the male. These two nuclei were then seen to undergo mitosis in the normal way, each giving rise to two 'chromatic loops' (*anses chromatiques*). The four loops thus produced were brought together in a single metaphase plate where each loop divided longitudinally into two secondary loops (Fig. 7). The latter were distributed to the two daughter cells in such a way that each received two male and two female

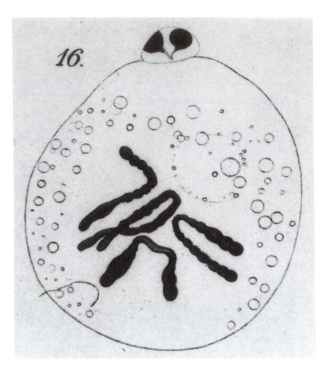

FIGURE 7 The four chromosomes (*anses chromatiques*) of *Ascaris megalocephala*, two paternal and two maternal, as seen by van Beneden. (Reprinted from *Archives of Biology*.)

loops. (The word chromosome to describe these *anses chromatiques*, *Stäbchen*, *Schleifen*, etc. was introduced by Waldeyer, but not until 1888.) van Beneden noted that the male and the female elements did not merge in the blastomere nuclei and regarded it as probable that they remained distinct in all the nuclei that were subsequently generated. van Beneden's account of the course of events in the nucleus of the fertilized egg has not since required any substantial modification. At a later date, van Beneden and Neyt (1887) accurately described the role of the centrosome in cell division and established the independent inheritance of this organelle. They showed that the centrosomes were derived from pre-existing centrosomes and that each of them divided into two before the nucleus itself divided. Similar conclusions were reached independently and at the same time by Boveri (1887b).

THE DETERMINANTS OF HEREDITY

Although it is difficult to avoid the impression that van Beneden was aware of the genetic consequences of what he had observed, he did not discuss these consequences explicitly in his paper. However, in the same year, Roux (1883) (Fig. 8) published a theoretical paper in support of the view that the intricate mechanisms of 'indirect' nuclear division were a device to ensure not only that the mass of the nucleus was equally partitioned between the two daughter cells, but also that the 'qualities' of the nucleus were also equally distributed. Roux proposed that each of the chromosomes carried a different genetic load. In the following year, Nägeli (1884) noted that the contribution of 'nutritive plasm' (cytoplasm) made to the fertilized egg by the oocyte was

FIGURE 8 Wilhelm Roux (1850–1924) argued that mitosis was a device to ensure that the qualitative properties of the cell nucleus were equally distributed to the two daughter cells. He proposed that each of the chromosomes carried a different genetic load. *(Courtesy of Gustav Fischer Verlag, Jena.)*

much greater than the contribution made by the sperm; but, as it had been known since Kölreuter's breeding experiments with tobacco plants that the *genetic* contributions of the male and the female parents were equal (Kölreuter 1761–1766), Nägeli concluded that the vectors of hereditary traits must be carried by something else which he called the 'idioplasm'. Nägeli did not believe that the idioplasm resided in the cell nucleus but envisaged it as a collection of long strands that passed from cell to cell independently of the nucleus. It was Hertwig (1884, 1885) (Fig. 9) who suggested that all the requirements of Nägeli's idioplasm would be met by the nuclei of the sperm and the oocyte. Indeed, he regarded it as very probable that it was Miescher's 'nuclein' that was responsible not only for fertilization but also for the transmission of hereditary traits. In fact, Haeckel had already suggested as early as 1866 that the nucleus was concerned with the transmission of heritable characteristics and the cytoplasm with the adaptation of the cell to its environment; but at that time such a conclusion could have been no more than an inspired conjecture. Direct experimental support for the idea that the nucleus was the vehicle by which inherited properties were transmitted was provided by Strasburger (1884). Working with orchids, Strasburger showed that when the pollen tube

FIGURE 9 Oscar Hertwig (1849–1922) thought it probable that the vectors of hereditary traits were composed of the 'nuclein' described by Friedrich Miescher. *(Photograph provided by Askan Hertwig, by courtesy of Dr. Paul Weindling.)*

penetrates down through the pistil into the embryo sac, the nucleus is pushed out through the end of the tube whereas the cytoplasm remains behind and is thus excluded from the fertilization process (the formal equivalence between this observation and the famous Hershey and Chase [1952] experiment with bacteriophage will not escape the modern reader). Heuser (1884), working with plants, and Rabl (1885) with salamander cells, concurred with van Beneden's view that the chromosomes were stable components transmitted from one cell generation to the next. Rabl actually proposed that the threads of chromatin into which a given chromosome dissolves when the nucleus enters the resting stage condense again into the same chromosome at the next mitosis. However, neither Heuser nor Rabl provided additional experimental evidence to support their conclusions. Weismann (1885) postulated on theoretical grounds that on fertilization a new combination of chromosomes and hence a new hereditary blueprint (*Erbanlage*) must be formed and suggested that the determinants of heredity were "arranged in a linear manner in the slender, thread-like loops" of the chromosomes. Weismann also insisted that at each generation a reduction must take place in the genetic material, and he argued that the probable mechanism by which the reduction was achieved was the karyokinesis of 'indirect' nuclear division with its longitudinal splitting of the chromosomes. But the decisive experimental evidence for the conclusion that the essential vectors of genetic information were the chromosomes was provided by Boveri (Fig. 10).

CONTINUITY AND INDIVIDUALITY OF CHROMOSOMES

Like van Beneden, to whom he gives every credit, Boveri worked initially with *Ascaris megalocephala*, but later also with the *univalens* variant which has only two chromosomes and thus offers exceptional material for the detailed study of chromosome morphology. Boveri (1887a, 1888) was able to provide

FIGURE 10   Theodor Boveri (1862–1915) established by direct experimental methods that individual chromosomes did indeed carry different genetic loads and that this individuality was stably maintained from one cell generation to the next. He later advanced the view that tumours were generated by genetic aberrations that occurred in somatic cells. He thought it likely that these aberrations resulted in losses of cell function. (From F. Baltzer 1962 in *Theodor Boveri, Leben und Werk* [*Courtesy of Wissenschaftliche Verlagsgesellschaft M.B.H., Stuttgart*].)

much more convincing evidence than had hitherto been available that the chromosomes formed at karyokinesis in the blastomeres had the same shape and the same disposition as the chromosomes of the fertilized egg. Boveri insisted that this observation had general validity and, on the strength of it, enunciated the principle of the 'continuity' of the chromosomes throughout interphase. The chromosomes were, in his view, "independent entities that retain their independence even in the resting nucleus". "What comes out of the nucleus", he concluded, "is what goes into it". This view was opposed by Hertwig, and notably by Fick (1899, 1907). The controversy continued well into the 20th century, and Boveri was still defending his position against Fick in 1909. Boveri next turned his attention to the question of qualitative differences between individual chromosomes, and for these studies he chose to work with sea urchin eggs, the material introduced by Hertwig. He already knew that the chromosomes retained their individuality from one cell generation to the next, that the developing egg received identical chromosome complements from the sperm nucleus and the egg nucleus, and, from the behaviour of haploid embryos, that each parental chromosome set was enough to support the normal development of the egg. Moreover, especially from the work of Montgomery (1901), there was a strong presumption that, as Roux (1883) had suggested much earlier, each of the chromosomes was qualitatively different from the others. Montgomery had examined the spermatogonial chromosomes of 42 species of *Hemiptera* (true bugs) and found that the chromosomes of any one individual differed greatly in size. In particular, he noted the huge disparity between the smallest (the sex chromosomes) and the largest. He also found that at meiosis, the paternal chromosomes always paired with the maternal, and he pointed out that this must also be the case with *Ascaris megalocephala var. univalens* since this contains only two chromosomes. It was thus difficult to avoid the inference that there must be some qualitative differences between the various chromosomes. This view was strongly supported by the work of McClung (1902) on the accessory chromosome in the sperm cells of grasshoppers. McClung found that this accessory chromosome was present in only half of the sperms formed and concluded that it must be responsible for determining the sex of the resulting individual. But it was another matter to provide direct experimental evidence of qualitative differences between chromosomes and to establish the generality of the principle. This Boveri did by studying the products of abnormal mitosis in sea urchin eggs. In this material the introduction of two sperms into the egg (dispermy) induces tripolar or tetrapolar mitoses and hence the distribution of different, and usually incomplete, chromosome sets to the two blastomeres. Dispermy was induced by exposing the egg to very high concentrations of sperm, but aberrant mitosis could also be produced by inhibiting the first cleavage division of the egg to produce a cell with four centrosomes that in due course generated a tetrapolar mitosis. Systematic examination of the development of these blastomeres containing different chromosome sets led inevitably to the conclusion that normal development required not simply a particular number of chromosomes but a particular combination of them, from which it followed that different chromosomes carried different genetic loads. This conclusion Boveri called the principle of the *individuality* of chromosomes as genetic determinants (*Verschiedenwertigkeit der Chromosomen als Erbträger*) (Boveri 1902, 1904, 1907).

Sutton's work was an extension of the observations made by Montgomery and McClung. In a paper that appeared in 1902, he showed that in the cells of the lubber grasshopper *Brachystola magna* each of the 11 pairs of chromosomes was morphologically distinguishable and clearly different from the accessory chromosomes. He thought it likely "that the constant morphological differences between the ordinary chromosomes are the visible expression of physiological or qualititative differences". Sutton was familiar with Boveri's work on blastomeres with abnormal chromosome complements and referred to this work in his paper, modestly but accurately describing his own observations as a morphological complement of Boveri's "beautiful experimental researches". It was E.B. Wilson, Sutton's teacher, who first referred to the qualitative individuality of chromosomes as the "Sutton-Boveri theory", but this eponym seems in retrospect to be the product of parochial or nepotistic partiality. Both Boveri (1902, 1903, 1904) and Sutton (1903) drew attention to the astonishing correspondence between the observations made on chromosomes in mitosis and the results obtained by Mendel, whose work was resurrected by de Vries, Correns, and Tschermak at the turn of the century. Correns himself drew the attention of de Vries to this parallelism.

TUMOUR CELLS

Boveri's first reference to the possible role of mitotic abnormalities in the genesis of tumours is to be found in his 1902 paper on multipolar mitoses. The idea was first put forward by Hansemann in 1890, but Boveri rightly considered that the model put forward by Hansemann was fundamentally incorrect. It is in the last paragraph of his 1902 paper that Boveri turns his attention to the problem of tumours, and he limits his discussion to the possibility that multipolar mitoses might be a causative factor. There is at this stage no generalised consideration of nuclear abnormalities as determinants of malignancy, but even in this first paper on the subject Boveri suggests that mitotic aberrations might be caused by physical or chemical agents and that they are not incompatible with a parasitic aetiology for cancer. But the monograph that he wrote on tumours in 1914, the year before he died, and that was translated into English by his widow in 1929, shows an insight and a prescience that are quite astonishing. Boveri begins by arguing that malignancy is due to a loss of normal function in the cell, and he then produces evidence from his work on sea urchin eggs that this loss of function does not result from loss of cytoplasm, an observation that had been made earlier by Wilson (1901). The functional loss must, he concludes, be due to an irreplaceable loss of nuclear material. Boveri considered that exponential multiplication was the normal steady state for cells and that inhibition of multiplication was imposed by the process of differentiation. His studies on the qualitative individuality of chromosomes led him to believe that certain specific chromosomes might be responsible for the inhibition of cell multiplication and that their elimination might result in progressive multiplication. This conclusion is so remarkably consonant with our modern view that it is worth quoting verbatim[1]:

> Another possibility is that in every normal cell there is a specific arrangement
> for inhibiting, which allows the process of division to begin only when the in-

[1]The extracts from Boveri's monograph on tumours are taken from Marcella Boveri's translation.

hibition has been overcome by a special stimulus. To assume the presence of definite chromosomes which inhibit division would harmonise best with my fundamental idea. If their inhibitory action were temporarily overcome by external stimuli, then cell division would follow. Cells of tumours with unlimited growth would arise if these 'inhibiting chromosomes' were eliminated.

Boveri did, however, envisage that functional losses could be produced not only by the elimination of whole chromosomes but also by the loss of parts of chromosomes, and he also envisaged the possibility that there might be chromosomes or combinations of chromosomes that stimulate cell multiplication. On the whole, he considered it more likely that a 'chromosome complex' rather than a single chromosome was the essential determinant of the malignant state. Although the monograph includes discussion of a model in which there is a balance between stimulatory and inhibitory chromosomes, the central theme running through the work is that the prime causes of the malignant phenotype are genetic losses.

By 1914, Boveri's view of the significance of mitotic abnormalities in the genesis of cancer had become much more sophisticated. It is no longer the mitotic abnormality itself that is the crucial factor, but a malfunction of some specific elements of the genetic machinery: "The essence of my theory", he states, "is not the abnormal mitosis, but a certain abnormal chromatin-complex, no matter how it arises". He also makes it clear that not all abnormal mitoses generate cancer. He is aware that most of them produce cells that do not survive, and that only rare combinations of chromosomes resulting from abnormal mitosis could contribute to the genesis of a tumour. Aberrant mitoses which, in 1902, Boveri thought might be the crucial events, he no longer regards as essential; and he emphasises that growth of a tumour can only result from the division of cells by bipolar mitosis. On the so-called 'hereditary' tumours in man, Boveri's views are also remarkably modern: "It is clear according to my theory", he explains, "that there may be a hereditary transmission only in the sense that a certain disposition is transmitted. It would suffice if the tumours which arise in many individuals were far less easily suppressed by their neighbouring tissues than in other individuals and if these qualities were inheritable". And he gives *Xeroderma pigmentosum* as an example. Moreover, Boveri had no doubt that, in general, tumours arose from single cells. "I am convinced", he declares, "that every theory of malignant tumours is wrong which does not take into account its unicellular origin". Finally, it is worth mentioning that Boveri's monograph on tumours contains a view of differentiation that also foreshadows our current concepts. On the various forms of differentiation he has this to say: "These diversities are not to be thought of as if the kinds of chromosomes in one tissue were different from those of another, for we know that the number of chromosomes is the same in different tissues, at least in some cases. Rather the differences in question must have their cause in that in every tissue, *certain parts* of chromosomes grow especially strong while in another tissue, they fall into the background or disappear entirely".

Four years before Boveri's monograph on tumours appeared, Morgan (1910a,b) published his first papers on the genetics of *Drosophila*, and thereafter it was the work of Morgan's *Drosophila* group that dominated the study of chromosomes and heredity (reviewed by Morgan, Bridges, and Sturtevant 1925). However, it was clear by the time Boveri laid down his pen that the cells of the body were organisms endowed with a stable heredity and hence, in principle, susceptible to genetic analysis. But two obstacles long hindered the application of genetic methods to somatic cells. The first was that these cells could not be serially cultivated as independent entities outside the body; and the second was that they did not, as far as was known, engage in sexual processes of any kind.

REFERENCES

Auerbach, L. 1874. *Zur Charakteristik und Lebensgeschichte der Zellkerne. Organologische Studien.* Heft I. E. Morgenstern, Breslau.

Baker, J.R. 1951. Remarks on the discovery of cell-division. *Isis* **42**: 285–287.

———. 1953. The cell-theory: A restatement, history and critique. Part IV. The multiplication of cells. *Q. J. Microsc. Sci.* **94**: 407–440.

———. 1955. The cell-theory: A restatement, history and critique. Part V. The multiplication of nuclei. *Q. J. Microsc. Sci.* **96**: 449–481.

Balbiani, E.G. 1876. Sur les phénomèmes de la division du noyau cellulaire. *C. R. Acad. Sci. Paris* **83**: 831–834.

Boveri, T. 1887a. Über die Befruchtung der Eier von *Ascaris megalocephala. Sitzungsber. Ges. Morphol. Physiol. München* **3**: 153.

———. 1887b. Zellenstudien I. Die Bildung der Richtungskörper bei *Ascaris megalocephala* und *Ascaris lumbricoides.* Jena. *Z. Naturwiss.* **21**: 423–515.

———. 1888. Zellenstudien II. Die Befruchtung und Teilung des Eies von *Ascaris megalocephala.* Jena. *Z. Naturwiss.* **22**: 685–882.

———. 1902. Über mehrpolige Mitosen als Mittel zur Analyse des Zellkerns. *Verh. Phys.-Med. Ges. Würzburg* **35**: 67–90.

———. 1903. Über die Konstitution der chromatischen Kernsubstanz. *Verh. Zool. Ges.* (*Versamml. Würzburg*) **13**: 10–33.

———. 1904. *Ergebnisse über die Konstitution des chromatischen Substanz des Zellkerns.* G. Fischer, Jena.

———. 1907. Zellenstudien VI. Die Entwicklung dispermer Seeigeleier. Ein Betrag zur Befruchtungslehre und zur Theorie des Kerns. Jena. *Z. Naturwiss.* **43**: 1–292.

———. 1909. Die Blastomerenkerne von *Ascaris megalocephala* und die Theorie der Chromosomenindividualität. *Arch. Zellforsch.* **3**: 181–268.

———. 1914. *Zur Frage der Entstehung maligner Tumoren.* G. Fischer, Jena.

Bütschli, O. 1873. Beiträge zur Kenntnis der freilebenden Nematoden. *Nova Acta Phys.-Med. Acad. Caesar. Leopold.-Carolinae Nat. Curios.* **36**: 1–144.

de Mirbel, C.F.B. 1835. Recherches anatomiques et physiologiques sur le Marchantia polymorpha. *Mém. Acad. Sci. Inst. France* **13**: 337–436.

Dumortier, B.C. 1832. Recherches sur la structure comparée et le développement des animaux et des végétaux. *Nova Acta Phys.-Med. Acad. Caesar. Leopold.-Carolinae Nat. Curios.* (part 1) **16**: 217–311.

Ehrenberg, C.G. 1838. *Die Infusionsthierchen als vollkommene Organismen.* Leopold Voss, Leipzig.

Fick, R. 1899. Mitteilungen über die Eireifung bei Amphibien. *Verh. Anat. Ges. Tübingen. Anat. Anz.* **16**: 94.

———. 1907. Vererbungsfragen, Reduktions—und Chromosomenhypothesen, Bastardregeln. *Ergeb. Anat. Entwicklungsgesch.* **16** (2 Abteil): 1–140.

Flemming, W. 1879. Beiträge zur Kenntnis der Zelle und ihrer Lebenserscheinungen. I. Theil. *Arch. Mikrosk. Anat.* **16**: 302–436.

———. 1880. Beiträge zur Kenntnis der Zelle und ihrer Lebenserscheinungen. II. Theil. *Arch. Mikrosk. Anat.* **18**: 151–259.

———. 1881. Beiträge zur Kenntnis der Zelle und ihrer Lebenserscheinungen. III. Theil. *Arch. Mikrosk. Anat.* **20**: 1–86.

———. 1882. *Zellsubstanz Kern und Zelltheilung.* F.C.W. Vogel, Leipzig.

Fol, H. 1876. Sur les phénomènes intimes de la division cellulaire. *C. R. Acad. Sci. Paris* **83**: 667–669.

———. 1877a. Sur les phénomènes intimes de la fécondation. *C. R. Acad. Sci. Paris* **84**: 268–271.

———. 1877b. Sur le premier développement d'une etoile de mer. *C. R. Acad. Sci. Paris* **84**: 357–360.

Haeckel, E. 1866. *Generelle Morphologie der Organismen: Allgemeine Grundzüge der organischen Formen-Wissenschaft, mechanisch begründet durch die von Charles Darwin reformirte Descendenz-Theorie.* Georg Reimer, Berlin.

Hansemann, D. 1890. Über asymmetrische Zellteilung in Epithelkrebsen und deren biologische Bedeutung. *Arch. Pathol. Anat.* **119**: 299–326.

Hershey, A.D. and M. Chase. 1952. Independent functions of viral protein and nucleic acid in growth of bacteriophage. *J. Gen. Physiol.* **36**: 39–56.

Hertwig, O. 1875. Beiträge zur Kenntnis der Bildung, Befruchtung und Theilung des thierischen Eies. I Theil. *Morphol. Jahrb.* **1**: 347–434.

———. 1877. Beiträge zur Kenntnis der Bildung, Befruchtung und Theilung des thierischen Eies. II Theil. *Morphol. Jahrb.* **3**: 271–279.

———. 1878. Beiträge zur Kenntnis der Bildung, Befruchtung und Theilung des thierischen Eies. III Theil. *Morphol. Jahrb.* **4**: 156–213.

———. 1884. Das Problem der Befruchtung und der Isotropie des Eies, eine Theorie der Vererbung. Jena. *Z. Naturwiss.* **18**: 21–23.

———. 1885. Das Problem der Befruchtung und der Isotropie des Eies. Jena. *Z. Naturwiss.* **18**: 276–381.

Heuser, E. 1884. Beobachtung über Zellkerntheilung. *Bot. Zentralbl.* **17**: 27–32; 57–59; 85–95; 117–128; 154–156.

Hofmeister, W. 1848. Ueber die Entwicklung des Pollens. *Z. Bot.* **6**: 425–434; 649–658; 670–674.

———. 1849. *Die Entstehung des Embryos der Phanerogamen.* Friedrich Hofmeister, Leipzig.

Hughes, A. 1959. *A history of cytology.* Abelard-Schuman, London and New York.

Keele, K.D. 1965. *William Harvey*, p.200. Thomas Nelson and Sons, London.

Kisch, B. 1954. Forgotten leaders in modern medicine: Robert Remak. *Trans. Am. Philos. Soc.* **44**: 227–296.

Kölreuter, J.G. 1761. *Vorläufige Nachricht von einigen das Geschlecht der Pflanzen betreffenden Versuchen und Beobachtungen.* Fortsetzung 1763; Zweyte Fortestzung 1764; Dritte Fortsetzung 1766. Gleditschische Buchhandlung, Leipzig.

Leydig, F. 1857. *Lehrbuch der Histologie des Menschen und der Thiere.* Meidinger Sohn, Frankfurt.

McClung, C.E. 1902. The accessory chromosome–sex determinant. *Biol. Bull.* **3**: 43–84.

Mohl, H. 1835. Doctoral thesis (cited by J. Sachs 1875).

———. 1837. Ueber die Vermehrung der Pflanzenzellen durch Theilung. *Flora* **20**: 1–16; 17–31.

———. 1839. Ueber die Entwicklung der Sporen von *Anthoceros laevis. Linnaea* **13**: 271–290.

Montgomery, T.H., Jr. 1901. A study of the chromosomes of the germ cells of metazoa. *Trans. Am. Philos. Soc.* **20**: 154–230.

Morgan, T.H. 1910a. Chromosomes and heredity. *Am. Nat.* **44**: 449–496.

———. 1910b. Sex-linked inheritance in *Drosophila. Science* **32**: 120–122.

Morgan, T.H., C.B. Bridges, and A.H. Sturtevant. 1925. The genetics of *Drosophila.* Martinus Nijhoff, 's-Gravenhage, Holland.

Müller, O.F. 1786. *Animalcula infusoria fluviatilia et marina.* N. Müller, Copenhagen.

Nägeli, C. 1844. Zellenkerne, Zellenbildung und Zellenwachstum bei der Pflanzen. *Z. Wiss. Bot.* **1**: 34–133.

———. 1884. *Mechanisch-physiologische Theorie der Abstammungslehre.* R. Oldenbourg, München and Leipzig.

Oken, L. 1805. *Die Zeugung.* Joseph Anton Goebhardt, Bamburg and Wurzburg.

———. 1831. *Lehrbuch der Naturphilosophie,* 2nd revised edition. Friedrich Frommann, Jena.

Rabl, C. 1885. Über Zellteilung. *Morphol. Jahrb.* **10**: 214–330.

Reichert, K.B. 1847. Bericht über die Leistungen in der mikroskopischen Anatomie des Jahres 1846. *Arch. Anat. Physiol,* pp. 1–67.

Remak, R. 1841a. Über Theilung rother Blutzellen beim Embryo. *Med. Z. Ver. Heilk. Pr.* **10:** 127.

———. 1841b. Leistungen im Gebiete der Physiologie im Jahre 1841. *Canstatts Jahresber. Ges. Med.* **1:** 17–18.

———. 1845. Ueber die Entwickelung der Muskelprimitivbündel. *Froriep's Notizen* **35:** 305–308.

———. 1852. Ueber extracellulare Entstehung thierischer Zellen und über Vermehrung derselben durch Theilung. *Arch. Anat. Physiol,* pp. 47–57.

———. 1854a. Ueber Theilung thierische Zellen. *Arch. Anat. Physiol.,* p. 376.

———. 1854b. Ein Beitrag zur Entwicklungsgeschichte der Krebshaften Geschwülste. *Dtsch. Klinik* **6:** 170–174.

———. 1855. *Untersuchungen über die Entwickelung der Wirbeltiere.* G. Reiner, Berlin.

———. 1858. Ueber die Theilung der Blutzellen beim Embryo. *Arch. Anat. Physiol.,* pp. 178–188.

———. 1862. Ueber die embryologische Grundlage der Zellentheorie. *Arch. Anat. Physiol.,* pp. 230–241.

Roux, W. 1883. Ueber die Bedeutung der Kerntheilungsfiguren. In *Gesammelte Abhandlungen über Entwickelungsmechanik der Organismen 1895,* pp. 125–143. Wilhelm Engelmann, Leipzig.

Sachs, J. 1875. *Geschichte der Botanik von 16 Jahrhundert bis 1860.* R. Oldenbourg, München.

Schleicher, W. 1878. Ueber den Teilungprozess der Knorpelzellen. *Zentralbl. Med. Wiss. Berlin,* pp. 418–419.

———. 1879. Die Knorpelzelltheilung. *Arch. Mikrosk. Anat.* **16:** 248–300.

Schleiden, M.J. 1838. Beiträge zur Phytogenesis. *Arch. Anat. Physiol.,* pp. 137–176.

Schwann, T. 1839. *Microskopische Untersuchungen ueber die Uebereinstimmung in der Struktur und dem Wachstum der Thiere und Pflanzen.* Sander'schen Buchhandlung, Berlin.

Selenka, E. 1878. *Zoologische Studien. Befruchtung des Eies von* Toxopneustes variegatus. Wilhelm Engelmann, Leipzig.

Singer, C. 1931. *A short history of biology,* p. 328. Clarendon Press, Oxford.

Strasburger, E. 1875. *Zellbildung und Zelltheilung,* 1st edition. Hermann Dabis, Jena.

———. 1879. Ueber ein zu Demonstrationen geeignetes Zelltheilungs-Objekt. Jena. *Z. Naturwiss.* **13** (*Sitzungsber.*): 93–104.

———. 1880. *Zellbildung und Zelltheilung,* 3rd edition. Hermann Dabis, Jena.

———. 1884. *Neue Untersuchungen über den Befruchtungsvorgang bei den Phanerogamen als Grundlage für eine Theorie der Zeugung.* G. Fischer, Jena.

Sutton, W.S. 1902. On the morphology of the chromosome group in *Brachystola magna. Biol. Bull.* **4:** 124–139.

———. 1903. The chromosomes in heredity. *Biol. Bull.* **4:** 231–251.

Trembley, A. 1744. Observations upon several newly discover'd species of fresh-water Polypi. *Philos. Trans.* **43:** 169–183.

———. 1747. Observations upon several species of small water insects of the *Polypus* kind. *Philos. Trans.* **44:** 627–655.

———. 1766. *Manuscript letter to Count Bentinck* (cited by J.R. Baker 1953).

Unger, F. 1841. Genesis der Spiralgefässe. *Linnaea,* p. 385–407.

———. 1844. Ueber das Wachsthum der Internodien. *Z. Bot.* **2:** 489–494.

van Beneden, E. 1883. Recherches sur la maturation de l'oeuf et la Fécondation. *Ascaris megalocephala. Arch. Biol.* **4:** 265–640.

van Beneden, E. and A. Neyt. 1887. Nouvelles recherches sur la fécondation et la division mitosique chez l'Ascaride mégalocéphale. *Bull. Acad. R. Belg. Sér. 3* **14:** 215–295.

Vasold, B. 1988. *Rudolph Virchow: Der Grosse Arzt und Politiker.* Deutsche Verlags-Anstalt, Stuttgart.

Vaucher, J.-P. 1803. *Histoire des conferves d'eau douce.* A Genève chez J.J. Paschoud.

Virchow, R. 1855. Cellular-Pathologie. *Arch. Pathol. Anat.* **8:** 3–39.

———. 1858. *Die Cellularpathologie in ihrer Begründung auf physiologische und pathologische Gewebelehre.* August Hirschwald, Berlin.

Waldeyer, W. 1888. Ueber Karyokinese und ihre Bezeihungen zu den Befruchtungsvorgängen. *Arch. Mikrosk. Anat.* **32:** 1–122.

Warneck, N. 1850. Über die Bildung und Entwickelung des Embryos bei den Gasteropoden. *Bull. Soc. Imp. Nat. Moscou* **23**: 90.

Weismann, A. 1885. *Die Kontinuität des Keimplasmas als Grundlage einer Theorie der Vererbung.* Gustav Fischer, Jena.

Wilson, E.B. 1901. Experimental studies in cytology. II. Some phenomena of fertilization and cell-division in etherized eggs. III. The effect on cleavage of artificial obliteration of the first cleavage-furrow. *Arch. Entwicklungsmech. Org.* **13**: 353–395.

2
SOMATIC CELLS OUTSIDE THE BODY

Reviews of the genesis of tissue culture usually begin by referring to the work of Wilhelm Roux (1885). I think this point of reference has been generally accepted because Ross G. Harrison (Fig. 11), whose papers (1907a,b) are normally credited with having initiated the explosive growth of tissue culture studies in modern times, described his own work as an extension of the methodology devised by Roux. This reference is more than a matter of courtesy, for Harrison, like Roux, was primarily concerned with embryonic development and both workers removed tissues from the embryo and maintained them *in vitro* in order to study the mechanisms of specific forms of differentiation. Roux's experiments, which involved the manipulation of frog and chick embryos in a number of different ways, were aimed at deciding whether differentiation at various sites could take place independently of stimuli provided by the surrounding tissues or whether interactions with other tissues was indispensable. Among the many experiments that Roux devised to analyse this question were some in which the neural plate of developing frog embryos was removed from the animal and maintained *in vitro* long enough to demonstrate that closure of the neural tube could take place without the pressure that was thought to be exerted by the surrounding tissues. Roux made no mention of whether the cells in his explanted tissues underwent multiplication, and he did not attempt to maintain the explant for any longer than was necessary to answer the embryological question in which he was interested.

Harrison also was not initially concerned with the question of cell multiplication *in vitro* but with the analysis of morphogenesis. The problem in which he was primarily interested was the mode of formation of nerve fibres. On the basis of histological work, Cajal (1907) was convinced that each nerve fibre was produced by protoplasmic outgrowth from a single nerve cell (the neuron doctrine of His and Forel), but decisive evidence for this doctrine was lacking. Harrison began by transplanting fragments from the nervous system of amphibian larvae to cavities in the embryo such as the ventricles of the brain or the pharynx, but no outgrowth of nerve fibres occurred at these sites. When, however, the transplants were made to other, solid tissue, sites, nerve fibres were formed that grew into the surrounding tissues. This finding argued against the idea that the nerve fibres were produced by elaboration of more primitive structures such as protoplasmic bridges, since the new fibres

FIGURE 11 Ross G. Harrison (1870–1959). Extending the studies of Wilhelm Roux (Fig. 8) on explanted tissues, Harrison developed a method for maintaining fragments of embryonic frog tissues in drops of clotted lymph. In these preparations, which could be maintained in a sterile condition for some weeks, cells were seen to undergo various forms of differentiation. These experiments are commonly regarded as the origin of modern tissue culture. *(Courtesy of the Cold Spring Harbor Laboratory Archives.)*

infiltrated tissues that were already organised in a different way. Harrison then excised small fragments from parts of the frog embryo that were known to give rise to nervous tissue, for example the medullary tube or the ectoderm of the branchial region, and explanted them into clotted lymph. The fragments were removed before any visible differentiation of nerve elements had taken place, and each was deposited on a coverslip in a drop of adult frog lymph which rapidly coagulated. The coverslip was then inverted over a well-slide to make a 'hanging-drop' preparation. If care was taken to ensure aseptic conditions, such hanging-drop preparations, when sealed with paraffin, could be kept alive for up to four weeks. Harrison was probably the first to see what we would now call an 'emigration zone'—a halo of cells that had moved out of the explant into the lymph clot. In this emigration zone he observed the formation of nerve fibres from protoplasmic extensions that were progressively spooled out from individual cells. He thus provided a definitive solution to the problem he had set himself. From explants of presumptive epidermis he saw in the emigration zone aggregates of cells that formed typical cuticular borders in which the cilia remained active for a week or more; and explants taken from embryonic myotomes released cells that developed into typical striated muscle fibres which, within two or three days, showed frequent contractions. Harrison realised at once that he had devised a method that would be of great value for the study of differentiation, but his initial papers make no mention of cell multiplication; and this is still true for the definitive account of his work that appeared three years later (Harrison 1910).

CELL MULTIPLICATION OUTSIDE THE BODY

It seems likely that Remak (1858), in his studies on the multiplication of chick embryo erythrocytes, was the first to observe the division of vertebrate cells outside the body, but there is no evidence of his having attempted to prolong the period of cell survival *in vitro* beyond what was necessary to enable him to observe the details of the mitotic process. von Recklinghausen (1866) kept preparations of frog blood free from bacterial or fungal contamination for up to 35 days in moist chambers and studied the development of erythrocytes in these chambers under varying conditions. Three to four days after removal of the blood from the body, he saw red cell precursors undergoing pigmentation and concluded that they must be newly formed cells. Such cells were seen in the chambers up to the 11th or 12th day and were especially frequent if the blood was withdrawn from animals actively undergoing some form of regeneration. von Recklinghausen also noted the presence of cells of other kinds and described appearances that he interpreted as 'coupling' between cells but that might have been instances of cell division. Normal erythrocyte precursors are, however, unpromising material for long-term culture as the cell division is soon followed by terminal differentiation which either expels the nucleus from the cell or condenses it into a dormant, genetically inactive, state. Arnold (1887) carried the study of cell multiplication *in vitro* a good deal further by extending the observations to leucocytes and other amoeboid cells found in amphibian tissues. Arnold inserted thin slices of porous elder pith into the dorsal lymph sac of frogs and left them there for many days. The interstices of the pith filled with lymph which soon clotted and thus formed a stable membrane. Polymorphonucleur leucocytes, eosinophils, mononuclear cells and, later, epithelial cells, migrated into the lymph clot and remained undisturbed when the preparation was subsequently removed from the lymph sac and transferred to a moist chamber. The chamber used by Arnold was based on that devised by Thoma (1878), in which cells could be examined in detail under the high power of the microscope. It was Arnold's successful use of lymph clot to provide a solid scaffolding into which cells could migrate that prompted Harrison's use of the same material. Arnold observed mononuclear cells undergoing mitosis in the moist chamber, but he also claimed to have seen cells dividing amitotically. He also described the formation of multinucleate cells by a process of nuclear division unaccompanied by cell division; but he did not see any unequivocal instance of cell fusion.

Although Ljunggren (1898) had shown that human skin could still be successfully grafted after being stored for weeks in ascitic fluid, and Haberlandt (1902) had attempted to propogate isolated vegetative cells from higher plants, Jolly (1903) seems to have been the first to set himself the specific problem of finding out just how long cell multiplication could continue outside the body. He had previously (Jolly 1898a,b,c) made a detailed study of the behaviour of different kinds of leucocytes *in vitro*, including cells freshly isolated from human blood, but these earlier studies were primarily concerned with the morphological features of the isolated cells rather than the length of their survival outside the body or their possible multiplication. In his 1903 paper, Jolly noted, without giving references, that von Recklinghausen, Ranvier and Cardile had previously observed that leucocytes could survive for long periods outside the body, and he confirmed these earlier observations. He found that leucocytes from the blood of the newt *Triton* could survive *in vitro* for a month. With respect to cell multiplication, he acknowledged that Strasburger and Flemming, whose contributions have already been described, had both observed division of erythrocytes from the blood of *Triton* for up to 24 hours after isolation, although these authors had considered 24 hours to be a long time for persistence of cell multiplication outside the body. Jolly greatly extended the time-scale. He withdrew blood by cardiac puncture from newts that were in the process of undergoing regeneration and showed that all stages of mitosis could still be observed in moist chambers for periods up to 15 days. He noted that, as time went by, mitosis became progressively slower, and in the later stages of the experiment he saw binucleate cells that were formed when division of the nucleus was successfully completed but the cell as a whole failed to divide. Binucleate cells arose more frequently when the preparations were subjected to low temperatures, an observation that had previously been made *in vitro* with eggs of various kinds. Beebe and Ewing (1906) maintained thin sections and fragments of an infectious canine lymphosarcoma *in vitro*, in various media and at different oxygen tensions. Cells in the periphery of the fragment appeared to be preserved for up to 48 hours in a medium containing serum, and there was some, but inconclusive, evidence of mitosis. When the fragments were maintained in blood, cells appeared to be preserved for up to 72 hours, but no evidence of mitosis was observed after 48 hours. This appears to have been the first report of mitosis in a solid tumour maintained outside the body, but lymphosarcomas are, of course, composed of cells of the lymphoid series, and cells of this type had previously been shown to survive for long periods *in vitro*.

THE BIRTH OF TISSUE CULTURE

All the work that I have so far described, including Harrison's experiments, formed an indispensable exordium to the vast modern movement in tissue culture, but the critical impulse came from the experiments of Burrows. Burrows was working in Carrel's department at the Rockefeller Institute but, under the influence of Harrison's papers of 1907 and 1910, moved to Harrison's laboratory at Yale in order to acquire the technique of tissue explantation that Harrison had devised. Burrows's aim was to apply the technique to warm-blooded animals. In his 1910 paper, Harrison had pointed out that clotted lymph was a far from ideal substrate for the support of the explanted cells: it was difficult to obtain in the amounts required and variable in quality, sometimes clotting too soon and sometimes not at all. Burrows chose the chick embryo as the source of his material and substituted plasma for lymph. The plasma was obtained in any amount desired from the carotid arteries of adult hens. The blood was collected into paraffin-lined tubes, and the separated plasma stored in the cold. It could be induced to clot when desired by raising the temperature to 39°C. Fragments of neural tubes, heart myotomes and skin were excised from 60-hour-old chick embryos and deposited in hanging-drop preparations of plasma clot, essentially as described by Harrison. Burrows observed interstitial connective tissue cells migrating out of the explants and noted, for the first time, that they actually multiplied in the plasma clot and continued to do so for up to 14 days. Burrows also introduced an efficient method for fixing and staining the cells in the clot and confirmed in the histological preparations that the emigration zone contained many mitotic figures. In 3% of the cases, muscular elements migrated out of the myotomes and underwent differentiation to form short chains of striated cells that contracted rhythmically in unison with the heart tissue from which they had emigrated. Like Harrison, Burrows saw axon cylinders grow out of the nerve cells. Burrows (1910) is the first account of chick embryo explantation in plasma clot.

After his sojourn with Harrison, Burrows returned to Carrel's laboratory, and the next paper in the series appeared as Carrel and Burrows (1910). This paper is essentially an extension of Burrows's work to a variety of adult tissues taken from different animal species. One cannot help wondering whether a more equitable name order might not have been Burrows and Carrel. Explants were made, from dogs, cats and frogs, of arterial sheath connective tissue, cartilage, peritoneal endothelium, bone, epidermis, thyroid, spleen and kidney. The emigration zones formed by these various explants were eventually dominated by only two cell types, one resembling connective tissue cells and the other epithelial cells, but in the initial stages cells resembling the tissue of origin were also seen in the clot, for example, tubular structures in the case of kidney explants and glandular cells in the case of thyroid explants. Mitoses were again seen in the emigration zones, but the nature of the cells in which they occurred could not be identified with certainty. In this paper, two further technical developments were reported: cultures that had stopped growing could be reactivated if they were transferred to fresh medium; and parts of the emigration zone itself could be *subcultivated* into a second plasma clot and would continue to grow there. It is clear that in this paper the emphasis is not only on the extension of the range of material that can be successfully explanted, but also on the continued subcultivation of the cells that migrate out of the explant. Carrel's assumption of the control of the work coincides with a change in the style of the papers that issue from his laboratory. The reports of the experiments become much more dramatic and are couched in such a way as to attract the maximum attention. For this there is always a heuristic justification, but in Carrel's case the drama is associated with a great deal of over-optimistic inaccuracy. For example, the principal conclusion drawn from the experiments described in this first paper of which Carrel is the leading author is that "the cultivation of normal cells would appear to be no more difficult than the cultivation of many microbes". While this was, at the time, a preposterous conclusion, it showed nonetheless that Carrel was fully conscious of the importance of applying microbiological methods to the study of animal cells. Nor did it escape him that the technique he was helping to develop might have an important bearing on the study of cancer. The successful explantation of a fragment of sarcoma was also reported in the Carrel and Burrows (1910) paper, and the implications of the work were discussed by Boveri (1914) in the celebrated monograph on malignant tumours that I have already discussed.

Carrel demonstrated his tissue cultures in Paris on 2 December 1910, but the demonstrations were greeted with great scepticism. Most observers considered that the tissues were merely surviving *in vitro* and that they showed profound signs of 'necrobiosis'. Carrel was challenged to show that the amount of growth seen could be accounted for by the number of mitoses. In primary explants, of course, the emigration zone is largely produced by movement of cells out of the explanted tissues, and many years were to elapse before quantitation of tissue culture reached a level that could permit this challenge to be met. The sceptical reaction to Carrel's demonstration is recorded in a paper by Jolly (1910). In Carrel and Burrows (1911), the question of cell multiplication *in vitro*, as opposed to mere cell survival, comes to the fore. The paper begins with a review of previous work on explanted animal cells and asserts that prior to the work of Burrows, only cell survival *in vitro*, but not cell multiplication, had been demonstrated. This is a curious conclusion, for specific reference is made to the paper by Jolly (1903), in which cell division *in vitro* was shown to continue for more than 15 days, and previous work on the multiplication of erythrocytes *in vitro* is ignored altogether. The paper does, however, contain a detailed examination of the claims of Leo Loeb. In a small monograph that he had published in 1897, Loeb claimed that he had cultivated animal tissues outside the body (Loeb 1897). But, as pointed out by Carrel and Burrows, this monograph contains no experimental evidence in support of the claim, and no such evidence was produced in the 13 years that elapsed between Loeb's claim and the publication of the papers by Carrel and Burrows. Loeb (1902a,b) did indeed describe the explantation of fragments of skin from guinea pig embryos into agar and coagulated serum, but these fragments were then inserted back into the body of the guinea pig, and subsequent observations were made only after the explants had been incubated for various periods *in vivo*. Cells were observed to grow into the agar gels, but this could hardly be described as cultivation of tissues outside the body.

In their 1911 paper, Carrel and Burrows note that cell multiplication was observed with certainty in only two cell types, connective tissue cells and epithelial cells; but subcultivation of the cells in the emigration zone was successfully achieved through *two* passages. Moreover, malignant cells from the Rous chicken sarcoma, the Ehrlich and Jensen rat sarcomas, a canine breast carcinoma, a primary human carcinoma of the breast and a human sarcoma of the tibula were successfully explanted. In the case of the Rous sarcoma, the explanted cells were shown to be capable of producing sarcomas when re-injected into the chicken, but this was almost certainly due to the release of free virus from the re-implanted cells rather than to their continued progressive growth in a histoincompatible host. In the 1911 Carrel and Burrows paper, we see further evidence of Carrel's equivocal influence on the field. Whereas, in 1910, he had claimed that growing animal cells *in vitro* appeared to be no more difficult than growing microbes, in 1911 he emphasizes the complexity of the procedures he adopts and exaggerates their difficulty. Even in the relatively simple matter of collecting sterile plasma, which was by that time already commonplace in many laboratories, he finds it necessary to describe his technique in elaborate detail. He insists that the tissues must be rapidly and carefully prepared, and that extreme precautions must be taken to ensure complete asepsis. As Harrison had previously pointed out, bacterial contamination of the tissue cultures was a problem, and aseptic precautions were necessary, but in Carrel's case these were expanded into a ritual that was no less exacting than that prevailing in hospital operating theatres. When Carrel moved from Harrison's hanging-drop preparations in well-slides to larger containers, glass flasks specially constructed to his own specifications (the Carrel flasks) were adopted. The final methodological conclusion drawn in the Carrel and Burrows 1911 paper is that "perfect teamwork of well trained assistants is necessary". All this deliberate complexity of operation created the impression that tissue culture was a monstrously difficult procedure and no doubt delayed progress in the field by discouraging many who did not have at their disposal the resources of the Rockefeller Institute.

Lambert and Hanes (1911a) were among the first to take up the techniques devised by Burrows and showed that when fragments of epithelial tumours were explanted, sheets of contiguous cells grew out of the explants, whereas connective tissue tumours generated "strings of irregularly shaped cells". In a second paper (1911b), they described changes in the morphology of the cells in the emigration zone, especially the connective tissue cells, in response to plasma from different animal species. In the same year, Burrows (1911) published an account of the behaviour of explants from different tissues of the chick embryo and provided a detailed description of the mode of formation of nerve fibres. Lambert (1912) also studied explants of various chick embryo tissues, including heart, intestine and spleen, and described differences in the morphology of both connective tissue cells and epithelial cells taken from different sites. He also noted the presence of multinucleate giant cells. Champy (1912, 1913) noticed that cells in culture often lost some of the specific features that characterised them in their normal habitat *in vivo* and coined the word *dedifferentiation* to describe this process. Lewis and Lewis (1911, 1912) made the first attempt to replace the complexity of a plasma clot by devising conditions in which explants of chick embryo tissues, and especially of the embryonic nervous system, produced emigration zones directly onto glass cover slips. This permitted much better definition of the cells than was possible in plasma clot. Lewis and Lewis were also the first to attempt to cultivate tissues in simple salt solutions of various kinds. They, however, were concerned with the morphological characteristics of the cells in the emigration zone and not with cell multiplication. Since Carrel and Burrows (1910) had shown that exhaustion of nutrients in the medium could limit the growth of explants, Burrows (1912) devised a perfusion chamber that provided a continuous supply of fresh medium to the cultures and thus achieved their survival and growth for longer periods.

IMMORTALITY OF CELLS IN CULTURE

Carrel (1912) bears the dramatic title *On the permanent life of tissues outside the body*. Clearly, if cells within the body were mortal, but cells outside it were immortal, then that would be a generalisation with monumental consequences not only for biology but even, perhaps, for theology. Needless to say, Carrel's paper did not establish the permanent life of tissues outside the body. What it did report was that explants of different tissues, and particularly explants of connective tissue, could be kept alive for much longer periods by frequent changes of medium and by the addition of embryo extract. A few of the cultures had been maintained for as long as 85 days at the time of writing, and explanted fragments of cardiac tissue were still beating at the beginning of the third month of culture. This paper was responsible for the subsequent widespread use of chick embryo extract in tissue cultures and initiated a prolonged series of attempts to identify and purify the stimulatory components. The more modest conclusion with which the paper ends is that the results described "may lead to the solution of the problem of permanent life of tissues *in vitro*". In Carrel (1913), the stimulatory power of tissue extract was examined further. Some stimulation was observed with several extracts, but embryo extracts and extracts of Rous sarcoma and adult spleen were found to be most effective. The growth-promoting properties of the extracts were reduced by heating at 56°C and abolished by heating at 70°C. They were also reduced by passage of the extracts through a Berkefeld filter (a bacterial filter made from diatomaceous earth) and abolished by passage through a Chamberland filter (made of unglazed porcelain). These preliminary observations suggested that the active principle might be a protein. Carrel initially contended that the effect of the tissue extracts was species-specific, a conclusion that was later invalidated by Carrel's own work and that of others. At this time, Carrel was joined by A.H. Ebeling who took over the management of the cultures of connective tissue cells that had been derived from explants of embryonic chick heart. All but one of these cultures died off or became contaminated with bacteria. The one remaining culture "arose indirectly from a fragment of heart which still pulsated after 104 days of life *in vitro*". (What precisely was meant by 'indirectly' is not clear.) The growth of the cells in this culture was initially very slow, but increased in subsequent passages. Eventually the culture was expanded into 30 subcultures, and by the time Ebeling (1913) wrote his paper, the cells had been maintained for over 12 months and 138 passages. Ebeling (1913) again bore a dramatic title: *The permanent life of connective tissue outside of the organism.*

The intervention of the First World War was perhaps responsible for the fact that we do not see important papers on tissue culture again until the early 1920s. The cultures described by Ebeling (1913), originally derived from chick embryo heart, were, however, maintained (Ebeling 1922), and they were eventually carried in continuous culture for 34 years before being finally closed down. It was the continued propagation of this cell line that gained credence for the doctrine that somatic cells were, in principle, immortal when cultivated in appropriate conditions outside the body. As will be seen later, this generalisation has since been subjected to the most profound modifications. Attempts were made in the post-First World War period to produce 'pure' strains of cells from different tissues. Pure in this context did not, of course, yet mean derived from a single clone. In fact it meant no more than homogeneous by morphological criteria. Fischer (1922) maintained a strain of epithelial cells from chick iris in continuous culture for a period of three months. Carrel and Ebeling (1922) stressed the importance of having pure strains for study and claimed to have derived a pure strain of mononuclear cells from the buffy coat of chicken blood. The cells were explanted into plasma clot and a segment of the primary emigration zone was cut out and subcultivated. The cells were maintained *in vitro* for three months, but no precise information was provided about mitotic activity. It was in this paper that the idea was first put forward that the mononuclear cells could undergo transformation into fibroblasts. This idea enjoyed widespread credence for many years and was not finally abandoned until the work of G.B. Mackaness in the 1950s, confirming an earlier observation by Moen (1935), demonstrated decisively that the apparent transformation of mononuclear cells into fibroblasts was actually to be explained by the overgrowth of fibroblasts that were present in the explants from the beginning. It now seems very unlikely that Carrel and Ebeling had pure cultures even by the inexact standards then operative. In Ebeling (1924) the production of pure cultures of epithelial cells was described, and these were maintained in continuous culture for 18 months; and in Ebeling (1925) the characteristics of a pure strain of thyroid cells were investigated.

ANALYSIS OF TISSUE EXTRACTS

Fischer (1923) showed that there was an inverse relationship between cell crowding and growth in tissue cultures, and this led him to advocate a new outlook on the biological significance of tissue growth *in vitro*. "Tissue cultures", he maintained, "must be regarded as regenerating tissue fragments, primitive cell states, or organism-like systems with strong correlations, and not as colonies of independent cell individuals" (Fischer 1946). This approach, which is essentially an extension of Harrison's work, was further developed by Strangeways and Fell (1926a,b), who sought not to produce maximum growth *in vitro*, but to establish cultural conditions in which normal development and normal patterns of differentiation could, as far as possible, be preserved. Tissue cultures of this kind, which eventually gave rise to what became known as 'organ cultures', yielded an immense amount of information in the ensuing decades, but they did not contribute in any important way to the development of somatic cell genetics. In the meantime, the search for the stimulatory components of tissue extracts continued. Carrel (1922) showed that leucocyte extracts were effective, and Champy (1922) demonstrated that thyroid extracts had a specific stimulatory effect. Carrel and Ebeling (1923) studied the effects of embryo extracts from different animal species on the growth of chick embryo fibroblasts, but their results did not support Carrel's earlier view that the stimulatory effect of embryo extracts was species-specific. Homologous and heterologous embryo extracts appeared to be equally effective, and much more effective than extracts of adult tissues. Baker and Carrel (1926a,b) undertook a systematic examination and partial fractionation of tissue extracts. They examined the dialyzable and non-dialyzable fractions and came to the conclusion (Carrel and Baker 1926) that 'proteoses' (large proteolytic fragments) from embryonic tissue, egg white, commercial fibrin, rabbit brain and other sources stimulated cell growth, but that 'peptones' (smaller proteolytic fragments) were inhibitory. Peptic digests of fibrin were found to be more stimulatory than embryo extract. Carrel and Baker came to the conclusion that the efficacy of embryo extracts was not due to the presence of a hormone but to the provision of nutrients in the form of proteoses. This conclusion seems at first sight at variance with the results reported earlier by Carrel (1913) which indicated that the stimulatory power of embryo extracts was diminished or abolished by bacterial filters. Proteoses would be expected to pass through bacteriological filters, although, of course, some adsorption of active material to the filter might well have occurred. The search for the active ingredients of tissue extracts, and especially extracts of embryonic tissues, continued intermittently for the next 30 years. Baker and Carrel (1928) studied the effect of digests of pure proteins, Willmer and Kendall (1932) the utilisation of proteoses. Fischer (1939) initially thought that nucleoprotein, and particularly ribonucleoprotein, was the single active component, but he later considered the effects of amino acids to be important (Fischer 1941). Doljanski and Werner (1945) fractionated adult tissue extracts with alcohol and examined the effects of lipid solvents. Morgan Harris (1952) tested alcoholic extracts of chick embryos. All this analytic work reached no clear conclusion and eventually gave way to more systematic studies on the growth requirements of animal cells that will be discussed later.

If genetic analyses of somatic cells were ever to be possible, it was clear that methods would have to be devised that would permit the progeny of a single cell to be isolated and then maintained in a state of continuous multiplication for long enough to generate cell populations that could be worked with. Carrel's claim that, under appropriate conditions, somatic cells could be propagated indefinitely, encouraged the hope that there would be no limitation on the amount of material that could be obtained once isolation of clonal populations had been achieved. However, the progressive development of tissue culture techniques in the period between the two wars and the extensive application of these techniques for a wide range of different biological assays revealed soon enough that very few normal adult tissues could be grown *in vitro* without difficulty, and some did not survive at all outside the body. The common experience was that cultures of connective tissue cells could be derived from explants of many tissues, and cultures of epithelial cells from a much narrower range; but there was singularly little success in establishing long-term cultures of the great majority of normal cells in the characteristic differentiated state that they had in the body. Although such cells could often be induced to emigrate out of an explant, they either failed to multiply or multiplied so slowly that the cultures were soon overgrown by the ubiquitous connective tissue cells. The chick embryo connective tissue cells maintained in continuous culture by Ebeling remained for many years the only ones for which permanent life *in vitro* could plausibly be claimed.

PERMANENT CELL LINES

Nothing comparable was achieved for mammalian cells until 1943, when the first permanent mouse cell line was established by Earle (Fig. 12) (Earle 1943a,b). The cells were originally derived from an explant of subcutaneous tissue from a C3H mouse and were at first cultivated in plasma clot. The experiments formed part of a programme aimed at inducing malignant changes in cells *in vitro*. The cells were cultivated for 200 days and then exposed at varying intervals to the carcinogen 20-methylcholanthrene. The cultures underwent marked morphological changes and eventually some sublines produced sarcomas when injected back into the host animal (Earle 1944). The cells

FIGURE 12 Wilton R. Earle (1902–1964), in collaboration with K.K. Sanford and G.D. Likely, produced the first clonal animal cell line, NCTC clone 929. *(Courtesy of Dr. Katherine Sanford.)*

that were propagated continuously *in vitro* were designated strain L and, in 1947, they were established as monolayer cultures that grew on glass in the absence of plasma clot (Evans and Earle 1947). At the same time, it was noticed that similar changes leading to the acquisition of the capacity to produce tumours also took place in control cultures that had not been exposed to 20-methylcholanthrene (Earle and Nettleship 1943; Nettleship and Earle 1943). All the sublines of strain L cells that were maintained in continuous culture over long periods eventually showed a morphology profoundly different from that of the connective tissue cells that grew out of the primary explant. This was the first description of what subsequently came to be known generically as 'transformation' of cells *in vitro*. The first human cell line to be permanently established was HeLa, which was derived from a rapidly growing cervical carcinoma (Gey, Coffman, and Kubicek 1952; Gey 1955). This also was originally grown in plasma clot, but was later established on a glass substrate. The transfer of cells growing on glass from one vessel to another was until 1953 achieved by mechanical means: the cells were scraped from the glass by a rubber policeman, and the cell aggregates thus liberated were dispersed by agitation. Cell numbers were estimated by counting the number of nuclei present in the dispersed cell suspension (Sanford et al. 1951). Rous, who was working at the Rockefeller Institute at the time that Carrel launched his tissue culture programme, was the first to use trypsin to liberate cells from plasma clot (Rous and Jones 1916). Rous was acutely aware of the importance of applying quantitative microbiological methods to tissue cultures and used trypsin not only to obtain suspensions of cells from fixed tissues, but also to 'plate out' the individual cells. Rous and Jones succeeded in cultivating the trypsinized cells through several passages, but the cultures eventually died out. Perhaps because of this, trypsin was not tried again until Moscona (1952) used the enzyme to release cell suspensions from fixed tissues in order to study the specificity of cell aggregation. Stimulated by Moscona's experiments, Scherer, Syverton, and Gey (1953) used trypsin to release monolayers of HeLa cells from a glass substrate; and thereafter trypsinization was rapidly adopted as the standard procedure for the subcultivation of cells in culture. With the L cell and HeLa as prototypes, other permanent cell lines were soon established: HEP2 from a carcinoma of the larynx (Moore, Sabachewsky, and Toolan 1955); KB from a carcinoma of the nasopharynx (Eagle 1955a); and Detroit 6, possibly from a metastatic carcinoma of the lung (Berman, Stulberg, and Ruddle 1955). Several thousand such cell lines derived from both neoplastic and normal tissues are now deposited in cell collections in many parts of the world.

Techniques of bulk cultivation, storage and general management of permanent cell lines underwent progressive development during the 1950s and 1960s. Collagenase, elastase and proteolytic enzymes other than trypsin were used to release cells directly from solid tissues and from glass or plastic culture flasks (Rinaldini 1958). Some cell lines were adapted to growth in suspension. The first of these was a malignant mouse lymphoblast line which was kept in suspension in a specially designed 'tumble-tube' (Owens, Gey, and Gey 1954). A little later, the A cell line was brought into suspension culture in rotating tubes or 'shaker flasks' (Earle et al. 1956). 'Spinner' flasks, in which the medium was continuously agitated by means of a magnetic stirrer, were introduced in response to increasing demands, both academic and industrial, for large-scale cell production (McLimans et al. 1957). Chemostats for the growth of animal cells were devised in order to permit continuous rather than batch culture, and eventually established cell lines were successfully grown in industrial fermentation vessels. It has not, however, been found possible, despite persistent efforts, to produce viable suspension cultures of cells freshly isolated from fixed tissues.

No less important than the development of efficient methods for growing cells *in vitro* was the development of methods for storing them. It was known that spermatozoa, skin and some tumours could be stored in the frozen state and remain viable after thawing, but until the 1950s it was generally believed that somatic animal cells were destroyed by freezing and thawing. So general was this belief that in experiments on the possible viral origin of human cancers, freezing and thawing of a cell suspension was held to be a secure way to ensure that no viable cells remained in the preparation. The essential problem was the disruption of the cell that resulted from the formation of ice crystals. This problem was solved in principle by Polge, Smith, and Parkes (1949) who first demonstrated the protective effect of adding glycerol to the preparation. Other antifreeze compounds, for example, glycol and dimethylsulphoxide, were soon tested and optimal conditions for freezing and thawing were determined (Molina 1962). The standardisation of these storage procedures enabled cell banks to be established (Hauschka, Mitchell, and Niederpruem 1959). Initially, these banks were maintained at –70°C and –80°C, but later, storage in liquid nitrogen was generally adopted. However, by far the most important technical advance in the field of cell and tissue culture after the Second World War was the introduction of antibiotics into medicine. Although the addition of antibiotics to culture media in due course brought its own problems, it so reduced the risk of bacterial contamination that what was once an exacting ritual became a procedure that could easily be carried out in any well found laboratory. This, more than anything else, made cell culture a feasible methodology for anyone interested in applying it.

DEVELOPMENT OF SIMPLIFIED CULTURE MEDIA

All these developments were necessarily accompanied by progressive improvement and simplification of culture media. White (1946, 1949) appears to have made the first attempt to replace biological fluids such as serum or embryo extract by synthetic media of known composition. White's media were essentially empirically derived mixtures based on the known nutritional requirements of animals. Although they permitted survival of chick embryo explants for some time, they did not support cell multiplication. Morgan, Morton, and Parker (1950) extended these observations. Their medium 199, a more complex mixture than White's medium, prolonged the survival of chick embryo cells *in vitro*, but again failed to support cell multiplication in the absence of serum. Fischer (1941, 1946) had shown that the dialyzed macromolecular components of chick embryo extract would not alone support cell growth, but growth could be restored if the dialysate was added back to the macromolecular residue. This observation formed the basis of the much more systematic analysis of the nutritional requirements of cells in culture undertaken by Eagle and his colleagues. Eagle (1955b,c) found that synthetic media would readily support the growth of HeLa and L cells if as little as 1–5% of dialyzed serum was added to the medium. The effect of omitting single defined components from the mixture could then be examined and those essential for growth determined. It transpired that the components required for growth *in vitro* were broadly similar for many established cell lines, irrespective of the species or tissue of origin. In addition to the eight classical 'essential' amino acids that were required to maintain nitrogen balance in man, five 'non-essential' amino acids were needed to support the growth of cells in culture. This discrepancy was attributed, plausibly, to the ability of the liver in the intact animal to synthesize these non-essential amino acids in sufficient quantities to meet metabolic needs, whereas cell lines *in vitro* were presumed to be unable to synthesize enough of them to support growth.

Eight vitamins were shown to be required, although there was reason to suppose that others that could not be synthesized by cells might be supplied as trace contaminants in the serum proteins that had to be added. It was later shown that dialyzed serum did indeed release essential growth factors of low molecular weight (Eagle 1960b). Only six inorganic electrolytes were found to be essential: potassium, sodium, calcium, magnesium, chloride and phosphate, although trace amounts of other, possibly essential, elements might have been added as contaminants. Eagle, Freeman, and Levy (1958) showed that the nutritional requirements of freshly isolated monkey kidney cells were very similar to those of established cell lines, the main differences being that freshly isolated cells required a high level of added glycine, and, unlike established cell lines, were able to use glutamic acid effectively as a substitute for glutamine. All the carbohydrate requirements of cells in culture could be met by glucose, although a number of other carbohydrates could, in appropriate concentrations, act as substitutes for glucose (Eagle et al. 1958). On the basis of these studies, Eagle (1959) devised a 'minimum essential medium' (MEM) which, with the addition of a small amount of serum or dialyzed serum, was capable of supporting the growth of a wide range of cells. Eagle's MEM was at once widely adopted and remains in use to the present day, although many modifications of it have since been introduced. (For a summary of Eagle's work, see Eagle [1960a]. The compositions of the media in common use are given in Paul [1975].)

The universal failure to achieve long-term growth of animal cells *in vitro* in the absence of at least some added serum or tissue protein led many workers to adopt the view that growth in completely protein-free medium would never be possible. This notion was finally dismissed by Evans et al. (1956a,b) who succeeded in growing sublines of L cells in a completely defined medium that contained no protein additives. The most thoroughly studied of these media was called NCTC109 which contained about 70 defined compounds but no doubt a number of undefined impurities. In these protein-free media, the L cells initially grew slowly and sporadically but eventually subpopulations emerged that grew well. This progressive adaptation appeared to result from overgrowth of variants that had a selective advantage in the serum-free medium (McQuilkin, Evans, and Earle 1957). Medium NCTC109 was assembled empirically and contained many compounds, and even groups of compounds, that have since been shown to be unnecessary. A simpler protein-free medium was devised by Waymouth (1959). At about the same time, Healy, Fisher, and Parker (1954, 1955) found that modifications of medium 199 that failed to support the growth of freshly isolated chick embryo cells allowed L cells to multiply for long periods; and eventually media based on 199 were devised that permitted indefinite proliferation of L cells without added serum protein (Parker, Castor, and McCulloch 1957). Other cell lines were soon shown to be capable of growth in serum-free media, and some of these grew without requiring the progressive selection of better adapted variants. It came to be generally accepted that animal cells did not, in principle, require protein supplements of any kind for growth *in vitro*, but the signal and persistent failure to grow freshly explanted cells in serum-free medium continued to support the idea that normal tissue cells had specific requirements that had not yet been defined and that were not shared by permanent cell lines. Some clarification of this problem was provided by Fisher, Puck, and Sato (1958) who showed that connective tissue cells would multiply only if they were attached to a solid substrate and that this attachment required the presence in the medium of a serum glycoprotein to which they gave the name fetuin. Although progress was slow, growth of freshly isolated cells in defined media was eventually achieved for some tissues, usually by the inclusion in the medium of hormones or other specific growth factors (for a review of this subject, see Mather 1984); but many normal cell types in adult tissues have still not been successfully grown *in vitro* either with or without the addition of serum or other biological fluids.

THE LIMITED LIFESPAN OF DIPLOID CELLS AND THE DEVELOPMENT OF ANEUPLOIDY

The fact that all permanently established cell lines were unmistakably different from the freshly isolated cells that gave rise to them, and the persistent failure to cultivate some somatic cells at all, fostered continuing doubts about Carrel's general thesis that outside the body somatic cells were, in principle, immortal. The development of satisfactory techniques for visualising the chromosomes of animal cells in culture reinforced these doubts, for it at once became apparent that all established cell lines were no longer diploid, but showed varying degrees of aneuploidy. Morgan Harris (1957) re-investigated the proliferative capacity of chick embryo cells *in vitro* and, unlike Carrel, found that their lifespan was limited. Several strains were established as monolayers on glass, but each of them, after a period of vigorous logarithmic growth, eventually underwent degeneration. This was the case whether the cells were subcultivated by trypsinization or by mechanical removal from the glass. Chick cells grown in plasma clot, the medium used by Carrel, also eventually degenerated (Parker 1961). Similar results were obtained with other diploid cells (Swim and Parker 1957; Madin 1959; Swim 1959). There has been much speculation about how Carrel came to obtain the results that he described. One possibility that has been suggested is that Carrel may have regularly re-seeded his culture with viable cells that could have been present in the chick embryo extract that he added to the medium (Morgan Harris 1964). I think this explanation is unlikely because the cells in Carrel's long-term cultures did not have the appearance of freshly isolated diploid fibroblasts, but clearly had what we would now regard as a 'transformed' morphology. Given the proximity of Rous in the same institute and the fact that Carrel himself tested the effects of Rous sarcoma extracts on his cultures, I think it much more probable that his immortal cell line was actually contaminated by Rous sarcoma virus and transformed by it. Unfortunately, the cell lines maintained for decades by Ebeling no longer exist, so that there is no possibility of testing this notion.

The common experience that diploid cells had only a limited lifespan in culture resurrected the possibility that normal cells contained a genetic programme that specified their destruction after a pre-determined number of cell generations. On the other hand, it remained possible that this limited lifespan was due to the accumulated toxicity of the admittedly imperfect cultural conditions that were then available. Puck and his colleagues (Puck 1958, 1959; Puck, Cieciura, and Robinson 1958) argued strongly in favour of the latter alternative. With media that had been tested for toxicity prior to use, and with meticulous control of pH and temperature, these workers succeeded in growing diploid human cells for up to a year without degeneration or progression to aneuploidy. Moser (1960) came to a similar conclusion. The question was, however, re-investigated exhaustively by Hayflick and Moorhead (1961) who were able to confirm that it was possible to maintain euploidy and satisfactory growth of human cells in culture for about a year, but thereafter degenerative changes set in and the only permanent cell lines that survived the phase of generalised cell destruction proved to be aneuploid. Hayflick and Moorhead isolated 25 different strains of human cells and managed to grow all of them in the euploid condition under routine cultural conditions for about 50 passages (approximately a year). Apparently no especially exacting control of physical conditions and no rigorous selection of non-toxic foetal sera were required to achieve this end. But between the 50th and the 60th passages, mitotic activity decreased in all 25 different strains and degeneration eventually supervened. This could not be prevented or reversed by any changes of media or cultural conditions. Similar results were obtained by Ferguson and Wansbrough (1962). Saksela and Moorhead (1963) demonstrated that during the phase of degeneration aneuploid cells began to appear in the cultures, and it was from these that the permanent cell lines appeared to evolve. This phenomenon was studied in greater detail in cultures of euploid human amnion cells. Such cultures could be maintained for long periods with little or no multiplication, and within these dormant populations variant colonies could be seen to arise. They were easily recognisable by their morphological characteristics even when they contained only a few cells, and they showed numerous mitoses when none were to be found in the surrounding background of normal cells (Zitcer and Dunnebacke 1957; Fogh 1961; Hayflick 1961). These observations left little doubt that the permanent cell lines derived from cultures of euploid cells were produced by the selective overgrowth of variants that had undergone profound genetic changes. There was every reason to believe that the variant colonies arose from single cells and that the genetic changes that conferred the ability to proliferate when the euploid population as a whole was either degenerating or dormant were stochastic events. The permanent cell lines that grew out of these variant colonies were all found to be aneuploid in some degree, and no permanent cell line with a strictly euploid chromosome constitution has yet been established. It remains an open question whether the observed finite lifespan of euploid cells is itself genetically determined. It may be that sustained proliferation in artificial culture which, even at its best, is far from physiological, may require genetic adaptations that are achieved by mechanisms whose visible manifestation is aneuploidy. This possibility will be discussed in more detail at a later stage.

CLONES OF SOMATIC CELLS

All these developments in the technique of cell culture were an indispensable prelude to the science of somatic cell genetics, but no formal genetic analysis of somatic cells could be envisaged until methods were devised that permitted such cells to be cloned. As mentioned earlier, Rous was fully aware of the importance of applying microbiological techniques to the cells of the body when, in 1916, he and Jones attempted to plate out trypsinized cells from fixed tissues in plasma clot. Although these trypsinized cell populations eventually died out under the conditions of culture then used, it remains surprising that some 40 years were to elapse before serious attempts were again made to apply microbiological techniques to animal cells. To some extent this inordinately long lag period was due to the growth of the idea that normal body cells could not survive except as components of an organised multicellular system. This idea had its origin in the observations of Fischer (1925) who became its leading exponent. Fischer showed that whereas colonies did arise from isolated scattered Rous sarcoma cells, no colonies arose from scattered normal connective tissue cells. Moen (1935), however, reported that colonies of cells did arise from occasional fibroblasts that contaminated exudates of mononuclear cells obtained from the peritoneal cavity of guinea pigs. These fibroblasts were carried through several passages of subculture in plasma clot. Although it is very probable that the original colonies described by Moen were derived from single cells, this could not at that time be formally demonstrated. The first formal demonstration that a single somatic cell could give rise to a clonal population capable of indefinite multiplication was not provided until 1948. Even so, the cell that gave rise to this first clonal population was not a normal euploid somatic cell, but an isolate from the L cell line that had already been in culture for some years and was almost certainly 'transformed' (Sanford, Earle, and Likely 1948).

The isolation of this first clonal cell line was a technical *tour de force*. Capillary pipettes lined with chicken plasma were used to pick off individual L cells which were then distributed along the length of the pipettes. These were then sealed at one end with a mixture of medium and chicken plasma and at the other end with a molten glass bead. The cells enclosed in the pipettes were incubated at 37°C for 15–20 hours and healthy single cells were located. The pipettes were then sterilized in chloroform and broken into fragments of 4–5 mm in length. Fragments containing only one cell were transferred to Carrel flasks and maintained in a mixture of 50% plasma and 50% conditioned medium, that is, medium in which some growth of cells had already occurred. It was found that only about 4% of these single isolated cells were still alive 48 hours later. In this small residue of viable cells, some then began to multiply and eventually grew out of the tips of the pipettes to form visible colonies. It was claimed that no single cells gave rise to colonies if medium was used that had not previously been conditioned. The first clonal cell line derived in this way was called NCTC-929 and was subsequently used in many laboratories for a variety of investigative purposes (Fig. 13). Other clonal lines were soon obtained by more simplified capillary tube techniques, and the cloning efficiency was improved by the use of better media (Likely, Sanford, and Earle 1952; Sanford et al. 1961). Although these experiments settled once and for all the fundamental question of the proliferative capacity of single animal cells *in vitro*, the technology, even when simplified, was much too complex to be generally adopted and too cumbersome to provide a basis for the application of quantitative microbiological methods.

DEVELOPMENT OF STANDARD TECHNIQUES FOR CELL CLONING

Earle had stressed the importance of conditioned medium for cloning and believed that the critical factor in the use of the capillary tube was that each isolated cell was able itself to 'condition' the very small volume of medium that surrounded it. Other cloning procedures that relied on severe limitation of the volume of medium to which each cell was exposed involved micromanipulation techniques such as those devised by de Fonbrune (1949). With micromanipulators it was possible to study the behaviour of single animal cells within minute droplets of medium suspended in layers of paraffin oil (Lwoff et al. 1955). Wildy and Stoker (1958) produced clones of HeLa cells within such microdroplets. However, the essential technological revolution was initiated by Puck (Fig. 14) and Marcus (Fig. 15) (see Puck and Marcus 1955). Instead of limiting the volume of medium to which each single cell was exposed, Puck and Marcus conditioned the medium as a whole by plating the single cells on a confluent layer of lethally irradiated cells. The colonies that grew out of the single cells were easily recognisable against the matt homogeneous background of the dying 'feeder' layer (Fig. 16). Initially it was thought that the conditioning effect of the feeder layer was critical, but it was soon found that, for HeLa cells, the feeder layer could be dispensed with.

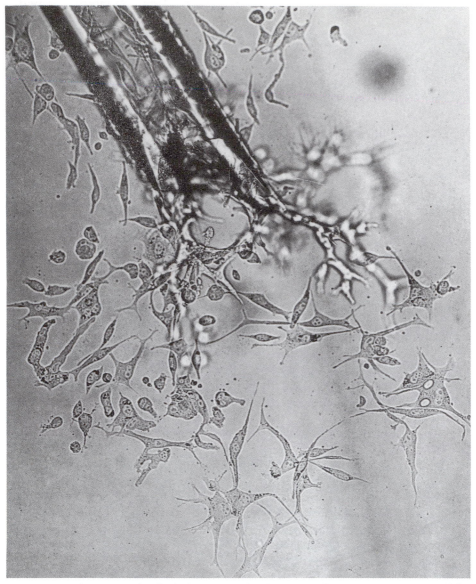

FIGURE 13 The origin of NCTC clone 929. The clonal population is growing out of the mouth of a glass capillary tube within which a single mouse cell had been isolated. (Reprinted, with permission, from Sanford, Earle, and Likely 1948.)

Puck, Marcus, and Cieciura (1956) showed that one line of HeLa cells gave a cloning efficiency of almost 100% in the absence of a feeder layer, and the cells in the clones grew logarithmically for 250 hours with a doubling time of less than 24 hours. The individual clones could be brought into suspension by trypsinization within stainless steel cylinders sealed to the floor of the culture vessel with silicone grease. These experiments provided the essential basis for what rapidly became the standard methodology for cloning animal cells. It was not long before several other permanent cell lines adapted to growth on

FIGURE 14 Theodore T. Puck (1916–), in collaboration with Philip I. Marcus (Fig. 15), devised the now standard method for cloning animal cells *in vitro*. Puck and Marcus also produced the first accurate single cell survival curve after X irradiation. *(Courtesy of Dr. Theodore Puck.)*

glass were found to generate colonies from single cells in a reproducible manner when plated out at an appropriate dilution. The question then arises why this was not done a decade earlier when the L cell line was first established and adapted to growth as a monolayer. One possible reason is that the media

FIGURE 15 Philip I. Marcus (1927–). *(Courtesy of Dr. Philip Marcus.)*

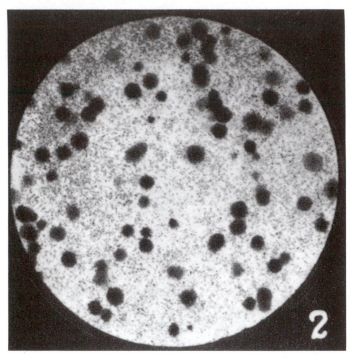

FIGURE 16   Clones growing from single HeLa cells plated onto a feeder layer of X-irradiated cells. (Reprinted, with permission, from Puck, Marcus, and Cieciura 1956.)

required to produce a high cloning efficiency are, for some cell lines, more exacting than those that will support the growth of bulk cultures. But media that would certainly have permitted the cloning of L cells were available long before anyone attempted the experiments that Puck and Marcus executed with such spectacular success in 1955. I think a more fundamental reason is that those who worked in the field of tissue culture at the time were simply not sufficiently impressed with the importance of applying quantitative microbiological techniques to somatic cells. The decisive impetus eventually came from the remarkable flow of new information generated by experiments with bacteriophages. (For an interesting, if partisan, account of the role of bacteriophage research in the birth of modern molecular biology, see Cairns, Stent, and Watson [1966].) The primary unit of genetic analysis in the case of the bacteriophage was the 'plaque'—a clear circular area produced in a lawn of bacteria by the lytic action of the phage. Plaque number and plaque morphology were the essential experimental parameters used, and they yielded insights of quite unprecedented profundity. After the Second World War, a number of physicists and others with a highly numerate background entered the field of biology via the study of bacteriophages, and, when they began to work with other organisms, they carried with them the concepts and methodology of phage genetics. Dulbecco (1952) first showed that single particles of an animal virus could produce lytic plaques in a lawn of confluent animal cells and thereby demonstrated that the methodology that had yielded such astonishing results with bacterial viruses was also applicable to animal viruses. Puck's clones of animal cells growing on a lethally irradiated feeder layer were an echo of the same methodology.

The cloning of euploid cells, and especially of cells freshly isolated from different organs, proved to be much more difficult. A feeder layer appeared to be essential, but, even so, cloning efficiencies with freshly isolated cells were very low compared with what could be achieved with permanent cell lines (Marcus, Cieciura, and Puck 1956; Marcus, Cieciura, and Fisher 1957). Rothfels, Kupelwieser, and Parker (1963) showed that, in the case of freshly isolated mouse embryo cells, no clones were produced with an inoculum of 3×10^3 cells per dish in the absence of a feeder layer. Progressive technical developments in due course increased the cloning efficiency of many cell types, including euploid cells. Glass vessels gradually gave way to plastic petri dishes that were maintained at constant temperature and pH in specially constructed incubators in which CO_2 tension could be accurately controlled. Media continued to improve. Ham (1963, 1965) formulated substantially better media for cell cloning (F10 and F12), and numerous other formulations were produced to meet specific cultural requirements. But despite all these improvements, it remained difficult to clone many diploid cells with any degree of efficiency; and it was not until 1993 that efficient cloning of euploid connective tissue cells in the absence of a feeder layer was finally achieved. Falanga and Kirsner (1993) showed that reduction of the oxygen tension in the gas phase of the tissue cultures from the usual 20% to 2% resulted in vigorous clonal growth of isolated single connective tissue cells.

Despite some serious limitations, it was obvious by the end of the 1950s that the problems of applying microbiological methods to the study of animal cells had in essence been solved. The genetic analysis of somatic cells could now begin.

REFERENCES

Arnold, J. 1887. Ueber Theilungsvorgänge an den Wanderzellen, ihre progressiven und regressiven Metamorphosen. *Arch. Mikrosk. Anat.* **30:** 205–310.

Baker, L.E. and A. Carrel. 1926a. Action on fibroblasts of the protein fraction of embryonic tissue extract. *J. Exp. Med.* **44:** 387–395.

———. 1926b. Effect of the amino acids and dialysable constituents of embryonic tissue juice on the growth of fibroblasts. *J. Exp. Med.* **44:** 397–407.

———. 1928. The effects of digests of pure proteins on cell proliferation. *J. Exp. Med.* **47:** 353–370.

Beebe, S.P. and J. Ewing. 1906. A study of the biology of tumour cells. *B. Med. J.* **2:** 1159–1160.

Berman, L., C.S. Stulberg, and F.H. Ruddle. 1955. Report of isolation of a strain of cells resembling epithelial cells from bone marrow of a patient with carcinoma of the lung. *Blood* **10:** 896–911.

Boveri, T. 1914. *Zur Frage der Entstehung maligner Tumoren.* G. Fischer, Jena.

Burrows, M.T. 1910. The cultivation of tissues of the chick-embryo outside the body. *J. Am. Med. Assoc.* **55:** 2057–2058.

———. 1911. The growth of tissues of the chick embryo outside the animal body with special reference to the nervous system. *J. Exp. Zool.* **10:** 63–84.

———. 1912. A method of furnishing a continuous supply of new medium to a tissue culture *in vitro. Anat. Rec.* **6:** 141–144.

Cairns, H.J.F., G.S. Stent, and J.D. Watson. 1966. *Phage and the origins of molecular biology.* Cold Spring Harbor Laboratory, Cold Spring Harbor, New York.

Cajal, S.R.y. 1907. Die Histogenetischen Beweise der Neuronentheorie von His und Forel. *Anat. Anz.* **30:** 113–144.

Carrel, A. 1912. On the permanent life of tissues outside the body. *J. Exp. Med.* **15:** 516–528.

———. 1913. Artificial activation of the growth *in vitro* of connective tissue. *J. Exp. Med.* **17:** 14–19.

———. 1922. Growth-promoting function of leucocytes. *J. Exp. Med.* **36:** 385–391.

Carrel, A. and L.E. Baker. 1926. The chemical nature of substances required for cell multiplication. *J. Exp. Med.* **44:** 503–521.

Carrel, A. and M.T. Burrows. 1910. Cultivation of adult tissues and organs outside the body. *J. Am. Med. Assoc.* **55:** 1379–1381.

———. 1911. Cultivation of tissues in vitro and its technique. *J. Exp. Med.* **13:** 387–396.

Carrel, A. and A.H. Ebeling. 1922. Pure cultures of large mononuclear leucocytes. *J. Exp. Med.* **36:** 365–377.

———. 1923. Action on fibroblasts of extracts of homologous and heterologous tissues. *J. Exp. Med.* **38:** 499–511.

Champy, C. 1912. Sur les phénomènes cytologiques qui s'observent das les tissus cultivés en dehors de l'organisme. I. Tissus épithéliaux et glandulaires. *C. R. Soc. Biol.* **72:** 987–988.

———. 1913. La dédifferenciation des tissus cultivés en dehors de l'organisme. *Bibl. Anat. Paris* **23:** 184–205.

———. 1922. L'action de l'extrait thyroïdien sur la multiplication cellulaire: Caractère électif de cette action. *Arch. Morphol.* fasc. **4:** 1–58.

de Fonbrune, P. 1949. *Technique de Micromanipulation.* Masson and Cie, Paris.

Doljanski, L. and H. Werner. 1945. Studies on growth-promoting factors of adult tissue extracts; precipitation with alcohol; action of lipid solvents. *Growth* **9:** 229–234.

Dulbecco, R. 1952. Production of plaques from monolayer tissue cultures by single particles of an animal virus. *Proc. Natl. Acad. Sci.* **38:** 747–752.

Eagle, H. 1955a. Propagation in a fluid medium of a human epidermoid carcinoma strain KB. *Proc. Soc. Exp. Biol. Med.* **89:** 362–364.

———. 1955b. The specific amino acid requirements of a mammalian cell (strain L) in tissue culture. *J. Biol. Chem.* **214:** 839–852.

———. 1955c. The specific amino acid requirements of a human carcinoma cell (strain HeLa) in tissue culture. *J. Exp. Med.* **102:** 37–48.

———. 1959. Amino acid metabolism in mammalian cell cultures. *Science* **130:** 432–437.

———. 1960a. Metabolic studies with normal and malignant human cells in culture. *Harvey Lect.* **54:** 156–175.

———. 1960b. The sustained growth of human and animal cells in a protein-free environment. *Proc. Natl. Acad. Sci.* **46:** 427–432.

Eagle, H., A.E. Freeman, and M. Levy. 1958. The amino acid requirements of monkey kidney cells in first culture passage. *J. Exp. Med.* **107:** 643–652.

Eagle, H., S. Barban, M. Levy, and H.O. Schultze. 1958. The utilization of carbohydrates by human cell cultures. *J. Biol. Chem.* **233:** 551–558.

Earle, W.R. 1943a. Changes induced in a strain of fibroblasts from a strain C3H mouse by the action of 20-methylcholanthrene. *J. Natl. Cancer Inst.* **3:** 555–558.

———. 1943b. Production of malignancy *in vitro*. IV. The mouse fibroblast cultures and changes seen in the living cells. *J. Natl. Cancer Inst.* **4:** 165–212.

Earle, W.R. 1944. A summary of certain data on the production of malignancy *in vitro*. In *American Association for the Advancement of Science Research Conference on Cancer*, pp. 139-153. Washington, D.C.

Earle, W.R. and A. Nettleship. 1943. Production of malignancy *in vitro*. V. Results of injections of cultures into mice. *J. Natl. Cancer Inst.* **4:** 213–228.

Earle, W.R., J.C. Bryant, E.L. Schilling, and V.J. Evans. 1956. Growth of cell suspensions in tissue culture. *Ann. N.Y. Acad. Sci.* **63:** 666–682.

Ebeling, A.H. 1913. The permanent life of connective tissue outside of the organism. *J. Exp. Med.* **17:** 273–284.

———. 1922. A ten year old strain of fibroblasts. *J. Exp. Med.* **35:** 755–759.

———. 1924. Cultures pures d'épithelium proliférant *in vitro* depuis dix-huit mois. *C.R. Soc. Biol.* **90:** 562–563.

———. 1925. A pure strain of thyroid cells and its characteristics. *J. Exp. Med.* **41:** 337–346.

Evans, V.J. and W.R. Earle. 1947. The use of perforated cellophane for the growth of cells in tissue culture. *J. Natl. Cancer Inst.* **8:** 103–119.

Evans, V.J., J.C. Bryant, M.C. Fioramonti, W.T. McQuilkin, K.K. Sanford, and W.R. Earle. 1956a. Studies of nutrient media for tissue cells *in vitro*. I. A protein-free chemically defined medium for cultivation of strain L cells. *Cancer Res.* **16:** 77–86.

Evans, V.J., J.C. Bryant, W.T. McQuilkin, M.C. Fioramonti, K.K. Sanford, B.B. Westfall, and W.R. Earle. 1956b. Studies on nutrient media for tissue cells *in vitro*. II. An improved protein-free chemically defined medium for long-term cultivation of strain L929 cells. *Cancer Res.* **16:** 87–94.

Falanga, V. and R.S. Kirsner. 1993. Low oxygen stimulates proliferation of fibroblasts seeded as single cells. *J. Cell. Physiol.* **154:** 506–510.

Ferguson, J. and A. Wansbrough. 1962. Isolation and long-term culture of diploid mammalian cell lines. *Cancer Res.* **22:** 556–562.

Fischer, A. 1922. A three months old strain of epithelium. *J. Exp. Med.* **35:** 367–372.

———. 1923. Contributions to the biology of tissue cells. 1. The relation of cell crowding to tissue growth *in vitro*. *J. Exp. Med.* **38:** 667–672.

———. 1925. Beitrag zur Biologie der Gewebezellen. Eine vergleichend-biologische Studie der normalen und malignen Gewebezellen *in vitro*. *Wilhelm Roux's Arch. Entwicklungsmech. Org.* **104:** 210–261.

———. 1939. Nature of the growth-accelerating substance of animal tissue cells. *Nature* **144:** 113.

———. 1941. Die Bedeutung der Aminosäuren für die Gewebezellen *in vitro*. *Acta Physiol. Scand.* **2:** 143–188.

———. 1946. *Biology of tissue cells*. Cambridge University Press, United Kingdom.

Fisher, H.W., T.T. Puck, and G. Sato. 1958. Molecular growth requirements of single mammalian cells: The action of fetuin in promoting cell attachment to glass. *Proc. Natl. Acad. Sci.* **44:** 4–10.

Fogh, J. 1961. Transformation of cultured human amnion cells. *Pathol. Biol.* **9:** 559–568.

Gey, G.O. 1955. Some aspects of the constitution and behaviour of normal and malignant cells maintained in continuous culture. *Harvey Lect.* **50:** 154–229.

Gey, G.O., W.D. Coffman, and M.T. Kubicek. 1952. Tissue culture studies on the proliferative capacity of cervical carcinoma and normal epithelium. *Cancer Res.* **12:** 264–265.

Haberlandt, C. 1902. Culturversuche mit isolierten Pflanzenzellen. *Sitzungsber. Berl. Acad. Wiss. Wien.* (Abt.1) **3:** 69–91.

Ham, R.G. 1963. An improved nutrient solution for diploid Chinese hamster and human cell lines. *Exp. Cell Res.* **29:** 515–526.

———. 1965. Clonal growth of mammalilan cells in a chemically defined synthetic medium. *Proc. Natl. Acad. Sci.* **53:** 288–293.

Harris, M. 1952. Growth factors in alcoholic extracts of chick embryos. *Growth* **16:** 215–230.

———. 1957. Quantitative growth studies with chick myoblasts in glass substrate cultures. *Growth* **21:** 149–166.

———. 1964. *Cell culture and somatic variation*, pp. 163-164. Holt, Reinhart, and Winston, New York.

Harrison, R.G. 1907a. Observations on the living developing nerve fiber. *Proc. Soc. Exp. Biol. Med.* **4:** 140–143.

———. 1907b. Observations on the living developing nerve fiber. *Anat. Rec.* **1:** 116–118.

———. 1910. The outgrowth of the nerve fiber as a mode of protoplasmic movement. *J. Exp. Zool.* **9:** 787–846.

Hauschka, T.S., J.T. Mitchell, and D.J. Niederpruem. 1959. A reliable frozen tissue bank: Viability and stability of 82 neoplastic and normal cell types after prolonged storage at –78°C. *Cancer Res.* **19:** 643–653.

Hayflick, L. 1961. The establishment of a line (WISH) of human amnion cells in continuous cultivation. *Exp. Cell Res.* **23:** 14–20.

Hayflick, L. and P.S. Moorhead. 1961. The serial cultivation of human diploid cell strains. *Exp. Cell Res.* **25:** 585–621.

Healy, G.M., D.C. Fisher, and R.C. Parker. 1954. Nutrition of animal cells in tissue culture. IX. Synthetic medium no. 703. *Can. J. Biochem. Physiol.* **32:** 327–337.

———. 1955. Nutrition of animal cells in tissue culture. X. Synthetic medium no. 858. *Proc. Soc. Exp. Biol. Med.* **89**: 71–77.

Jolly, J. 1898a. Sur les mouvements amiboïdes des globules blancs du sang dans la leucémie. *C. R. Soc. Biol.* **5**: 30–32.

———. 1898b. Sur les mouvements amiboïdes et sur le noyau des cellules éosinophiles. *C. R. Soc. Biol.* **5**: 554–556.

———. 1898c. Sur la dégénérescence du noyau des cellules lymphatiques *"in vitro"*. *C. R. Soc. Biol.* **5**: 702–704.

———. 1903. Sur la durée de la vie et de la multiplication des cellules animales en dehors de l'organisme. *C. R. Soc. Biol.* **55**: 1266–1268.

———. 1910. A propos de communications de MM. A. Carrel et Montrose T. Burrows sur la culture des tissues. *C.R. Soc. Biol.* **69**: 470–473.

Lambert, R.A. 1912. Variations in the character of growth in tissue cultures. *Anat. Rec.* **6**: 91–108.

Lambert, R.A. and F.M. Hanes. 1911a. Characteristics of growth of sarcoma and carcinoma cultivated *in vitro*. *J. Exp. Med.* **13**: 495–504.

———. 1911b. The cultivation of tissue in plasma from alien species. *J. Exp. Med.* **14**: 129–138.

Lewis, M.R. and W.H. Lewis. 1911. The cultivation of tissues from chick embryos in solutions of NaCl, $CaCl_2$, KCl and $NaHCO_3$. *Anat. Rec.* **5**: 277–285.

Lewis, W.H. and M.R. Lewis. 1912. The cultivation of sympathetic nerves from the intestine of chick embryos in saline solutions. *Anat. Rec.* **6**: 7–32.

Likely, G.D., K.K. Sanford, and W.R. Earle. 1952. Further studies on the proliferation *in vitro* of single isolated tissue cells. *J. Natl. Cancer Inst.* **13**: 177–184.

Ljunggren, C.A. 1898. Von der Fähigkeit des Hautepithels ausserhalb des Organismus sein Leben zu behalten, mit Berücksichtigung der Transplantation. *Dtsch. Z. Chir.* **47**: 605–615.

Loeb, L. 1897. *Ueber die Entstehung von Bindegewebe, Leucocyten und roten Blutkörperchen aus Epithel und über eine Methode isolierte Gewebstheile zu züchtern*, p. 41. M. Stern and Co., Chicago.

———. 1902a. Über das Wachstum des Epithels. *Wilhelm Roux's Arch. Entwicklungsmech. Org.* **13**: 487–506.

———. 1902b. On the growth of epithelium in agar and blood-serum in the living body. *J. Med. Res.* **8**: 109–115.

Lwoff A., R. Dulbecco, M. Vogt, and M. Lwoff. 1955. Kinetics of the release of poliomyelitis virus from single cells. *Virology* **1**: 128–139.

Madin, S.H. 1959. Tissue culture in veterinary medical resarch. *Adv. Vet. Sci.* **5**: 329–417.

Marcus, P.I., S.J. Cieciura, and H.W. Fisher. 1957. Clonal growth *in vitro* of human cells with fibroblastic morphology. Comparison of growth and genetic characteristics of single epitheloid and fibroblast-like cells from a variety of human organs. *J. Exp. Med.* **106**: 145–158.

Marcus, P.I., S.J. Cieciura, and T.T. Puck. 1956. Clonal growth *in vitro* of epithelial cells from normal human tissues. *J. Exp. Med.* **104**: 615–628.

Mather, J.P. 1984. *Mammalian cell culture. The use of serum-free hormone-supplemented media*. Plenum Press, New York and London.

McLimans, W.F., E.V. Davis, F.L. Glover, and G.W. Rake. 1957. The submerged culture of mammalian cells. The spinner culture *J. Immunol.* **79**: 428–433.

McQuilkin, W.T., V.J. Evans, and W.R. Earle. 1957. The adaptation of additional lines of NCTC clone 929 (strain L) cells to chemically defined protein-free medium NCTC 109. *J. Natl. Cancer Inst.* **19**: 885–907.

Moen, J.K. 1935. The development of pure cultures of fibroblasts from single mononuclear cells. *J. Exp. Med.* **61**: 247–260.

Molina, S.W. 1962. The low-temperature preservation of tissue and cell cultures. *Technical bulletin F. 1649*. Linde Company (Division of Union Carbide Corp.), New York.

Moore, A.E., L. Sabachewsky, and H.W. Toolan. 1955. Culture characteristics of four permanent lines of human cancer cells. *Cancer Res.* **15**: 598–602.

Morgan, J.F., H.J. Morton, and R.C. Parker. 1950. Nutrition of animal cells in tissue culture. I. Initial studies on a synthetic medium. *Proc. Soc. Exp. Biol. Med.* **73**: 1–8.

Moscona, H. 1952. Cell suspensions from organ rudiments of chick embryos. *Exp. Cell*

Res. **3:** 535–539.

Moser, H. 1960. Modern approaches to the study of mammalian cells in culture. *Experientia* **16:** 385–398.

Nettleship, A. and W.R. Earle. 1943. Production of malignancy *in vitro*. VI. Pathology of tumours produced. *J. Natl. Cancer Inst.* **4:** 229–248.

Owens, O.H., M.K. Gey, and G.O. Gey. 1954. Growth of cells in agitated fluid medium. *Ann. N.Y. Acad. Sci.* **58:** 1039–1055.

Parker, R.C. 1961. *Methods of tissue culture,* 3rd edition. Hoeber, New York.

Parker, R.C., L.N. Castor, and E.A. McCulloch. 1957. Altered cell strains in continuous culture: A general survey. *Spec. Publ. N.Y. Acad. Sci.* **5:** 303–313.

Paul, J. 1975. *Cell and tissue culture,* 5th edition. Churchill Livingstone, Edinburgh, London, and New York.

Polge, C., A.V. Smith, and A.S. Parkes. 1949. A revival of spermatozoa after vitrification and dehydration at low temperature. *Nature* **164:** 666.

Puck, T.T. 1958. Growth and genetics of somatic mammalian cells *in vitro. J. Cell. Comp. Physiol.* (suppl. 1.) **52:** 287–311.

———. 1959. Quantitative studies on mammalian cells *in vitro. Rev. Mod. Physiol.* **31:** 433–448.

Puck, T.T. and P.I. Marcus. 1955. A rapid method for viable cell titration and clone production with HeLa cells in tissue culture: The use of X-irradiated cells to supply conditioning factors. *Proc. Natl. Acad. Sci.* **41:** 432–437.

Puck, T.T., S.J. Cieciura, and A. Robinson. 1958. Genetics of somatic mammalian cells. III. Long-term cultivation of euploid cells from human and animal subjects. *J. Exp. Med.* **108:** 945–956.

Puck, T.T., P.I. Marcus, and S.J. Cieciura. 1956. Clonal growth of mammalian cells *in vitro*. Growth characteristics of colonies from single HeLa cells with and without a 'feeder' layer. *J. Exp. Med.* **103:** 273–284.

Remak, R. 1858. Ueber die Theilungder Blutzellen beim Embryo. *Arch. Anat. Physiol.,* pp. 178–188.

Rinaldini, L.M.J. 1958. The isolation of living cells from animal tissues. *Int. Rev. Cytol.* **7:** 587–647.

Rothfels, K.H., E.B. Kupelwieser, and R.C. Parker. 1963. Effects of X-irradiated feeder layers on mitotic activity and development of aneuploidy in mouse-embryo cells *in vitro. Can. Cancer Conf.* **5:** 191–223.

Rous, P. and F.S. Jones. 1916. A method of obtaining suspensions of living cells from the fixed tissues and for the plating out of individual cells. *J. Exp. Med.* **23:** 549–555.

Roux, W. 1885. Beiträge zur Entwicklungsmechanik des Embryos. *Z. Biol.* **21:** 411–526.

Saksela, E. and P.S. Moorhead. 1963. Aneuploidy in the degenerative phase of serial cultivation of human cell strains. *Proc. Natl. Acad. Sci.* **50:** 390–395.

Sanford, K.K., W.R. Earle, and G.D. Likely. 1948. The growth *in vitro* of single isolated cells. *J. Natl. Cancer Inst.* **9:** 229–246.

Sanford, K.K., A.B. Cavalesky, L.T. Dupree, and W.R. Earle. 1961. Cloning of mammalian cells by a simplified capillary technique. *Exp. Cell Res.* **23:** 361–372.

Sanford, K.K., W.R. Earle, V.J. Evans, H.K. Waltz, and J.E. Shannon. 1951. The measurement of proliferation in tissue cultures by enumeration of cell nuclei. *J. Natl. Cancer Inst.* **11:** 773–795.

Scherer, W.F., J.T. Syverton, and G.O. Gey. 1953. Studies on the propagation of poliomyelitis viruses. IV. Viral multiplication in a stable strain of human malignant cells (strain HeLa) derived from an epidermoid carcinoma of the cervix. *J. Exp. Med.* **97:** 695–709.

Strangeways, T.S.P. and H.B. Fell. 1926a. Experimental studies on the differentiation of embryonic tissues growing *in vivo* and *in vitro*. I. The development of the undifferentiated limb-bud (a) when subcutaneously grafted into the post-embryonic chick and (b) when cultivated *in vitro. Proc. R. Soc. Lond. B Biol. Sci.* **99:** 340–366.

———. 1926b. Experimental studies on the differentiation of embryonic tissues growing *in vivo* and *in vitro*. II. The development of the isolated early embryonic eye of the fowl when cultivated *in vitro. Proc. R. Soc. Lond. B Biol. Sci.* **100:** 273–283.

Swim, H.E. 1959. Microbiological aspects of tissue culture. *Annu. Rev. Microbiol.* **13:** 141–176.

Swim, H.E. and R.F. Parker. 1957. Discussion: Cells in continuous culture. *Spec. Publ. N.Y. Acad. Sci.* **5**: 351–355.

Thoma, R. 1878. Ueber entzündliche Störungen des Capillarkreislaufes bei Warmblütern. *Arch. Pathol. Anat.* **74**: 360–393.

von Recklinghausen, F.D. 1866. Ueber die Erzeugung von rothen Blutkörperchen. *Arch. Mikrosk. Anat.* **2**: 137–139.

Waymouth, C. 1959. Rapid proliferation of sublines of NCTC clone 929 (strain L) mouse cells in a simple chemically defined medium (MB752/1). *J. Natl. Cancer Inst.* **22**: 1003–1017.

White, P.R. 1946. Cultivation of animal tissues *in vitro* in nutrients of precisely known constitution. *Growth* **10**: 231–289.

———. 1949. Prolonged survival of excised animal tissues *in vitro* in nutrients of known constitution. *J. Cell. Comp. Physiol.* **34**: 221–241.

Wildy, P. and M. Stoker. 1958. Multiplication of solitary HeLa cells. *Nature* **181**: 1407–1408.

Willmer, E.N. and L.P. Kendall. 1932. The utilization of proteoses by chicken heart fibroblasts growing *in vitro*. *J. Exp. Biol.* **9**: 149–179.

Zitcer, E.M. and T.H. Dunnebacke. 1957. Transformation of cells from the normal human amnion into established strains. *Cancer Res.* **17**: 1047–1053.

3
CYTOGENETICS

EARLY ATTEMPTS TO DETERMINE
THE CHROMOSOME NUMBER IN MAN

The large size and the relatively small number of the chromosomes in certain plants made *Vicia, Trillium, Lilium* and *Tradescantia* the classical materials for cytological study. By 1932, when C.D. Darlington wrote his celebrated monograph *Recent Advances in Cytology,* the analysis of chromosome mechanisms in plants had become a fine art. The consequences of variation in chromosome number had been explored; duplications, deletions, inversions and translocations had been studied in detail; heterochromatin had been defined. *Pari passu,* the polytene chromosomes of *Drosophila* had permitted a large and progressively increasing number of mutations to be mapped to precise locations within the chromosome set. But the chromosomes of mammals and in particular those of man remained, if not a closed book, one that was very difficult to decipher. Most accounts of the origin of human cytogenetics begin with the work of Hansemann (1890, 1891a,b), but Hansemann himself refers to earlier observations by Hauser who estimated that the number of chromosomes in man lay between eight and twelve. Before 1921, all chromosome counts on mammalian somatic cells were made on mitotic figures seen in thin tissue sections. Hansemann, in discussing methodological limitations, admitted that it was rarely possible to arrive at an accurate figure because of the large number of chromosomes and the errors inherent in making counts on tissue sections. He was convinced, however, that Hauser's estimate was too low. Hansemann counted 18 chromosomes in one case, 24 in another. In one rather dispersed mitotic figure in an endothelial cell, examined before the chromosomes had divided, he counted more than 14. He concluded, without guaranteeing accuracy, that the number must be greater than 24. Hansemann's primary interest was in the chromosomal constitution of human tumours. He confirmed and extended the observations of several earlier workers who had noted the presence of abnormal mitotic figures in tumours, and argued that the abnormal chromosome constitution produced by aberrant mitoses was an essential determinant of tumorigenesis. This view was accepted by no one until it was taken up and developed with great virtuosity almost a quarter of a century later by Boveri (1914). In his 1882 paper, to which reference has already been made, Flemming includes observations on mitosis in human corneal epithelium in an eye that had been surgically removed. He found clear evidence of 'indirect' cell division and, in one case (Fig. 11 in the paper), produced a drawing of a mitotic figure in which the chromosomes were well enough dispersed for a count to have been attempted; but there is no mention of chromosome number in this paper. Ten years later (Flemming 1892), he turned his attention to this problem. The impulse was provided by his correspondence with von Bardeleben, the editor of the *Anatomischer Anzeiger* in which Flemming's paper eventually appeared. von Bardeleben believed that the normal chromosome number in man was 16, and this prompted Flemming to resurrect the corneal preparations that he had made a decade earlier and to examine them. Flemming specifically mentions the cell illustrated in Figure 11 of the 1882 paper, from which he derived a chromosome count of more than 16. Flemming searched systematically through the whole series of preparations and arrived at a probable figure of 24. He was, in any case, convinced that the figure was greater than 22 but probably less than 28. Just how inaccurate these counts were can be judged by his conclusion that 24 was also the normal chromosome number for *Salamandra, Mus, Salmo, Rana, Triton, Helix, Lilium* and several other plants.

The first study to yield consistent results within reach of what we now know to be the correct chromosome number for man was that of von Winiwarter (1912). Working in van Beneden's laboratory in the University of Liège, von Winiwarter made a systematic study of sections of testicular fragments from four men aged 21, 23, 25 and 41 years. The first part of the paper deals with the histology and development of the testicular epithelium and the Sertoli cells; the second part concentrates on the specific problem of establishing the exact chromosome number in man. von Winiwarter is very conscious of the problems raised by the large number and small size of the human chromosomes, especially as the observations were made entirely on tissue sections. Nonetheless, the meticulous standards set by van Beneden must have had a profound effect, for the quality of the results presented by von Winiwarter were of a quite different order from all those that had preceded him. In the case of spermatogonial mitoses, counts on 32 of the best preparations, each one chosen from a separate section, yielded 47 chromosomes in 29 cells, 46 in 2 cells, and 49 in 1 cell. For mitoses in the first spermatocyte division, which was easier to study than the spermatogonial division because of the reduction in chromosome number, the results on the 60 best preparations were 24 chromosomes in 57 cells, 25 in 2 cells, and 23 in 1 cell. von Winiwarter was naturally puzzled to find that the reduction division apparently generated 24 chromosomes out of 47 and suggested that perhaps during sectioning the blade had divided one of the chromosomes longitudinally into two. In the secondary spermatocytes, the counts on the 25 best preparations were 24 chromosomes in 15 cells and 23 chromosomes in the other 10 cells. Given the intrinsic limitations of estimating human chromosome number in tissue sections, these results were quite remarkable.

von Winiwarter's findings were strongly reinforced by the observations of Painter (1921, 1923). Painter (1923) lists 26 previous publications that contain estimates of the chromosome number in man: all of them offer variable counts well below the figures given by von Winiwarter. Like the latter, Painter worked on sections of testicular tissue but stressed the importance of examining fresh material. This was obtained from three inmates of the Texas State Insane Asylum through the good offices of Dr. T.E. Cook, a physician at that institution. Removal of the testes was judged to be desirable because of "excessive self-abuse, coupled with certain phases of insanity". Two of the patients were black and one a young white. The material was fixed for the most part in Bouin's solution, and the sections, cut at a thickness of 4–8 μm, were stained with iron haematoxylin. Painter's first report on the human material (1921) refers to his earlier work on spermatogenesis in the opossum in which a diploid chromosome number of 22 was established and an X,O system of sex chromosomes. For man, Painter found a diploid chromosome number of 45–48 and an X,Y system of sex chromosomes. He argued that with an X,Y sex system, an even number of chromosomes was to be expected, thus either 46 or 48. Painter (1923) provides the detailed evidence for an X,Y sex system: the presence of two disparate chromosomes that did not pair with each other and that segregated at the first maturation division, the X going to one pole and the Y to the other. In this paper, Painter reached the conclusion that the diploid chromosome number was 48: 23 autosomes and two X chromosomes in the female; 23 autosomes, an X and a Y in the male. This conclusion was widely accepted and remained the standard, and apparently uncontested, view of the subject until 1956. Given that Painter's conclusion was eventually shown to be incorrect, it is perhaps worth mentioning that Hsu (1979) in his history of cytogenetics, recounts that he was able to re-examine Painter's original preparations and was amazed that any numerical conclusion could be drawn from material of such poor cytogenetic quality.

It remains a matter of conjecture why Painter's results were so widely accepted when, at the same time, Oguma and Kihara (1923), also working on sections of testis, came to a different conclusion. Like Painter, these workers studied a surgical specimen, in this case removed from a 19-year-old Japanese who was castrated because of tuberculosis of the epididymis. The fixatives used included the procedure described by Painter for his study of spermatogenesis in the opossum, and the sections cut did not exceed 5 μm in thickness. Oguma and Kihara arrived at a figure of 47 for the diploid chromosome set, 23 pairs of autosomes and one large heterochromatic chromosome without a partner, which they were convinced was an X chromosome. They did not discern a Y chromosome and suggested that the female sex constitution was XX and the male XO. They regarded their findings as essentially concordant with those of von Winiwarter and concluded therefore that the chromosome constitution of the Japanese was the same as that of the European. It seems possible that Painter's results attracted greater attention than those of Oguma and Kihara because Painter published in English in a major American journal, whereas Oguma and Kihara published their preliminary report in a Japanese journal (Oguma and Kihara 1922) and their definitive report in French in a French journal (Oguma and Kihara 1923).

THE SQUASH TECHNIQUE

It was clear from the disparity of the results obtained that some methodological improvement was required that would yield cytological preparations with better definition than was possible in tissue sections. For plant material, this was provided by the introduction of the squash technique (*die Nukleal-Quetschmethode*) for which Heitz (1936) is usually given the credit. However, this technique was actually devised much earlier by Belling (1921, 1926, 1927) who applied it first to plant cells and later also to human cells. In his 1921 paper, Belling studied a variety of plants but obtained especially favourable results with *Datura* where squeezing out the anthers could release up to 1000 pollen mother cells onto one slide. These were then fixed in acetic alcohol, stained with acetocarmine and immobilized under a coverslip. One 'tap' on the coverslip over the desired cell dislodged the cytoplasm, and a second tap brought the chromosomes into the one focal plane. In the 1926 paper, gentle pressure on the coverslip with a small roll of paper replaced the two taps previously used. This procedure did not appear to disrupt or damage the chromosomes and counts were made on the pollen mother cells of hyacinth and *Datura*. It is the 1927 paper that describes the application of this gentle pressure technique to human material: fragments of a femoral sarcoma removed from a female. Fourteen chromosome counts were made with numbers ranging from 40 to 50. Belling admits to being unable to count most preparations because of chromosome clumping, but he found that the clearest preparations were to be seen in cells at prophase. Belling assumed, without any additional evidence, that Painter's figure of 48 chromosomes for the normal human karyotype was correct. While squash preparations of fixed mammalian tissue were an improvement on tissue sections, the results obtained, even in the most favourable circumstances, remained variable and suspect. Still further methodological advances were required.

THE CHROMOSOMES OF CELLS IN CULTURE

The next important step was taken by Kemp (1929). Kemp was convinced that sections of tissues were of little use in determining chromosome number and thought it of great importance to examine somatic cells other than those of the germ line in the testis. Kemp worked in Copenhagen where Fischer had already established a thriving programme of research in tissue culture, and this perhaps provided the impetus to examine the chromosomes of somatic cells multiplying *in vitro*. Cells in culture not only reduced some of the difficulties posed by the focal depth of different sections, they also permitted large numbers of mitotic figures to be collected. Kemp explanted tissues from the spleen, liver and heart of four human embryos, three male and one female, removed at operation. The cells that emigrated were for the most part fibroblasts. To increase the proportion of cells in mitosis, a partial synchronization of the cultures was attempted; they were maintained at room temperature for 1–2 days and then returned to 37°C. Several thousand mitoses were accumulated, and the 25 best preparations were examined in detail. The photographs reproduced in the paper are far from clear, due in large part to residual problems with the focal plane. The chromosome counts were apparently made from diagrammatic representations of what was observed at high power, but in the construction of these diagrams an element of interpretation seems to have been inevitable. Kemp found 48 chromosomes to be the normal diploid number but confessed that "in many cases there was an element of uncertainty with respect to one or two chromosomes". He was, however, convinced that the deviation from 48 was never more than one or two. In considering the general implications of his results, Kemp observed that previous studies on somatic cells would not have led one to expect that in these the chromosome number would be the same as in the sex cells (spermatogonia). Table 1 in

Makino's book on human chromosomes (1975) lists 21 references to estimates of the diploid human chromosome number published between 1882 and 1955. These range from 18 to 91. Twelve of them record either 47 or 48 chromosomes in somatic cells, but none proposes 46.

COLCHICINE AND HYPOTONIC SOLUTIONS

Although tissue cultures were certainly a decided advance on tissue sections, after fixation of the cells, the chromosomes were rarely dispersed enough to permit accurate counts. A further advance was made by Blakeslee and Avery (1937) and Levan (1938) who introduced colchicine to block cells at metaphase. Colchicine was first used in plants, where it was found to have three main actions. First, cells could be held in the blocked condition for long enough to permit the accumulation of increasing numbers of metaphases suitable for cytological examination. Second, by inhibiting the formation of the spindle, the drug produced a substantial dispersion of the chromosomes that were otherwise closely grouped together or clumped. And third, it caused the chromosomes to condense or contract even further than normal with the result that the resolution of individual chromosomes was greatly enhanced. Nonetheless, for cells with relatively high numbers of chromosomes, such as those of man, accurate and reproducible chromosome counts remained difficult to obtain. The next, and in some respects crucial, development for the study of mammalian cells was the introduction of a period of exposure to hypotonic solutions before the cells were fixed. The first, and by a long way, to study the effect of hypotonic solutions on cells in culture were members of a Russian group whose work appeared in the 1930s. Zhivago, Morosov, and Ivanickaya (1934) made a systematic study of the effect of hypotonicity on mitosis in tissue cultures of embryonic heart; they reported their findings in German in the Proceedings of the Academy of Sciences of the USSR. Aisenberg (1935) studied the effects of both hypotonicity and hypertonicity and published an account of the work in a French journal. Some members of this group studied human chromosomes using the techniques they had developed (Andres and Jiv 1935, 1936; Andres and Navashin 1936). Perhaps because publications from this source ceased in 1937 (the influence of Lysenko?), these highly original contributions were consigned to oblivion until they were resurrected by Hungerford in 1978. Those who, in the 1950s, vied for priority in the rediscovery of the uses of hypotonicity appear to have been totally unaware of the Russian work. In the same year that Zhivago et al. published their work on mammalian cells in culture, Slifer (1934), who was working on insect development, described the effect of an anisotonic balanced salt solution on the behaviour of grasshopper embryos. But Slifer was not concerned with cytogenetics, whereas the study of chromosomes was the principal theme of the papers that emanated from the Russian group.

It was not until 1952 that the effect of hypotonicity was again systematically investigated. Hughes (1952) showed that hypotonic solutions arrested mitosis in tissue cultures derived from chick frontal bone. The cells were arrested in prophase or metaphase, and the chromosomes were scattered throughout the cell instead of moving to the metaphase plate and there dividing. The effect was found to be partially reversible. Hughes was not, however, concerned with cytogenetic analysis, and it appears that the first to use hypotonicity specifically to enhance cytological preparations for chromosome analysis were Makino and Nishimura (1952). Their initial observations were made on preparations of insect testes which were exposed for 5–10 minutes to distilled (or tap) water before fixation. The paper itself does not give any indication of why this procedure was introduced, but some anecdotal information on this score is available and will be discussed presently. A 5-minute exposure at room temperature was found to be adequate for most material, but, for bird tissues, water at 38°C was found to be useful. A range of fixatives was tested, and dilute solutions of glacial acetic acid were found to give the best results (3–5% was no worse than 10–50%). Squash preparations of the metaphases were produced in the usual way and the chromosomes were stained with basic fuchsin. Thirty-two species of invertebrates and sixteen species of vertebrates, including seven mammals, were examined, but not man. The photographs in the paper show well dispersed chromosomes, but they are probably not good enough for accurate counts in species containing a high diploid chromosome number.

In the same year, Hsu (1952) published a paper on the karyotype of man. The study was made on cells cultured from human embryonic skin and spleen. The spleen cultures appear to have yielded more dispersed and better defined chromosomes than the skin cultures. The photographs presented are of a higher quality than those of Makino and Nishimura, and many of the metaphases appear to have been good enough for chromosome counts. Of 124 cells counted, 48 chromosomes were found in 91 cells, 49 in 4 cells, 47 in 11 cells, 45 in 5 cells, and 44 in 1 cell. From an historical point of view, it is of interest that no mention of hypotonicity is made in the main body of the paper. The fact that the cells had been exposed to hypotonic solutions is mentioned only in an addendum attached at a later stage. In this addendum, Hsu states that it was subsequently discovered that the cultures had been accidentally washed with hypotonic tyrode solution before fixation. The addendum also contains the following statement: "Furthermore, it was found that Dr. Arthur Hughes of the Strangeways Research Laboratory, Cambridge, England had been carrying out experiments on the effect of hypotonicity upon dividing cells and his findings were almost identical with ours". There is an acknowledgement in the addendum that Hughes had sent Hsu an advance copy of his paper before publication. What is not clear is whether Hsu became aware of the accidental use of a hypotonic solution in his own experiments before he had heard of Hughes' work. In a history of cytogenetics that he subsequently wrote (1979), Hsu elaborates on the circumstances surrounding the accident. It appears that neither the source of the error nor the identity of the technician who made it was ever actually established, but a process of exclusion is said to have ruled out all other possibilities. It is difficult to envisage how, of the many variables that might have been involved, the conclusion could have been reached that accidental use of a hypotonic solution was responsible, unless there was *some* indication in the preparations themselves that hypotonicity was involved, or unless this idea was suggested to the author from some other source. As far as I am aware, none of Hsu's accounts of this work claims that it was some property of the preparations themselves that suggested accidental exposure to a hypotonic environment. With Hsu and Pomerat (1953), treatment of cells with a hypotonic solution before fixation becomes a systematic procedure. This paper refers to the work of Hughes, but claims that, although Hsu's discovery was accidental, it was made independently. The chromosomes of several species of laboratory animal were examined: the diploid number for the mouse was found to be 40 and for the guinea pig, 64. The work of Makino and Nishimura is also mentioned in this paper but criticised on two grounds: first, because the Japanese authors applied the squash technique to organised tissues and not to cells in culture; and second, because it had been shown by other workers that pure water damages cells and causes them to burst. (This is, of course, true, but might not be acutely relevant to organised tissues where the added water would to a varying extent be mixed with extracellular fluid.) Hsu (1979) recounts that, when he finally met Makino, he learned that Makino's discovery of the usefulness of tap water was also accidental. Apparently Makino had left his testicular preparations in water because his work was interrupted by a distraction that took him away from the specimens.

ASCITES TUMOURS

After 1953, pre-treatment with a hypotonic solution, colchicine and the 'squash' were routinely incorporated into the procedures used to display chromosomes in mammalian cells, and various detailed recipes were offered (see, for example, Ford and Hamerton 1956a). It was generally agreed that, where they could be obtained, cells in culture yielded the best preparations. However, at about the same time, an additional source of excellent cytological material became available in the form of ascites tumours. These were tumours that grew spontaneously as a single cell suspension in the peritoneal cavity or could be induced to do so by repeated passage. The first of these, a rat sarcoma, was described by Yoshida in 1949. This tumour was examined cytologically by Makino (1951, 1952), Makino and Kano (1951a), Yosida (1952) and Nakahara (1952) and shown to be aneuploid. Detailed examination of the karyotype after passage of the tumour in syngeneic and foreign hosts led these authors to conclude that the tumour was driven by a 'stem line' characterised by a clear modal chromosome number. Cells were indeed generated with a wide spread of chromosome numbers, but these were not thought to contribute significantly to the growth of the tumour. The stem line concept appears to have originated in these experiments and will be discussed in greater detail later. A new set of rat ascites tumours, the MTK sarcomas, were produced by Makino and Kano (1951b) and, like the Yoshida sarcoma, were found to have aneuploid chromosome constitutions. A systematic study of mouse ascites tumours was initiated by Klein (1951), who showed by microspectrophotometric methods that these cells were not euploid and that there was substantial variation in the DNA content from cell to cell. Hauschka and Levan (1951) examined the chromosomes of five such tumours and confirmed that they were indeed aneuploid and that different tumours had different modal chromosome numbers. A further set of three mouse ascites tumours was examined by Levan and Hauschka (1952) and 16 more by Hauschka and Levan (1953). These authors found that there was a change in modal chromosome number when the tumours were passaged through a mouse of foreign genotype and concluded that there was constant remodelling of the karyotype in response to changes in the environment.

THE KARYOTYPE OF MAN

Although Hsu's paper on the human chromosome set examined after accidental treatment of the preparation with a hypotonic solution appeared in 1952, and hypotonicity combined with colchicine became standard procedure shortly thereafter, it is a remarkable fact that four years were to elapse before the true chromosome number for man was established. The decisive paper is Tjio (Fig. 17) and Levan (Fig. 18) (1956). This describes a study of tissue culture cells derived from four aborted human embryos. The cells were exposed to colchicine and a hypotonic solution before fixation, and the chromosome preparations were made by the squash technique. In all four cases, 46 chromosomes were found. The authors came to the conclusion that the 2n number for man was indeed 46, not 48, but with some trepidation. So heavy was the weight of the 48 chromosomes tradition that Tjio and Levan felt obliged to present their conclusion with the most guarded modesty: "It is hard to avoid the conclusion that this would be the most natural explanation of our observations". Hsu (1979), looking back ruefully, felt that it was indeed the universal acceptance of 48 as the correct figure that prevented him from counting accurately the number of chromosomes in his well spread cells. Ford and Hamerton (1956b), working with squashes of testicular cells from three patients, confirmed that the diploid number for man was, as Tjio and Levan had found, 46 and added the additional evidence that the haploid number was indeed 23. In the procedures used to demonstrate the chromosomes of mammalian cells, the main technical difficulty that remained was that the squash technique was highly sensitive to the vigour of the squash. If not vigorous enough, the chromosomes would not be distributed in the one focal plane, and if too vigorous, cells might be broken and chromosomes dislodged. The latter possibility tended to make cytogeneticists suspicious of lower chromosome numbers than they anticipated. This difficulty was overcome by the introduction of the 'air-drying' or 'flame-drying' technique (Rothfels and Siminovitch 1958; Tjio and Puck 1958). It was found that when the preparations were simply dried in a stream of air, the surface tension generated as the film of fluid evaporated flattened the cells gently and spread the chromosomes for display in the one focal plane. The rupture of cells and loss of chromosomes that marred the squash technique were essentially eliminated by this procedure. Since flaming the slides proved to be unnecessary, the air-drying technique of Rothfels and Siminovitch rapidly became the standard procedure.

CHROMOSOME ABNORMALITIES AND HUMAN GENETIC DISEASE

With the final establishment of the correct chromosome number in man and the availability of reliable methods for obtaining chromosome preparations of high quality, a worldwide search began for chromosome abnormalities associated with human genetic disease. The first success to be reported was for mongolism. (To avoid racial offence this is now referred to as Down's syndrome, but the racial views held by Down would hardly commend themselves to a modern liberal reader. The title of Down's original paper was *Observations on an ethnic classification of idiots*.) There was every reason to expect

FIGURE 17 Joe-Hin Tjio (1919–), in collaboration with Albert Levan (Fig. 18), established that the correct chromosome number of man was 46. *(Courtesy of Dr. Joe-Hin Tjio.)*

that abnormalities in chromosome number would have phenotypic consequences in man. To begin with, there were Boveri's classical experiments on the consequences of abnormal mitoses in sea urchin eggs, and Morgan, Bridges, and Sturtevant (1925) had shown that chromosome imbalance could produce some intersexual types in *Drosophila.* Waardenburg (1932), in an essay on mongolism, urged cytogeneticists to examine the chromosomes of patients with this condition and argued that either loss or duplication of a whole

FIGURE 18 Albert Levan (1905–). *(Courtesy of Dr. Nils Ringertz.)*

chromosome or part of a chromosome might be responsible. Bleyer (1934) considered that mongolism was a "gametic mutation of a degressive type" and suggested that it might be caused by a trisomy. Snell (1935) showed that chromosome imbalance in mice was frequently associated with anencephaly and embryonic death. In 1958, at a conference in Montreal, Lejeune (Fig. 19) announced that in connective tissue cells explanted from nine mongol children he had found 47 chromosomes, the additional chromosome being a small acrocentric. It was not at that time possible to determine exactly which chromosome was involved. These observations were published in Lejeune, Gautier, and Turpin (1959) and were confirmed within a few months by several other groups. Jacobs et al. (1959) found the additional small acrocentric chromosome in bone marrow cells from three male and three female patients, and identical results were obtained in both bone marrow cells and skin fibroblast cultures by Böök, Fraccaro, and Lindsten (1959). Ford (Fig. 20) et al. (1959b) found 48 chromosomes in a patient showing both mongolism and Klinefelter's syndrome: 44 autosomes, the additional small acrocentric and an XXY sex chromosome constitution. Ford et al. (1959a) found another sex chromosome anomaly in a case of gonadal dysgenesis (Turner's syndrome). This group of papers, all appearing in the same year, may be regarded as marking the birth of clinical cytogenetics. Thereafter, each year brought its consignment of papers describing chromosome abnormalities that were associated with clinical conditions in man.

To bring some order into the nomenclature for the human karyotype, a meeting was arranged in Denver in April 1960 that gathered together most of the leading figures in cytogenetic research. Extensive measurements of arm length and centromere position by Tjio and others eventually permitted a division of the human chromosome set into seven groups, group 1 being the largest. Within each group, the individual chromosomes were also numbered according to size, although uncertainty remained in some of the groups. The

FIGURE 19 Jérôme Lejeune (1926–1994) was the first to discover a chromosome abnormality associated with a human genetic disease. He found an additional small acrocentric chromosome in patients with mongolism (Down's syndrome). *(Courtesy of Dr. Jérôme Lejeune.)*

FIGURE 20 Charles E. Ford (1912–) found an abnormal sex chromosome constitution (XXY) in Klinefelter's syndrome. (*Courtesy of the Archives of the Sir William Dunn School of Pathology, University of Oxford.*)

additional acrocentric chromosome in mongolism was agreed to be either 21 or 22. This nomenclature was eventually agreed by 14 signatories (and three eminent neutral councillors) and became known as the Denver Convention (1962). Within two years, the following aberrant karyotypes associated with clinical abnormalities in man had been identified (Ford 1962):

- Sex chromosome anomalies:
  XXY47 in Klinefelter's syndrome; XO45 in Turner's syndrome; XXX47 in a phenotype dubbed 'superfemale' and associated with mental defect; XY46 associated with a female phenotype; XX46 in true hermaphroditism; X, defective X, 46 in a syndrome showing low intelligence and poor sexual development.

- Autosome anomalies:
  21 trisomy 47 in mongolism; 17 or 18 trisomy 47 in mental retardation with a large misshapen head; 13 or 15 trisomy 47 in a syndrome showing multiple defects including anophthalmia, deafness and hare lip.

Some presumptive translocations were also reported about which there were differences in interpretation.

SEX CHROMATIN AND THE INACTIVATION OF THE X CHROMOSOME

The frequent involvement of the sex chromosomes in genetic abnormalities reinforced the intense interest that had been generated by the discovery of Barr and Bertram (1949) that male and female cell nuclei could be distinguished in interphase. Working on neurones in the cat, Barr and Bertram found that the nuclei in the female showed a small, densely staining accumulation of chromatin that was absent in the male. They originally called this body a 'nuclear satellite', but it soon became known as the Barr body or as the sex chromatin. Its presence in human cells (Moore and Barr 1954) made it a useful adjunct for diagnostic purposes. Five years were to elapse before it could be shown decisively in man and in the rat that the Barr body was formed from a single X chromosome (Barr 1959; Ohno, Kaplan, and Kinosita 1959; Ohno and Makino 1961). The fact that it was only one of the two X chromosomes in the female that contributed to the formation of the Barr body and the pattern of inheritance of certain X-linked characteristics in the mouse led Mary Lyon (Fig. 21) to formulate what for some time was known as the Lyon hypothesis (Lyon 1961, 1962). She postulated that during embryonic development one of the two X chromosomes is rendered permanently inactive by a process of chromatin condensation (heterochromatinization). Which of the two X chromosomes was inactivated was thought to be, at least to a first approximation, a random event. To accommodate the genetic data, the hypothesis required that the cells in which the paternal X was inactivated would generate progeny with an inactivated paternal X, and cells in which the maternal X was inactivated would similarly generate progeny with an inactivated maternal X. The tissues of the adult female would thus be a mosaic in which about half the cells had an inactivated paternal X and half an inactivated maternal X. Although initially the subject of some heated controversy, the Lyon hypothesis so neatly explained a variety of otherwise unconnected genetic and cytogenetic observations that it soon ceased to be a hypothesis and became a fact. It was one of the most brilliant and illuminating conjectures in the history of embryology.

FIGURE 21 Mary Lyon (1925–) postulated that during embryonic development one of the two X chromosomes in the female was rendered permanently inactive: the Lyon hypothesis. *(Courtesy of Dr. Mary Lyon.)*

AUTORADIOGRAPHY AND THE CELL CYCLE

Further light on the behaviour of the X chromosome was shed by the development of autoradiographic techniques that permitted the resolution of events taking place not only within single nuclei but even within single chromosomes. The earliest applications of autoradiography to single cells were made in plants by Pelc and his colleagues using radioactive phosphorus (Donniah and Pelc 1950; Howard and Pelc 1951a,b). In 1953, Howard and Pelc showed in the root cells of *Vicia* that radioactive phosphorus was incorporated into DNA only at one particular stage in the period between mitoses. Walker and Yates in 1952 and Swift in 1953 had already established by microspectrophotometric methods that the doubling of DNA occurred not throughout the whole of interphase, but in a limited and well-defined segment of it, preceded and succeeded by periods in which the DNA content of the cell was constant. These observations, reinforced by the metabolic studies of Howard and Pelc, delineated what became known as the cell cycle: the period of DNA replication, designated the S (for synthetic) phase, was preceded by a G1 period in which no synthesis of DNA occurred and succeeded by a G2 period in which there was similarly no DNA synthesis but in which other events essential for mitosis were thought to take place. The work of Howard and Pelc was expanded by the experiments of Taylor (1953) who studied the incorporation of radioactive phosphorus into the chromosomes of cells undergoing mitosis and meiosis in *Tradescantia* and *Lilium*. Taylor and Taylor (1953), working with *Tradescantia* and *Lilium*, simultaneously administered ^{35}S to label proteins and ^{32}P to label nucleic acids and they were able to discriminate between the two labels by treating the preparations with trypsin before submitting them to autoradiography. Whereas protein synthesis was found to take place continuously, DNA synthesis in cells undergoing either mitosis or meiosis was again shown to be limited to one particular stage in the cell cycle.

The introduction of tritium-labelled compounds greatly increased the precision of autoradiographic procedures. The low energy of the tritium radiation yielded autoradiographs with a very much reduced range of particle scatter and permitted accurate analysis of individual chromosomes, parts of chromosomes and chromatids. The first tritiated compound to be used was tritiated thymidine. This was synthesized because it was already known that ^{15}N-thymidine and ^{14}C-thymidine were incorporated specifically into DNA, not RNA, and could therefore be used to study DNA synthesis. Taylor, Woods, and Hughes (1957) first used tritiated thymidine to study DNA replication in *Vicia*. The autoradiographs produced were sharp enough to permit the conclusion that at mitosis each daughter chromosome received one newly synthesized chromatid and one chromatid that had been formed before exposure to the isotope, a result that was consistent with the semi-conservative model for DNA replication proposed by Watson and Crick. Lima de Faria (1959a), using tritiated thymidine, showed that in rye plants the heterochromatic regions replicated late in the S phase of DNA synthesis. Lima de Faria (1959b) also appears to have been the first to publish results on the incorporation of tritiated thymidine into animal cells. Taylor (1960) made a systematic study of chromosome replication in Chinese hamster cells and showed that there was an ordered temporal sequence in the replication of the individual chromosomes and that this pattern of replication was maintained from one cell generation to the next. Taylor also observed that the sex chromosomes were among the last to be replicated. German and Bearn (1961) showed that a pattern of asynchronous chromosome replication was also present in human cells. German (1962) found that in human cells one of the chromosomes then classified as a member of the C group replicated late, and he thought it likely that this was the inactive heterochromatic X. Morishima, Grumbach, and Taylor (1962) provided further information about the asynchronous replication pattern of human chromosomes and were able to confirm by autoradiographic methods that it was indeed the inactivated X chromosome that replicated late. In the years that followed, autoradiographic procedures were used extensively to study the replication pattern of chromosomes in cells of various kinds. A bibliography of this work is given in German (1966) and a review in German (1967).

SOURCES OF MATERIAL: TISSUES AND BLOOD

By 1960, when the Denver Convention for the classification of human chromosomes was agreed, there were essentially only three methods that could be used to obtain human material suitable for cytogenetic analysis. Squash preparations of testicular material were still in use, but they were, of course, limited to studies on the male and were constrained by the availability of suitable clinical material. Tissue cultures were widely used and were generally held to yield the best cytological preparations. But there was the risk (not great for human cells) that chromosome changes might occur during the period of cell cultivation *in vitro.* Freshly isolated cultures were recommended, and these were generally made from skin biopsies. Puck, Cieciura, and Robinson (1958) had introduced a useful simplification of the routine procedure for skin biopsy. They simply abraded an area of skin and removed the scab two or three days later. The underside of the scab contained many multiplying cells which grew well *in vitro* when fragments of the scab were explanted. The third method, regarded by Ford (1962) as the most reliable at that time, was marrow culture. Marrow specimens were originally used for cytogenetic studies in laboratory animals which were injected with a dose of colchicine 1–2 hours before the marrow specimen was taken. This procedure was obviously inapplicable to man, but the difficulty was overcome by the development of short-term marrow cultures which could, for cytogenetic purposes, be treated in the same way as other tissue cultures. Even so, taking marrow from patients was not, and still is not, a trivial procedure, and marrow culture has never become routine. But in the late 1950s and early 1960s, a fourth technique made its appearance and proved eventually to be a major contribution to human cytogenetics and especially in the study of haematological malignancies. This was the technique of peripheral blood culture.

Reference has already been made to the Russian workers who first studied the effects of hypotonic solutions on mitotic chromosomes in culture (Zhivago, Morosov, and Ivanickaya 1934; Aisenberg 1935). This same group was also the first to use cultures of peripheral blood for the study of chromosomes (Chrustschoff, Andres, and Iljina-Kakujewa 1931; Andres and Zhivago 1933; Chrustschoff 1935). These papers were published in well known German and English language journals, but, like the work on hypotonicity, were soon forgotten. Chrustschoff (1935) described karyological observations on cultures of normal blood, Andres and Zhivago (1933) reported similar observations on cultures of leukaemic blood. Whereas cultures of leukaemic blood may contain many cells in mitosis, in normal blood, mitosis is usually seen only in the large lymphocytes (lymphoblasts). These are present in very small numbers relative to other leucocytes and they do not, in any case, multiply for long *in vitro*. This limitation on the use of normal blood for cytogenetic purposes was overcome in 1958 by a circuitous route. Osgood and Brooke (1955) had developed a gradient method for separating leukocytes from peripheral blood and had succeeded in establishing continuous cultures of lymphocytes from leukaemic blood fractionated by this method. To facilitate the removal of red cells, Osgood and Krippaehne (1955) used phytohaemagglutinin, an extract of the red kidney bean (*Phaseolus vulgaris*), to clump the red cells together. Nowell, Hungerford, and Brooks (1958) noticed that the phytohaemagglutinin stimulated the multiplication of the small lymphocytes, which were present in blood in much larger numbers, and these stimulated cells continued to multiply *in vitro* for long enough to permit karyological investigations to be made. Using short-term cultures in which the lymphocytes were stimulated to multiply by phytohaemagglutinin and then exposed to both colchicine and a hypotonic solution, Moorhead et al. (1960) were able to make chromosome preparations of high quality from both normal and leukaemic human blood. Hungerford et al. (1959) used peripheral blood culture to ascertain the chromosome constitution of a human phenotypic intersex. Farnes et al. (1964) found that peripheral blood lymphocytes could also be stimulated to multiply by an extract of pokeweed (*Phytolacca americana*), and a number of other compounds have since been found to have this property. Some of these have found special uses, but phytohaemagglutinin has remained the most commonly used reagent for cytological work on peripheral blood.

ANEUPLOIDY AND THE EVOLUTION OF KARYOTYPES

Mention has already been made of the observation that the chromosome constitutions of all established mammalian cell lines were in some degree aneuploid. This finding raised a number of important questions. How stable was the karyotype of somatic cells in their normal habitat *in vivo*? Was aneuploidy inevitable *in vitro*? How was it generated? And, of primary interest, what was the relationship between the generation of aneuploidy and carcinogenesis? Because of the inadequacy of the techniques then available for displaying mammalian chromosomes, and the consequent variability of the chromosome numbers proposed for man and other animals, some workers continued to believe, even as late as 1950, that the cells of the body did indeed have variable chromosome numbers (Timonen and Therman 1950). However, the refinement of cytological methods made it progressively clearer that this was not the case. Levan (1956a) made a careful examination of human tissues *in vivo* and after explantation *in vitro*, and established beyond reasonable doubt that the chromosome number of somatic cells was constant. But in the same study he observed that the cells of tumours had aneuploid chromosome constitutions. Beatty (1957) found constancy of chromosome number in the cells of the corneal epithelium of the mouse. The more extensive studies of Levan (1959) and of Hsu (1959) confirmed that the chromosome number was constant in somatic cells *in vivo* but that aneuploidy was characteristic of both tumours and permanent cell lines. Hsu (1961) found some polyploidy in somatic cells *in vivo*, especially in rodent liver. While admitting the possibility that mitotic irregularities might occur *in vivo*, Hsu reported that in his experience they were very difficult to find. The detailed studies of Tjio and Puck (1958) and of Hayflick and Moorhead (1961) on the chromosome constitution of cells freshly isolated from mammalian tissues have already been discussed. This work left little doubt that very powerful mechanisms existed in the body to maintain the constancy of the chromosome constitution in somatic cells.

With residual uncertainty in the identification of some of the human chromosomes and the almost complete inscrutability of the mouse chromosome set, composed entirely of acrocentric chromosomes that were difficult to distinguish, mammals with more amenable chromosome constitutions were eagerly sought. The Chinese hamster was introduced into cytogenetic studies by Yerganian (1952) who had discovered that it had a low chromosome number and that the individual chromosomes differed greatly in size. The normal chromosome complement of this animal was soon established and the sex chromosomes identified (Yerganian 1959). Yerganian also found, as others had done with cells from different species, that when permanent cell lines were derived from Chinese hamster cells they too became aneuploid. However, one established cell line that grew rapidly was found to maintain what at that time appeared to be a normal euploid chromosome set (Yerganian and Leonard 1961). This raised the possibility that aneuploidy, although a regular concomitant of the establishment of permanent cell lines, was not an indispensable causal factor. This view was reinforced by the observations of Ruddle (1961) on an established line of pig kidney cells that were propagated *in vitro* for five years. Both the original stock cultures and a number of clonal derivatives were all found to have 38 chromosomes, the diploid number for the pig. Permanent lymphoid cell lines derived from peripheral blood cultures were also usually found to have a diploid chromosome number. Further developments in techniques for the identification of individual chromosomes, which will be discussed presently, revealed, however, that these established lines, although diploid in chromosome number, nonetheless had multiple structural aberrations within the individual chromosomes. This was true even for the diploid human cell lines that were selected for vaccine production such as Hayflick's WI-38; and it was also true for the diploid lymphocyte cell lines. It was eventually agreed that no established or permanent cell line was strictly euploid.

FORMATION OF POLYPLOID CELLS

Aneuploid cell lines in culture were often observed to have a mode in the subtetraploid region, and there were good grounds for supposing that such cell populations were derived by chromosome loss from tetraploid cells. It therefore seemed likely that the prior formation of polyploid cells might be an important element in the generation of aneuploidy. During the 1950s, several mechanisms for the generation of polyploidy were discovered. As early as 1916, Macklin described the formation of tetraploids from binucleate cells; and this phenomenon was studied in greater detail by Fell and Hughes (1949). The binucleate cell was usually found to arise from the failure of cytokinesis: the chromosomes divided normally at the metaphase plate but cell division did not go to completion so that the two daughter nuclei were reconstituted within the one cell instead of in two daughter cells. Binucleate cells were also sometimes formed by the coalescence of two daughter cells. Within the binucleate cell, a single spindle was commonly formed, and the chromosomes of both nuclei were aligned along the one metaphase plate. Division of the cell then gave rise to two tetraploid daughter cells each containing the chromosome sets of both the nuclei in the original binucleate cell. This process was termed 'teloreduplication' by Moorhead and Hsu (1956). Another mechanism was given the designation C mitosis (C for colchicine) because it was found to involve defective formation of the spindle, as produced by colchicine. The chromosomes that resulted from C mitosis were usually reconstituted within a single interphase nucleus which was thus, in principle, tetraploid. 'Endomitosis' was a term invented by Geitler (1937) who first described the phenomenon in the water-striders *Gerris lateralis* and *Gerris lacustris*. The chromosomes were reduplicated during interphase in the normal way, but at mitosis the nuclear membrane did not disappear and tetraploidization resulted. Levan and Hauschka (1953) described yet another mechanism of tetraploidization to which they gave the name 'endoreduplication'. In this case, after replication of the chromosomes, mitosis failed to occur and a second round of replication took place.

Tetraploid cells, and less commonly cells of higher ploidy, were found to be constantly generated in many cell populations in culture, but the mechanisms by which they were generated varied from one cell line to another. For example, Chu, Sanford, and Earle (1958) found that endoreduplication was common in the fibroblastic L cell line, but Chu and Giles (1958) found that it was uncommon in cultures of HeLa cells. Ruddle (1961) found that in clonal populations of pig cells, clones that on the whole showed a diploid chromosome number nonetheless contained occasional tetraploid or near tetraploid cells. On continued cultivation, however, new modes, usually in the subtetrapoloid or hypertriploid range, gradually appeared. It seemed very probable that the subtetraploid cells were derived from the tetraploids by mechanisms involving chromosome loss. Several such mechanisms have been described. In cultures of HeLa cells, multipolar mitoses were found to be common, particularly in multinucleate cells, but tripolar mitoses were also seen in mononucleate cells (Hsu 1954; Hsu and Moorhead 1957). Such mitoses in tetraploid cells could, of course, readily produce subtetraploid daughter cells. 'Non-disjunction' was a name given to a mitotic aberration in which three copies of one of the chromosomes were distributed to one of the daughter cells and only one copy to the other daughter cell. As will be discussed later in connection with mouse lymphoid tumours, trisomy for an autosome may, under certain conditions, confer a selective growth advantage, presumably by increasing the gene dosage for one or more genes located on that chromosome. Other mechanisms such as 'lagging', in which one of the chromosomes failed to join the metaphase plate, and losses involving chromatids were also described.

Although the commonest mode of production of subtetraploid cells was by reduction of tetraploid cells, the reverse of this process was also found to occur. Hsu, Billen, and Levan (1961) found that in some cases there was an initial production of subdiploid cells which later doubled up to produce sub-tetraploids. It seemed likely that chromosome losses would be more readily tolerated in tetraploid cells in which there was a redundancy of genetic information than in diploid cells where a net loss of autosomes was likely to be lethal or at least disadvantageous. But with the development of new cytological techniques having a much greater resolution, it was soon revealed that pseudodiploid or subdiploid cells invariably contained rearranged chromosome sets. These new techniques showed further that structural alterations such as deletions, translocations, inversions and duplications, which had been thoroughly studied in plant chromosomes, also occurred in mammalian cells. All these studies concurred in the general conclusion that, *in vitro*, somatic cells exhibited a much higher level of genomic instability than they did *in vivo*, and this instability provided a source of variation on which the selective pressures exerted by growth *in vitro* could operate. Ruddle (1961) showed that this variation could not be eliminated, or even reduced by, cloning. He found, indeed, that diversification of the karyotype was initially accentuated by cloning. It seemed likely that the stresses imposed by the cloning procedure actually increased the incidence of mitotic aberrations and hence the variability of observed karyotypes. It was clear by the end of the 1950s that some stabilising factor that operated *in vivo* was lost from mammalian cells on continued cultivation *in vitro,* and it is only within the last couple of years that we have begun to have some glimmer of what this factor might be. This is a subject that I shall discuss in the final chapter of this book when I consider the mode of action of tumour suppressor genes.

STRUCTURAL ABNORMALITIES AND MARKER CHROMOSOMES

One of the important by-products of the instability of the karyotype of animal cells *in vitro* was the spontaneous generation of marker chromosomes. The overwhelmingly plausible assumption that underlay the use of marker chromosomes was that any cell population characterised by the presence of a specific chromosome abnormality in all or the great majority of the cells must have been derived from a single progenitor in which this abnormality first occurred. Such cytological markers were crucial for the analysis of cell lineage, both in normal development and in the study of tumours. In mouse cells, in which all the chromosomes are normally telocentric, by far the commonest chromosome marker was formed by the fusion of two telocentrics to form a large metacentric (Hsu and Klatt 1958; Rothfels and Parker 1959). These so-called Robertsonian metacentrics were generally supposed to arise from the fusion of the two terminal or subterminal centromeres of the telocentric chromosomes, but Hsu, Billen, and Levan (1961) thought it more probable that the metacentrics were formed by breakage of the centromeres followed by fusion of the sister chromatids. Robertsonian fusions also occur as a polymorphism in mouse populations, the extreme case being the tobacco mouse (*Mus poschiavinus*) in which many metacentrics are present (Gropp, Tettenborn, and von Lehmann 1970). Given the cytogenetic opacity of the normal mouse karyotype at that time, any abnormality that served to identify individual chromosomes was valuable. In populations of human and Chinese hamster cells, the reverse process was also observed: the formation of telocentric chromosomes from metacentrics, presumably by breakage of the centromere (Chu and Giles 1958; Ford and Yerganian 1958). A wide range of other structural abnormalities were in due course recorded: dicentrics, abnormally long chromosomes, acentric fragments and minute chromosomes. One of the important practical uses of such markers was that they provided a reliable tag for the identification of cell populations *in vitro*. This became a serious problem when it was shown that cells maintained in continuous culture could easily be contaminated by others being grown in the laboratory at the same time. Hsu and Klatt (1958) described the contamination of primary human cultures by L cells; Ford and Yerganian (1958) the contamination of Chinese hamster cells by HeLa cells; and Rothfels et al. (1959) cross-contamination in cell lines from mouse, monkey and man. As a consequence of these observations, periodic karyological examination of cultures maintained for long periods was adopted as a routine precautionary measure.

Systematic attempts to generate new chromosome markers were made by exposing cell cultures to ionizing radiation. It was known from studies in plants and in *Drosophila* that X irradiation could induce breaks in chromosomes (Muller 1954; Lea 1955; Swanson 1957). Puck (1958), studying the relationship between X irradiation and reproductive death in euploid human cells, observed that after as little as 50–150 rads, ring chromosomes, dicentrics and other structural rearrangements appeared in the cultures. Wakonig and Ford (1960) reported the appearance of ring chromosomes, minute chromosomes and chromatid exchanges in cultures of Chinese hamster cells after X irradiation. Ruddle (1961) made a systematic study of the cytological consequences of X irradiation in his cultures of pig cells. He found that new markers were generated after irradiation in the range of 300–800 rads. These included new telocentric and metacentric chromosomes. Ruddle isolated clones carrying these markers and was thus able to provide information about their stability.

The growth of mammalian cytogenetics coincided with a rising tide of interest in viruses as possible aetiological agents in the generation of tumours. Since, by the 1960s, it was the generally held view that events of a mutational kind in somatic cells were involved in some way in the genesis of cancer, it was not surprising that the discovery of viruses that could induce morphological transformation of euploid cells *in vitro* and, at several removes, induce tumours in experimental animals, should be quickly followed by cytological investigation of cells infected with such viruses. One such virus, which was shown by Shein and Enders (1962) and Koprowski et al. (1962) to produce characteristic morphological changes in cultures of human cells, was an isolate from monkey tissues that was given the name simian virus 40. Moorhead and Saksela (1963) and Black and Rowe (1963) showed that morphological transformation induced in human and golden hamster cells by simian virus 40 was associated with non-random chromosome aberrations that included aneuploidy, trisomy and monosomy. Similar effects were produced by polyoma virus, an endemic resident in certain populations of wild mice (Vogt and Dulbecco 1960, 1963). Lehman and Defendi (1970) observed that perturbation of DNA synthesis occurred very quickly after infection with simian virus 40, and Hirai, Lehman, and Defendi (1971) showed that re-initiation of DNA synthesis could occur within one cell cycle. Polyploid and aneuploid cells appeared within a few cell divisions together with a range of other chromosome abnormalities. Several other viruses, including some that produced only transient infections in cells, were subsequently shown to produce chromosome aberrations. However, in the context of carcinogenesis, three decades were to elapse before some of the cytological consequences of viral infection could be reduced to biologically comprehensible molecular terms.

TUMOURS AND THE STEM LINE CONCEPT

It was the challenge of the cancer problem more than anything else that drove the development of somatic cell genetics. Furth and Kahn (1937) had shown that leukaemia in the mouse could be transmitted by a single cell; and Ishibashi (1950) demonstrated that this was also true for the Yoshida ascites sarcoma. These experiments opened the possibility of examining the stem line concept in a more direct way. Hauschka and Levan (1958) studied clonal populations of the Ehrlich and Krebs 2 ascites tumours, which were also found to be transmissible by a single cell. They found that individual clones had different karyotypes defined by marker chromosomes and numerical modes; that the clones differed in their malignancy as assessed by take incidence and rate of growth *in vivo;* and that the chromosomal and biological characteristics of each clone were often maintained on serial transfer. These findings showed unequivocally that many different cells in an ascites tumour were capable of progressive growth *in vivo*, albeit at different rates, and that the sharply defined concept of the stem line, as originally proposed by Makino, was not tenable. The experiments of Hauschka and Levan (1958) suggested that it might be difficult to make a formal distinction between a stem line and a simple numerical mode. Heroic attempts were made to penetrate further into the mouse karyotype by detailed analysis of chromosome length. Levan (1956b) studied three strains of the TA3 mouse mammary adenocarcinoma which had been converted to the ascitic form. One of these strains was more or less diploid, the other two subtetraploid. Visible structural changes were seen more frequently in the subtetraploid cells, but measurement of chromosome length revealed that the 'diploid' cells did not have a karyotype that corresponded exactly to that found in normal spermatogonial cells but had undergone many 'cryptostructural changes'. Ising (1955, 1958) showed that marked changes of karyotype occurred when ascites tumours were passaged in a foreign host. When the mouse Ehrlich ascites tumour was passaged through the hamster, there was a fall in the modal chromosome number from 79 to 72, but measurement of chromosome lengths revealed an overall loss of about 20%. It seemed possible that this loss represented the elimination of chromosomes or parts of chromosomes bearing genes that specified antigens against which the hamster mounted an immunological reaction. There was little change in the mode when the tumour was passaged in mice. The stem line concept was analysed further in solid human tumours by microspectrophotometric methods. Stich and Steele (1962) showed that in some tumours a genuine stem line did appear to exist. In such cases, all the cells at metaphase had the same DNA content which was halved at telophase, but there was a wide scatter of DNA values in interphase cells. This result indicated that only cells having a DNA content within a particular narrow range actually completed mitosis. In other cases, however, multiple stem lines appeared to be present within the one tumour; and in others again no dominant stem cell mode could be detected.

ANEUPLOIDY AND CARCINOGENESIS

A critical question at this time was the relationship between aneuploidy and carcinogenesis. An orthodox view, expounded by Hauschka (1961) and Hsu (1961), was that the chromosomal constitution of cell populations *in vitro* was constantly undergoing evolution in response to changes in selective pressures, and that this was, in principle, also true for the growth of tumour cells. The aneuploidy was thus envisaged as a source of genetic variation from which, in classical Darwinian terms, selective forces operating in the host would encourage the emergence of genotypes increasingly competent for progressive growth *in vivo*. The germ of this idea is already to be found in the work of Winge (1927, 1930). Winge's first paper dealt with crown gall tumours in the beet (*Beta vulgaris*). Tumours produced by infection of the plant with *Bacterium tumefaciens* were examined but also spontaneous tumours. Winge found that the cells of the tumours contained 36 chromosomes instead of the normal diploid 18. Occasional octoploid cells were also seen. Winge was aware that polyploidy could occur without tumour formation but argued that different responses might be expected to occur in different tissues and different plant species. In his second paper, Winge examined the chromosome constitution of epithelial tumours produced by painting coal tar on the skin of mice. Chromosome counts were made on sections of the tumours and were obviously subject to serious errors, but the histograms presented in the paper show one mode in the diploid range and one in the tetraploid. Winge noted, however, that whereas in the crown gall tumours in the beet the chromosome numbers were exactly tetraploid or octoploid, in the mouse tumours the chromosome number was variable. Winge concluded that these tumours were produced by cells that had acquired an abnormal chromosome constitution, and, in particular, cells that had lost certain chromosomes and duplicated others. However, this Darwinian interpretation of the significance of aneuploidy was not universally accepted. Morgan Harris (1964), for example, thought it possible that the constant remodelling of the karyotype might simply be a reflection of 'genetic drift' of no selective significance. Bayreuther (1960) maintained that many, indeed most, primary tumours had a euploid chromosome constitution and that aneuploidy and other forms of chromosome abnormality were secondary events. Bayreuther's observations were, however, called into serious question by most other workers in the field. Ford, Hamerton, and Mole (1958) found aneuploidy and chromosome markers in primary reticular neoplasms in the mouse. Hellström (1959) found aneuploidy, mainly in the hyperdiploid-triploid-hypotetraploid range, in 14 primary mouse fibrosarcomas. Hauschka (1961) found that 76% of 104 untreated human neoplasms were aneuploid, and some of the remainder were 'pseudodiploid'. Miller (1961), on the other hand, found predominantly euploid karyotypes in the early stages of mouse leukaemia. Given the detailed measurements of Levan (1956b), which indicated that such apparently diploid karyotypes concealed numerous 'cryptostructural' changes, the apparent absence of chromosome abnormalities, especially in the mouse, was generally regarded as less telling than their presence.

Whether aneuploidy was a precursor of tumorigenicity or a secondary complication in cells already tumorigenic was resolved in the case of epidermal cells by Levan and Biesele (1958). These authors established a strain of cells explanted from mouse embryonic skin and monitored both the morphological changes taking place *in vitro* and the tumorigenicity of the cells on continued cultivation. The viability of the cells began to decline after two or three passages and this was accompanied by the emergence of foci of cells showing morphological transformation. The cultures had become generally aneuploid after 12 passages, but no tumours arose from the cells injected into appropriate hosts until passage 22. Levan (1958) reviewed the evidence on this question and came to the general conclusion that aneuploidy reflected continuous structural remodelling of the genotype until eventually a variant was produced that could grow progressively *in vivo*. A much later detailed study of cells transformed by simian virus 40 confirmed these conclusions. Although, as previously described, major changes in the number and structure of the chromosomes occur very quickly after infection of cells with simian virus 40, Gee and Harris (1979) found that when diploid mouse embryo fibroblasts were transformed by this virus, there was a very long lag, up to 100 passages in some cases, before the cells were able to produce tumours. This view of aneuploidy was strongly supported by the study of pre-cancerous lesions in man. Spriggs, Boddington, and Clarke (1962), Stanley and Kirkland (1968), and Spriggs, Bowey, and Cowdell (1971) showed that aneuploidy and other chromosome abnormalities appeared in lesions of the uterine cervix long before the emergence of tumours. Spriggs (1974) reported that in inflammatory lesions of the cervix a normal karyotype was found. Where there was mild dysplasia, most of the cells were diploid although occasional tetraploids were seen; but in severely dysplastic conditions and in what was classified as *carcinoma-in-situ*, aneuploidy was the rule. When frank cancers emerged, a narrowing of the mode and the appearance of marker chromosomes supported the view that the tumours were clonal outgrowths arising from a background of cells with disordered chromosome complements.

Atkin and Baker (1966), who studied five tumours in detail, found marker chromosomes in 700 out of 711 metaphases. This, together with other similarities in the karyotypes produced by the cells of any one tumour, led these authors to conclude, like Spriggs and his colleagues, that each tumour was composed of cells derived from a single progenitor in which the marker chromosome first arose. Atkin (1970, 1974), reviewing his own extensive studies on human tumours and those of other workers, reached the following conclusions:

- The vast majority of human tumours were aneuploid; they commonly had two modes, one in the subtetraploid region and one in the diploid region.

- Marker chromosomes indicating a rearrangement of the karyotype were present in most tumours that had an approximately diploid mode, but were less common in the subtetraploid tumours.

- No two tumours had a similar chromosome constitution even when they were of the same type.

The evidence was thus overwhelmingly in favour of the view that the tumours were clonal in origin. Essentially similar views were reached by Sandberg and Hossfeld (1970) and by Makino (1975). The studies by Makino and other Japanese workers included karyological analysis of 78 cases of cancerous effusions, which gave better chromosome preparations than solid tumours, but the results still failed to reveal any specific karyotype that was characteristic for a particular kind of tumour.

THE PHILADELPHIA CHROMOSOME

Although this massive effort to make sense of the karyological changes seen in cancer cells resulted in a notable increase in our understanding of how genetic variation could be magnified by chromosome instability and how selective pressures both *in vivo* and *in vitro* could result in the emergence of new genotypes and hence new phenotypes, it utterly failed to identify any specific chromosomal change that might plausibly be supposed to have a direct causative role in the generation of a tumour—with one possible exception. In 1960, Nowell and Hungerford described a minute chromosome that was regularly found in peripheral blood in human chronic myeloid leukaemia. It was named the Philadelphia chromosome and its presence in chronic myeloid leukaemia was rapidly confirmed in literally thousands of other cases. The discovery of the Philadelphia chromosome was facilitated by the fact that it is a very small element and hence easily recognisable and also because there is usually no other gross karyotypic abnormality in this condition. The Philadelphia chromosome was found in about 80% of cases of chronic myeloid leukaemia, but some 20%, which were distinguishable on clinical grounds, did not show it. In cases of chronic myeloid leukaemia that did show the Philadelphia chromosome in the cells of the peripheral blood, the chromosome was found to be absent in lymphoid organs such as spleen and lymph nodes; and when the peripheral blood was exposed to phytohaemagglutinin, which stimulated the multiplication of the lymphoid cells, a mixture of cells was found, some containing the Philadelphia chromosome and some not. All this amounted to strong evidence that this particular chromosome abnormality was specifically associated with the leukaemic condition in one particular cell lineage. Prior to 1970, a revolutionary year for human cytogenetics, the Philadelphia chromosome remained for a decade the only chromosomal abnormality that offered any encouragement for the hope that a cytogenetic basis for tumour formation would one day be revealed.

THE DISCOVERY OF CHROMOSOME BANDING

At some time in the late 1960s, it occurred to Torbjörn Caspersson (Fig. 22) at the Karolinska Institute in Stockholm that if chromosomes were stained with a fluorochrome that was coupled to an alkylating agent, then DNA regions rich in guanine and cytosine would be cross-linked and would stain more heavily than those rich in adenine and thymine. A quinacrine mustard having the required chemical characteristics was synthesized by E.J. Modest at the Boston Children's Cancer Foundation where Caspersson was engaged as a consul-

FIGURE 22 Torbjörn O. Caspersson (1910–), in collaboration with Lore Zech (Fig. 23), discovered chromosome banding. *(Courtesy of Dr. Nils Ringertz.)*

tant. This compound was tested in Stockholm on chromosome preparations from *Vicia faba*, *Trillium* and Chinese hamster, and the first results were published by Caspersson et al. in 1968. The plants were first subjected to low temperature and starvation as described by McLeish (1953) to display the heterochromatic regions of the chromosomes, and characteristic banding patterns were observed. This paper was mainly concerned with defining what regions in the chromosome were the ones that showed bright fluorescence, but in Caspersson, Zech (Fig. 23), et al. (1969a), there is a plate showing the banding patterns of all 12 chromosomes of *Vicia faba*, and most of them can be readily distinguished by their banding patterns. Similar results were obtained with *Trillium* and *Scilla sibirica*. Experiments with various quinacrine mustards and with quinacrine itself showed that, in addition to the alkylation of the DNA guanines, as originally envisaged, the fluorescent compounds exhibited ionic binding to the DNA through their basic side chains and also binding by intercalation. There is, however, no mention in the paper of the possibility that the banding patterns could be used to identify individual chromosomes. But Caspersson, Zech, et al. (1969b), which describes tests with various fluorescent dyes and mustards on the chromosomes of *Vicia*, *Trillium* and *Scilla*, contains a clear statement of the profoundly important observation that the fluorescence pattern given by each individual chromosome in the set was highly characteristic. Caspersson, Zech, and Johansson (1970a) showed that the banding patterns produced by quinacrine mustards could be used to identify human chromosomes, but not all the human chromosomes were actually identified in this paper. In Caspersson, Zech, and Johansson (1970b), however, the complete set is identified and a karyotype presented. The fluorescent banding patterns were scanned by microspectrophotometry which was shown to be more ac-

FIGURE 23 Lore Zech (1923–). *(Courtesy of Dr. Lore Zech.)*

curate than the eye but which also reflects Caspersson's devotion to instrumentation. Caspersson et al. (1970d) describes the use of television techniques for the rapid identification of human chromosomes. In Caspersson et al. (1970c), the value of fluorescent banding in distinguishing chromosomes 4 and 5 and in identifying individual chromosomes in the 6–12 group was demonstrated; and Caspersson et al. (1970b) showed that extra chromosomes in the G group could be distinguished by their banding pattern. The definitive paper on the human chromosome set was Caspersson, Lomakka, and Zech (1971). The banding patterns of some 5000 chromosomes from 14 healthy patients were examined by microspectrophotometric techniques and the range of variation between different individuals established. The banding patterns of Chinese hamster chromosomes were presented in Caspersson, Simonsson, and Zech (1970).

The detail revealed in the quinacrine mustard banding patterns was reproducible enough to permit major structural aberrations to be detected. Caspersson, Lindsten, and Zech (1970a) showed that the chromosome abnormality in Lejeune's *cri du chat* syndrome was a deletion or translocation in the distal part of the short arm of human chromosome 5; and Caspersson, Lindsten, and Zech (1970b) analysed a variant of Turner's syndrome in which the usual 45, XO chromosome constitution was replaced by 46, one apparently normal X and one abnormal metacentric having the size of chromosome 3. This was shown to be an isochromosome of the short arm of the X chromosome. Caspersson et al. (1970a) identified the Philadelphia chromosome as a truncated form of chromosome 22. This brave new world of banded chromosomes dominated the Paris Conference of 1971 where the term Q banding was adopted and the nomenclature of the human karyotype standardised. Caspersson et al. (1971) showed that individual human chromosomes could be identified against a background of mouse chromosomes within hybrid cells (which will be discussed later); and it was not long before every chromosome in the mouse karyotype was accurately identified. This had profound consequences, for a long tradition of mouse genetics had provided a large inventory of linkage groups. Mouse stocks could now be analysed and any translocations or other abnormalities identified. Cytological identification of linkage groups became possible, and the break points of many translocations were soon accurately localised. A summary of the progress achieved in mouse cytogenetics within a couple of years of the discovery of chromosome banding is given in Miller and Miller (1972).

Caspersson's original idea that quinacrine mustards would bind specifically to the GC rich regions of the DNA proved in practice to be incorrect. It turned out to be more probable that the brightest fluorescence was associated with the AT rich region. Weisblum and De Haseth (1972) showed with purified DNA solutions that regions containing higher AT/CG ratios gave brighter fluorescence. Since quinacrine does not have any special affinity for AT base pairs, it appeared that the binding was influenced in a complex way by the base composition of the DNA. Caspersson, Zech, and Modest (1970) stressed that quinacrine mustards were superior to quinacrine for chromosome banding, but since these mustards were difficult to obtain and the banding patterns produced by quinacrine were essentially the same as those given by the mustards, quinacrine was quickly adopted as the standard reagent. But other fluorochromes that gave different banding patterns were soon developed. Hoechst 33258 gave particularly bright staining of the centromeric areas of mammalian chromosomes (Hilwig and Gropp 1972). The antibiotic olivomycin, which binds specifically to the GC components of the DNA, was found to give a banding pattern which was the reverse of that given by quinacrine, that is, those bands that gave bright fluorescence with quinacrine gave weaker fluorescence with olivomycin and vice versa. This pattern of staining was named R banding (R for reverse) (van de Sande, Lin, and Jorgenson 1977). R banding was also produced by DNase I digestion of chromosomes stained with chromomycin (Schweizer 1977). Fluorescein-conjugated antibodies against specific nucleotides or short sequences of bases generated another range of banding patterns (Miller and Erlanger 1975). A fluorescent antibody directed against methylcytosine illuminated the heterochromatic regions. Quinacrine was also found to give particularly bright fluorescence with the Y chromosome in man. This could be distinguished even in interphase nuclei and was therefore useful for diagnostic purposes (Pearson, Bobrow, and Vosa 1970).

GIEMSA BANDING

A development which, because of its practical simplicity, proved to be of major importance was the discovery of the banding patterns produced by the classical Giemsa stain. This was originally devised by Gustav Giemsa in the 19th century and was used initially for staining *Spirochaeta pallida*. It was derived from the Romanowsky group of stains and is a complex mixture of methylene azure, eosin, glycerin and methyl alcohol. It was eventually adopted as a routine stain for haematological preparations, and it was for this reason that the Giemsa banding pattern of chromosomes was first seen in preparations of peripheral blood (Nowell, Hungerford, and Brooks 1958; Hungerford et al. 1959). The Giemsa stain was found to react preferentially with constitutive heterochromatin (Arrighi and Hsu 1971), and the resulting pattern of chromosome staining was named G banding. Various modifications of the staining procedure were tried with air- or flame-dried chromosome spreads, and a detailed, reproducible pattern of bands eventually emerged. A number of marginally different recipes were advocated (Drets and Shaw 1971; Patil, Merrick, and Lubs 1971; Sumner, Evans, and Buckland 1971). At the Paris Conference (1971), a detailed comparison was made between Q banding and G banding, and it was shown that the two sets of banding patterns were exactly equivalent. Since staining with Giemsa does not require ultraviolet optics and is permanent, Giemsa banding rapidly displaced quinacrine banding. Many subsequent refinements were made of which perhaps the most important was the introduction of trypsin treatment into the G-banding protocol (Seabright 1971, 1973). In the definitive procedure that was finally adopted, more bands were revealed than could be detected by quinacrine staining and the bands were sharper. A procedure for R banding was also devised with the Giemsa stain (Dutrillaux and Lejeune 1971). A modification of the R-banding Giemsa procedure was found to give differential staining of the nucleolus organiser regions (Matsui and Sasaki 1973), but this stain was hard to control and was soon replaced by an ammoniacal silver stain (Howell, Denton, and Diamond 1975). It is difficult to overestimate the change produced in the field of cytogenetics by the discovery of chromosome banding. A torrent of new information of unparalleled precision was unleashed that continues to the present day. A recent review lists 329 reproducibly identifiable bands in the human chromosome set (Mitelman and Heim 1988). A catalogue of the observations that have been made in mammalian cytogenetics during the quarter of a century that has elapsed since Caspersson's original papers appeared lies outside the scope of this book. Interested readers are referred to the plethora of reviews, catalogues and, more recently, computer databases, in which this wealth of information has been assembled.

HYBRIDIZATION OF NUCLEIC ACIDS *IN SITU*

There are, however, two developments that need to be discussed in the present context, the first because it constituted a decisive step in the application of molecular techniques to chromosome cytology, and the second because it opened the way to a functional analysis of the cytogenetic aberrations associated with tumour formation. Gall and Pardue (1969) were the first to localise a specific gene to a particular site in the chromosome. The technique that they used relied on the work of Doty (Doty et al. 1960) and others who had shown that oligonucleotide chains that were complementary to each other annealed (hybridized) to form much more stable complexes than chains that were not in register. As will be discussed in more detail later, this general principle was elaborated into a widely applicable methodology in which nucleic acid hybridization was used to identify and isolate stretches of DNA or RNA that were complementary to defined sequences of nucleotides, or nearly so. Gall and Pardue (1969) applied DNA-RNA hybridization to locate the genes coding for ribosomal RNA. They used cultures of *Xenopus laevis* cells to obtain tritiated ribosomal RNA and then hybridized the labelled RNA to amphibian oocytes at the pachytene stage of meiosis. At this stage the nucleus is enlarged and the ribosomal RNA genes, amplified about a thousand times, are located on one side of the nucleus as a cap. Gall and Pardue found that, in autoradiographs, the labelled ribosomal RNA was concentrated over the cap. They also studied the distribution of the ribosomal genes in the polytene chromosomes of *Drosophila*, *Rhynchosciara* and *Sciara*. In order to obtain ribosomal RNA with a high enough specific radioactivity to permit detection in autoradiographs, the labelled ribosomal RNA was obtained by transcribing the amplified ribosomal genes of *Xenopus* oocytes *in vitro* in the presence of tritium-labelled nucleotides. Pardue and Gall (1970) also identified the location of the highly repetitious 'satellites' in mouse chromosomes (see Chapter 6). Since some 10% of mouse DNA is composed of such satellites, it was a relatively simple matter to isolate and purify the satellite DNA and use it as a template to synthesize highly radioactive complementary RNA *in vitro*. Jones (1970) also localised the satellite regions in mouse chromosomes using tritiated DNA as the radioactive probe, but the results obtained with DNA-DNA hybridization were not as clear as those obtained by Pardue and Gall with RNA-DNA hybridization. The experiments of Gall and Pardue were the first occasion on which probes composed of highly radioactive nucleic acids were used to locate complementary regions in organised chromosomes. It was a methodology which, when fully developed, played a major part in bringing molecular and cell biology together.

SPECIFIC CHROMOSOME ABNORMALITIES IN HAEMATOLOGICAL MALIGNANCIES

The second of these two major developments that were made possible by the discovery of chromosome banding was the elucidation in biological terms of the characteristic chromosome abnormalities found in chronic myeloid leukaemia and in Burkitt's lymphoma. Rowley (1973) showed that the Philadelphia chromosome was not produced by a deletion in chromosome 22, but a translocation between chromosome 22 and chromosome 9. About half of the long arm of one chromosome 22, including the middle Q band, was moved to a terminal position on the long arm of one chromosome 9 (and, presumably, only a small piece of the chromosome 9 was translocated to chromosome 22). Chromosome 22 was found to be involved in all cases showing a Philadelphia chromosome, but the other chromosome involved in the translocation was not always chromosome 9; others might be 2, 6, 7, 11, 13, 16, 17, 19, 21 or a homologous 22. These findings not only delineated the crucial role of a locus on chromosome 22, but also demonstrated that breaks and translocations did not at all occur in a random fashion as had once been supposed. Rowley noted further that during blast crises trisomies often occurred. The key question, of course, was whether the Philadelphia translocation was the initiating event in the genesis of the leukaemia or one that occurred subsequently during the development of the disease. Martin et al. (1980) and Fialkow et al. (1981) examined this question using a methodology initially devised by Linder and Gartler (1965). Since, as previously described, paternal and maternal X chromosomes are inactivated at random in human females, any gene located on the X chromosome would be of paternal origin, and hence presumably active, in half the cells in a sample of tissue and would be of maternal origin, and hence presumably inactive, in the other half. Linder and Gartler (1965) noted that the enzyme glucose-6-phosphate dehydrogenase, which maps to the X chromosome, showed a dimorphism that could be revealed by a difference in electrophoretic mobility. Using this difference, they were able to show that whereas normal tissues showed both paternal and maternal forms of the enzyme, leiomyomas generally showed only one form. This they interpreted as evidence that the tumours were probably clonal in origin. The interpretation of this kind of experiment has since been the subject of a good deal of controversy hinging mainly on how small a sample of tissue would have to be before the presence of only one form of the enzyme might be expected on stochastic grounds. On the strength of their analysis of the distribution of the dimorphic glucose-6-phosphate dehydrogenase in chronic myeloid leukaemia, Martin et al. (1980) and Fialkow et al. (1981) concluded that the leukaemia arose initially as a clone of cells that did not show a Philadelphia chromosome, but that this abnormality appeared later. On the other hand, Hamada and Uchino (1982), examining survivors of the atomic bomb, found the Philadelphia chromosome in virtually 100% of cases before the development of clinical evidence of leukaemia.

In 1972, Manolov and Manolova noticed that in five out of six freshly isolated Burkitt's lymphomas and in seven out of nine cell lines derived from such lymphomas, there was an additional band at the end of the long arm of one chromosome 14. Zech et al. (1976), exploring this aberration further, found that the end of one chromosome 8 was consistently absent and suggested that it was this that was translocated to chromosome 14, a situation reminiscent of what Rowley had found for the Philadelphia chromosome. In the meantime, cytogenetic studies in the mouse revealed that in leukaemias produced by radiation or by chemical carcinogens, there was a regular appearance of trisomy for chromosome 15, and sometimes also for chromosome 17 (Wiener et al. 1978a,b). Wiener et al. (1978c) showed that the essential element of the trisomy was located in the distal portion of chromosome 15. Further analysis indicated that, quite generally in mouse T cell leukaemias and plasmacytomas, the distal portion of chromosome 15 was translocated either to the distal part of chromosome 12 or, less frequently, to chromosome 6. Since it was known that in mice the gene coding for the heavy chain of the immunoglobulin molecule was located on chromosome 12 (Meo et al. 1980), and that for the light chain on chromosome 6, Klein (1981) suggested that the biological consequence of the translocation was the transfer of some gene normally located on chromosome 15 to a position in close proximity to an immunoglobulin locus. 'Oncogenes', of which much more will be said in Chapter 6, had meanwhile come into prominence, and Klein proposed that the critical gene on chromosome 15 was an oncogene which was induced to become active or to overact when it was translocated to an immunoglobulin region where the level of transcription was high. Klein also argued that the translocations seen in Burkitt's lymphomas were formally equivalent to those seen in mouse plasmacytomas and resulted in a similar enhancement of oncogene action.

By 1982, chromosome regions regularly involved in haematological malignancies had been identified in chronic myeloid leukaemia (long arm of chromosome 9 to chromosome 22), acute myeloblastic leukaemia (long arm of chromosome 21 to chromosome 8), and acute promyelocytic leukaemia (long arm of chromosome 17 to chromosome 15) (Rowley 1982). In Burkitt's lymphoma and in B cell acute lymphocytic leukaemia, three related translocations had been found: chromosome 8 to chromosome 2, 14 or 22. Detailed analysis of a complex translocation indicated that translocation of 8 to 14 was the constant and decisive event. 1982 was also the year in which the translocations seen in chronic myeloid leukaemia and in Burkitt's lymphoma were reduced to molecular terms. Hagemeijer et al. (1982) showed in interspecific hybrid cells in which the Philadelphia chromosome was the only human element, that it was indeed an oncogene that was translocated to the immunoglobulin locus. Using a probe for the Abelson virus, these authors demonstrated that the critical gene translocated from chromosome 9 to chromosome 22 was the cellular homologue of the Abelson viral oncogene and that the translocation was reciprocal. Dalla-Favera et al. (1982) and Taub et al. (1982) similarly showed that the (8;14) translocation characteristic of Burkitt's lymphoma involved the transposition of the cellular homologue of the *myc* viral oncogene, normally located on chromosome 8, to the immunoglobulin locus on chromosome 14. These papers constituted the first reduction of a cytological abnormality to molecular terms and opened the gateway to what was soon to become a major field of enquiry (Rowley 1990).

A RECURRENT CHROMOSOME ABNORMALITY IN A SOLID TUMOUR

Because of the ready accessibility of the material, leukaemias, for more than a decade, provided most of the precise information on the relationship between chromosome aberrations and the malignant state. Before 1982, a recurrent chromosome abnormality had been detected in only one solid tumour: retinoblastoma. This tumour was known to exist in two forms, one in which the predisposition to develop the tumour was inherited in a Mendelian fashion as a highly penetrant autosomal dominant, and one that occurred sporadically. Knudson (1971), basing his argument on the analysis of epidemiological data, suggested that the predisposition to develop the tumour was determined by a recessive mutation in the germ line, but that the tumour itself was generated by a second genetic event that occurred in a somatic cell and that rendered the mutation functionally homozygous. Knudson's model for retinoblastoma stimulated a search for cytogenetic evidence that might support it. Francke (1976) drew attention to the fact that the cells of retinoblastomas consistently showed abnormalities involving chromosome 13; and Yunis and Ramsay (1978) described an interstitial deletion in the long arm of chromosome 13 in such cells. These observations were the starting point of a molecular dissection of this region of the chromosome, and this eventually resulted in the isolation of the retinoblastoma gene (*Rb1*), the first gene of this kind to be fully characterised. A recurrent cytogenetic abnormality was the starting point of several other molecular analyses that eventually resulted in the isolation of genes closely involved in the genesis of tumours. This work is discussed at some length in Chapter 6. A review in 1988 concluded that of the 329 chromosome bands that had then been identified, only 71 were consistently involved in rearrangements in primary tumours (Mitelman and Heim 1988). With the massive effort now being put into the complete decipherment of the human genome, it does not seem wildly improbable to suggest that most of these rearrangements will in due course be reduced to molecular terms.

REFERENCES

Aisenberg, E.J. 1935. De l'effet de l'hypo- et de l'hypertonie sur les mitoses. *Bull. Histol. Appl.* **12**: 100–122.

Andres, A.H. and B.V. Jiv. 1935. Der Chromosomenbestand im embryonalen Soma des Menschen. *Biol. Zh.* **4**: 489–504.

———. 1936. Somatic chromosome complex of the human embryo. *Cytologia* **7**: 371–388.

Andres A.H. and M.S. Navashin. 1936. Morphological analysis of human chromosomes. *Proc. Maxim Gorky Med.-Genet. Res. Inst.* **4**: 506–524.

Andres, A.H. and P. Zhivago. 1933. Karyologische Studien an myeloidischer Leukämie des Menschen. *Folia Haematol.* **49**: 1–20.

Arrighi, F.E. and T.C. Hsu. 1971. Localization of heterochromatin in human chromosomes. *Cytogenetics* **10**: 81–86.

Atkin, N.B. 1970. *Genetic concepts and neoplasia* (Symposium 1969, Houston), pp. 36-56. Williams and Wilkins, Baltimore.

———. 1974. Chromosomes in human malignant tumors: A review and assessment. In *Chromosomes and cancer* (ed. J. German), pp. 375–422. John Wiley and Sons, New York.

Atkin, N.B. and M.C. Baker. 1966. Chromosome abnormalities as primary events in human malignant disease: Evidence from marker chromosomes. *J. Natl. Cancer Inst.* **36**: 539–559.

Barr, M.L. 1959. Sex chromatin and phenotype in man. *Science* **130**: 676–685.

Barr, M.L. and E.G. Bertram. 1949. A morphological distinction between neurones of the male and female, and the behaviour of the nuclear satellite during accelerated nucleoprotein synthesis. *Nature* **163**: 676–677.

Bayreuther, K. 1960. Chromosomes in primary neoplastic growth. *Nature* **186**: 6–9.

Beatty, R.A. 1957. Chromosome constancy in the corneal epithelium of the mouse. *Chromosoma* **8**: 585–596.

Belling, J. 1921. On counting chromosomes in pollen-mother cells. *Am. Nat.* **55**: 573–574.

———. 1926. The iron-acetocarmine method of fixing and staining chromosomes. *Biol. Bull.* **50**: 160–162.

———. 1927. The number of chromosomes of cancerous and other human tumours. *J. Am. Med. Assoc.* **88**: 396.

Black, P.H. and W.P. Rowe. 1963. Transformation in hamster kidney monolayers by vacuolating virus SV-40. *Virology* **19**: 107–108.

Blakeslee, A.F. and A.G. Avery. 1937. Methods of inducing doubling of chromosomes in plants. *J. Hered.* **28**: 392–411.

Bleyer, A. 1934. Indications that mongoloid imbecility is a gametic mutation of degressive type. *Am. J. Dis. Child.* **47**: 342–348.

Böök, J.A., M. Fraccaro, and J. Lindsten. 1959. Cytogenetical observations in mongolism. *Acta Paediatr. Scand.* **48**: 453–468.

Boveri, T. 1914. *Zur Frage der Entstehung maligner Tumoren.* G. Fischer, Jena.

Caspersson, T., J. Lindsten, and I. Zech. 1970a. Identification of the abnormal B group chromosome in the 'cri du chat' syndrome by QM-fluorescence. *Exp. Cell Res.* **61**: 475–476.

———. 1970b. The nature of structural X chromosome aberrations in Turner's syndrome as revealed by quinacrine mustard fluorescence analysis. *Hereditas* **66**: 287–292.

Caspersson, T., G. Lomakka, and L. Zech. 1971. The 24 fluorescence patterns of the human metaphase chromosomes—Distinguishing characters and variability. *Hereditas* **67**: 89–102.

Caspersson, T., E. Simonsson, and L. Zech. 1970. UV-absorption and quinacrine mustard fluorescence patterns for chromosome aberration study in Chinese hamster. *Exp. Cell Res.* **63**: 243–244.

Caspersson, T., L. Zech, and C. Johansson. 1970a. Differential binding of alkylating fluorochromes in human chromosomes. *Exp. Cell Res.* **60**: 315–319.

———. 1970b. Analysis of human metaphase chromosome set by aid of DNA-binding fluorescent agents. *Exp. Cell Res.* **62**: 490–492.

Caspersson, T., L. Zech, and E.J. Modest. 1970. Fluorescent labelling of chromosomal DNA: Superiority of quinacrine mustard to quinacrine. *Science* **170**: 762.

Caspersson, T., G. Gahrton, J. Lindsten, and L. Zech. 1970a. Identification of the Philadelphia chromosome as a number 22 by quinacrine mustard fluorescence analysis. *Exp. Cell Res.* **63:** 238–240.

Caspersson, T., M. Hulten, J. Lindsten, and L. Zech. 1970b. Distinction between extra G-like chromosomes by quinacrine mustard fluorescence analysis. *Exp. Cell Res.* **63:** 240–243.

Caspersson, T., L. Zech, C. Johansson, and E.J. Modest. 1970c. Identification of human chromosomes by DNA-binding fluorescent agents. *Chromosoma* **30:** 215–227.

Caspersson, T., J. Lindsten, G. Lomakka, H. Wallman, and L. Zech. 1970d. Rapid identification of human chromosomes by TV-techniques. *Exp. Cell Res.* **63:** 477–479.

Caspersson, T., L. Zech, H. Harris, F. Wiener, and G. Klein. 1971. Identification of human chromosomes in a mouse/human hybrid by fluorescence techniques. *Exp. Cell Res.* **65:** 475–478.

Caspersson, T., L. Zech, E.J. Modest, G.E. Foley, U. Wagh, and E. Simonsson. 1969a. Chemical differentiation with fluorescent alkylating agents in *Vicia faba* metaphase chromosomes. *Exp. Cell Res.* **58:** 128–140.

———. 1969b. DNA-binding fluorochromes for the study of the organization of the metaphase nucleus. *Exp. Cell Res.* **58:** 141–152.

Caspersson, T., S. Farber, G.E. Foley, J. Kudynowski, E.J. Modest, E. Simonsson, U. Wagh, and L. Zech. 1968. Chemical differentiation along metaphase chromosomes. *Exp. Cell Res.* **49:** 219–222.

Chrustschoff, G.K. (asst. by E.A. Berlin). 1935. Cytological investigations on cultures of normal human blood. *J. Genet.* **31:** 243–261.

Chrustschoff, G.K., A.H. Andres, and W.I. Iljina-Kakujewa. 1931. Kulturen von Blutleukozyten als Methode zum Studium des menschlichen Karyotypus. *Anat. Anz.* **73:** 159–168.

Chu, E.H.Y. and N.H. Giles. 1958. Comparative chromosomal studies on mammalian cells in culture. I. The HeLa strain and its mutant clonal derivatives. *J. Natl. Cancer Inst.* **20:** 383–401.

Chu, E.H.Y., K.K. Sanford, and W.R. Earle. 1958. Comparative chromosome studies on mammalian cells in culture. II. Mouse sarcoma-producing cell strains and their derivatives. *J. Natl. Cancer Inst.* **21:** 729–752.

Dalla-Favera, R., M. Bregni, J. Erikson, D. Patterson, R.C. Gallo, and C.M. Croce. 1982. Human c-*myc* onc gene is located on the region of chromosome 8 that is translocated in Burkitt lymphoma cells. *Proc. Natl. Acad. Sci.* **79:** 7824–7827.

Darlington, C.D. 1932. *Recent advances in cytology*. J. and A. Churchill, London.

Denver Convention. 1962. Proposed standard system of nomenclature for human mitotic chromosomes, appendix II. *In Methodology in human genetics* (ed. W.J. Burdette), pp. 317–376. Holden-Day, San Francisco.

Donniah, I. and S.R. Pelc. 1950. Autoradiographic technique. *Br. J. Radiol.* **23:** 184–192.

Doty, P., J. Marmur, J. Eigner, and C. Schildkraut. 1960. Strand separation and specific recombination in deoxyribonucleic acids: Physical chemical studies. *Proc. Natl. Acad. Sci.* **46:** 461–476.

Drets, M.E. and M.W. Shaw. 1971. Specific banding patterns of human chromosomes. *Proc. Natl. Acad. Sci.* **68:** 2073–2077.

Dutrillaux, B. and J. Lejeune. 1971. Sur une nouvelle technique d'analyse du caryotype humain. *C.R. Acad. Sci. Paris* **272:** 2638–2640.

Farnes, P., B.E. Barker, L.E. Brownhill, and H. Fanger. 1964. Mitogenic activity of *Phytolacca americana* (pokeweed). *Lancet* **II:** 1100–1101.

Fell, H.B. and A.F. Hughes. 1949. Mitosis in the mouse: A study of living and fixed cells in tissue culture. *Q. J. Microsc. Sci.* **90:** 355–380.

Fialkow, P.J., P.J. Martin, V. Najfeld, G.K. Penfold, R.J. Jacobson, and J.A. Hansen. 1981. Evidence for a multistep pathogenesis of chronic myelogenous leukemia. *Blood* **58:** 158–163.

Flemming, W. 1882. Beiträge zur Kenntniss der Zelle und ihrer Lebenserscheinungen. III Theil. *Arch. Mikrosk. Anat.* **20:** 1–86.

———. 1892. Ueber die Chromosomenzahl beim Menschen. *Anat. Anz.* **14:** 171–174.

Ford, C.E. 1962. Methods in human cytogenetics. In *Methodology in human genetics* (ed. W.J. Burdette), pp. 337–381. Holden-Day, San Francisco.

Ford, C.E. and J.L. Hamerton. 1956a. A colchicine, hypotonic citrate squash sequence for mammalian chromosomes. *Stain Technol.* **31**: 247–251.

———. 1956b. The chromosomes of man. *Nature* **178**: 1020–1023.

Ford, C.E., J.L. Hamerton, and R.H. Mole. 1958. Chromosomal changes in primary and transplanted reticular neoplasms of the mouse. *J. Cell. Comp. Physiol.* (suppl. 1) **52**: 235–269.

Ford, C.E., K.W. Jones, P.E. Polani, J.C. De Almedia, and J.H. Briggs. 1959a. A sex chromosome anomaly in a case of gonadal dysgenesis (Turner's syndrome). *Lancet* **I**: 711–713.

Ford, C.E., K.W. Jones, O.J. Miller, U. Mittwoch, L.S. Penrose, M. Ridler, and A. Shapiro. 1959b. The chromosomes in a patient showing both mongolism and the Klinefelter's syndrome. *Lancet* **I**: 709–710.

Ford, D.K. and G. Yerganian. 1958. Observations on the chromosomes of Chinese hamster cells in tissue culture. *J. Natl. Cancer Inst.* **21**: 393–425.

Francke, U. 1976. Retinoblastoma and chromosome 13. *Cytogenet. Cell Genet.* **16**: 131–134.

Furth, J. and M.C. Kahn. 1937. The transmission of leukaemia of mice with a single cell. *Am. J. Cancer* **31**: 276–282.

Gall, J.G. and M.L. Pardue. 1969. Formation and detection of RNA-DNA hybrid molecules in cytological preparations. *Proc. Natl. Acad. Sci.* **63**: 378–383.

Gee, C.J. and H. Harris. 1979. Tumorigenicity of cells transformed by simian virus 40 and of hybrids between such cells and normal diploid cells. *J. Cell Sci.* **36**: 223–240.

Geitler, L. 1937. Die Analyse des Kernbaus und der Kernteilung der Wasserläufer *Gerris lateralis* und *Gerris lacustris* (Hemiptera heteroptera) und die Somadifferenzierung. *Z. Zellforsch. Mikrosk. Anat.* **26**: 641–672.

German, J. 1962. DNA synthesis in human chromosomes. *Trans. N.Y. Acad. Sci.* **24**: 395–407.

———. 1966. A bibliography on autoradiographic studies of mammalian chromosomes. *Ann. Génét.* **9**: 137–140.

———. 1967. Autoradiographic studies of human chromosomes: A review. In *Proceedings of the 3rd International Congress on Human Genetics*, pp. 123–136. Johns Hopkins University Press, Baltimore.

German, J.L. and A.G. Bearn. 1961. Asynchronous thymidine uptake by human chromosomes. *J. Clin. Invest.* **40**: 1041–1042.

Gropp, A., U. Tettenborn, and E. von Lehmann. 1970. Chromosomenvariation vom Robertson'schen Typus der Tabakmaus, *M. poschiavinus*, und ihren Hybriden mit der Laboratoriummaus. *Cytogenetics* **9**: 9–23.

Hagemeijer, A., D. Bootsma, N.K. Spurr, N. Heisterkamp, J. Groffen, and J.R.A. Stevenson. 1982. A cellular oncogene is translocated to the Philadelphia chromosome in chronic myelocytic leukemia. *Nature* **300**: 765–767.

Hamada, N. and H. Uchino. 1982. Chronologic sequence in appearance of clinical and laboratory findings characteristic of chronic myelocytic leukemia. *Blood* **51**: 843–850.

Hansemann, D. 1890. Über asymmetrische Zellteilung in Epithelkrebsen und deren biologische Bedeutung. *Arch. Pathol. Anat.* **119**: 299–326.

———. 1891a. Karyokinese und Cellularpathologie. *Berl. Klin. Wochenschr.* **28**: 1039–1042.

———. 1891b. Ueber pathologische Mitosen. *Arch. Pathol. Anat.* **123**: 356–370.

Harris, M. 1964. *Cell culture and somatic variation*, p. 228. Holt, Rinehart, and Winston, New York.

Hauschka, T.S. 1961. The chromosomes in ontogeny and oncogeny. *Cancer Res.* **21**: 957–974.

Hauschka, T.S. and A. Levan. 1951. Characterization of five ascites tumours with respect to chromosome ploidy. *Anat. Rec.* **111**: 467.

———. 1953. Inverse relationship between chromosome ploidy and host specificity of sixteen transplantable tumors. *Exp. Cell Res.* **4**: 457–467.

———. 1958. Cytologic and functional characterization of single cell clones isolated from the Krebs -2 and Ehrlich ascites tumors. *J. Natl. Cancer Inst.* **21**: 77–135.

Hayflick, L. and P.S. Moorhead. 1961. The serial cultivation of diploid cell strains. *Exp. Cell Res.* **25**: 585–621.

Heitz, E. 1936. Die Nukleal-Quetschmethode. *Dtsch. Bot. Ges.* **53**: 870–878.

Hellström, K.E. 1959. Chromosomal studies on primary methylcholanthrene-induced sarcomas in the mouse. *J. Natl. Cancer Inst.* **23**: 1019–1033.

Hilwig, I. and A. Gropp. 1972. Staining of constitutive heterochromatin in mammalian chromosomes with new fluorochrome. *Exp. Cell Res.* **75**: 122–126.

Hirai, K., J.M. Lehman, and V. Defendi. 1971. Re-initiation within one cell cycle of the deoxyribonucleic acid synthesis induced by simian virus 40. *J. Virol.* **8**: 828–835.

Howard, A. and S.R. Pelc. 1951a. Nuclear incorporation of P^{32} as demonstrated by autoradiographs. *Exp. Cell Res.* **2**: 178–187.

———. 1951b. Synthesis of nucleoproteins in bean root cells. *Nature* **167**: 599–601.

———. 1953. Synthesis of deoxyribonucleic acid in normal and irradiated cells and its relation in chromosome breakage. *Heredity* (suppl.) **6**: 261–273.

Howell, W.M., T.E. Denton, and R.J. Diamond. 1975. Differential staining of the satellite regions of human acrocentric chromosomes. *Experientia* **31**: 260–262.

Hsu, T.C. 1952. Mammalian chromosomes *in vitro*. I. The karyotype of man. *J. Hered.* **43**: 167–172.

———. 1954. Cytological studies on HeLa, a strain of human cervical carcinoma. I. Observations on mitosis and chromosomes. *Texas Rep. Biol. Med.* **12**: 833–846.

———. 1959. Numerical variation in chromosomes of higher animals. In *Developmental cytology* (ed. D. Rudrich), pp. 47–62. The Ronald Press, New York.

———. 1961. Chromosomal evolution in cell populations. *Int. Rev. Cytol.* **12**: 69–161.

———. 1979. *Human and mammalian cytogenetics: An historical perspective.* Springer Verlag, New York, Berlin, and Heidelberg.

Hsu, T.C. and O. Klatt. 1958. Mammalian chromosomes *in vitro*. IX. On genetic polymorphism in cell populations. *J. Natl. Cancer Inst.* **21**: 437–473.

Hsu, T.C. and P.S. Moorhead. 1957. Mammalian chromosomes *in vitro*. VII. Heteroploidy in human cell strains. *J. Natl. Cancer Inst.* **18**: 463–471.

Hsu, T.C. and C.M. Pomerat. 1953. Mammalian chromosomes *in vitro*. II. A method for spreading the chromosomes of cells in tissue. *J. Hered.* **44**: 23–29.

Hsu, T.C., D. Billen, and A. Levan. 1961. Mammalian chromosomes *in vitro*. XV. Patterns of transformation. *J. Natl. Cancer Inst.* **27**: 515–541.

Hughes, A. 1952. Some effects of abnormal tonicity on dividing cells in chick tissue cultures. *Q. J. Microsc. Sci.* **93**: 207–219.

Hungerford, D.A. 1978. Some early studies of human chromosomes, 1879-1955. *Cytogenet. Cell Genet.* **20**: 1–11.

Hungerford, D.A., A.J. Donnelly, P.C. Nowell, and S. Beck. 1959. The chromosome constitution of a human phenotypic intersex. *Am. J. Hum. Genet.* **11**: 215–236.

Ishibashi, K. 1950. Studies on the number of cells necessary for the transplantation of the Yoshida sarcoma. *Gann* **41**: 1–14.

Ising, U. 1955. Chromosome studies in Ehrlich mouse ascites cancer after heterologous transplantation through hamsters. *Br. J. Cancer* **9**: 592–599.

———. 1958. Effect of heterologous transplantation on chromosomes of ascites tumors. A contribution to our knowledge of environmental influence on tumor cells. *Acta Pathol. Microbiol. Scand.* (suppl.) **127**: 1–102.

Jacobs, P.A., A.G. Baikie, W.M. Court Brown, and J.A. Strong. 1959. The somatic chromosomes in mongolism. *Lancet* **I**: 710–712.

Jones, K.W. 1970. Chromosomal and nuclear location of mouse satellite DNA of individual cells. *Nature* **225**: 912–915.

Kemp, T. 1929. Ueber das Verhalten der Chromosomen in den somatischen Zellen des Menschen. *Z. Mikrosk. Anat. Forsch.* **16**: 1–20.

Klein, G. 1951. Comparative studies of mouse tumors with respect to their capacity for growth as 'ascites tumors' and their average nucleic acid content per cell. *Exp. Cell Res.* **2**: 518–573.

———. 1981. The role of gene dosage and genetic transposition in carcinogenesis. *Nature* **294**: 313–318.

Knudson, A.G. 1971. Mutation and cancer: Statistical study of retinoblastoma. *Proc. Natl. Acad. Sci.* **68**: 820–823.

Koprowski, H., J.A. Ponten, F. Jensen, R.G. Ravdin, P. Moorhead, and E. Saksela. 1962. Transformation of cultures of human tissue infected with simian virus 40. *J. Cell.*

Comp. Physiol. **59:** 281–286.

Lea, D.E. 1955. *Actions of radiations on living cells,* 2nd edition. Cambridge University Press, United Kingdom.

Lehman, J.M. and V. Defendi. 1970. Changes in deoxyribonucleic acid synthesis regulation in Chinese hamster cells infected with simian virus 40. *J. Virol.* **6:** 738–749.

Lejeune, J., M. Gautier, and R. Turpin. 1959. Etude des chromosomes somatiques de neuf enfants mongoliens. *C. R. Acad. Sci. Paris* **248:** 1721–1722.

Levan, A. 1938. The effect of colchicine on root mitosis in *Allium. Hereditas* **24:** 471–486.

———. 1956a. Chromosome studies on some human tumours and tissues of normal origin grown *in vivo* and *in vitro* at the Sloan-Kettering Institute. *Cancer* **9:** 648–663.

———. 1956b. The significance of polyploidy for the evolution of mouse tumors. Strains of the TA3 mammary adenocarcinoma with different ploidy. *Exp. Cell Res.* **11:** 613–629.

———. 1958. Cancerogenesis. A genetic adaptation on the cellular level. In *Achtste Jaarboek van Kankeronderzoek en Kankerbestrijding in Nederland,* pp. 110–126. Carl Bloms Boktryckeri, Lund.

———. 1959. Relation of chromosome status to the origin and progression of tumours: The evidence of chromosome number. In *Genetics and cancer,* pp. 151–182. University of Texas Press, Austin.

Levan, A. and J.J. Biesele. 1958. Role of chromosomes in cancerogenesis, as studied in serial tissue culture of mammalian cells. *Ann. N.Y. Acad. Sci.* **71:** 1022–1053.

Levan, A. and T.S. Hauschka. 1952. Chromosome numbers of three mouse ascites tumours. *Hereditas* **38:** 251–255.

———. 1953. Endomitotic reduplication mechanisms in ascites tumours of the mouse. *J. Natl. Cancer Inst.* **14:** 1–43.

Lima de Faria, A. 1959a. Differential uptake of tritiated thymidine into hetero and euchromatin in *Melanoplus secale. J. Biophys. Biochem. Cytol.* **6:** 457–466.

———. 1959b. Incorporation of tritiated thymidine into meiotic chromosomes. *Science* **130:** 503–504.

Linder, D. and S.M. Gartler. 1965. Glucose-6-phosphate dehydrogenase mosaicism: Utilization as a cell marker in the study of leiomyomas. *Science* **150:** 67–69.

Lyon, M.F. 1961. Gene action in the X chromosome of the mouse (*Mus musculus*). *Nature* **190:** 372–373.

———. 1962. Sex chromatin and gene action in mammalian X-chromosome. *Am. J. Hum. Genet.* **14:** 135–148.

Macklin, C.C. 1916. Binucleate cells in tissue culture. *Contr. Embryol.* **4:** 69-106. Carnegie Institution of Washington, D.C.

Makino, S. 1951. Some observations on the chromosomes of the Yoshida sarcoma cells based on the homoplastic and heteroplastic transplantation. *Gann* **42:** 87–90.

———. 1952. Cytologic studies of cancer. III. The characteristics and individualities of chromosomes in tumor cells of the Yoshida sarcoma which contribute to the growth of the tumour. *Gann* **43:** 17–34.

———. 1975. *Human chromosomes,* pp. 429–516. North Holland Publishing, Amsterdam and Oxford.

Makino, S. and K. Kano. 1951a. Cytological studies of cancer. II. Daily observations on the mitotic frequency and the variation of the chromosome number in tumour cells of the Yoshida sarcoma through a transplant generation. *J. Fac. Sci. Hokkaido Univ. Ser. VI Zool.* **10:** 225–242.

———. 1951b. Cytologic studies on cancer. IV. General characteristics of the MTK sarcomas, new ascites tumours of rats produced by the administration of azo dye. *J. Fac. Sci. Hokkaido Univ. VI Zool.* **10:** 289–301.

Makino, S. and I. Nishimura. 1952. Water pre-treatment squash technique. *Stain Technol.* **27:** 1–7.

Manolov, G. and Y. Manolova. 1972. Marker band in one chromosome 14 from Burkitt lymphomas. *Nature* **237:** 33–34.

Martin, P.J., V. Najfeld, J.A. Hansen, G.K. Penfold, R.J. Jacobson, and P.J. Fialkow. 1980. Involvement of the B-lymphoid system in chronic myelogenous leukaemia. *Nature* **287:** 49–50.

Matsui, S. and M. Sasaki. 1973. Differential staining of nucleolus organizers in mammalian chromosomes. *Nature* **246**: 148–150.

McLeish, J. 1953. The action of maleic hydrazide in *Vicia*. *Heredity* (suppl.) **6**: 125–147.

Meo, T., J. Johnson, C.V. Beechey, S.J. Andrews, J. Peters, and A.G. Searle. 1980. Linkage analyses of murine immunoglobulin heavy chain and serum prealbumin genes establish their location on chromosome 12 proximal to the T(5;12) 31H breakpoint in band 12F1. *Proc. Natl. Acad. Sci.* **77**: 550–553.

Miller, D.A. and O.J. Miller. 1972. Chromosome mapping in the mouse. *Science* **178**: 949–955.

Miller, J.F.A.P. 1961. Etiology and pathogenesis of mouse leukemia. *Adv. Cancer Res.* **6**: 291–368.

Miller, O.J. and B.F. Erlanger. 1975. Immunochemical probes of human chromosome organisation. *Pathobiol. Ann.*, pp. 71–103.

Mitelman, F. and S. Heim. 1988. Consistent involvement of only 71 of the 329 chromosomal bands of the human genome in primary neoplasia-associated rearrangements. *Cancer Res.* **48**: 7115–7119.

Moore, K.L. and M.L. Barr. 1954. Nuclear morphology, according to sex, in human tissues. *Acta Anat.* **21**: 197.

Moorhead, P.S. and T.C. Hsu. 1956. Cytological studies of HeLa, a strain of human cervical carcinoma. III. Durations and characteristics of the mitotic phases. *J. Natl. Cancer Inst.* **16**: 1047–1066.

Moorhead, P. and E. Saksela. 1963. Non-random chromosomal aberrations in SV40-transformed human cells. *J. Cell. Comp. Physiol.* **62**: 57–83.

Moorhead, P.S., P.C. Nowell, W.J. Mellman, D.M. Batipps, and D.A. Hungerford. 1960. Chromosome preparations of leukocytes cultured from human peripheral blood. *Exp. Cell Res.* **20**: 613–616.

Morgan, T.H., C.B. Bridges, and A.H. Sturtevant. 1925. The genetics of *Drosophila*. *Bibliogr. Genet.* **2**: 3–262.

Morishima, A., M.M. Grumbach, and J.H. Taylor. 1962. Asynchronous duplication of human chromosomes and the origin of sex chromatin. *Proc. Natl. Acad. Sci.* **48**: 756–763.

Muller, H.J. 1954. The nature of the genetic effects produced by radiation. In *Radiation biology* (ed. A Hollaender), vol. 1, part 1, pp. 351–374. McGraw Hill, New York.

Nakahara, H. 1952. A study of the chromosomes in the Yoshida sarcoma cells transplanted into mice. *Jpn. J. Genet.* **27**: 25–27.

Nowell, P.C. and D.A. Hungerford. 1960. A minute chromosome in human chronic granulocytic leukemia. *Science* **132**: 1497.

Nowell, P.C., D.A. Hungerford, and C.D. Brooks. 1958. Chromosomal characteristics of normal and leukaemic human leukocytes after short term tissue culture. *Proc. Am. Assoc. Cancer Res.* **2**: 331–332.

Oguma, K. and H. Kihara. 1922. A preliminary report on the human chromosomes. *Zool. Mag. Tokyo* **34**: 424–435.

———. 1923. Etude des chromosomes chez l'homme. *Arch. Biol.* **33**: 493–514.

Ohno, S. and S. Makino. 1961. The single-X nature of sex chromatin in man. *Lancet* **I**: 78–79.

Ohno, S., W.D. Kaplan, and R. Kinosita. 1959. Formation of the sex chromatin by a single X chromosome in liver cells of *Rattus norvegicus*. *Exp. Cell Res.* **18**: 415–418.

Osgood, E.E. and J.H. Brooke. 1955. Continuous tissue culture of leukocytes from human leukaemic bloods by application of 'gradient' principle. *Blood* **10**: 1010–1022.

Osgood, E.E. and M.L. Krippaehne. 1955. The gradient tissue culture method. *Exp. Cell Res.* **9**: 116–127.

Painter, T.S. 1921. The T-chromosome in mammals. *Science* **53**: 503–504.

———. 1923. Studies in mammalian spermatogenesis. II. The spermatogenesis of man. *J. Exp. Zool.* **37**: 291–335.

Pardue, M.L. and J.G. Gall. 1970. Chromosomal localization of mouse satellite DNA. *Science* **168**: 1356–1358.

Paris Conference. 1971. Standardization in human cytogenetics. *Birth Defects Orig. Artic. Ser.* **8**: 1-46.

Patil, S.R., S. Merrick, and H.A. Lubs. 1971. Identification of each human chromosome with a modified Giemsa stain. *Science* **173**: 821–822.

Pearson, P.L., M. Bobrow, and C.G. Vosa. 1970. Technique for identifying Y chromosomes in human interphase nuclei. *Nature* **226:** 78–80.

Puck, T.T. 1958. Action of radiation on mammalian cells. III. Relationship between reproductive death and induction of chromosome anomalies by X-irradiation of euploid human cells *in vitro. Proc. Natl. Acad. Sci.* **44:** 772–780.

Puck, T.T., S.J. Cieciura, and A. Robinson. 1958. Genetics of somatic mammalian cells. III. Long-term cultivation of euploid cells from human and animal subjects. *J. Exp. Med.* **108:** 945–956.

Rothfels, K.H. and R.C. Parker. 1959. The karyotypes of cell lines recently established from normal mouse tissues. *J. Exp. Zool.* **142:** 507–520.

Rothfels, K.H. and L. Siminovitch. 1958. An air-drying technique for flattening chromosomes in mammalian cells grown *in vitro. Stain Techol.* **33:** 73–77.

Rothfels, K.H., A.A. Axelrad, L. Siminovitch, E.A. McCulloch, and R.C. Parker. 1959. The origin of altered cell lines from mouse, monkey and man, as indicated by chromosome and transplantation studies. *Can. Cancer Conf.* **3:** 189–214.

Rowley, J.D. 1973. A new consistent chromosomal abnormality in chronic myelogenous leukemia identified by quinacrine fluorescence and Giemsa staining. *Nature* **243:** 290–293.

———. 1982. Identification of the constant chromosome regions involved in human hematologic malignant disease. *Science* **216:** 749–751.

———. 1990. Molecular cytogenetics: Rosetta Stone for understanding cancer. *Cancer Res.* **50:** 3816–3825.

Ruddle, F.H. 1961. Chromosome variation in cell populations derived from pig kidney. *Cancer Res.* **21:** 885–894.

Sandberg, A.A. and D.K. Hossfeld. 1970. Chromosomal abnormalities in human neoplasia. *Annu. Rev. Med.* **21:** 379–408.

Schweizer, D. 1977. R-banding produced by DNase I digestion of chromomycin-stained chromosomes. *Chromosoma* **64:** 117–124.

Seabright, M. 1971. A rapid banding technique for human chromosomes. *Lancet* **II:** 971–972.

———. 1973. Improvement of trypsin method for banding chromosomes. *Lancet* **I:** 1249–1250.

Shein, H.M. and J.F. Enders. 1962. Transformation induced by simian virus 40 in human renal cell cultures. I. Morphology and growth characteristics. *Proc. Natl. Acad. Sci.* **48:** 1164–1172.

Slifer, E.H. 1934. Insect development. VI. The behaviour of grasshopper embryos in anisotonic, balanced salt solution. *J. Exp. Zool.* **67:** 137–157.

Snell, G.D. 1935. The induction by X-rays of hereditary changes in mice. *Genetics* **20:** 545–567.

Spriggs, A.I. 1974. Cytogenetics of cancer and precancerous states of the cervix uteri. In *Chromosomes and cancer* (ed. J. German), pp. 423–450. John Wiley and Sons, New York.

Spriggs, A.I., M.M. Boddington, and C.M. Clarke. 1962. Carcinoma-in-situ of the cervix uteri. *Lancet* **I:** 1383–1384.

Spriggs, A.I., C.E. Bowey, and R.H. Cowdell. 1971. Chromosomes of pre-cancerous lesions of the cervix uteri. *Cancer* **27:** 1239–1254.

Stanley, M.A. and J.A. Kirkland. 1968. Cytogenetic studies of endometrial carcinoma. *Am. J. Obstet. Gynecol.* **102:** 1070–1079.

Stich, A.F. and H.O. Steele. 1962. DNA content of tumor cells. III. Mosaic composition of sarcomas and carcinomas in man. *J. Natl. Cancer Inst.* **28:** 1207–1218.

Sumner, A.T., H.J. Evans, and R.A. Buckland. 1971. A new technique for distinguishing between human chromosomes. *Nat. New Biol.* **232:** 31–32.

Swanson, C.P. 1957. *Cytology and cytogenetics.* Prentice Hall, New Jersey.

Swift, H. 1953. Quantitative aspects of nuclear nucleoprotein. *Int. Rev. Cytol.* **2:** 1–76.

Taub, R., I. Kirsch, C. Morton, G. Lenoir, D. Swam, S. Aaronson, and P. Leder. 1982. Translocation of the *c-myc* gene into the immunoglobulin heavy chain locus in human Burkitt lymphoma and murine plasmacytoma cells. *Proc. Natl. Acad. Sci.* **79:** 7837–7841.

Taylor, J.H. 1953. Autoradiographic detection of incorporation of P^{32} into chromosomes during meiosis and mitosis. *Exp. Cell Res.* **4:** 169–179.

————. 1960. Asynchronous duplication of chromosomes in cultured cells of Chinese hamster. *J. Biophys. Biochem. Cytol.* **7**: 455–464.

Taylor, J.H. and S.H. Taylor. 1953. The autoradiograph—A tool for cytogeneticists. *J. Hered.* **44**: 129–132.

Taylor, J.H., P.S. Woods, and W.L. Hughes. 1957. The organization and duplication of chromosomes as revealed by autoradiographic studies, using tritium labelled thymidine. *Proc. Natl. Acad. Sci.* **43**: 122–128.

Timonen, S. and E. Therman. 1950. Variation in the somatic chromosome number in man. *Nature* **166**: 995–996.

Tjio, J.H. and A. Levan. 1956. The chromosome number of man. *Hereditas* **42**: 1–6.

Tjio, J.H. and T.T. Puck. 1958. Genetics of somatic mammalian cells. II. Chromosome constitution of cells in tissue culture. *J. Exp. Med.* **108**: 259–262.

van de Sande, J.H., C.C. Lin, and K.F. Jorgenson. 1977. Reverse banding on chromosomes produced by a guanine-cytosine specific DNA binding antibiotic: Olivomycin. *Science* **195**: 400–402.

Vogt, M. and R. Dulbecco. 1960. Virus-cell interaction with a tumour-producing virus. *Proc. Natl. Acad. Sci.* **46**: 365–370.

————. 1963. Steps in the neoplastic transformation of hamster embryo cells by polyoma virus. *Proc. Natl. Acad. Sci.* **49**: 171–179.

von Winiwarter, H. 1912. Etudes sur la spermatogénèse humaine. I. Cellule de Sertoli II Hétérochromosome et mitoses de l'épithélium séminal. *Arch. Biol.* **27**: 91–190.

Waardenburg, P.J. 1932. Mongolismus (Mongoloid Idiotie). In Das menschliche Auge und seine Erbanlagen. *Bibliogr. Genet.* **7**: 44–48.

Wakonig, R. and D.K. Ford. 1960. Chromosome aberrations in irradiated cells of Chinese hamster grown in tissue culture. *Can. J. Zool.* **38**: 203–207.

Walker, P.M.B. and H.B. Yates. 1952. Nuclear components of dividing cells. *Proc. R. Soc. Lond. B Biol. Sci.* **140**: 274–299.

Weisblum, B. and P. De Haseth. 1972. Quinacrine—A chromosome stain specific for deoxyadenylate-deoxythymidilate-rich regions in DNA. *Proc. Natl. Acad. Sci.* **69**: 629–632.

Wiener, F., S. Ohno, J. Spira, N. Haran-Ghera, and G. Klein. 1978a. Chromosomal changes (trisomy 15 and 17) associated with tumor progression in leukemias induced by radiation leukemia virus (RadLV). *J. Natl. Cancer Inst.* **61**: 227–237.

————. 1978b. Chromosome changes (trisomy 15) in murine T-cell leukemia induced by 7,12 dimethylbenz (a) anthracene (DMBA). *Int. J. Cancer* **22**: 447–453.

————. 1978c. Cytogenetic mapping of the trisomic segment of chromosome 15 in murine T-cell leukaemia. *Nature* **275**: 658–660.

Winge, Ø. 1927. Zytologische Untersuchungen über die Natur maligner Tumoren. I. 'Crown Gall' der Zuckerrübe. *Z. Zellforsch. Mikrosk. Anat.* **6**: 397–423.

————. 1930. Zytologische Untersuchungen über die Natur maligner Tumoren. II. Teerkarzinome bei Mäusen. *Z. Zellforsch. Mikrosk. Anat.* **10**: 683–735.

Yerganian, G. 1952. Cytogenetic possibilities with the Chinese hamster *Cricetulus barabensis griseus. Genetics* **37**: 638–639.

————. 1959. Chromosomes of the Chinese hamster *Cricetulus griseus.* I. The normal complement and identification of sex chromosomes. *Cytologia* **24**: 66–75.

Yerganian, G. and M.J. Leonard. 1961. Maintenance of normal *in situ* chromosomal features in long term tissue cultures. *Science.* **133**: 1600–1601.

Yoshida, T. 1949. The Yoshida sarcoma, an ascites tumour. *Gann* **40**: 1–21.

Yosida, T.H. 1952. Cytologic studies on cancer. V. Heteroplastic transplantation of the Yoshida sarcoma with special regard to the behaviour of tumor cells. *Gann* **43**: 35–43.

Yunis, J.J. and N. Ramsay. 1978. Retinoblastoma and sub-band deletion of chromosome 13. *Am. J. Dis. Child.* **132**: 161–163.

Zech, L., U. Haglund, K. Nilsson, and G. Klein. 1976. Characteristic chromosomal abnormalities in biopsies and lymphoid cell lines from patients with Burkitt and non-Burkitt lymphomas. *Int. J. Cancer* **17**: 47–56.

Zhivago, P., B. Morosov, and A. Ivanickaya. 1934. Über die Einwirkung der Hypotonie auf die Zellteilung in den Gewebkulturen des embyronalen Herzens. *Dokl. Akad. Nauk. USSR.* **3**: 385–386.

4
GENETICS WITHOUT SEX

GENETIC VARIANTS IN SOMATIC CELLS

In a Harvey lecture that summarised his painstaking work on the nutritional requirements of animal cells in culture, Eagle (1960) drew two principal conclusions. The first was that, with a few minor variations, all mammalian cells in culture, whether freshly isolated or long established, whether tumorigenic or not, and irrespective of their tissue of origin or morphological type, had essentially similar nutritional requirements. The second was that the specific differentiated traits that distinguished the cells of one organ from another were not expressed in cell lines propagated *in vitro*. Eagle, Piez, and Fleischman (1957) had indeed isolated a variant HeLa cell culture that managed to encompass a limited conversion of phenylalanine to tyrosine. Herzenberg and Roosa (1959) had shown that mouse lymphoma cells required added pyruvate for growth; and a similar requirement was reported by Eagle and Oyama (Eagle 1960) for embryonic mouse cells. But these nutritional variants could easily be accounted for by metabolic adaptations, perhaps involving changes in enzyme concentrations, and no strong claim was made that they represented auxotrophic nutritional mutants in the conventional sense. On the other hand, Puck (1959) claimed that mutants of mammalian cells could readily be isolated by the single-cell plating technique that he had devised, although he made no formal distinction between mutants, as defined by stable changes in the DNA of the cells, and variants that were thought not to involve such changes. If these cells with altered nutritional requirements were indeed mutants in a classical sense and if, as in microorganisms, such mutations were usually recessive, the claim that they could easily be obtained in mammalian cells raised a major conceptual difficulty. For in diploid cells, any recessive mutation involving an autosomal gene would have to be present in the homozygous condition to be detectable as a phenotypic change; and this would occur with much too low a frequency to permit ready isolation of the mutant.

The first systematic attempt to investigate this problem was made by Szybalski and his colleagues who introduced 8-azaguanine resistance as a mutational marker apparently produced in a single step (Szybalski and Smith 1959a; Szybalski and Szybalska 1962). Szybalski, Szybalska, and Brockman (1961) showed that 8-azaguanine-resistant mutants lacked the enzyme inosinic acid pyrophosphorylase (now known as hypoxanthine-guanine phosphoribosyl transferase: HPRT) which is required for the incorporation of exogenous hypoxanthine into nucleic acids. When *de novo* synthesis of purines is blocked by the folic acid antagonist amethopterin, normal cells can overcome the block by incorporating exogenous hypoxanthine, and they are killed by exogenous 8-azaguanine because this cytotoxic analogue is incorporated into nucleic acids by the same pathway. Cells lacking inosinic acid pyrophosphorylase cannot incorporate exogenous 8-azaguanine and are thus resistant to its cytotoxic actions. Such resistant cells were, however, found in wild-type populations at a level of about 0.1%, so that a procedure had to be devised to eliminate such pre-existing variants before quantatitive studies on mutational frequency could be attempted. This was achieved by exploiting a differential between the pre-existing variants and 8-azaguanine-resistant cells in their requirement for exogenous hypoxanthine when blocked by amethopterin. When pre-existing variants were eliminated in this way, a 'mutational frequency' of 3×10^{-6} 'mutations' per cell per generation was obtained. Lieberman and Ove (1959), studying puromycin resistance by the Delbrück-Luria fluctuation test, obtained a mutational frequency of 3.6×10^{-6} mutations per generation, which is in remarkably good, but perhaps fortuitous, agreement with the figure provided by Szybalski and his colleagues.

If these drug-resistant variants were caused by conventional mutations, then it was reasonable to suppose that their frequency would be increased by mutagens. However, Szybalski and Smith (1959b) found that when Detroit 98 cells, a human epithelial line, were exposed to mutagenic doses of ultraviolet light, the incidence of 8-azaguanine-resistant cells was reduced. In these experiments, however, the incidence of spontaneous variants was very high: 5×10^{-4} per cell per generation. Szybalski, Szybalska, and Ragni (1962) found no increase in the incidence of 8-azaguanine-resistant variants after treatment of the cells with nitrogen mustards, triethylene melanine, β-propriolactone or halogen-substituted thymidine analogues. Hsu and Somers (1962) and Kit et al. (1963) showed that resistance to the thymidine analogue 5-bromo-deoxyuridine was nonetheless associated with loss of the enzyme thymidine kinase. Between 1959 and 1962, numerous workers produced populations of cells that were resistant to folic acid antagonists, purine and pyrimidine analogues, steroids, antibiotics and metal ions, but the precise nature of the genetic or non-genetic changes that underlay these variations remained obscure.

In the absence of any mating system for somatic cells, attempts were made to analyse this question further by means of DNA transfection, a technique that had proven to be highly informative in the genetic analysis of bacteria (Szbalska and Szybalski 1962). The results obtained were, however, inconsistent and difficult to interpret. Bradley, Roosa, and Law (1962) found that resistance to 8-azaguanine could indeed be conferred on sensitive cells by exposing them to preparations of DNA extracted from 8-azaguanine-resistant cells; but, unfortunately, they also found that resistance could be conferred by DNA from 8-azaguanine-sensitive cells, which appeared to indicate that the effect was non-specific. Szybalski, Szybalska, and Ragni (1962), on the other hand, obtained a different result when reversion of analogue-resistant cells was studied by means of DNA transfection. They found that when cells resistant to azahypoxanthine were treated with DNA from wild-type cells or cells resistant to 8-azaguanine, the incidence of revertants was greatly increased from a base-line level of 2×10^{-7} per cell per generation to a level of 1.2×10^{-4} per cell per generation; and the effect was said to be proportional to the amount of DNA added. Moreover, the revertants isolated after treatment with exogenous DNA were described as having a spectrum of sensitivity to guanine and hypoxanthine analogues that more closely resembled the cells from which the DNA was extracted than that found in spontaneous revertants. But, unlike the findings described by Bradley, Roosa, and Law (1962), Szybalski, Szybalska, and Ragni found that transfection of DNA from analogue-resistant to analogue-sensitive cells did not enhance mutational frequency in the forward direction. The effects produced by DNA transfection in animal cells were obviously complex, and the claim that specific analogue-resistance markers had been transferred from one cell type to another by this means was not generally accepted. Many years were to elapse before a convincing demonstration of marker transfer by DNA transfection was finally achieved in animal cells.

MUTATION

The fundamental question remained unanswered: it was still not clear that any of the extensive range of variants that had now been generated was in fact produced by genetic mutation in the classical sense. Gartler and Pious (1966), Breslow and Goldsby (1969), Coffino and Scharff (1971), and Levisohn and Thompson (1972), working with different cell types and different markers, had all found that the emergence of variants was much too frequent to be accounted for by random mutation; and several authors continued to argue strongly for the view that these variants arose from stable physiological changes of a non-genetic character. Morgan Harris (1967) had observed that when cultures of pig kidney cells were exposed to puromycin, large colonies grew out of cell aggregates at concentrations of the drug that were lethal for sparse cultures. Harris noted that the strong influence of cell density on the results obtained made it very difficult to calculate mutation rates, and he emphasised that it was necessary to distinguish between genuine mutations, for which there was no decisive evidence, and "refractory responses by sensitive cells", that is, phenotypic modulation. Another way of exploring this by then much vexed question was to examine the effect of chromosome ploidy on the frequency of emergence of drug-resistant variants. For recessive mutations, systematic increases in ploidy would be expected to produce systematic reductions in mutational frequency. This approach had yielded interpretable and consistent results with yeast cells. Morgan Harris (1971a), by blocking mitosis with colchicine, succeeded in establishing a polyploid series of the V79 strain of Chinese hamster cells. The chromosome number in these cells ranged from 2n to 16n, and they all multiplied at much the same rate. Again applying a modification of the Delbrück-Luria fluctuation test, Harris compared the frequency of emergence of 8-azaguanine-resistant variants in diploid, tetraploid and octoploid cells. The estimated 'mutational frequency' was about 10^{-5}, but it either remained more or less constant with increasing ploidy or showed a small decline, but not at all what would be expected if the variants were genuine mutants, whether dominant, co-dominant or recessive. Similar experiments were done with variants resistant to heat shock. The cells were heated in suspension at 43–47°C, and heat-resistant variants were obtained at a calculated mutational frequency of 10^{-6}; but again no interpretable relationship between ploidy and mutational frequency was observed. From these results

Morgan Harris drew the conclusion that both the drug-resistant and the heat-shock-resistant variants were not produced by genuine mutations but by "stable shifts in phenotypic expression" (Harris 1971b).

A similar conclusion was drawn by Mezger-Freed (1972, 1974) from studies on haploid and diploid cell lines derived from frog embryos. Freed and Mezger-Freed (1970) had established two haploid cell lines from androgenetic (haploid) embryos of *Rana pipiens* and, at the time that their paper was submitted for publication, had maintained one line for 150 cell generations and the other for 200. *Grosso modo*, the karyotypes of the cell lines were very similar to that seen in the cells of the embryo itself. However, when arm lengths and centromere positions were compared, statistically significant deviations were found, as had previously been described by Levan for pseudodiploid populations of human tumour cells. These deviations ranged from 4–11% of the chromosome length and were found to involve both gains and losses of chromosome material. That these cells were pseudodiploid and not strictly euploid turned out to be an important consideration in the controversy that subsequently arose in connection with the interpretation that Mezger-Freed gave to her results. Mezger-Freed (1972) studied the effects of a range of mutagens on the incidence of analogue-resistant variants in the two haploid and in diploid cell lines. Resistance to 15 µg/ml of bromodeoxyuridine was used as the mutational marker, and the mutagens included agents that reacted with DNA in different ways. Treatment with mutagens was found in some cases to increase the incidence of bromodeoxyuridine-resistant variants, but in others this incidence was reduced. Even with the same mutagen, the responses given by the two haploid cell lines differed. The frequency with which resistant variants appeared in the haploid cells was about 5% of the value given by diploid cells, which was entirely inconsistent with what was to be expected for a recessive mutation. Mezger-Freed suggested that the analogue resistance was conferred by phenotypic modulation of membrane permeability, a view supported by measurements of tritiated thymidine uptake. Mezger-Freed (1974) describes similar experiments with some acridine mustard compounds known to be mutagenic in bacteria. In these experiments the differences between haploid and diploid cells were again found to be far too small to accommodate a model in which the variants were produced by classical recessive mutations; in the latter case, the mutation rate to be expected in cells of different ploidy would be the rate for a single copy of the locus raised to a power equal to the ploidy of the cell.

The relationship between ploidy and mutational frequency was re-examined in greater detail by Chasin (1973). A pseudodiploid Chinese hamster cell line was compared with a tetraploid subline derived from it. Reversion of a glycine auxotrophic variant to glycine independence occurred with the same frequency in the diploid and the tetraploid cells, as would be expected for a dominant mutation; but the incidence of 6-thioguanine-resistant variants was found to be 25 times lower in the tetraploids than in the pseudodiploids. Since resistance to 6-thioguanine was known to be a recessive character, a decrease in its incidence with increasing ploidy was to be expected, but the decrease observed was not nearly big enough to be accommodated by a model involving nothing more than conventional recessive mutation. It was clear that some event that occurred much more frequently than the usual rate of mutation was involved. Chasin suggested that this event might be some form of chromosome segregation, broadly defined as any chromosomal event that occurred at a higher order of frequency than classical mutation. Since the gene coding for the enzyme involved in resistance to 6-thioguanine (HPRT) was known to be located on the X chromosome, the results would be explained by frequent elimination of an X chromosome from the tetraploid cells.

STRUCTURAL MUTANTS

It was clear that the decisive evidence required to demonstrate that the variant was produced by a mutation in the orthodox sense was the demonstration that the enzyme responsible for the metabolic abnormality had undergone a structural change. Before 1975, there were very few pieces of structural evidence of this kind, and most of them were rather indirect. Beaudet, Roufa, and Caskey (1973), studying HPRT-variants in Chinese hamster cells, found that the cells produced a protein that cross-reacted with antibody directed against HPRT but that was enzymatically inactive. Albrecht, Biedler, and Hutchinson (1972) found that variants with a defect in dihydrofolate reductase activity produced an enzyme that showed an altered response to inhibitors. Chan, Whitmore, and Siminovitch (1972) found that variants resistant to α-amanitin produced altered forms of the enzyme RNA-polymerase II that were no longer sensitive to the inhibitor. Chasin et al. (1974) made a detailed study of an auxotrophic mutant of a Chinese hamster cell line isolated after exposure to the mutagen ethylmethanesulphonate. This variant required glycine for growth. The synthesis of glycine from serine is catalyzed by the enzyme serine hydroxymethyl transferase, which is found both in the mitochrondria and in the cytosol of fractionated cells. The enzyme associated with the mitochondrial fraction has a specific activity about 20 times greater than the cytosolic enzyme and is much more resistant to thermal denaturation. Chasin et al. found that the auxotrophic variant had completely lost all mitochondrial enzyme activity. Revertants could be induced by mutagenesis, and, when these were examined, it was found that about a third of the enzyme activity had been restored to the mitochondrial fraction, but the mitochondrial enzyme was now more sensitive to heat denaturation than the wild type. These results, although not decisive, strongly supported the view that the auxotrophy had been produced by a mutation in the structural gene.

AUXOTROPHIC MUTANTS

In 1967, Puck and Kao introduced a new procedure that was specificially designed to select for auxotrophic mutants. The cells were first exposed to bromodeoxyuridine in a medium from which the specified component was omitted and were then exposed to visible light. Cells that were able to grow in the absence of this component incorporated the bromodeoxyuridine and were subsequently killed by exposure to the visible light. Auxotrophs, unable to grow in the absence of the specified component, did not incorporate the bromodeoxyuridine and were therefore not killed by the visible light. Most of the work on mutagenesis from Puck's laboratory was done with CHO cells, an established line derived originally from Chinese hamster ovary cultures in which spontaneous transformation had taken place (Tjio and Puck 1958). The original cell line had 21 chromosomes, but a subclone CHOki was selected for general use because it contained only 20 chromosomes. The first auxotrophic variant isolated from CHO cells after chemical mutagenesis required glycine, adenine and thymidine for growth and was found to be deficient in the enzyme folylpolyglutamate synthetase (Kao and Puck 1968). In the same year, Chu and Malling (1968), using the selective procedure devised by Szybalski, isolated HPRT-variants from Chinese hamster cells after treating the cultures with a chemical mutagen. In both cases, the incidence of the metabolic variants was greatly increased by chemical mutagenesis. This was also true for synchronized hamster cells treated with nitrosoguanidine (Orkin and Littlefield 1971) and for variants isolated from hamster cells after exposure to X irradiation (Chu 1971). In a review published in 1982, Puck and Kao listed some 50 auxotrophic mutants that had thus far been isolated from cultures of CHO and other Chinese hamster cell lines, but it is of interest that even at this late date, the authors added a footnote to the effect that they made no distinction between mutants and variants.

The case against metabolic variants in cell culture being genuine mutants was seriously undermined by a thorough analysis of the question by De Mars (1974). De Mars pointed out first that, despite some reports to the contrary, there was ample evidence that the incidence of metabolic variants was substantially enhanced by known mutagens and by X rays; and second, that there were serious technical flaws in the experiments of Morgan Harris and Mezger-Freed from which the conclusion was drawn that there was no relationship between ploidy and mutational frequency. In neither of these two sets of experiments were there adequate controls for spontaneous reversion, and no information was provided about the number of X chromosomes that the cells contained—essential information because the metabolic variants were selected for their resistance to 8-azaguanine, and the gene usually responsible for conferring this resistance (HPRT) was known to be located on the X chromosome. The X linkage of HPRT excluded 8-azaguanine resistance from the general argument that recessive mutations would not be found in genuinely euploid cells because two alleles are normally present; but the work of Rappaport and De Mars (1973) showed that diaminopurine-resistant variants could also be readily isolated from human fibroblasts, and the gene responsible for diaminopurine resistance (adenine phosphoribosyl transferase: APRT) was known to map to an autosome. How was this to be accounted for? De Mars explained that some individuals in any population would be heterozygous for the autosomal gene one was interested in, so that in cultures made from different individuals one would expect to find great variation in the number of mutants that could be detected. In some cultures, those with two active alleles, one might find no mutants, but in those with only one active allele one might expect a mutational frequency comparable to that found for X-linked genes. In fluctuation tests on cultures from three unrelated males and one female, who may be presumed to have had only one active X chromosome, De Mars found that 8-azaguanine-resistant variants arose with an average frequency of 5×10^{-6} per generation, with a range of $0.5–37 \times 10^{-6}$. Diaminopurine-resistant mutants were obtained in about 1 in 20 to 1 in 5 cultures. In cultures from 13 individuals taken from 11 unrelated families and treated with the mutagen N-methyl-N'-nitro-N-nitrosoguanidine (MNNG), diaminopurine-resistant mutants arose with a frequency of $10^{-5}–10^{-4}$ per cell per generation for the cells that survived the mutagenic treatment. Spontaneous diaminopurine-resistant mutants arose in three of the cultures with an incidence of 10^{-7}–10^{-5} per cell per generation, a figure comparable to that obtained for 8-azaguanine-resistant mutants. These results thus agreed tolerably well with the predictions imposed by genetic theory, and they lent strong support to the view that these analogue-resistant variants were indeed classical mutations.

However, there was still a problem to be solved for the large number of apparently recessive auxotrophic variants easily selected in CHO cells. Many of these involved genes that were known to map to different autosomes, and it was difficult to reconcile the very high mutational frequency with genetic theory if two functional alleles were present in these cells. This problem was systematically discussed in an influential article by Siminovitch (1976) who, like De Mars, argued strongly for the view that in CHO, as in other, cells, most auxotrophic and drug-resistant variants were indeed produced by classical mutations. Siminovitch assembled and discussed the cases where the incidence of such variants was substantially enhanced by mutagenesis and concluded that there were strong technical grounds for doubting the validity of experiments in which such enhancement was not observed. A more telling point was the assembly of data in which a range of variants had been shown to produce structurally modified proteins. Siminovitch's list contains some 20 different kinds of variant, including eight auxotrophs, and, in almost all categories, examples were given in which there was strong, if indirect, evidence that a structural modification of a key protein had taken place. Like Chasin, Siminovitch was highly critical of the observations made by Morgan Harris and Mezger-Freed purporting to show no systematic relationship between mutational frequency and ploidy. With respect to the findings of Puck and others on CHO cells, Siminovitch argued that these were explicable if many loci in CHO cells were present in the hemizygous or heterozygous condition. Although the CHO line and the clonal derivative commonly used were classified as pseudodiploid, there is little doubt that in this cell, as in others that had been systematically examined from this point of view, extensive rearrangements of the karyotype were present. Although formal demonstration of extensive hemizygosity in CHO cells was not provided, and has not been provided to the present day, Siminovitch's argument was generally accepted, and the unexpectedly high mutational frequency of apparent recessives ceased to be regarded as a serious objection to the conclusion that most of the variants obtained in established cell lines after mutagenesis were in fact mutants.

LOSS OF DIFFERENTIATED TRAITS

However, the loss of differentiated traits that occurred in virtually all normal tissues on explantation did not, on the face of it, appear to be easily explicable by the selective overgrowth of undifferentiated mutants. Sato, Zaroff, and Mills (1960) did indeed argue that this was the case, but there was strong experimental evidence to the contrary. To begin with, the process of dedifferentiation (here used simply to describe the loss of observable differentiated functions) appeared to involve the whole of the explanted population in a systematic manner, and there was nothing about the character of the change to suggest that it was based on a stochastic process such as random mutation (Willmer 1960; Levintow and Eagle 1961; Morris 1962). Moreover, Ebner, Hageman, and Larson (1961) had shown in primary cultures of bovine cells that although there was a generalised decline in specialised functions, individual functions did not decline in parallel. Production of lactose disappeared within 24 hours, but β-lactoglobulin production declined much more slowly to reach a lower plateau in about two weeks. The decisive experiment was done by Hilfer (1962) on thyroid cells freshly explanted from chick embryos. These cells formed epithelial sheets that remained in good condition for a week or more, but they did not multiply. Nonetheless, the amount of thyroxine that they produced declined precipitously and none could be detected after five days. Triiodothyronine production fell to zero within three days. Numerous earlier studies of enzyme reduction and enzyme loss in tissue cultures, although not decisive, certainly supported Hilfer's conclusion that regulatory processes rather than genetic events were responsible for the rapid loss of differentiated functions *in vitro*. Evidence was also provided that the re-acquisition of differentiated traits by cells that had lost them was similarly mediated by regulatory processes. As early as 1924, Ebeling had shown that sheets of iris epithelium could be grown continuously for a year or more without producing any pigment, but they could regularly be induced to undergo pigmentation if they were transferred to a nutritionally poor medium. Holtzer et al. (1960) and Stockdale et al. (1963), studying the loss of specialised function in cultures of cartilage cells, found that if trypsinized cells were grown as monolayers they failed to form cartilage, but if they were grown in aggregates they did so. Over a ten day period in culture, monolayer cells progressively lost their ability to form cartilage when reaggregated. It seemed remotely improbable that such changes could have a mutational basis.

STABILISATION OF DIFFERENTIATED TRAITS

The failure of most normal tissue cells to express their characteristic differentiated traits on continued cultivation *in vitro* gave no great hope that genetic analysis of such cells would yield much information about differentiation. But it had been observed that certain tumour cells, unlike their normal progenitors, did continue to synthesize their specialised products *in vitro*. Waltz et al. (1954) had shown that cells derived from a hydatidiform mole continued to secrete gonadotrophic hormone when grown *in vitro*; Schindler, Day, and Fischer (1959) had demonstrated that cultures from a mast cell tumour synthesized 5-hydroxytryptamine and histamine; and Day and Green (1962) had reported that the mast cells also synthesized amines. These promising results with tumour cells prompted Sato to explore the possibility of extending the range of tumours from which to derive cell lines that continued to synthesize the specialised products characteristically made by the tumours *in vivo*. The approach that Sato and his colleagues adopted was to subject the tumour cell populations to alternating passages through the animal and through culture *in vitro*. This approach was devised by Buonassisi, Sato, and Cohen (1962), and its aim was to select for continued expression of specific differentiated products by passage of the tumour cells through the animal, and then to select for growth *in vitro* by explantation of the tumour. The expectation was that by alternating passage *in vivo* with passage *in vitro*, cells would eventually be selected that grew well *in vitro*, but continued to synthesize differentiated products. Yasumura, Tashjian, and Sato (1966) demonstrated dramatically that this was indeed the case. Four specialised tumours were subjected to this alternating *in vivo/in vitro* passage: a Leydig cell tumour that produced steroids, a melanoma that formed pigment and two pituitary tumours that secreted hormones. The tumours were grown *in vitro* for 3–10 days, passaged through the animal for 3–6 cycles, and then cloned by Puck's procedure, but without feeder layers. The isolated clones were then expanded and tested for the production of the specialised product. In this way, cell lines that produced γ^4-3-keto-steroids were derived from the Leydig cell tumour, pigmented lines were derived from the melanoma, and one line that secreted growth hormone and one that secreted a substance that appeared to be adrenocorticotrophic hormone were derived from the pituitary tumours. Augusti-Tocco and Sato (1969) derived functional cell lines from neuroblastoma cells by the same procedure. The neuroblastoma appeared to be composed of immature neuroblasts, but *in vitro* the cells took on the appearance of mature neurones and generated axons. After alternating *in vivo/in vitro* passage and subsequent cloning, cell lines were produced that synthesized neurotransmitters, choline acetylase, tyrosine hydroxylase and acetylcholinesterase. The cloned cell lines produced these specialised compounds in amounts comparable to those found in the original tumours. Sato and his colleagues stressed the importance of cloning to eliminate undifferentiated cells that might otherwise overgrow the cultures, and of supplying the cells with exogenous hormones in order to maintain the differentiated state. Hayashi and Sato (1976) and Mather and Sato (1977) succeeded in growing the pituitary cell line and the melanoma in serum-free medium without loss of the differentiated function by adding the appropriate hormones and transferrin to the medium. The techniques elaborated by Sato and his colleagues were widely adopted, and it was not long before a wide spectrum of highly differentiated cell lines derived from tumours became available. Indeed, there were eventually very few tissue types that were not represented in this array.

The need to add appropriate hormones was also generally acknowledged. Hutchings and Sato (1978) showed that HeLa cells could be grown in serum-free medium if this was supplemented with hormones, and Barnes and Sato (1979) showed that this was also true for human mammary cells. Coon (1964) appears to have been the first to obtain clones of euploid cells that retained their specialised function and to show (Coon 1966) that the expression of this function could be stably maintained. Coon worked with cartilage and pre-cartilage cells from chicken embryos. Occasional clones that were visibly cartilagenous were picked off and expanded. Cahn and Cahn (1966) achieved the same thing with retinal pigment cells. In the years that followed, libraries of highly differentiated cell types were accumulated and stored in cell repositories; and although these differentiated cells provided exceptional material for a variety of purposes, they did not in the end prove in themselves to be particularly useful for the genetic analysis of differentiation. Variants that lost specific differentiated functions were all too easy to obtain, but painstaking analysis usually revealed that the loss could be reinstated by the addition of higher concentrations of some particular hormone or growth factor, or by other modifications of the medium. Where apparently genuine mutants were isolated, they were usually found to have affected a hormone receptor or some element in a generalised intracellular regulatory system such as that mediated by cyclic adenosine monophosphate (AMP). Goss (1993), reviewing decades of work on the somatic cell genetics of hepatoma differentiation, was unable to identify a single mutant isolated *in vitro* that threw any important light on the process of liver differentiation. The further analysis of differentiation required the development not only of new methods, but also of new ideas.

GENETIC ANALYSIS OF RADIATION DAMAGE

Perhaps the most important contributions made by somatic cell genetics in the period before the development of parasexual methods were in the field of radiation biology. Prior to Puck's work on cell cloning, radiation biology was at best a semi-quantitative subject and, at the level of the cell, beset with data that were little more than anecdotal. The paper by Puck and Marcus (1956), which produced the first accurate single cell survival curve after X irradiation, transformed the subject. The cells used were a strain of HeLa cells that gave a 100% cloning efficiency. Each cell produced a macroscopic colony within 15 days, and this was adopted as the experimental end point. When the survival of single cells was plotted against the X-ray dose, a typical curve was obtained that showed an initial shoulder extending to about 75r and thereafter a linear logarithmic decline. Puck and Marcus considered that the survival curve was best accommodated by a 'two-hit' mechanism. The reciprocal of the slope of the exponential region of this curve on a semi-logarithmic plot yields the dose of X rays that is needed to reduce the number of surviving cells to 37%. This value, initially called D37, but later D0, was used for comparative purposes as a convenient measure of the radiosensitivity of cell populations, and it was at once widely adopted. The D37 value for the HeLa cells used in the original experiments of Puck and Marcus was found to be 96r. This radiation sensitivity was tens to hundreds of times greater than that of any microorganism for which an equivalent function had been derived. It was found that at about 100r the growth of the X-irradiated cells began to show a delay, but with doses up to as much as 800r the cells could still go through a few divisions and make an abortive clone. The formation of giant cells was a characteristic feature of irradiated cultures. These resulted from continued growth of cells in which mitosis was inhibited by the radiation. Even after 19,000r, 5–10% of the irradiated cells were still capable of forming giants. It was clear that to produce a rapid disintegration of these cells by irradiation, very high doses indeed were required. Puck and Marcus concluded that the essential damage done by the radiation was to produce a genetic defect, but they did not believe that this could be the simple inactivation of a single gene. They thought it more likely that the effect was exerted primarily at the level of the chromosome.

Puck et al. (1957) used the same technique to measure the radiosensitivity of a wide range of cells both normal and malignant. These included diploid and polyploid cells, cells explanted from both adult and embryonic tissues, freshly isolated cells and long established cell lines. The mean lethal dose (D37) for all these cell types was found to be contained within the limits of 50–150r. Abortive colonies and giant cells were formed in all cell types. Although the survival curves were generally similar, there appeared to be systematic differences between epithelial cells and fibroblasts. All the epithelial cells studied were more radioresistant than the fibroblasts and gave survival curves best fitted by a two-hit model, whereas the curves for fibroblasts could be fitted equally well by a two-hit or a one-hit model. The mean lethal dose

(D37) for fibroblasts was in the region of 60r. Among the cells that survived irradiation with a dose of 500–900r there was a high frequency of 'mutants', but their characteristics were not precisely defined. They fell into three general classes: cells that failed to grow in the semi-synthetic medium normally used by these authors (a synthetic medium to which dialyzed macromolecular components were added), but which did grow in medium containing whole serum; cells that showed an altered colonial morphology; and cells with altered chromosome constitutions.

The quantitative aspects of the work of Puck and his colleagues were subjected to critical evaluation by Elkind (1961) (Fig. 24), who challenged the conclusion that the survival curves necessarily indicated either a two-hit or a one-hit mechanism. Elkind made a special study of the significance of the threshold region or 'shoulder' of the survival curves. Alper, Gillies, and Elkind (1960) were the first to define and make systematic use of the 'extrapolation number' in the analysis of the sigmoidal survival curves. This number is obtained by extrapolating to the ordinate the exponential region of a semi-logarithmic plot of the survival curve. Although always greater than one, it was found to vary not only from one cell type to another but also with the one cell type under different experimental conditions. Elkind and Sutton (1960), in a paper that has now become classical, set out to examine whether the sublethal damage sustained by the cells at low doses of radiation was heritable in so far as this could be measured by the survival of the progeny of the sublethally irradiated cells. Elkind and Sutton showed that by the time the delay in cell division induced by the radiation was terminated, the survival curves given by the irradiated cells were essentially similar to those given by the initial unirradiated cell population. This result indicated that surviving cells rapidly repaired the damage inflicted by radiation, and that, as far as survival was concerned, by the time a cell had divided once after its initial exposure to radiation, it had already eliminated its sublethal or 'recessive' lethal damage (Elkind, Sutton, and Moses 1961).

Puck's experiments were done on cultures equilibrated in air, but it was known that in bacteria sensitivity to radiation could be modified by the presence or absence of oxygen (Alper and Howard-Flanders 1956). Dewey (1960) was the first to show an effect of anoxia on the radiation sensitivity of animal cells. Dewey showed with human cells in culture that the survival curves after radiation in oxygen did not differ significantly from those in air, the calculated D37 value being 118.8 ± 3.9r. But in nitrogen, this value rose to 263.1 ± 16.6r, giving an N_2/O_2 ratio of about 2.2. Anoxia clearly made the cells more resistant to radiation. Elkind et al. (1964) examined the effect of hypoxia in greater detail using Chinese hamster cells and an experimental protocol that involved two doses of radiation. They found that the repair of sublethal radiation damage did not require aerobic metabolism; but reduced oxygen tension did affect the progression of the cells through the period of division delay. The complex oscillations seen in the survival curves were shown to be a composite of oxygen-insensitive radiation repair and oxygen-sensitive progression of the cells through the cell cycle (Elkind and Whitmore 1967). The interaction of repair and progression was analysed further by examining the temperature dependence of the two processes and their sensitivity to inhibitors of DNA, RNA and protein synthesis. Repair of sublethal radiation damage was found to be only weakly temperature-dependent. Hypoxic cells could completely

FIGURE 24 Mortimer Elkind (1922–), in collaboration with H. Sutton, showed that, when animal cells were exposed to radiation, sublethal damage in those that survived was rapidly and completely eliminated. *(Courtesy of Dr. Mortimer Elkind.)*

repair this damage at room temperature. However, progression through the cell cycle was very sensitive to reduction in temperature (Elkind 1967). Inhibition of protein synthesis by puromycin and of DNA synthesis by high concentrations of thymidine had no effect on repair, but puromycin did slow down progression (Elkind, Moses, and Sutton-Gilbert 1967). Elkind, Whitmore, and Alescio (1964) found, however, that the recovery of mammalian cells from sublethal irradiation was impaired by actinomycin D, an antibiotic whose inhibitory action was thought at that time to be entirely due to its ability to block the synthesis of RNA. Actinomycin D at an appropriate concentration was found to suppress the initial shoulder in single cell survival curves and to produce a large reduction in the capacity of the cells to repair sublethal radiation damage (Elkind 1967). This effect was not correlated with the overall amount of RNA synthesized, and the suggestion was made that it might have been due to the suppression of some particular RNA. The molecular characteristics of the binding of actinomycin D to DNA had not then been elucidated in molecular terms, and the possibility that the bound actinomycin D might itself impair the process of DNA repair was not considered.

A further refinement in the analysis of radiation damage was achieved by analysing the effect of radiation given at different points in the cell cycle. This work was initiated by Tolmach and Terasima (1961) who obtained synchronized populations of cells by collecting mitoses and then subjecting the synchronized cells to radiation at different points in the cell cycle. The cells appeared to be most sensitive to killing by radiation at the stage of mitosis itself, that is, at the time the mitoses were collected. The next most sensitive phase was 12–15 hours later (probably the second half of S phase), and after that came a period at 18–20 hours after collection of the mitoses (the G2 phase). The least sensitive period was at 3–7 hours after collection (the G1 phase). The calculated D37 was found to increase 2.5 fold between the most radiosensitive and the least sensitive phases. Sinclair and Morton (1963, 1965) also studied the responses of partially synchronized cells to radiation delivered at different points in the cell cycle. The degree of synchronization was in this case monitored by tritiated thymidine incorporation. These authors found that the maximum resistance to X rays coincided almost exactly with the period of maximum tritiated thymidine labelling. This result was obviously not in agreement with the observations of Terasima and Tolmach, but both sets of experiments concurred in finding substantial fluctuations in the D37 at different stages in the cell cycle.

The work of Puck, Elkind and others greatly clarified our understanding of radiation damage and its repair in isolated cell populations, but the overall findings obtained *in vitro* met with considerable resistance from radiotherapists who were convinced from their clinical experience that in the body different cell types showed a much greater range of variation in radiosensitivity than the results of cell survival curves *in vitro* indicated. The first attempt to derive an accurate post-irradiation cell survival curve *in vivo* was made by Hewitt and Wilson (1959a,b). They used for their studies a mammalian leukaemia that was capable of generating malignant tumours in a genetically compatible host with inocula of very small numbers of cells. The leukaemic animals were irradiated from a cobalt-60 source and the malignant cells then transplanted to a new host. The end point of the titration was the production of tumours on transplantation. When the radiation dose for cobalt-60 was converted to the equivalent dose of X rays, the D37 for the leukaemic cells was found to be about 122 rad in one set of experiments and about 140 rad in another. These figures were not far removed from those obtained by Puck and others for irradiation *in vitro*. McCulloch and Till (1960) used a similar transplantation technique to measure the radiation sensitivity of normal bone marrow cells. In this case, mice were lethally irradiated and the end point of the measurement was their rescue by intravenous injection of marrow cells. These cells were taken from animals that had been given doses of radiation in the appropriate range. Post-irradiation cell survival curves constructed in this way showed a systematic relationship between cell survival and radiation dose, with a D37 value of 105 ± 24 rad. A more refined technique for measuring radiosensitivity *in vivo* was devised by Till and McCulloch (1961). They discovered that marrow cells injected intravenously into genetically compatible mice produced in the spleen colonies of cells that were easily detectable on gross inspection as nodules. They found further that there was a linear relationship between the number of cells injected and the number of nodules produced. By taking the marrow cells from animals that had received graded doses of radiation, remarkably accurate survival curves could be constructed for the marrow cells irradiated *in vivo*. These curves showed the same initial shoulder as that seen in the survival curves of cells irradiated *in vitro* and gave an extrapolation number of about 2. Converting the gamma rays produced by cobalt-60 to the equivalent X-ray dose, the D37 for marrow cells irradiated *in vivo* in this way was found to be 105 ± 24 rad.

As measured by cell survival curves, the sensitivity of leukaemic cells and normal marrow cells to radiation was thus not very different from their sensitivity to radiation *in vitro*. But radiotherapists remained puzzled by the fact that at some sites radiation produced rapid cellular depletion whereas at others it did not. This question was systematically investigated by Puck (1964). The femoral bone marrow of mice was irradiated and the marrow cavity then thoroughly evacuated to permit enumeration of the cells remaining. The rate of cell depletion was found to be too low to be detected at doses of 24–33 rad, became detectable at 48 rad, and reached a maximum at about 190 rad. This maximum was maintained without further deviation even with doses close to 2000 rad. Puck found that at least the major part of the cell depletion seen in marrow could be accounted for by inhibition of cell reproduction, and this inhibition *in vivo* corresponded satisfactorily with the results given by single cell survival curves *in vitro*. No evidence was found that radiation induced or accelerated other processes of cell removal even at doses as high as 2000 rad. Puck considered that what he had found for marrow was true for all organs and concluded that the large variation in the apparent radiosensitivity of different organs was due essentially to regional differences in the rate of cell turnover. Another clinical preoccupation resolved by the analysis of cell survival curves was the possible role of hypoxic cells in determining the response of tumours to radiation. Elkind, Withers, and Belli (1968) compared the data derived from studies on cells irradiated *in vitro* under aerobic and hypoxic conditions with the responses of human tumours given fractionated radiation therapy. The conclusion reached by these authors was that the clinical data available at that time indicated that if the human tumours initially contained hypoxic cells, these cells were able to repair sublethal damage and did not affect the overall radiation response of the tumours. The meticulous data extracted from the analysis of cell survival curves were a major contribution to our understanding of the response of cells to radiation both *in vitro* and *in vivo* and did much to dispel the vague conjectures generated by imperfectly analysed clinical experience. But what genes were responsible for the repair of radiation damage and where they were located required the development of more penetrating genetic methods than could be provided by cells whose genetic repertoire was limited to vegetative propagation.

CELL 'TRANSFORMATION'

The second major theme that formed the subject of intensive investigation during this period was the phenomenon of cell 'transformation' and especially cell transformation induced by the so-called oncogenic viruses. The elucidation of the mode of action of very small viruses, such as polyoma and simian virus 40, which had only enough DNA to code for three or four genes, appeared to open the possibility that the genetic basis of malignancy might be simply explained. Originally Earle, and later others, had shown that transformation of cells could occur in cell cultures spontaneously, or at least without the conscious addition of exogenous viruses. The overall impression to be gained from these early experiments was that transformation was a relatively infrequent and largely unpredictable event, and even the salient features that characterised the transformed cell were not precisely defined. A major clarification of the phenomenon was provided by Todaro and Green (1963). They showed that with mouse embryo cells, transformed cell lines that were capable of indefinite propagation grew out of the cultures regularly. Their emergence was preceded by a period of serious decline in the growth rate, but this was followed by a progressive acceleration that eventually restored the growth rate to its initial level. This occurred before the appearance of any major karyotypic rearrangements or obvious changes in morphology. At this stage the cells showed three characteristics that later became diagnostic features for transformed cells:

- They were able to grow from much smaller inocula than untransformed cells. With cultures of primary cells, there was usually no growth from inocula of 3×10^4 cells per 50-mm petri dish, but after 67 cell generations *in vitro* the established cells grew at approximately 50% of the normal rate from inocula of this size, and after 107 cell generations optimal growth was achieved.

- The established cells grew to a much higher saturation density, reaching levels of up to 10^7 cells per dish.

- The established cells showed multilayering: primary cultures grew only as a monolayer and therefore ceased growing at a lower cell density than the established cells, which were able to grow on top of one another. This form of growth had been shown by Vogt and Dulbecco (1960) to be characteristic of cells transformed by polyoma virus and to be associated with the ability to produce tumours in appropriate hosts.

CONTACT INHIBITION

In the course of their experiments, Todaro and Green isolated the 3T3 cell line, which was subsequently widely used for the study of transformation. This line, although established, had a very flat morphology and showed marked inhibition of growth when the cell cultures reached confluence. Todaro and Green called this effect 'contact inhibition of growth', and Todaro, Green, and Goldberg (1963) showed that it was abolished or greatly reduced when the cells were transformed by polyoma virus or simian virus 40. The transformed cells could easily be recognised as well defined colonies of multilayered growth against a background monolayer of untransformed cells. The term 'contact inhibition' has given rise to a great deal of confusion. It was first used by Abercrombie (Fig. 25) to describe not inhibition of growth, but inhibition of locomotion. Abercrombie and Heaysman (1953, 1954) found that when two

FIGURE 25 Michael Abercrombie (1912–1979) first described and measured contact inhibition of cell locomotion. (*Courtesy of the Biographical Memoirs of Fellows of the Royal Society.*)

explants of normal fibroblasts were confronted and the cells emigrating from each of them finally formed a continuous sheet, their rate of locomotion was much reduced. They also noticed that normal fibroblasts avoided crawling over each other, so that there were fewer overlaps than would be expected if the cells were distributed at random. It was this avoidance of overlapping locomotion that generated the monolayers that characterised the growth of these cells. Abercrombie and Ambrose (1958) showed that when two normal fibroblasts came into contact with each other, the ruffled membrane that normally indicated the direction of locomotion of the cell was suppressed, and the cell then changed direction. This re-orientation of cell movement was termed 'locomotor inactivation'. On the other hand, it was found that several different lines of mouse sarcoma cells were not inhibited in this way when they came into contact with normal fibroblasts, whether mouse or chick (Abercrombie and Heaysman 1954; Abercrombie and Ambrose 1958). This was also shown to be true for cells transformed by viruses (Abercrombie 1963). Abercrombie, Heaysman, and Karthauser (1957) suggested that loss of contact inhibition of locomotion might form a basis not only for multilayering of cell cultures but also for the difference between invasive and normal growth *in vivo*. Further evidence in support of this idea was presented by Abercrombie (1961) and Abercrombie and Ambrose (1962).

Contact inhibition of growth as described by Todaro and Green was a much less well defined phenomenon and one that appeared to be very sensitive to cultural conditions. Stanners, Till, and Siminovitch (1963) made a careful study of the serum requirements of freshly isolated hamster embryo cells and hamster cell lines transformed by strains of polyoma virus. They showed that untransformed cells had a higher requirement for serum in the medium than transformed cells and suggested that this differential might be used to provide a selective technique for the transformed cells. Stanners (1963) showed that low serum concentration (2% foetal calf serum in medium 1066) did indeed provide a robust selection procedure for this purpose. Another version of contact inhibition of growth was introduced by Dulbecco (1969, 1970) under the term 'topoinhibition'. Topoinhibition was used to describe the inhibition of DNA synthesis seen in cells that had established extensive contacts with each other. The inhibition was released when a confluent culture was wounded; this permitted cells to migrate out onto the bare area and thus reduce the contact that they had with each other. Reinitiation of DNA synthesis under these conditions was shown to depend on the addition of serum to the medium, but normal cells had a much higher serum requirement in this respect than transformed cells. Stanners (1963) also showed that transformed cells were able to form colonies under a layer of agar, Todaro and Green (1963) having previously shown that the growth of normal cells was arrested under agar. MacPherson and Montagnier (1964) went further and demonstrated that transformed cells could actually generate colonies within a layer of soft agar. Cloning in semi-solid medium, to begin with in agar but later in other gels such as methylcellulose, soon became a standard technique for selecting transformed cells and measuring their growth potential.

Because cells that grew in semi-solid medium frequently produced tumours when injected into appropriate animals in high enough numbers, cloning in semi-solid medium was advocated by some authors as a good *in vitro* marker for tumorigenicity, but more extensive studies soon demonstrated that this correlation broke down too often to be a reliable marker. Later work showed that neither multilayering nor growth in semi-solid medium were defining characteristics of transformed cells. Both effects were found to be very sensitive to serum concentration; and Kruse and Miedema (1965) showed that a wide variety of cells, including untransformed fibroblasts, greatly exceeded their normal saturation densities in perfusion chambers that provided a constant supply of fresh medium. A range of established cell lines from human and rodent sources, including sarcomas and carcinomas, produced thick sandwiches of cells when grown in the perfusion chambers, and even standard untransformed human cell strains such as WISH and WI38 showed multilayering several cells deep. These experiments made it clear that for all cell types the limits of growth (the saturation density) were governed by the nutrient supply. Moreover, Peehl and Stanbridge (1981) eventually showed that even growth in semi-solid medium was a moveable criterion. Normal human fibroblasts from foreskin and foetal lung were found to be capable of generating large colonies in methylcellulose medium with a cloning efficiency approaching 50% if the concentration of foetal calf serum in the medium was raised to 20% and hydrocortisone was added at a concentration of 10 µg/ml.

CELL 'TRANSFORMATION' BY VIRUSES

The cardinal morphological features of cells transformed by polyoma virus, namely, their much more rounded character and their growth as multilayers,

FIGURE 26 Renato Dulbecco (1914–), in collaboration with M. Vogt, demonstrated that single cells infected with polyoma virus generated clones in which the morphology and the cultural characteristics of the constituent cells were stably transformed. *(Courtesy of the Imperial Cancer Research Fund.)*

had originally been described by Vogt and Dulbecco (Fig. 26) (1960), Sachs and Medina (1961), Stoker and MacPherson (1961), and Sachs, Medina, and Berwald (1962), but Vogt and Dulbecco (1963) reported that not all the transformed colonies were morphologically similar. Stanners (1963) extended this observation to show that transformed colonies exhibited a continuous spectrum of morphologies that ranged from marginal deviations from the normal to highly irregular accumulations of multilayered cells. In general, each morphological type bred true on subculture. The fact that the one virus could result in the generation of a range of different colonial morphologies obviously had important implications for the mode of action of the virus in producing the transformation. This was explored further by di Mayorca et al. (1969) and by Dulbecco and Eckhart (1970) using temperature-sensitive mutants of the polyoma virus (Eckhart 1969). Four groups of temperature-sensitive mutants were isolated, two affecting early functions and inhibiting the synthesis of DNA, and two affecting late functions implicated in the synthesis of viral capsid proteins. Dulbecco and Eckhart showed that one of the temperature-sensitive mutants that they examined rendered topoinhibition of the cells temperature-dependent, but in these same cells growth in agar and the serum requirement for the initiation of DNA synthesis in the wounded culture were not temperature-dependent. These authors concluded that the results obtained with the temperature-sensitive mutants indicated that the polyoma virus did affect an essential aspect of the transformation process; but they also indicated that different aspects of the transformed phenotype were regulated independently and must therefore be secondary consequences of the viral infection. The decisive evidence for independent regulation of the cardinal features of transformation was provided by Pollack, Green, and Todaro (1968) who studied flat revertants of 3T3 cells transformed by simian virus 40. These revertants showed a saturation density comparable to that seen with untransformed cells, but the serum requirement for the release of topoinhibition after wounding of the culture remained that of transformed cells. In his 1969 paper, Dulbecco also discussed the phenomenon of abortive transformation. Polyoma virus was found to give rise to many transformed colonies that sustained a little growth but then stopped. The interpretation given by Dulbecco to this phenomenon was that abortive transformants were cells that had taken up the virus but failed to integrate it into a stable state with the result that the viral genes were subsequently lost. Methods did not at that time permit a decisive demonstration that this was indeed the case.

When cells were infected with polyoma virus they produced two major new antigens. One of these had a nuclear location and was named the T antigen (Sabin and Koch 1963a,b, 1964; Pope and Rowe 1964); the other was a cell surface antigen detected by transplantation (Habel 1961; Sjögren, Hellström, and Klein 1961). Sachs (1967) argued that the only essential element in producing transformation was the T antigen; the surface change he regarded as a secondary effect. However, Dulbecco (1969) considered that the T antigen was excluded as the key operative because in 3T3 cells transformed by a temperature-sensitive mutant of the polyoma virus, transformation was produced at the permissive temperature without the production of T antigen. Dulbecco's view was that the surface antigen was the essential factor. Further evidence on this question was provided by Black and Todaro (1965) who showed that weanling hamster kidney cells (WHK) and adult human skin fibroblasts generated foci of transformation when infected with a simian virus 40-adenovirus 7 hybrid virus. The infected cells showed all the morphological features of transformation and produced both the simian virus 40 nuclear T antigen and the so-called adenovirus 'tumour antigen'. However, in coverslip preparations some of the cells did not show these antigens. Huebner et al. (1963) discovered that hamster cells could be transformed by the highly oncogenic adenovirus type 12; but it was later shown that this was also the case with the weakly oncogenic adenovirus type 3 (Freeman et al. 1967a) and adenovirus type 2 which fell into neither of these categories (Freeman et al. 1967b). Duff and Rapp (1971, 1973) showed that herpes simplex virus types 1 and 2 were also able to induce transformation *in vitro*, and it soon transpired that several other viruses, whether oncogenic or not, had this ability.

CELL 'TRANSFORMATION' BY X RAYS AND CHEMICAL CARCINOGENS

A systematic study of transformation produced by X rays and by chemical carcinogens was undertaken by Sachs and his collaborators. Berwald and Sachs (1963, 1965) showed that typically transformed clones could be produced in cultures of normal hamster cells by treating them with chemical carcinogens, and Borek and Sachs (1966) showed that this could also be done by exposing the cultures to X irradiation. Under the experimental conditions used by these authors, no spontaneous transformations appear to have occurred in untreated cultures. Comparing the incidence of transformed colonies produced by polyoma virus with those produced by chemical carcinogens and X rays under the same conditions, these authors found that 2% of the cells were transformed by polyoma virus, 3–20% by chemical carcinogens, and 0.5–2% by X rays. These figures were much too high for the results to be explicable simply by the selection of pre-existing mutants, but they also showed that the efficiency of quite non-specific agencies such as X rays in transforming cells was not significantly different from that of the so-called oncogenic viruses. As MacPherson and Montagnier (1964) had previously shown for polyoma virus, there was a systematic relationship between the dose of carcinogen applied and the number of transformed colonies produced (Huberman and Sachs 1966). These results bore heavily on the fundamental significance of the role of viruses in generating tumours.

The main issue was whether an oncogenic virus like polyoma or simian virus 40 had a specific gene or set of genes that both initiated neoplastic transformation and thereafter maintained the neoplastic state, or whether, at the other extreme, the virus did not do much more than X rays, that is perturb the genome in a great variety of ways which provided the raw material on which selection *in vivo* could operate to permit the emergence of tumorigenic variants. Several substantial pieces of evidence argued in favour of a mode of action more closely approaching the latter position than the former. Reference has already been made to the very wide range of morphologies generated by infection with polyoma virus, to the finding that different features of the transformed phenotype were regulated independently, and to the observation that morphological transformation could take place in the absence of detectable T antigen production. These observations argued strongly for a concatenation of secondary effects rather than a single pleiotropic event. But the work of Black and Rowe (1965) succeeded in dissociating morphological transformation from tumorigenicity altogether. They showed that BHK21 cells (baby hamster kidney fibroblasts) transformed by DNA from simian virus 40 could be cloned and re-cloned efficiently in agar even though they retained a normal morphology. And, when injected into hamsters, these morphologically normal cells nonetheless produced progressive tumours in six out of seven animals. Moreover, only 3 of 22 transformed lines examined produced T antigen, and the cells that did produce it were not more tumorigenic than those that did not. Observations of this kind gradually moved workers in the field to the view that in generating tumours, the so-called oncogenic viruses acted only indirectly. The term 'hit and run' was adopted to describe mechanisms of carcinogenesis in which the virus produced an initial perturbation of the genome of the cell, but was thereafter expendable. Galloway and McDougall (1983) demonstrated this effect with herpes simplex viruses inactivated by ultraviolet light; and Smith and Campo (1988), working with mouse cells transformed by DNA from bovine papilloma virus, showed that the viral DNA was necessary for the initiation of the transformed phenotype, but not for its maintenance. Dulbecco (1969) had argued that the key element in determining transformation by polyoma virus was the transplantation antigen detected on the cell surface; but eventually this, too, was formally eliminated as an essential determinant of tumorigenicity. Klein and Harris (1972), using parasexual methods that will be discussed in the next chapter, showed that the polyoma surface antigen could continue to be fully expressed in cells without conferring on them the ability to grow progressively in the animal.

REFERENCES

Abercrombie, M. 1961. Behaviour of normal and malignant connective tissue cells *in vitro*. *Can. Cancer Conf.* **4**: 101–117.

———. 1963. Contact-dependent behaviour of normal cells and the possible significance of surface changes in virus-induced transformation. *Cold Spring Harbor Symp. Quant. Biol.* **27**: 427–431.

Abercrombie, M. and E.J. Ambrose. 1958. Interference microscope studies of cell contacts in tissue culture. *Exp. Cell Res.* **15**: 332–345.

———. 1962. The surface properties of cancer cells. *Cancer Res.* **22**: 525–548.

Abercrombie, M. and J.E.M. Heaysman. 1953. Social behaviour of cells in tissue culture. I. Speed of movement of chick heart fibroblasts in relation to their mutual contacts. *Exp. Cell Res.* **5**: 111–131.

———. 1954. Social behaviour of cells in tissue culture. II. Monolayering of fibroblasts. *Exp. Cell Res.* **6**: 293–306.

Abercrombie, M., J.E.M. Heaysman, and H.M. Karthauser. 1957. Social behaviour of cells in tissue culture. III. Mutual influence of sarcoma cells and fibroblasts. *Exp. Cell Res.* **13**: 276–292.

Albrecht, A.M., J.L. Biedler, and D.J. Hutchinson. 1972. Two different species of dihydrofolate reductase in mammalian cells differentially resistant to amethopterin and methasquin. *Cancer Res.* **32**: 1539–1546.

Alper, T. and P. Howard-Flanders. 1956. Role of oxygen in modifying the radiosensitivity of *E. coli* B. *Nature* **178**: 978–979.

Alper, T., N.E. Gillies, and M.M. Elkind. 1960. The sigmoid survival curve in radiobiology. *Nature* **186**: 1062–1063.

Augusti-Tocco, G. and G. Sato. 1969. Establishment of functional clonal lines of neurons from mouse neuroblastoma. *Proc. Natl. Acad. Sci.* **64**: 311–315.

Barnes, D. and G. Sato. 1979. Growth of a human mammary tumour cell line in a serum-free medium. *Nature* **281**: 388–389.

Beaudet, A.L., D.J. Roufa, and C.T. Caskey. 1973. Mutations affecting the structure of hypoxanthine-guanine phosphoribosyl transferase in cultured Chinese hamster cells. *Proc. Natl. Acad. Sci.* **70**: 320–324.

Berwald, Y. and L. Sachs. 1963. *In vitro* cell transformation with chemical carcinogens. *Nature* **200**: 1182–1184.

———. 1965. *In vitro* cell transformation with chemical carcinogens. *J. Natl. Cancer Inst.* **35**: 641–661.

Black, P.H. and W.P. Rowe. 1965. Increase in the malignant potential of BHK-21 cells by SV40 DNA without persistent new antigen. *Proc. Natl. Acad. Sci.* **54**: 1126–1133.

Black, P.H. and G.J. Todaro. 1965. *In vitro* transformation of hamster and human cells with the adeno 7-SV40 hybrid virus. *Proc. Natl. Acad. Sci.* **54**: 374–381.

Borek, C. and L. Sachs. 1966. *In vitro* cell transformation by X-irradiation. *Nature* **210**: 276–278.

Bradley, T.R., R.A. Roosa, and L.W. Law. 1962. Transformation studies with mammalian cells in culture. *J. Cell. Comp. Physiol.* **60**: 127–137.

Breslow, R.E. and R.A. Goldsby. 1969. Isolation and characterization of thymidine transport mutants of Chinese hamster cells. *Exp. Cell Res.* **55**: 339–346.

Buonassisi, V., G. Sato, and A.I. Cohen. 1962. Hormone-producing cultures of adrenal and pituitary tumor origin. *Proc. Natl. Acad. Sci.* **48**: 1184–1190.

Cahn, R.D. and M.B. Cahn. 1966. Heritability of cellular differentiation. Clonal growth and expression of differentiation in retinal pigment cells *in vitro*. *Proc. Natl. Acad. Sci.* **55**: 106–114.

Chan, V.L., G.F. Whitmore, and L. Siminovitch. 1972. Mammalian cells with altered forms of RNA polymerase II. *Proc. Natl. Acad. Sci.* **69**: 3119–3123.

Chasin, L.A. 1973. The effect of ploidy on chemical mutagenesis in cultured Chinese hamster cells. *J. Cell. Physiol.* **82**: 299–307.

Chasin, L.A., A. Feldman, M. Konstam, and G. Urlaub. 1974. Reversion of a Chinese hamster cell auxotrophic mutant. *Proc. Natl. Acad. Sci.* **71**: 718–722.

Chu, E.H.Y. 1971. Mammalian cell genetics. III. Characterization of X-ray-induced forward mutations in Chinese hamster cell cultures. *Mutat. Res.* **11**: 23–34.

Chu, E.H.Y. and H.V. Malling. 1968. Mammalian cell genetics. II. Mutational chemical induction of specific locus mutations in Chinese hamster cells *in vitro. Proc. Natl. Acad. Sci.* **61:** 1306–1312.

Coffino, P. and M.D. Scharff. 1971. Rate of somatic mutation in immunoglobulin production by mouse myeloma cells. *Proc. Natl. Acad. Sci.* **68:** 219–223.

Coon, H.G. 1964. The retention of differentiated function among clonal and subclonal progeny of precartilage and cartilage cells from chicken embryos. *J. Cell Biol.* **23:** 20A.

———. 1966. Clonal stability and phenotypic expression of chick cartilage cells *in vitro. Proc. Natl. Acad. Sci.* **55:** 66–73.

Day, M. and J.P. Green. 1962. The uptake of amino acids and the synthesis of amines by neoplastic mast cells in culture. *J. Physiol.* **164:** 210–226.

De Mars, R. 1974. Resistance of cultured human fibroblasts and other cells to purine and pyrimidine analogues in relation to mutagenesis detection. *Mutat. Res.* **24:** 355–364.

Dewey, D.L. 1960. Effect of oxygen and nitric oxide on the radiosensitivity of human cells in tissue culture. *Nature* **186:** 780–782.

di Mayorca, G., J. Callender, G. Marin, and K. Giordano. 1969. Temperature-sensitive mutants of polyoma virus. *Virology* **38:** 126–133.

Duff, R. and F. Rapp. 1971. Oncogenic transformation of hamster cells after exposure to herpes simplex virus type 2. *Nat. New Biol.* **233:** 48–50.

———. 1973. Oncogenic transformation of hamster embryo cells after exposure to inactivated herpes simplex virus type 1. *J. Virol.* **12:** 209–217.

Dulbecco, R. 1969. Cell transformation by viruses. *Science* **166:** 962–968.

———. 1970. Topoinhibition and serum requirement of transformed and untransformed cells. *Nature* **227:** 802–806.

Dulbecco, R. and W. Eckhart. 1970. Temperature dependent properties of cells transformed by a thermosensitive mutant of polyoma virus. *Proc. Natl. Acad. Sci.* **67:** 1775–1781.

Eagle, H. 1960. Metabolic studies with normal and malignant human cells in culture. *Harvey Lect.* **54:** 156–175.

Eagle, H., K.A. Piez, and R. Fleischman. 1957. The utilization of phenylalanine and tyrosine for protein synthesis by human cells in tissue culture. *J. Biol. Chem.* **228:** 847–861.

Ebeling, A.H. 1924. Cultures pures d'épithelium proliférant *in vitro* depuis dix-huit mois. *C. R. Soc. Biol.* **90:** 562–563.

Ebner, K.E., E.C. Hageman, and B.L. Larson. 1961. Functional biochemical changes in bovine mammary cell cultures. *Exp. Cell Res.* **25:** 555–570.

Eckhart, W. 1969. Complementation and transformation of temperature-sensitive mutants of polyoma virus. *Virology* **38:** 120–125.

Elkind, M.M. 1961. Radiation responses of mammalian cells. In Fundamental aspects of radiosensitivity. *Brookhaven Symp. Biol.* **14:** 220–245.

———. 1967. Sublethal X-ray damage and its repair in mammalian cells. In *Radiation research 1966* (ed. G. Silini), pp. 558–586. North Holland Publishing, Amsterdam.

Elkind, M.M. and H. Sutton. 1960. Radiation response of mammalian cells grown in culture. I. Repair of X-ray damage in surviving Chinese hamster cells. *Radiat. Res.* **13:** 556–593.

Elkind, M.M. and G.F. Whitmore. 1967. The radiobiology of cultured mammalian cells. Gordon and Breach Science Publishers, New York.

Elkind, M.M., W.B. Moses, and H. Sutton-Gilbert. 1967. Radiation response of mammalian cells grown in culture. VI. Protein, DNA and RNA inhibition during the repair of X-ray damage. *Radiat. Res.* **31:** 156–173.

Elkind, M.M., H. Sutton, and W.B. Moses. 1961. Postirradiation survival kinetics of mammalian cells grown in culture. *J. Cell. Comp. Physiol.* (suppl. 1) **58:** 113–134.

Elkind, M.M., G.F. Whitmore, and T. Alescio. 1964. Actinomycin D: Suppression of recovery in X-irradiated mammalian cells. *Science* **143:** 1454–1457.

Elkind, M.M., H.R. Withers, and J.A. Belli. 1968. Intracellular repair and the oxygen effect in radiobiology and radiotherapy. *Radiat. Ther. Oncol.* **3:** 55–87.

Elkind, M.M., T. Alescio, R.W. Swan, W.B. Moses, and H. Sutton. 1964. Recovery of hypoxic mammalian cells from sub-lethal X-ray damage. *Nature* **202:** 1190–1193.

Freed, J.J. and L. Mezger-Freed. 1970. Stable haploid cultured cell lines from frog embryos. *Proc. Natl. Acad. Sci.* **65:** 337–344.

Freeman, A.E., E.A. Vanderpool, P.H. Black, H.C. Turner, and R.J. Huebner. 1967a. Transformation of primary rat embryo cells by a weakly oncogenic adenovirus-type 3. *Nature* **216:** 171–173.

Freeman, A.E., P.H. Black, E.A. Vanderpool, P.H. Henry, J.B. Austin, and R.J. Huebner. 1967b. Transformation of primary rat embryo cells by adenovirus type 2. *Proc. Natl. Acad. Sci.* **58:** 1205–1212.

Galloway, D.A. and J.K. McDougall. 1983. The oncogenic potential of herpes simplex viruses: Evidence for a "hit-and-run" mechanism. *Nature* **302:** 21–24.

Gartler, S.M. and D.A. Pious. 1966. Genetics of mammalian cell cultures. *Humangenetik* **2:** 83–114.

Goss, S.J. 1993. A fresh look at the somatic cell genetics of hepatoma differentiation. *J. Cell Sci.* **104:** 231–235.

Habel, K. 1961. Resistance of polyoma virus immune animals to transplanted polyoma tumors. *Proc. Soc. Exp. Biol. Med.* **106:** 722–725.

Harris, M. 1967. Phenotypic expression of drug resistance. *J. Natl. Cancer Inst.* **38:** 185–192.

———. 1971a. Polyploid series in mammalian cells. *Exp. Cell Res.* **66:** 329–336.

———. 1971b. Mutation rates in cells at different ploidy levels. *J. Cell. Physiol.* **78:** 177–184.

Hayashi, I. and G.H. Sato. 1976. Replacement of serum by hormones permits growth of cells in a defined medium. *Nature* **259:** 132–134.

Herzenberg, L.A. and R.A. Roosa. 1959. Serine, glycine and certain α-keto acids as alternative growth factors for a mouse lymphoid neoplasm in cell culture. *Fed. Proc.* **18:** 401.

Hewitt, H.B. and C.W. Wilson. 1959a. A survival curve for mammalian cells irradiated *in vivo. Nature* **183:** 1060–1061.

———. 1959b. A survival curve for mammalian leukaemia cells irradiated *in vivo* (implications for the treatment of mouse leukaemia by whole-body irradiation. *Br. J. Cancer* **13:** 69–75.

Hilfer, S.R. 1962. The stability of embryonic chick thyroid cells *in vitro* as judged by morphological and physiological criteria. *Dev. Biol.* **4:** 1–21.

Holtzer, H., J. Abbott, J. Lash, and S. Holtzer. 1960. The loss of phenotypic traits by differentiated cells *in vitro*. I. Dedifferentiation of cartilage cells. *Proc. Natl. Acad. Sci.* **46:** 1533–1542.

Hsu, T.C. and C.E. Somers. 1962. Properties of L cells resistant to 5-bromodeoxyuridine. *Exp. Cell Res.* **26:** 404–410.

Huberman, E. and L. Sachs. 1966. Cell susceptibility to transformation and cytotoxicity by the carcinogenic hydrocarbon benzo[a]pyrene. *Proc. Natl. Acad. Soc.* **56:** 1123–1129.

Huebner, R.J., W.P. Rowe, H.C. Turner, and W.T. Lane. 1963. Specific adenovirus complement-fixing antigens in virus-free hamster and rat tumors. *Proc. Natl. Acad. Sci.* **50:** 379–389.

Hutchings, S.E. and G.H. Sato. 1978. Growth and maintenance of HeLa cells in serum-free medium supplemented with hormones. *Proc. Natl. Acad. Sci.* **75:** 901–904.

Kao, F.T. and T.T. Puck. 1968. Genetics of somatic mammalian cells. VII. Induction and isolation of nutritional mutants in Chinese hamster cells. *Proc. Natl. Acad. Sci.* **60:** 1275–1281.

Kit, S., D.R. Dubbs, L.J. Piekarski, and T.C. Hsu. 1963. Deletion of thymidine kinase activity from L cells resistant to bromodeoxyuridine. *Exp. Cell Res.* **31:** 297–312.

Klein, G. and H. Harris. 1972. Expression of polyoma-induced transplantation antigen in hybrid cell lines. *Nature* **237:** 163–164.

Kruse, P.F. and E. Miedema. 1965. Production and characterization of multiple-layered populations of animal cells. *J. Cell Biol.* **27:** 273–279.

Levintow, L. and H. Eagle. 1961. Biochemistry of cultured mammalian cells. *Annu. Rev. Biochem.* **30:** 605–640.

Levisohn, S.R. and E.B. Thompson. 1972. Tyrosine amino-transferase induction regulation variant in tissue culture. *Nat. New Biol.* **235:** 102–104.

Lieberman, J. and P. Ove. 1959. Estimation of mutation rates with mammalian cells in culture. *Proc. Natl. Acad. Sci.* **45:** 872–877.

MacPherson, I. and L. Montagnier. 1964. Agar suspension culture for the selective assay of cells transformed by polyoma virus. *Virology* **23:** 291–294.

Mather, J. and G. Sato. 1977. Hormones and growth factors in cell cultures: Problems and perspectives. In *Proceedings of the International Workshop for Cell Tissue and Organ Culture in Neurobiology* (ed. S. Federoff), pp. 619–630. Academic Press, New York.

McCulloch, E.A. and J.E. Till. 1960. The radiation sensitivity of normal mouse bone marrow cells determined by quantitative marrow transplantation into irradiated mice. *Radiat. Res.* **13** 115–125.

Mezger-Freed, L. 1972. Effect of ploidy and mutagens on bromodeoxyuridine resistance in haploid and diploid frog cells. *Nat. New Biol.* **235:** 245–246.

———. 1974. An analysis of survival in haploid and diploid cell cultures after exposure to ICR acridine half-mustard compounds mutagenic for bacteria. *Proc. Natl. Acad. Sci.* **71:** 4416–4420.

Morris, C.C. 1962. Maintenance and loss in tissue culture of specific cell characteristics. *Adv. Appl. Microbiol.* **4:** 117–212.

Orkin, S.H. and J.W. Littlefield. 1971. Nitrosoguanidine mutagenesis in synchronized hamster cells. *Exp. Cell Res.* **66:** 69–74.

Peehl, D.M. and E.J. Stanbridge. 1981. Anchorage-independent growth of normal human fibroblasts. *Proc. Natl. Acad. Sci.* **78:** 3053–3057.

Pollack, R., H. Green, and G.J. Todaro. 1968. Growth control in cultured cells: Selection of sublines with increased sensitivity to contact inhibition and decreased tumor-producing ability. *Proc. Natl. Acad. Sci.* **60:** 126–133

Pope, J.H. and W.P. Rowe. 1964. Detection of specific antigen in SV40-transformed cells by immunofluorescence. *J. Exp. Med.* **120:** 121–127.

Puck, T.T. 1959. Quantitative studies of mammalian cells *in vitro*. *Rev. Mod. Physiol.* **31:** 433–448.

———. 1964. Cellular aspects of the mammalian radiation syndrome: Nucleated cell depletion in the bone marrow. *Proc. Natl. Acad. Sci.* **52:** 152–160.

Puck, T.T. and P.I. Marcus. 1956. Action of X-rays on mammalian cells. *J. Exp. Med.* **103:** 653–666.

Puck, T.T. and F.T. Kao. 1967. Genetics of somatic mammalian cells. V. Treatment with 5-bromodeoxyuridine and visible light for isolation of nutritionally deficient mutants. *Proc. Natl. Acad. Sci.* **58:** 1227–1234.

———. 1982. Somatic cell genetics and its application to medicine. *Annu. Rev. Genet.* **16:** 225–271.

Puck, T.T., D. Morkovin, P.I. Marcus, and S.J. Cieciura. 1957. Action of X-rays on mammalian cells. II. Survival curves of cells from normal human tissues. *J. Exp. Med.* **106:** 485–50.

Rappaport, H. and R. De Mars. 1973. Diaminopurine-resistant mutants of cultured diploid human fibroblasts. *Genetics* **75:** 335–345.

Sabin, A.B. and M.A. Koch. 1963a. Evidence of continuous transmission of noninfectious SV40 viral genome in most or all SV40 hamster tumor cells. *Proc. Natl. Acad. Sci.* **49:** 304–311.

———. 1963b. Behavior of noninfectious SV40 viral genome in hamster tumor cells: Induction of synthesis of infectious virus. *Proc. Natl. Acad. Sci.* **50:** 407–417.

———. 1964. Source of genetic information for specific complement-fixing antigens in SV40 virus-induced tumors. *Proc. Natl. Acad. Sci.* **52:** 1131–1138.

Sachs, L. 1967. An analysis of the mechanism of neoplastic cell transformation by polyoma virus, hydrocarbons and X-irradiation. *Curr. Top. Dev. Biol.* **2:** 129–150.

Sachs, L. and D. Medina. 1961. *In vitro* transformation of normal cells by polyoma virus. *Nature* **189:** 457–458.

Sachs, L., D. Medina, and Y. Berwald. 1962. Cell transformation by polyoma virus in clones of hamster and mouse cells. *Virology* **17:** 491–493.

Sato, G., L. Zaroff, and S.E. Mills. 1960. Tissue culture populations and their relation to the tissue of origin. *Proc. Natl. Acad. Sci.* **46:** 963–972.

Schindler, R., M. Day, and G.A. Fischer. 1959. Cultures of neoplastic mast cells and their synthesis of 5-hydroxytryptamine and histamine *in vitro*. *Cancer Res.* **19:** 47–51.

Siminovitch, L. 1976. On the nature of hereditable variation in cultured somatic cells. *Cell* **7**: 1–11.

Sinclair, W.K. and R.A. Morton. 1963. Variations in the X-ray response during the division cycle of partially synchronized Chinese hamster cells in culture. *Nature* **199**: 1158–1160.

———. 1965. X-ray and ultraviolet sensitivity of synchronized Chinese hamster cells at various stages of the cell cycle. *Biophys. J.* **5**: 1–25.

Sjögren, H.O., J. Hellström, and G. Klein. 1961. Transplantation of polyoma virus-induced tumors in mice. *Cancer Res.* **21**: 329–337.

Smith, K.J. and M.S. Campo. 1988. "Hit and run" transformation of mouse C127 cells by bovine papillomavirus type 4: The virus DNA is required for the initiation but not for maintenance of the transformed phenotype. *Virology* **169**: 39–47.

Stanners, C. 1963. Studies on the transformation of hamster embryo cells in culture by polyoma virus. II. Selective techniques for the detection of transformed cells. *Virology* **21**: 464–476.

Stanners, C.P., J.E. Till, and L. Siminovitch. 1963. Studies on the transformation of hamster embryo cells in culture by polyoma virus. I. Properties of transformed and normal cells. *Virology* **21**: 448–463.

Stockdale, F.E., J. Abbott, S. Holtzer, and H. Holtzer. 1963. The loss of phenotypic traits by differentiated cells. II. Behaviour of chondrocytes and their progeny *in vitro*. *Dev. Biol.* **7**: 293–302.

Stoker, M.G.P. and I.A. MacPherson. 1961. Studies on transformation of hamster cells by polyoma virus *in vitro*. *Virology* **14**: 359–370.

Szybalska, E.H. and W. Szybalski. 1962. Genetics of human cell lines. IV. DNA-mediated heritable transformation of a biochemical trait. *Proc. Natl. Acad. Sci.* **48**: 2026–2034.

Szybalski, W. and M.J. Smith. 1959a. Genetics of human cell lines. I. 8-azaguanine resistance, a selective 'single-step' marker. *Proc. Soc. Exp. Biol. Med.* **101**: 662–666.

———. 1959b. Effect of ultraviolet light on mutation to 8-azaguanine resistance in a human cell line. *Fed. Proc.* **18**: 336.

Szybalski, W. and E.H. Szybalska. 1962. Approaches to the genetic analysis of mammalian cells. Drug sensitivity as a genetic marker. *Univ. Mich. Med. Bull.* **28**: 277–293.

Szybalski, W., E.H. Szybalska, and D.W. Brockman. 1961. Biochemical basis of sequential mutations towards resistance to purine analogs in human cell lines. *Proc. Am. Assoc. Cancer Res.* **3**: 272.

Szybalski, W., E.H. Szybalska, and G. Ragni. 1962. Genetic studies with human cell lines. *Natl. Cancer Inst. Monogr.* **7**: 75–89.

Till, J.E. and E.A. McCulloch. 1961. A direct measurement of the radiation sensitivity of normal mouse bone marrow cells. *Radiat. Res.* **14**: 213–222.

Tjio, J.H. and T.T. Puck. 1958. Genetics of somatic mammalian cells. II. Chromosomal constitution of cells in tissue culture. *J. Exp. Med.* **108**: 259–263.

Todaro, G.J. and H. Green. 1963. Quantitative studies of the growth of mouse embryo cells in culture and their development into established lines. *J. Cell Biol.* **17**: 299–313.

Todaro, G.J., H. Green, and B.D. Goldberg. 1963. Transformation of properties of an established cell line by SV40 and polyoma virus. *Proc. Natl. Acad. Sci.* **51**: 66–73.

Tolmach, L.J. and T. Terasima. 1961. Variations in X-ray sensitivity during the division cycle of HeLa cells. *Radiat. Res.* **14**: 512.

Vogt, M. and R. Dulbecco. 1960. Virus-cell interaction with a tumour-producing virus. *Proc. Natl. Acad. Sci.* **46**: 365–370.

———. 1963. Steps in the neoplastic transformation of hamster embryo cells by polyoma virus. *Proc. Natl. Acad. Sci.* **49**: 171–179.

Waltz, A.K., W.W. Tullner, V.J. Evans. R. Hertz, and W.R. Earle. 1954. Gonadotrophic hormone secretion from hydatid mole grown in tissue culture. *J. Natl. Cancer Inst.* **14**: 1173–1185.

Willmer, E.N. 1960. *Cytology and evolution.* Academic Press, New York.

Yasumura, Y., A.H. Tashjian, and G.H. Sato. 1966. Establishment of four functional, clonal strains of animal cells in culture. *Science* **154**: 1186–1189.

5
PARASEXUAL GENETICS

THE DISCOVERY OF SOMATIC CELL HYBRIDIZATION

In 1960, there appeared in the *Comptes Rendus des Séances de l'Académie des Sciences* an enigmatic paper by Barski (Fig. 27), Sorieul, and Cornefert. It described a strange phenomenon that occurred in a mixed culture of two mouse cell lines. Both of these lines were subclones of a single clone originally isolated from a culture of connective tissue explanted from a C3H mouse. One of these lines produced a high incidence of tumours when injected back into C3H mice, the other a low incidence. Barski's intention in putting the cells together was to see if there was any 'transfer of characters' from one cell type to the other. Sorieul, who was responsible for the cytogenetic monitoring of the two cell types, made the crucial observation (Ephrussi and Sorieul 1962b). He found that in the mixed cultures there were cells that appeared to contain the chromosome complements of both parent cells. This observation provoked no general interest, and where it was noticed, it was greeted with scepticism. Some cytogeneticists thought that these composite karyotypes might simply be an artefact resulting from the fortuitous overlap of two separate karyotypes. However, in a second paper, Barski, Sorieul, and Cornefert (1961), by isolating cell lines with these composite karyotypes, provided decisive evidence that Sorieul's original observation was not an artefact. Sorieul then left Barski's laboratory and joined Ephrussi (Fig. 28) at Gif-sur-Yvette. Sorieul and Ephrussi (1961) confirmed the original observations of Barski, Sorieul, and Cornefert (1960) but under rather more carefully controlled conditions; and Ephrussi and Sorieul (1962a) showed that such composite or hybrid cells could arise in mixed cultures of mouse cells of different genetic origin. One of the original cell lines used by Barski, Sorieul, and Cornefert (C3H genotype) produced hybrids when grown in mixed culture with a conjunctival cell line derived from a C3H mouse originating in a different laboratory, and also with a cell line derived from a Swiss mouse and transformed by polyoma virus. This was confirmed by Gershon and Sachs (1963) who also produced hybrids between two mouse cell lines bearing different histocompatibility antigens. Ephrussi et al. (1964) showed further that one of the mouse cell lines used by Barski, Sorieul, and Cornefert (1960) could also generate hybrids when cocultivated with normal skin fibroblasts derived from a newborn CBA mouse bearing the T6 translocation. Ephrussi and Sorieul (1962b) made the important observation that, on continued cultivation *in vitro*, the hybrid cells that they had studied showed a slow but progressive reduction in chromosome number. The two essential requirements of a genetic system, namely the conjunc-

FIGURE 27   Georges Barski (1909–1985). During the course of an experiment designed by Barski for another purpose, Serge Sorieul noticed in mixed cultures of two different mouse cell lines mitotic figures that appeared to combine the chromosome sets of both parent cells. This was the first indication that the somatic cells of animals might undergo some form of hybridization. *(Courtesy of Prof. R. Flamant.)*

tion of two different genomes and their subsequent segregation, were thus, in principle, met even if only by a very circuitous route. This was the last paper on which Serge Sorieul's name appeared. At this point he fell prey to the saddest of illnesses and his untimely death at the age of 32 removed from the scene the discoverer of somatic cell hybridization.

THE ORIGIN OF HYBRID CELLS

The mode of origin of these composite cells remained obscure. Ephrussi appears to have assumed from the beginning that they were formed by cell fusion, but Barski and Belehradek (1963), using time-lapse cinematography, observed cell interactions that they interpreted as the transfer of a nucleus from one cell to another. In Ephrussi and Sorieul (1962b), the possibility was discussed that the hybrid cells might have arisen from multinucleate cells induced by viruses, although Ephrussi later doubted whether virus-induced multinucleate cells were capable of multiplication (Ephrussi and Weiss 1965; Ephrussi [1965–1970], correspondence). Ephrussi and Sorieul (1962b) made

FIGURE 28 Boris Ephrussi (1901–1979). Together with Sorieul, Ephrussi confirmed the initial observations of Sorieul and Barski, cloned the hybrid mouse cells and showed that on continued cultivation they sustained a progressive loss of chromosomes. It was Ephrussi's advocacy that drew attention to the potential usefulness of these hybrid cells for genetic analysis. *(Courtesy of Dr. Nils Ringertz.)*

reference to the work of Roizman (1962) on polykaryocytosis induced by viruses, but they did not seem to be aware of the substantial body of earlier work that had been done on multinucleate cells and especially on the mechanisms by which binucleate cells generate mononucleates at mitosis. This earlier work is notable not only for its extent but also for its depth.

The first description of multinucleate cells in vertebrate tissues appears to have been given by Müller (1838) in a microscopical study that he made on some 400 tumour specimens collected from the surgical clinics in Berlin. Robin (1849) noted their presence in bone marrow, Rokitansky (1855) in tuberculous tissue, and Virchow (1858) in a variety of normal tissues and in both inflammatory and neoplastic lesions. The different views held by Remak and Virchow on the biological significance of multinucleation have been discussed in Chapter 1. By the time Langhans (1868, 1870) wrote his classical papers on giant cells, an extensive literature about them already existed. The view that at least some of these cells were produced by fusion of mononucleate cells derived from the work of de Bary (1859), who observed that the life cycle of certain myxomycetes involved the fusion of single cells to form multinucleate plasmodia. Lange (1875) appears to have been the first to describe a process of this sort in vertebrates. Lange observed the coalescence of blood-borne amoeboid cells in the frog; and similar observations were made a little later by Cienkowski (1876), Buck (1878), and Geddes (1880) in invertebrates. Metchnikoff (1884) considered that the fusion of phagocytic cells to form plasmodia was a characteristic cellular defence mechanism in both vertebrates and invertebrates. It is very probable that some of the inflammatory lesions in which multinucleate cells were noticed in the last century were caused by viruses, although, of course, the viral aetiology of these lesions was not recognised until much later. The earliest reports of multinucleate cells in lesions that can with certainty be identified as of viral origin appear to be those of Luginbühl (1873) and Weigert (1874) (quoted by Krauss 1884), who described such cells at the periphery of smallpox pustules. Unna (1896) noticed them in the skin lesions of chicken-pox, and Warthin (1931) in the tonsils of patients with measles. Lambert (1912) appears to have been the first to describe the formation of multinucleate cells in tissue cultures; but 15 years later, Lewis (1927) was able to list 21 references to observations of this kind.

Warthin's observations on the tonsils of measles patients prompted Enders and Peebles (1954) to examine the effect of measles virus on tissue cultures. These authors found that the virus induced the cells in culture to fuse together to form multinucleated syncytia. A similar observation was made by Henle, Deinhardt, and Girardi (1954) with mumps virus, by Chanock (1956) with the virus of infantile croup and by Marston (1958) with a virus of the parainfluenza group. Numerous other examples of this phenomenon have since been described. Okada (1958, 1962) demonstrated that Ehrlich ascites tumour cells in suspension could be rapidly fused together to form multinucleate giant cells by high concentrations of HVJ (haemolytic virus of Japan), another member of the parainfluenza group. Whether vertebrate cells containing larger numbers of nuclei were capable of multiplication or of generating viable daughter cells remained for decades a matter of controversy, but as early as 1916, Macklin showed that binucleate cells in chick embryo tissue cultures could undergo mitosis, and that the mitosis sometimes gave rise to two mononucleate daughter cells. Macklin described how, in such cases, the chromosomes from both nuclei became aligned along a single equatorial plate and were then distributed by normal cell division to the two daughter cells. Macklin also observed various forms of irregular mitosis in binucleate cells, including tripolar mitosis. Fell and Hughes (1949) described essentially the same process in binucleate mouse cells in culture. Here, synchronous mitosis of the two nuclei again collected all the chromosomes along a single equatorial plate, and cell division gave rise to mononucleate daughter cells with abnormally large nuclei apparently containing twice the normal number of chromosomes. By 1960, when Barski, Sorieul, and Cornefert published their first account of hybrid cell formation, it was already known that cells in culture could fuse with each other spontaneously, that fusion could be induced at will by the use of certain viruses, and that binucleate cells could give rise to mononucleate daughters in which chromosomes from both the nuclei in the original binucleate cell were included in a single nucleus. It remains very surprising that for several years after their discovery by Sorieul, the origin of hybrid cells remained shrouded in mystery.

SELECTION OF HYBRID CELLS

All of the hybrids isolated by Ephrussi and his colleagues until the end of 1964 were identified by the presence of parental marker chromosomes, and further investigation of the hybrid cells was limited to karyological monitoring (Ephrussi et al. 1964). Some of these hybrids showed a moderate selective ad-

FIGURE 29 John Littlefield (1925–). By combining the selective systems developed by Szybalski, Szybalska, and Ragni (1962) and Kit et al. (1963), Littlefield devised a procedure for the selective isolation of hybrid animal cells. *(Courtesy of the Archives of the Sir William Dunn School of Pathology, University of Oxford.)*

vantage over their parent cells (as did the original hybrids isolated by Barski, Sorieul, and Cornefert [1960]), so that isolation of hybrid clones presented no great problem. But this was not generally the case, and a more systematic method for selecting the hybrids was obviously required. This was provided by Littlefield (1964) (Fig. 29), using a combination of the selective procedures worked out by Szybalski, Szybalska, and Ragni (1962) and by Kit et al. (1963). One of the parental cells was made resistant to 8-azaguanine and thus lacked the enzyme hypoxanthine guanine phosphoribosyltransferase (HPRT), the other was made resistant to 5-bromodeoxyuridine and lacked the enzyme thymidine kinase. In the HAT medium devised by Hakala and Taylor (1959), which contained hypoxanthine, thymidine and aminopterin, neither of the parental cells could grow because they lacked an indispensable component of the salvage pathway that was required for their survival when folic acid synthesis was blocked by aminopterin. But, in the hybrid cells, complementation of both the parental enzyme deficiences occurred, and this enabled the hybrids to grow in the HAT medium. Littlefield's procedure was rapidly adopted and became a standard technique for isolating hybrid cells. It had the disadvantage that drug-resistant variants of the cells to be fused had first to be selected, and for certain markers this raised the possibility that unwanted changes of phenotype might be induced as a secondary consequence of the selection. Nonetheless, for the vast majority of cases, the Littlefield procedure provided all that was necessary to permit informative hybrids to be isolated. Where the morphology or growth characteristics of the hybrids differed substantially from those of the parent cells, hybrid clones could sometimes be isolated when only one of the parent cells harboured a selectable drug-resistant marker.

VIRUS-INDUCED CELL FUSION

Before 1965, cell hybridization had been observed only in crosses between mouse cells and, except for two cases where one of the parental cells was apparently a normal fibroblast, only between established cell lines. In February of that year, a paper published in *Nature* by Harris and Watkins greatly extended the scope of somatic cell hybridization and opened up a new range of experimental possibilities. Harris (Fig. 30) and Watkins (Fig. 31) showed that cells of human and murine origin could be fused together at will to produce viable interspecific heterokaryons. The technique exploited the well-known ability of certain viruses to induce cell fusion and, in particular, was based on the work of Okada (1958, 1962) and Okada and Tadokoro (1962), who had shown not only that Ehrlich ascites cells could be rapidly fused together by high concentrations of HVJ virus, but also that the virus retained its ability to fuse cells even after its power to replicate had been completely destroyed by

FIGURE 30 Henry Harris (1925–), in collaboration with John F. Watkins (Fig. 31), showed that an inactivated virus could be used to amalgamate cells from different animal species into viable composite units. This procedure provided a general method for fusing together cells from virtually any tissue and any species. The photograph shows Harris fusing human and mouse cells together in 1965. *(Courtesy of the Archives of the Sir William Dunn School of Pathology, University of Oxford.)*

FIGURE 31   John F. Watkins (1927–). *(Courtesy of the Archives of the Sir William Dunn School of Pathology, University of Oxford.)*

irradiation with ultraviolet light. Using irradiated Sendai virus (a strain of HVJ), Harris and Watkins fused together Ehrlich ascites cells with HeLa cells and thus produced heterokaryons that contained within the one cell nuclei of human and murine origin (Fig. 32). Okada and his colleagues were at that time primarily interested in the mechanism of virus-induced cell fusion and their publications contained no information about the viability of the fused cells or their metabolic potential after fusion. Harris and Watkins showed not only that both human and mouse nuclei in the fused cells synthesized RNA and replicated their DNA, but also that the interspecific heterokaryons were capable of undergoing mitosis (Fig. 33). Mitotic figures were observed in which both telocentric mouse chromosomes and metacentric human chromosomes could readily be discerned. This was confirmed in a detailed karyological study of the hybrid mitoses by Harris et al. (1965). In the same year, Harris (1965) showed that highly differentiated normal cells such as macrophages, lymphocytes and erythrocytes, could also be fused together to produce viable heterokaryons. This indicated that cell fusion could be achieved not only between cells of widely different species, but also across extremes of differentiation. It was clear that inactivated virus offered a general method for bringing different vertebrate genotypes together within the one cell.

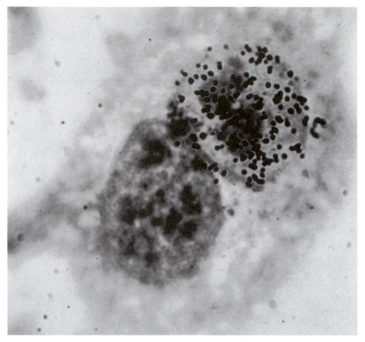

FIGURE 32 Autoradiograph showing a heterokaryon produced by fusing a labelled human cell with an unlabelled mouse cell. The human nucleus in the heterokaryon is labelled, but the mouse nucleus is not. (From the original series of experiments described by Harris and Watkins 1965.)

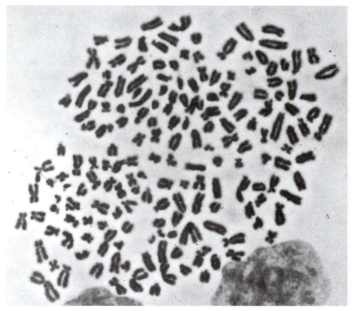

FIGURE 33 Mitosis in a hybrid produced by the fusion of human with mouse cells. Both human and mouse chromosomes are present. (Reprinted, with permission, from Harris et al. 1965 [copyright Macmillan].)

MITOSIS AND MULTIPLICATION OF HYBRID CELLS

Although hybrid mitoses involving both human and mouse chromosomes were described in the first study on HeLa-Ehrlich heterokaryons by Harris and Watkins (1965), and small clones of mononucleate hybrid cells arising from these heterokaryons were subsequently detected by Watkins and Grace (1967), no interspecific hybrid cell line was isolated from this original cross. The mononucleate hybrid cells formed in this combination grew much more slowly than the parental cells and, since these lacked selectable drug-resistant markers, the hybrids were rapidly overgrown. However, stimulated by the experiments of Harris and Watkins (Ephrussi 1972; Weiss 1992), Ephrussi and Weiss (1965) set up mixed cultures of 5-bromodeoxyuridine-resistant mouse L cells and rat embryo fibroblasts and, by selecting in HAT medium, which eliminated the 5-bromodeoxyuridine-resistant L cells, succeeded in isolating a line of rat-mouse hybrid cells. During the course of 1965, Okada and Murayama, and Okada, Murayama, and Tadokoro published further observations on multinucleate cells fused together by inactivated HVJ virus. Like Harris and Watkins (1965), to whom they refer, Okada and Murayama (1965a) found that they could fuse together established cell lines from different species (KB cells from man with L cells or Ehrlich ascites cells from the mouse and with PS cells from the pig). This was, moreover, the first paper by Okada and his colleagues to make any mention of the fate of the cells after fusion. Okada and Murayama showed that multinucleate KB cells were capable of synthesizing RNA and DNA, but no information was provided about the metabolic activity of interspecific heterokaryons, nor were any observations recorded on mitosis in the fused cells or on their chromosome constitution. Some of these results were also published in Okada and Murayama (1965b). In both of their papers (1965a,b), Okada and Murayama mention that an earlier account of the work was reported at the 17th Meeting of the Japan Society for Cellular Chemistry held in November of 1964. The paper delivered at that meeting was subsequently published in Japanese (Okada, Murayama, and Tadokoro 1965). It shows that a wide range of established and malignant cell lines were susceptible to fusion by HVJ virus, and it extends an earlier observation of Okada and Tadokoro (1963) that freshly isolated and fully differentiated somatic cells fused poorly. It does not, however, report interspecific cell fusion, nor does it provide any information about the viability or metabolic activity of fused cells. Surprisingly, Okada, Murayama, and Tadokoro (1965) were unable to induce monocytes or lymphocytes to fuse under the action of HVJ.

The first interspecific hybrid cell line to be isolated from cells fused by inactivated virus was reported by Yerganian and Nell (1966). They fused together pseudodiploid cells from two different species of hamster and found that the interspecific hybrids rapidly overgrew the parental cells. In order to compare the hybrids produced by inactivated Sendai virus with those arising spontaneously in mixed cultures, Engel, McGee, and Harris (1969) fused together the 8-azaguanine-resistant and 5-bromodeoxyuridine-resistant cell lines from which Littlefield (1964) had previously obtained spontaneous hybrids. They found that the growth potential, the initial chromosome constitution and the subsequent karyological evolution of the hybrid cells were essentially the same in the two sets of experiments. The yield of hybrid clones was, however, greatly increased by the use of the inactivated virus. Similar observations were made by Siniscalco, Knowles, and Steplewski (1969) with hybrids between human diploid cell strains bearing different metabolic defects. It thus became clear that inactivated Sendai virus could be used to produce hybrids from virtually any pair of vertebrate cells irrespective of their species of origin or the tissue from which they were derived. It was rapidly adopted as a standard reagent in the burgeoning science of somatic cell genetics and remained so until it was displaced by chemical fusogens a decade after its introduction.

HETEROKARYONS

Controlled cell fusion also gave birth to an entirely new field of investigation: the analysis of animal cell heterokaryons. Artificial heterokaryons appear first to have been produced from plant protoplasts by Michel (1937) who used a mechanical procedure to fuse together protoplasts from different plant species and genera. These fused protoplasts did not survive for long, and although Michel was aware of the experimental possibilities offered by interspecific heterokaryons, his research was not further pursued, and it was not a stimulus for the work on animal heterokaryons initiated 30 years later. Harris (1965), studying the synthesis of RNA and DNA in heterokaryons made by fusing fibroblastic cells with macrophages, lymphocytes and nucleated erythrocytes, found that the regulation of nucleic acid synthesis in the heterokaryon was controlled by positive signals: whenever a cell that did not make a particular class of nucleic acid, either RNA or DNA, was fused with one that did, synthesis was initiated in the nucleus of the inactive partner. In this way, nuclei engaged in different patterns of nucleic acid synthesis and at different stages of the cell cycle were brought into register with the result that, in many of the fused cells, all the nuclei entered mitosis together. This synchronization of nuclear events was studied in detail by Johnson and Harris (1969a,b,c) who found persistent asynchrony more common in heterokaryons made with widely different cell types than in fused cells of the same type. Although a careful scrutiny of earlier literature could have solved the mystery, the mode of formation of mononucleate hybrid cells remained a matter of controversy for some years after their discovery. Harris (1970), using time-lapse cinematography, showed, as Macklin (1916) and Fell and Hughes (1949) had done long before, that when two nuclei in a binucleate heterokaryon entered mitosis together, the two sets of chromosomes commonly joined a single metaphase plate and were then symmetrically distributed to two mononucleate daughter cells each of which could subsequently be shown to contain within a single nucleus the chromosomes of both parent cells. The mode of formation of the 'spontaneous' hybrids discovered by Sorieul was thus no longer in serious doubt.

One particular family of heterokaryons became an object of special study. Harris and his colleagues had shown that when chick erythrocyte nuclei, which were genetically inert and conventionally thought to be in the process of dissolution, were incorporated into combinations with metabolically active cells, the erythrocyte nuclei were reactivated (Harris 1965, 1967; Harris et al. 1966). They enlarged, resumed the synthesis of RNA, formed nucleoli, replicated their DNA and finally entered mitosis (Appels, Bell, and Ringertz 1975). Chick-specific antigens (Harris et al. 1969; Ringertz et al. 1971) and enzymes

(Harris and Cook 1969; Kit et al. 1974) were also shown to be synthesized in these heterokaryons. Since erythrocytes constitute the most extreme form of differentiation seen in vertebrates, these experiments demonstrated that so long as a cell retained its nucleus, all the phenotypic limitations imposed by differentiation were, in principle, reversible. The biochemical and biophysical changes that took place during the reactivation of the erythrocyte nucleus were studied exhaustively by Ringertz and his colleagues. These studies (for reviews, see Ringertz and Bolund 1974; Appels and Ringertz 1975) provided fundamental new insights into nuclear physiology. However, as the whole subject of nuclear reactivation has been given detailed treatment by Ringertz and Savage in their book on hybrid cells (1976), there is little point in reviewing it again here.

GENETIC COMPLEMENTATION IN HETEROKARYONS

The most important genetic contribution made by the use of heterokaryons was the analysis of complementation in cells carrying inherited metabolic defects. The first study of this kind was done with cells from patients with *Xeroderma pigmentosum*, a autosomal recessive disease in which the skin is pathologically sensitive to sunlight. It was known that this sensitivity was determined by a genetic defect in the mechanisms that repair DNA damage inflicted by ultraviolet light, but essentially nothing was known about the number of mutations that might be involved, nor was it at all clear that the clinical heterogeneity of the syndrome had its basis in genetic heterogeneity. The first attempt to resolve this sort of question by the use of heterokaryons was made by de Weerd-Kastelein, Keijzer, and Bootsma (1972). Giannelli and Croll (1971), using incorporation of tritiated thymidine as the index, had previously shown that the defect in DNA repair exhibited by *Xeroderma pigmentosum* cells could be corrected when they were fused with normal fibroblasts. De Weerd-Kastelein, Keijzer, and Bootsma showed that no restoration of DNA repair occurred when cells from the same individual were fused with each other, but when cells from two individuals having different clinical manifestations of the disease were fused, DNA repair was effectively restored in both nuclei. This complementation of genetic defects provided the first direct evidence that the mutations in these clinically different conditions involved different elements in the pathway of DNA repair. These studies were extended to other cases of *Xeroderma pigmentosum* by de Weerd-Kastelein et al. (1973), Kraemer, Coon, and Robbins (1973), de Weerd-Kastelein, Keijzer, and Bootsma (1974), and Kraemer et al. (1975). By 1976, at least six complementation groups had been identified for *Xeroderma pigmentosum* and others were added in later years. Similar studies with heterokaryons identified different complementation groups in maple syrup disease (Lyons, Cox, and Dancis 1973), Tay-Sachs and Sandhoff's disease (Galjaard et al. 1974; Migeon, Norum, and Corsaro 1974), gangliosidosis (Galjaard et al. 1975), and cobalamin deficiency (Gravel et al. 1975). Complementation studies with heterokaryons have remained to the present day a powerful techique for investigating not only the mutational basis of inherited human diseases, but also the genetic regulatory mechanisms involved in differentiation (see, for example, Rastinejad and Blau 1993).

CHROMOSOME SEGREGATION AND GENE MAPPING IN HYBRID CELLS

The general applicability of Sendai virus-induced cell fusion unleashed a torrent of publications that described the production of hybrids from parental cells of the most widely (in some cases even grotesquely) different genotypes. But by far the most useful combination from the genetic point of view turned out to be hybrids between human and rodent cells. It was known that all hybrid cells progressively lost chromosomes on continued cultivation, but for the limited number of hybrids that had been studied before the species barrier was broken, this loss was slow and unpredictable. However, when Weiss (Fig. 34) and Green (Fig. 35) (see Weiss and Green 1967) produced hybrid lines from crosses between thymidine kinase-deficient (5-bromodeoxyuridine-resistant) mouse L cells and a diploid strain of human fibroblast (WI-38), they found that the hybrids rapidly eliminated three-quarters or more of the human chromosomes but retained essentially all of the mouse chromosome set. These cells containing partial complements of human chromosomes in a mouse genetic background were found to express human surface antigens; but, more important, the fact that they were selected in HAT medium, in which cells lacking thymidine kinase could not grow, indicated that they were surviving on the strength of the thymidine kinase contributed by one of the

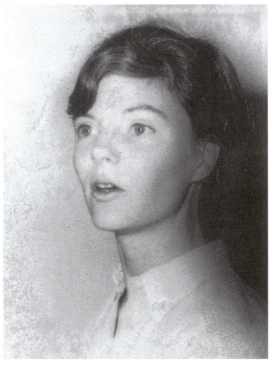

FIGURE 34 Mary Weiss (1941–), in collaboration with Howard Green (Fig. 35), showed that man-mouse hybrid cells selectively eliminated human chromosomes. This asymmetric chromosome loss produced hybrid cells with partial human chromosome complements. By correlating the retention or loss of a specific human marker with the retention or loss of a particular chromosome, Weiss and Green were able to assign the gene coding for that marker to an identifiable human chromosome (synteny). *(Courtesy of Dr. Howard Green.)*

FIGURE 35 Howard Green (1925–). *(Courtesy of Dr. Howard Green.)*

human chromosomes. Analysis of the chromosome composition of a number of independently derived clones permitted the identification of a human chromosome common to them all, and the conclusion was therefore drawn that the gene for thymidine kinase must be located on that particular chromosome. Strong evidence in support of this conclusion was provided by the systematic elimination of this chromosome from the hybrid cells when they were back-selected in 5-bromodeoxyuridine. The chromosome was initially thought to be a member of the C group, but Migeon and Miller (1968), examining crosses between the same thymidine kinase-deficient L cells and euploid cells lacking HPRT, came to the conclusion that the chromosome implicated by Weiss and Green was a member of the E, not the C, group. This assignation was accepted by Matsuya, Green, and Basilico (1968). With the advent of chromosome banding techniques, Miller et al. (1971) finally showed that the chromosome in question was number 17. Thymidine kinase was thus the first human gene to be localised to a particular chromosome by means of somatic cell hybridization. It was the swallow that made a summer.

At the time it was not at all clear, nor is it to the present day, why in certain combinations one set of parental chromosomes in the hybrid cells was preferentially eliminated. Studies in heterokaryons had shown that with widely different genotypes nuclear asynchrony was common, and there was some fragmentary evidence to suggest that the chromosomes of lagging nuclei might fail to make the necessary attachment to the metaphase plate. But preferential elimination of chromosomes was not determined solely by species differences. Minna and Coon (1974) found that if an established, rapidly growing human cell line was fused with euploid mouse cells that grew more slowly, it was the mouse chromosomes that were preferentially eliminated. Minna, Marshall, and Shaffer-Berman (1976) showed that it was in general the case that when highly differentiated euploid cells were crossed with established heteroploid cell lines, the euploid chromosomes were preferentially eliminated irrespective of the species of origin of the parent cells. Kao and Puck (1970) found that human chromosomes were more radically eliminated from crosses between human and Chinese hamster cells than from similar crosses between human and mouse cells, but the latter remained the preferred material largely because of the ease with which the metacentric human chromosomes could be distinguished from the telocentric mouse chromosomes. Westerveld et al. (1971) showed that hybrids between human lymphocytes and Chinese hamster cells eliminated human chromosomes more rapidly than similar hybrids made with human fibroblasts. Since lymphocytes do not adhere to the plastic or glass of culture flasks and can thus readily be removed from mixed cell cultures, Nabholz, Miggiano, and Bodmer (1969) routinely used crosses between established mouse cells and human lymphocytes for mapping purposes.

'EXTINCTION' OF DIFFERENTIATIED TRAITS

Although there were a number of experimental situations in which it would have been very useful to be able to determine the direction or, better still, the specificity of chromosome loss in hybrid cells, exploration of the mechanisms that governed this loss was largely abandoned in the rush to map human genes by the novel parasexual methods that cell fusion had made available. The classical approach to the study of human genetics was statistical analysis of meiotic recombination. But for many human genetic diseases, informative families are rare and pedigrees often faulty or incomplete. There was thus intense and continuous pressure to find new approaches to the mapping of human genes, and the opportunity provided by the findings of Weiss and Green was eagerly grasped. However, gene mapping via somatic cell hybridization had from the beginning two serious drawbacks. The first of these was that in many cases the abnormality that characterised a particular human genetic disease involved a biochemical marker that was not expressed by tissue cells in culture; and, in some cases, the biochemical abnormality was not even known. This meant that there was a large area of human genetics to which somatic cell hybridization could not, in principle, contribute. The second drawback had its origin in an observation made by Davidson, Ephrussi, and Yamamoto (1966, 1968). These authors found that when pigmented melanoma cells from the Syrian hamster were crossed with unpigmented mouse L cells, all hybrid clones were unpigmented. Silagi (1967) confirmed that this was also the case for crosses between pigmented and fibroblastic cells from the same species (mouse). In the latter case, the relative chromosomal stability of the hybrids made it very unlikely that the loss of pigmentation was due to chromosome elimination. Moreover, Fougère, Ruiz, and Ephrussi (1972) and Davidson (1972) showed that when near-tetraploid pigmented melanoma cells were fused with near-diploid L cells, some of the hybrid clones remained pigmented, thus indicating that abrogation of pigmentation was an effect subject to gene dosage. This virtually immediate loss of a differentiated trait when specialised cells were fused with fibroblasts was dubbed 'extinction' by

Ephrussi, and it was soon found to occur in other crosses of the same type. Schneider and Weiss (1971) showed that tyrosine aminotransferase, an enzyme activity that characterised liver cells, was extinguished in hybrids between relatively differentiated hepatoma cells and fibroblasts; and Weiss and Chaplain (1971) showed that this enzyme activity reappeared in some of the subclones made from this cross, perhaps as a consequence of chromosome loss. This indicated that, in at least some of the cells, extinction of the differentiated trait was not due to elimination of the structural gene. This conclusion was decisively confirmed by the demonstration that extinction of tyrosine aminotransferase took place in heterokaryons made from similar parent cells, where the question of chromosome elimination did not arise (Thompson and Gelehrter 1971). Gordon and Cohn (1970) showed that markers specific for macrophages were rapidly extinguished in heterokaryons made by fusing macrophages with melanocytes. The mechanisms responsible for the extinction of differentiated traits in hybrid cells remained the subject of intensive investigation over many years, but the underlying biochemistry is still incompletely resolved (for a recent review, see Goss 1993). Nonetheless, the fact that such extinction commonly did occur in the continued presence of the relevant structural genes meant that there was little chance that the genes determining markers of tissue differentiation could be mapped by the method introduced by Weiss and Green. It was clear that, at least for the immediate future, mapping by somatic cell hybridization would be limited to genes that were expressed constitutively in culture. But that was scope enough.

SELECTIVE SYSTEMS FOR GENE MAPPING

The method used by Weiss and Green (1967) to establish the location of the human thymidine kinase gene relied on the fact that this gene was selectable in an appropriate medium, and confirmation of the localisation was obtained by back-selection against the gene. But there were at the time very few human genes that could be selectively retained in, or selectively eliminated from, interspecific hybrid cells. This initially imposed a further limitation on the Weiss and Green procedure and stimulated an intensive search for additional human markers that could be manipulated in this way. Puck et al. (1971) introduced the use of cytotoxic antisera directed against human cell surface antigens to select against specific human chromosomes, and Wuthier, Jones, and Puck (1973), using this procedure, established a linkage between a human cell surface antigen (named A_L) and the lactic dehydrogenase A gene. The two genes were subsequently shown to map to human chromosome 11 and the A_L antigen was identified as glycophorin, a prominent surface element in human red cells (Jones, Wuthier, and Puck 1975; Jones et al. 1976). The use of cytotoxic antibodies enabled Van Someren et al. (1974a) to assign the HLA histocompatibility genes to human chromosome 6 and Goodfellow et al. (1975) to assign the β_2-microglobulin gene to human chromosome 15. Dendy and Harris (1973) showed that diphtheria toxin, which is about 100,000 times more lethal to human than to mouse cells, could be used as a selective system for man-mouse hybrid cells, and this permitted Creagan, Chen, and Ruddle (1975) to locate the gene for the diphtheria toxin receptor in human cells to chromosome 5. Kucherlapati, Baker, and Ruddle (1975) similarly showed that ouabain was about 1000 times more lethal to human than to rodent cells and could therefore also be used to provide a selective system for man-mouse hybrids. Resistance to ouabain showed partial dominance in hybrid cells, so that if a recessive selectable marker such as thioguanine-resistance was introduced into ouabain-resistant cells, the resultant doubly-marked cells could be fused with any other cells to yield hybrids that could readily be isolated in an appropriate selective medium containing ouabain. Doubly-marked cells that yielded easily selectable hybrids when fused with other cells became known as 'universal fusers'. Miller et al. (1974), using resistance to polio virus as a selective system, were able to assign the polio virus receptor gene to human chromosome 19.

THE DETERMINATION OF 'SYNTENY'

However, it soon became apparent that selective systems were not indispensable for the assignment of human genes to particular chromosomes. If a sufficient number of independently isolated man-mouse hybrid clones were examined, the more or less random elimination of the human chromosomes permitted a correlation to be established between the presence or absence of a particular chromosome and the presence or absence of the human marker one was interested in. A high degree of concordance between marker and chromosome in such segregated hybrids was found in practice to provide a reliable chromosome assignment for the marker, a form of linkage for which the term 'synteny' was adopted. Creagan and Ruddle (1975) introduced the idea of screening panels of hybrid cell clones selected to provide a maximally informative representation of human chromosomes. This approach was rapidly adopted by many laboratories and soon became established as a standard technique for determining synteny. It was well known at the time that the same enzyme in different animal species often showed variations in amino acid sequence that were enough to permit the enzymes from two different species to be distinguished by their electrophoretic mobility. Meera Kahn and his colleagues (Meera Khan 1971; Van Someren et al. 1974b) established suitable electrophoretic conditions for separating many human enzymes from their hamster equivalents in extracts of man-hamster hybrid cells; and with minor modifications these procedures could also be used to separate human from mouse enzymes. Simple electrophoretic procedures thus made enzymes an especially attractive and facile set of markers for gene mapping. In a single paper, Ruddle et al. (1971) recorded the synteny relationships of 17 human enzymes, established by screening panels of interspecific hybrid cells. Where electrophoretic methods failed to separate the human enzyme from its rodent equivalent, kinetic or antigenic differences could sometimes be used to facilitate identification of the human component (Boyd and Harris, 1973; Palser and McAlpine 1976; Shimizu et al. 1976). The torrent of papers reporting the assignment of human genes to particular chromosomes by the analysis of highly segregated interspecific hybrids is recorded in the Human Gene Mapping Conferences I–V that were held in New Haven in 1973, Rotterdam in 1974, Baltimore in 1975, Winnipeg in 1977 and Edinburgh in 1979. In the decade that followed the original Weiss and Green (1967) paper, more than 100 human genes were localised in this way, and although much more refined techniques for gene mapping have since been developed, the assignation of genes to particular chromosomes by means of highly segregated hybrid cells continues to the present day.

But merely to establish synteny, to locate a gene to some undetermined position within a whole chromosome, is a hugely approximate kind of gene mapping. Compared with what was then possible with bacteria or yeasts, determining synteny relationships was very largely a matter of obtaining information for its own sake; only rarely did the information illuminate function or shed new light on the genetic organisation of somatic cells. Refinement of the localisation could sometimes be achieved by using human cells that carried chromosome translocations, or by exploiting chromosome aberrations that arose spontaneously in the hybrid cell cultures. For example, Boone, Chen, and Ruddle (1972) were able to assign the gene for human thymidine kinase activity to the long arm of chromosome 17 by analysing hybrid cells in which a translocation had occurred that involved human chromosome 17 and a mouse chromosome. Further precision in the localisation of the thymidine kinase gene was made possible by the fortuitous circumstance that adenovirus 12 integrates into chromosome 17 at a site close to this gene. The virus induces visible chromosome deletions, and by correlating the positions of these deletions with the presence or absence of thymidine kinase activity, McDougall, Kucherlapati, and Ruddle (1973) concluded that the gene was located in the proximal region of chromosome 17q22. Numerous other cases of regional localisation of genes by means of chromosome translocations or deletions detectable in hybrid cells were soon reported in the literature, but since informative chromosome aberrations become available only by chance, such events could never have provided a systematic approach to regional mapping; and except where a break point actually involved the gene itself, the degree of localisation that could be inferred from a visible translocation remained very approximate.

TRANSFER OF CHROMOSOMES AND SUBCHROMOSOMAL FRAGMENTS

Attempts were made to increase the power of these mapping procedures and to render them less dependent on chance chromosome elimination or rearrangement. McBride and Ozer (1973) showed that it was possible to introduce isolated metaphase chromosomes into cells in culture and to obtain relatively stable pseudohybrids in which genes located on the transferred chromosomes were stably retained. McBride and Ozer transferred the HPRT gene derived from isolated Chinese hamster chromosomes to mouse cells and showed by electrophoretic and chromatographic methods that the enzyme activity characteristic of Chinese hamster HPRT was present in the mouse cells. This demonstration removed the cardinal objection made to previous experiments of this kind, namely that the appearance of an enzyme activity previously absent might have been due to reversion of a mutated host gene or to activation of a silent gene. The observations of McBride and Ozer were confirmed and extended to human genes by Wullems, van der Horst, and Bootsma (1975), Willecke and Ruddle (1975), and Burch and McBride (1975). These authors found that it was generally the case that only chromosomal fragments were stably transferred from isolated metaphase chromosomes. This permitted Klobutcher and Ruddle (1979) to correlate the size of the transferred fragments with the expression of three linked genes on human chromosome 17 and hence to deduce their order. Transfer of genes by fragments too small to be detected by light microscopy was also observed in certain combinations of fused cells (Schwartz, Cook, and Harris 1971; Boyd and Harris 1973). These submicroscopic fragments were often formed by a process originally called 'chromosome pulverization' but, with greater understanding, later renamed 'premature chromosome condensation' (PCC). Johnson and Harris (1969a,b,c) had shown that when cells of widely different genotypes were fused together, synchrony of mitosis was often not achieved in the heterokaryons, and the chromosomes of the lagging nuclei were sometimes pulverized when the heterokaryon entered mitosis. Johnson and Rao (1970, 1971), examining this phenomenon more closely in synchronized cells, showed that the appearance of the interphase nuclei forced to enter mitosis prematurely depended on the stage of the cell cycle in which they found themselves at the time. Nuclei in the G1 phase produced thin, extended, single-stranded filaments, nuclei in G2 produced thicker, double-stranded filaments, and nuclei in S produced irregular chromatin fragments connected by a thin strand. These prematurely condensed chromosomes revealed a more detailed pattern of Giemsa bands than that seen in conventional mitotic preparations and should, in principle, have permitted a higher degree of cytological resolution (Unakul et al. 1973; Röhme 1974; Sperling and Rao 1974). But the technical difficulty of standardising banding patterns seen in PCC seems to have discouraged the widespread use of this procedure for high resolution mapping. PCC proved, however, to be very useful in facilitating the analysis of chromosome damage produced by X rays, ultraviolet light and alkylating agents (Waldren and Johnson 1974; Hittelman and Rao 1974a,b, 1975; Schor, Johnson, and Waldren 1975). A less capricious method for introducing single chromosomes into animal cells than a transfer of isolated metaphase chromosomes was devised by Ege and Ringertz (1974). They showed that micronuclei produced by treating cells with colchicine or other mitotic inhibitors could be isolated as 'microcells' by the enucleation technique discovered by Carter (1967, 1972) and developed further by Prescott, Myerson, and Wallace (1972). This involves treating the cells with the toxic antibiotic cytochalasin, which disrupts cytoplasmic microfilaments, and then subjecting them to centrifugation. Nuclei and micronuclei, being denser than the cytoplasm, are released from the cells as spheroidal units containing a rim of cytoplasm enclosed in cell membrane. The microcells derived from micronuclei vary in size depending on how many chromosomes they contain, but Ege and Ringertz (1974) demonstrated by Feulgen photometry that the smallest of them contained an amount of DNA equivalent to a single chromosome. Ege, Krondahl, and Ringertz (1974) showed that the microcells isolated in this way could be fused with other cells by means of inactivated Sendai virus and could thus serve as vectors for the transfer of single chromosomes. Enucleation coupled with cell fusion was used to form various kinds of reconstituted cells in which complete or reduced chromosome sets were integrated into foreign cytoplasm (Ringertz and Savage 1976). These various technical developments permitting the transfer of nuclei, partial chromosome sets or single chromosomes from one cell to another proved to be of great value in the analysis of nucleocytoplasmic relationships; and, in some cases, the transfer of a single chromosome served to establish beyond doubt the presence and biological function of an important gene whose location had been inferred but remained in doubt. But none of these techniques produced major advances in regional gene mapping. Somatic cell genetics at this point was still without any formal method for solving even the simplest of problems in topographical analysis, for example, how to determine the linear order of three linked genes and the distances between them.

GENE MAPPING BY MARKER SEGREGATION INDUCED BY RADIATION

A systematic and generally applicable method for the regional mapping of human genes was eventually provided by Goss (Fig. 36) and Harris (1975, 1977a,b). The technique devised by these authors rested on the well known observation that X irradiation of cells gave rise to chromosome breaks and that the number of breaks produced, at least in plant cells and in *Drosophila*, was, over a certain range, a simple function of the radiation dose. Goss and Harris reasoned that the chance that any two genes on the one chromosome would be segregated by a break would be in some way proportional to the distance between them: genes close together ought to be segregated less frequently by a given dose of radiation than genes far apart. If then the theory held in practice, it should be possible with a suitable dose of radiation to estimate the relative distance between genes from the frequency with which they were segregated by chromosome breaks; and from the relative distances between genes it should be possible to deduce their order. Goss and Harris (1975) first explored whether the theory held for the simple case of the human X chromosome which offered the technical advantage of containing a marker (HPRT) that could be selectively retained in hybrid cells and thus could serve as a reference point. The segregation frequencies of four enzymes that mapped to the X chromosome were examined: HPRT, glucose-6-phosphate dehydrogenase, 3-phosphoglycerate kinase, and α-galactosidase A. Chinese hamster

FIGURE 36 Stephen Goss (1952–). Using hybrids between rodent cells and lethally irradiated human cells, Goss and Henry Harris (Fig. 30) devised the first systematic method for determining the order of human genes along the chromosome and the distances between them. *(Courtesy of the Archives of the Sir William Dunn School of Pathology, University of Oxford.)*

cell lines were fused with human lymphocytes that had been given doses of gamma irradiation ranging from 10–40 Jkg⁻¹, and the frequency with which each of the four human genes was retained in the resulting hybrid cells determined. From these figures, it was possible to calculate the relative distances of each of these genes from the others and hence to establish their order. The results obtained were found to be in good agreement with the conclusions that had been drawn from cytogenetic observations.

Determining the order and spacing of these X-linked genes was greatly facilitated by the presence of the selectable X-linked marker HPRT. Genes known to map to autosomes, which were scored as controls in the experiments, were found to be largely lost from these hybrids between hamster cells and X-irradiated human lymphocytes. If the Goss and Harris procedure had been applicable only to genes linked to a selectable marker, that would have imposed severe limitations on its usefulness for, as mentioned previously, there were at that time rather few selectable markers whose chromosome location was known. However, Goss and Harris (1977b) were able to show that the method could be generalised to include markers that were not linked to a selectable gene. In crosses between a pseudodiploid mouse cell line and suitably irradiated normal human fibroblasts, broken human chromosomes were found to be retained in the hybrids with a much higher frequency than in similar crosses with irradiated lymphocytes, and this permitted unselected genes to be scored in essentially the same way as the genes on the selectable X chromosome. Eight markers that were known to map to chromosome 1 were examined. Chromosome 1 was chosen for two reasons. First, it was the longest human chromosome and thus, in principle, provided the most exacting test of the method; and second, the eight genes that were known to map to it constituted the largest collection then available on any one chromosome of markers that could be scored *in vitro*. The segregation frequencies of all eight genes were determined, as had been done for the X-linked genes, and it was again found that the relative distances between them, and hence their order, could be sensibly calculated from the segregation data. It thus proved possible to construct a map that showed the regional localisation of all eight genes on chromsome 1, and this map also agreed with the information that had been obtained by cytogenetic methods. However, the statistical map went a good deal further, not only in the precision of the localisation, but also in providing new information (subsequently confirmed) that cytogenetic methods had not yet yielded.

The two great advantages of the Goss and Harris procedure were first, that it provided the desperately needed formal method for determining intergenic distances and gene order; and second, that it dispensed with microscopic cytogenetics, a laborious skill that took a long time to acquire and that was always in short supply. The method as used for the selectable X-linked genes was adopted by other workers, and genes mapped by what became known as the Goss-Harris technique made their appearance from time to time in McKusick's great compilations of data on human genes (McKusick 1978). However, the general method, as illustrated by the mapping of unselected genes on chromosome 1, did not attract much attention. Part of the reason for this may have been that a preliminary account of the data on the X-linked genes was presented in *Nature*, which ensured a wide audience, whereas the data on chromosome 1 was published only in an orthodox and conservative cell biology journal. But a more fundamental reason was probably the fact that too few markers were then available to offer many opportunities for the useful application of the generalised statistical treatment devised by Goss and Harris (1977b). More than a decade was to elapse, during which advances in nucleic acid technology yielded a plenitude of suitable markers, before the Goss-Harris technique was again applied in a systematic fashion to the mapping of the human genome. The startling recent applications of this methodology will be discussed in the next chapter.

FUSION OF PLANT CELLS AND THE PRODUCTION OF HYBRID PLANTS

Although, as mentioned earlier, plant protoplasts from different species had been fused together to produce transient heterokaryons as early as 1937 (Michel 1937), it was the spectacular harvest yielded by the experimental fusion of animal cells that prompted a revival of interest in plant cell fusion. The prospects that could be envisaged for the successful hybridization of plant cells were even more dramatic than those offered by animal cells, for one overriding reason. Whereas there seemed to be no likelihood that new individuals could be generated from single somatic animal cells, this had been achieved for some plant cells. Steward, Mapes, and Mears (1958) and Blakely and Steward (1964) had shown that single carrot cells could generate calluses from which carrot plants could develop. Vasil and Hildebrandt (1965) succeeded in generating flowering tobacco plants from single *Nicotiana* cells in microcultures, and Joshi and Ball (1968) showed that this could also be done with single cell cultures derived from groundnuts (*Arachis hypogaea*). It therefore seemed possible that hybrid plants might be produced from different species, or even different genera, if whole plants could be generated from fused plant protoplasts. Many different procedures were devised for the isolation of plant protoplasts (for review, see Cocking 1972), and a systematic search was made for reagents that could induce protoplasts to fuse together. The first chemical reagent to be used for fusing cells was lysolethicin (Howell and Lucy 1969), but many others were subsequently tested (see, for example, Lucy et al. 1971; Ahkong et al. 1973; Cramp and Lucy 1974). A variety of recipes for media that would support the growth of plants from isolated protoplasts also emerged. The first hybrid plant to be produced from the fusion of somatic cell protoplasts was a cross between two species of tobacco (*Nicotiana glauca* x *N. lansdorffii*) (Carlson, Smith, and Dearing 1972). Isolation of this hybrid was achieved by the use of auxotrophic mutants that permitted a selective medium to be formulated in which the hybrid cells, but neither of their parents, could grow (Carlson, 1970). Melchers and Labib (1974) used sensitivity to light as a selective system for isolating somatic cell tobacco hybrids. Although these first hybrid plants derived from fused protoplasts involved species that could be crossed in other ways, it was not long before hybrids were produced from quite different and incompatible species. Melchers, Sacristan, and Holder (1978) succeeded in regenerating from fused somatic cell protoplasts flowering hybrids between potato and tomato plants. Although such totally novel crosses appeared to open a brave new world for agriculture, it turned out in practice that none of the parasexual plant hybrids produced by protoplast fusion had any important agricultural advantages. It was not until methods were devised for inserting specific foreign genes into plant cells that real prospects for crop improvement emerged.

CHEMICAL FUSOGENS

Plant protoplast fusion did, however, yield one important technological advance that was of general use not only for plant, but also for animal, cells. Among the many chemical fusogens that were tried on plant protoplasts, one turned out to be particularly effective. Kao and his colleagues (Constabel and Kao 1974; Kao and Michayluk 1974; Kartha et al. 1974) showed that the water-soluble polymer, polyethylene glycol, readily induced the formation of het-erokaryons from plant protoplasts of different species and even genera. Under optimal conditions, a heterokaryon yield of up to 20% was obtained, and some of the fused protoplasts were subsequently shown to divide. Polyethylene glycol was rapidly adopted for experiments involving plant cell fusion, and Pontecorvo (1975) showed that it could also be used to fuse animal cells together. Although the time of exposure of the cells to polyethylene glycol and the concentration of the reagent were critical (Pontecorvo, Riddle, and Hales 1977), conditions were soon standardised and, for most purposes, poly-ethylene glycol eventually displaced inactivated Sendai virus as the standard reagent for fusing cells.

THE PRODUCTION OF MONOCLONAL ANTIBODIES

Of the many uses to which cell fusion was put, by far the most important practical application was the development of a system for producing mono-clonal antibodies of predetermined specificity. The letter to *Nature* by Köhler and Milstein (1975) announcing this advance was the decisive event, but it was not widely appreciated at the time that this work was the last stage in a long history of previous experiments that provided an indispensable method-ological background. Many workers during the 1950s and early 1960s contributed to the gradual realisation that the proteins secreted by individual myeloma tumours were homogeneous molecules of which some had antibody activity (for review of this early work, see Kunkel 1964). Plasma cell tumours of the mouse and other laboratory animals were known to produce single antibodies, but it was the development of reproducible techniques for the production of experimental plasma cell tumours and myelomas that brought their secretion products within the range of systematic investigation (Merwin and Algire 1959; Potter and Boyce 1962). Schubert, Jobe, and Cohn (1968) found that some mouse myelomas produced antibody that precipitated nucleic acid bases and nitrophenyl derivatives; and Potter and Leon (1968) showed that others produced antibodies that precipitated pneumococcal polysaccharide. Pettengill and Sorenson (1967) succeeded in growing my-eloma cells in suspension culture, and myelomas were cloned in agar by Horibata and Harris (1970) and by Coffino, Laskov, and Scharff (1970).

The lack of any method for obtaining pure cultures of normal lymphocytes able to produce a single specified antibody was widely recognised as a serious impediment to progress in the structural analysis of antibody specificity. Several groups attempted to overcome this barrier by the application of cell fusion techniques. The hope was that the production of a specific antibody by a lymphoid cell might be stabilised if that cell was fused with one that was capable of vigorous growth *in vitro*. It had been shown as early as 1965 that normal lymphocytes could be fused with other cell types and that the lymphocyte nucleus in the fused cell was genetically active (Harris 1965). But it was not until 1970 that the first experiment was done to see whether antibody production persisted when a lymphoid cell was fused with an established cell line (Periman 1970). Periman used a fibroblastic cell line and found that some antibody production did persist in the hybrid, but at a very low level. Parkman, Hagemeier, and Merler (1971), in a similar experiment, found some expression of membrane-bound antibody, but this proved to be transient. Coffino, Laskov, and Scharff (1970) and Klein and Wiener (1971), studying similar crosses, found that antibody production was extinguished. All these experiments were probably examples of the extinction of differentiated traits originally observed by Ephrussi and his colleagues in crosses between specialised cells and fibroblasts. The experiments of Mohit and Fan (1971), however, constituted a new departure. They fused together two cells of the same general differentiation lineage: a mouse myeloma that produced immunoglobulin and free kappa chains and a mouse lymphoma that did not produce any antibody. In this case, production of antibody was not extinguished; the hybrid cells produced the antibodies made by the myeloma parent cell at about half the original level. The results described by Mohit and Fan were probably the first example, although it was not fully appreciated at the time, of what later came to be regarded as a general rule, namely, that the extinction seen when specialised cells were fused with fibroblasts was not seen when these cells were fused with others of the same differentiation lineage. Schwaber and Cohen (1973) found that when antibody-producing mouse myeloma cells were fused with human peripheral blood lymphocytes, one of the hybrid clones isolated produced both human and mouse immunoglobulin. This was not, however, the first example of antibody production in a normal lymphocyte being stabilised by fusion of the lymphocyte with a tumour cell of the same lineage. Trujillo et al. (1970), stimulated by clinical observations made by Sinkovics, Drewinko, and Thornell (1970), co-cultivated a mouse lymphoma cell line with an explant from the spleen of a mouse immune to the lymphoma, and from these mixed cultures hybrids arose that produced antibodies against mouse leukaemia virus (for review, see Sinkovics 1982). At a later stage, Szpirer, Szpirer, and Wanson (1980) showed that the expression of liver markers by normal hepatocytes could similarly be stabilised in culture if the hepatocytes were fused with established hepatomas.

Parasexual somatic cell genetics was introduced into Milstein's laboratory by Cotton (Fig. 37) in order to explore the phenomenon known as 'allelic exclusion' (Cotton 1994). This term was used to describe the observation first made by Weiler (1965) and Pernis et al. (1965) that when lymphoid cells produce immunoglobulin, only one of the two allelic genes is expressed. The experiment described by Schwaber and Cohen (1973) indicated that in the man-mouse hybrid clone that produced immunoglobulins of both species, allelic exclusion had not occurred. Cotton examined this question systematically in a cross between a mouse and a rat myeloma and also found no evidence of allelic exclusion (Cotton and Milstein 1973). Bloom and Nakamura (1974) found no evidence of either extinction or allelic exclusion in a cross between two human lymphoid cell lines. Köhler and Milstein (1975) showed

FIGURE 37 Richard Cotton (1940–). *(Courtesy of the Archives of the Sir William Dunn School of Pathology, University of Oxford.)*

FIGURE 38 Georges Köhler (1946–1995). *(Courtesy of Dr. César Milstein.)*

FIGURE 39 César Milstein (1927–). *(Courtesy of Dr. César Milstein.)*

The work of Cotton, Köhler and Milstein resulted in the development of a general method for producing monoclonal antibodies of predetermined specificity.

that this was also true for hybrids between two mouse myelomas. The final step in the production of monoclonal antibodies of predetermined specificity was taken by Köhler (Fig. 38) and Milstein (Fig. 39) (see Köhler and Milstein 1975), who fused mouse myeloma cells with cells taken from the spleen of mice immunized against sheep red cells. The hybrid cells were cloned in agar and, in one experiment, as many as 10% of them could be shown to produce antibody against sheep red cells. All of these early experiments involving the fusion of cells of the lymphoid series, including the work described in the paper by Köhler and Milstein in 1975, were done with inactivated Sendai virus; but since in that year polyethelyne glycol was shown to be an effective fusogen for animal cells, further development and standardisation of the technique of monoclonal antibody production was based on the use of this reagent (Köhler and Milstein 1976). Galfré et al. (1977) and Williams, Galfré, and Milstein (1977) provided the first examples of the practical application of monoclonal antibodies as tools for the identification, and eventually purification, of specific antigens. (This account of the development of monoclonal antibodies leans heavily on Cotton [1994] which should be consulted for greater detail.)

REFERENCES

Ahkong, Q.F., D. Fisher, W. Tampion, and J.A. Lucy. 1973. The fusion of erythrocytes by fatty acids, esters, retinol and alpha-tocopherol. *Biochem. J.* **136**: 147–155.

Appels, R. and N.R. Ringertz. 1975. Chemical and structural changes within chick erythrocyte nuclei introduced into mammalian cells by cell fusion. *Curr. Top. Dev. Biol.* **9**: 137–166.

Appels, R., P.B. Bell, and N.R. Ringertz. 1975. The first division of HeLa x chick erythrocyte heterokaryons. Transfer of chick nuclei to daughter cells. *Exp. Cell Res.* **92**: 79–86.

Barski, G. and J. Belehradek. 1963. Transfert nucléaire intercellulaire en cultures mixtes *in vitro*. *Exp. Cell Res.* **29**: 102–111.

Barski, G., S. Sorieul, and F. Cornefert. 1960. Production dans des cultures *in vitro* de deux souches cellulaires en association, de cellules de caractère "hybride". *C. R. Acad. Sci. Paris* **251**: 1825–1827.

———. 1961. "Hybrid" type cells in combined cultures of two different mammalian cell strains. *J. Natl. Cancer Inst.* **26**: 1269–1291.

Blakely, L.M. and F.C. Steward. 1964. Growth and organized development of cultured cells. V. The growth of colonies from free cells on nutrient agar. *Am. J. Bot.* **51**: 780–791.

Bloom, H.D. and F.T. Nakamura. 1974. Establishment of a tetraploid immunoglobulin producing cell line from the hybridization of two human lymphocyte lines. *Proc. Natl. Acad. Sci.* **71**: 2689–2692.

Boone, C., T.-R. Chen, and F.H. Ruddle. 1972. Assignment of three human genes to chromosomes (LHD-A to 11, TK to 17 and IDH to 20) and evidence for translocation between human and mouse chromosomes in somatic cell hybrids. *Proc. Natl. Acad. Sci.* **69**: 510–514.

Boyd, Y.L. and H. Harris. 1973. Correction of genetic defects in mammalian cells by the input of small amounts of foreign genetic material. *J. Cell Sci.* **13**: 841–861.

Buck, E. 1878. Einige Rhizopodenstudien. *Z. Wiss. Zool.* **30**: 1–49.

Burch, J.W. and O.W. McBride. 1975. Human gene expression in rodent cells after uptake of isolated metaphase chromosomes. *Proc. Natl. Acad. Sci.* **72**: 1797–1801.

Carlson, P.S. 1970. Induction and isolation of auxotrophic mutants in somatic cell cultures of *Nicotiana tabacum*. *Science* **168**: 487–489.

Carlson, P.S., H.H. Smith, and R.D. Dearing. 1972. Parasexual interspecific plant hybridization. *Proc. Natl. Acad. Sci.* **69**: 2292–2294.

Carter, S.B. 1967. Effects of cytochalasins on mammalian cells. *Nature* **213**: 261–266.

———. 1972. The cytochalasins as research tools in cytology. *Endeavour* **31**: 77–82.

Chanock, R.M. 1956. Association of a new type of cytopathogenic myxovirus with infantile croup. *J. Exp. Med.* **104**: 555–576.

Cienkowski, L. 1876. Ueber einige Rhizopoden und verwandte Organismen. *Arch. Mikrosk. Anat.* **12**: 15–50.

Cocking, E.C. 1972. Plant cell protoplasts. Isolation and development. *Annu. Rev. Plant Physiol.* **23**: 29–50.

Coffino, P., R. Laskov, and M.D. Scharff. 1970. Immunoglobulin production. Method for detecting and quantitating variant myeloma cells. *Science* **167**: 186–188.

Constabel, F. and K.N. Kao. 1974. Agglutination and fusion of plant protoplasts by polyethylene glycol. *Can. J. Bot.* **52**: 1603–1606.

Cotton, R.G.H. 1994. The road to monoclonal antibodies. In *The legacy of cell fusion* (ed. S. Gordon), pp. 151–166. Oxford University Press, United Kingdom.

Cotton, R.G.H. and C. Milstein. 1973. Fusion of two immunoglobulin-producing myeloma cells. *Nature* **224**: 42–43.

Cramp, F.C. and J.A. Lucy. 1974. Glycerol monooleate as a fusogen for the formation of heterokaryons and interspecific hybrid cells. *Exp. Cell Res.* **87**: 107–110.

Creagan, R.P. and F. Ruddle. 1975. The clone panel: A systematic approach to gene mapping using interspecific somatic cell hybrids: Human gene mapping 2. *Birth Defects. Orig. Artic. Ser.* **11**: 112–113.

Creagan, R.P., S. Chen, and F.H. Ruddle. 1975. Genetic analysis of the cell surface. Association of human chromosome 5 with sensitivity to diphtheria toxin in mouse-human somatic cell hybrids. *Proc. Natl. Acad. Sci.* **72**: 2237–2241.

Davidson, R.L. 1972. Regulation of melanin synthesis in mammalian cells: Effect of gene dosage on the expression of differentiation. *Proc. Natl. Acad. Sci.* **69**: 951–955.

Davidson, R.L., B. Ephrussi, and K. Yamamoto. 1966. Regulation of pigment synthesis in mammalian cells as studied by somatic hybridization. *Proc. Natl. Acad. Sci.* **56**: 1437–1440.

———. 1968. Regulation of melanin synthesis in mammalian cells as studied by somatic hybridization. I. Evidence for negative control. *J. Cell. Physiol.* **72**: 115–127.

de Bary, A. 1859. Die Mycetozoen. Ein Beitrag zur Kenntnis der niedersten Thiere. *Z. Wiss. Zool.* **10**: 88–175.

Dendy, P.R. and H. Harris. 1973. Sensitivity to diphtheria toxin as a species-specific marker in hybrid cells. *J. Cell Sci.* **12**: 831–837.

de Weerd-Kastelein, E.A., W. Keijzer, and D. Bootsma. 1972. Genetic heterogeneity of *Xeroderma pigmentosum* demonstrated by somatic cell hybridization. *Nat. New Biol.* **238**: 80–83.

———. 1974. A third complementation group in *Xeroderma pigmentosum*. *Mutat. Res.* **22**: 87–91.

de Weerd-Kastelein, E.A., W.J. Kleijer, M.L. Sluyter, and W. Keijzer. 1973. Repair replication in heterokaryons derived from different repair-deficient *Xeroderma pigmentosum* strains. *Mutat. Res.* **19**: 237–243.

Ege, T. and N.R. Ringertz. 1974. Preparation of microcells by enucleation of micronucleate cells. *Exp. Cell Res.* **87**: 378–382.

Ege, T., U. Krondahl, and N.R. Ringertz. 1974. Introduction of nuclei and micronuclei into cells and enucleated cytoplasms by Sendai virus induced fusion. *Exp. Cell Res.* **88**: 428–432.

Enders, J.F. and T.C. Peebles. 1954. Propagation in tissue cultures of cytopathogenic agents from patients with measles. *Proc. Soc. Exp. Biol. Med.* **86**: 277–286.

Engel, E., B.J. McGee, and H. Harris. 1969. Cytogenetic and nuclear studies on A9 and B82 cells fused together by Sendai virus. The early phase. *J. Cell Sci.* **5**: 93–120.

Ephrussi, B. 1972. *Hybridization of somatic cells*. Princeton University Press, Princeton, New Jersey.

———. 1965–1970. Correspondence with Henry Harris (deposited in the Contemporary Medical Archives Centre of the Wellcome Institute for the History of Medicine, London).

Ephrussi, B. and S. Sorieul. 1962a. Nouvelles observations sur l'hybridation "in vitro" de cellules de souris. *C. R. Acad. Sci. Paris* **254**: 181–182.

————. 1962b. Mating of somatic cells *in vitro. Univ. Mich. Med. Bull.* **28:** 347–363.

Ephrussi, B. and M.C. Weiss. 1965. Interspecific hybridization of somatic cells. *Proc. Natl. Acad. Sci.* **53:** 1040–1042.

Ephrussi, B., L.J. Scaletta, M.H. Stenchever, and M.C. Yoshida. 1964. Hybridization of somatic cells *in vitro. Symp. Int. Soc. Cell Biol.* **3:** 13–25.

Fell, H.B. and A.F. Hughes. 1949. Mitosis in the mouse: A study of living and fixed cells in tissue cultures. *Q. J. Microsc. Sci.* **90:** 355–380.

Fougère, C., F. Ruiz, and B. Ephrussi. 1972. Gene dosage dependence of pigment synthesis in melanoma x fibroblast hybrids. *Proc. Natl. Acad. Sci.* **69:** 330–334.

Galfré, G., S.C. Howe, C. Milstein, G.W. Butcher, and J.C. Howard. 1977. Antibodies to major histocompatability antigens produced by hybrid cell lines. *Nature* **266:** 550–552.

Galjaard, H., A. Hoogeveen, H.A. de Wit-Verbeek, A.J.J. Reuser, W. Keijzer, A. Westerveld, and D. Bootsma. 1974. Tay-Sachs and Sandhoffs disease. Intergenic complementation after somatic cell hybridization. *Exp. Cell Res.* **87:** 444–448.

Galjaard, H., A. Hoogeveen, W. Keijzer, H.A. de Wit-Verbeek, A.J.J. Reuser, M.W. Ho, and D. Robinson. 1975. Genetic heterogeneity in GM1-gangliosidosis. *Nature* **257:** 60–62.

Geddes, P. 1880. On the coalescence of amoeboid cells into plasmodia. *Proc. R. Soc. Lond.* **30:** 252–255.

Gershon, D. and L. Sachs. 1963. Properties of a somatic hybrid between mouse cells with different genotypes. *Nature* **198:** 912–913.

Giannelli, F. and P. Croll. 1971. Complementation *in vitro* between fibroblasts from normal subjects and patients with *Xeroderma pigmentosum. Clin. Sci.* **40:** 27.

Goodfellow, P., E. Jones, V. van Heyningen, E. Solomon, R. Kennet, M. Bobrow, and W.F. Bodmer. 1975. Linkage relationships of the HL-A system and β_2 microglobulin: Human gene mapping 2. *Birth Defects Orig. Artic. Ser.* **11:** 162–167.

Gordon, S. and Z. Cohn. 1970. Macrophage-melanocyte heterokaryons. I. Preparation and properties. *J. Exp. Med.* **131:** 981–1003.

Goss, S.J. 1993. A fresh look at the somatic cell genetics of hepatoma differentiation. *J. Cell Sci.* **104:** 231–235.

Goss, S.J. and H. Harris. 1975. New method for mapping genes in human chromosomes. *Nature* **255:** 680–684.

————. 1977a. Gene transfer by means of cell fusion. I. Statistical mapping of the human X-chromosome by analysis of radiation-induced gene segregation. *J. Cell Sci.* **25:** 17–37.

————. 1977b. Gene transfer by means of cell fusion. II. The mapping of 8 loci on human chromosome 1 by statistical analysis of gene assortment in somatic cell hybrids. *J. Cell Sci.* **25:** 39–58.

Gravel, R.A., M.J. Mahoney, F.H. Ruddle, and L.E. Rosenberg. 1975. Genetic complementation in heterokaryons of human fibroblasts defective in cobalamin metabolism. *Proc. Natl. Acad. Sci.* **72:** 3181–3185.

Hakala, M.T. and E. Taylor. 1959. The ability of purine and thymine derivatives and of glycine to support the growth of mammalian cells in culture. *J. Biol. Chem.* **234:** 126–128.

Harris, H. 1965. Behaviour of differentiated nuclei in heterokaryons of animal cells from different species. *Nature* **206:** 583–588.

————. 1967. The reactivation of the red cell nucleus. *J. Cell Sci.* **2:** 23–32.

————. 1970. *Cell fusion: The Dunham Lectures.* Oxford University Press, London and New York.

Harris, H. and P.R. Cook. 1969. Synthesis of an enzyme determined by an erythrocyte nucleus in a hybrid cell. *J. Cell Sci.* **5:** 121–134.

Harris, H. and J.F. Watkins. 1965. Hybrid cells derived from mouse and man. Artificial heterokaryons of mammalian cells from different species. *Nature* **205:** 640–646.

Harris, H., E. Sidebottom, D.M. Grace, and M.E. Bramwell. 1969. The expression of genetic information. A study with hybrid animal cells. *J. Cell Sci.* **4:** 499–525.

Harris, H., J.F. Watkins, C.E. Ford, and G.I. Schoefl. 1966. Artificial heterokaryons of animal cells from different species. *J. Cell Sci.* **1:** 1–30.

Harris, H., J.F. Watkins, G.L.M. Campbell, E.P. Evans, and C.E. Ford. 1965. Mitosis in hybrid cells derived from mouse and man. *Nature* **207:** 606–608.

Henle, G., F. Deinhardt, and A. Girardi. 1954. Cytolytic effects of mumps virus in tissue cultures of epithelial cells. *Proc. Soc. Exp. Biol. Med.* **87:** 386–393.

Hittelman, W.N. and P.N. Rao. 1974a. Premature chromosome condensation. I. Visualization of X-ray induced chromosome damage in interphase cells. *Mutat. Res.* **23:** 251–258.

————. 1974b. Premature chromosome condensation. II. The nature of chromosome gaps produced by alkylating agents and ultraviolet light. *Mutat.Res.* **23:** 259–266.

————. 1975. The nature of adriamycin-induced cytotoxicity in Chinese hamster cells as revealed by premature chromosome condensation. *Cancer Res.* **35:** 3027–3035.

Horibata, K. and A.W. Harris. 1970. Mouse myelomas and lymphomas in culture. *Exp. Cell Res.* **60:** 61–77.

Howell, J.I. and J.A. Lucy. 1969. Cell fusion induced by lysolecithin. *FEBS Lett.* **4:** 147.

Johnson, R.T. and H. Harris. 1969a. DNA synthesis and mitosis in fused cells. I. HeLa homokaryons. *J. Cell Sci.* **5:** 603–624.

————. 1969b. DNA synthesis and mitosis in fused cells. II. HeLa-chick erythrocyte heterokaryons. *J. Cell Sci.* **5:** 625–643.

————. 1969c. DNA synthesis and mitosis in fused cells. III. HeLa-Ehrlich heterokaryons. *J. Cell Sci.* **5:** 645–697.

Johnson, R.T. and P.N. Rao. 1970. Mammalian cell fusion. Induction of premature chromosome condensation in interphase nuclei. *Nature* **226:** 717–722.

————. 1971. Nucleo-cytoplasmic interactions in the achievement of nuclear synchrony in DNA synthesis and mitosis in multinucleate cells. *Biol. Rev.* **46:** 97–155.

Jones, C., P. Wuthier, and T.T. Puck. 1975. Genetics of somatic cell surface antigens. III. Further analysis of the A_L marker. *Somatic Cell Genet.* **1:** 235–246.

Jones, C., F.-T. Kao, B. Moore, D. Patterson, and T.T. Puck. 1976. Human gene locations achieved by means of human-Chinese hamster (CHO-K1) auxotrophic cell hybridization: Human gene mapping 3. *Birth Defects. Orig. Artic. Ser.* **12:** 387–390.

Joshi, P.C. and E. Ball. 1968. Growth of isolated palisade cells of *Aradis hypogaea in vitro*. *Dev. Biol.* **17:** 308–325.

Kao, F.T. and T.T. Puck. 1970. Linkage studies with human-Chinese hamster cell hybrids. *Nature* **228:** 329–332.

Kao, K.N. and M.R. Michayluk. 1974. A method for high-frequency intergeneric fusion of plant protoplasts. *Planta* **115:** 355–367.

Kartha, K.K., O.L. Gamborg, F. Constabel, and K.N. Kao. 1974. Fusion of rapeseed and soybean protoplasts and subsequent division of heterokaryocytes. *Can. J. Bot.* **52:** 2435–2536.

Kit, S., D.R. Dubbs, L.J. Piekarski, and T.C. Hsu. 1963. Deletion of thymidine kinase activity from L cells resistant to bromodeoxyuridine. *Exp. Cell Res.* **31:** 297–312.

Kit, S., W.-C. Leung, G. Jorgensen, D. Trkula, and D.R. Dubbs. 1974. Acquisition of chick cytosol thymidine kinase activity by thymidine kinase-deficient mouse fibroblast cells after fusion with chick erythrocytes. *J. Cell Biol.* **63:** 505–514.

Klein, E. and F. Wiener. 1971. Loss of surface-bound immunoglobulin in mouse A9 and human lymphoblast hybrid cells. *Exp. Cell Res.* **67:** 251.

Klobutcher, L.A. and F.H. Ruddle. 1979. Phenotype stabilization and integration of transferred material in chromosome-mediated gene transfer. *Nature* **280:** 657–660.

Köhler, G. and C. Milstein. 1975. Continuous cultures of fused cells secreting antibody of predefined specificity. *Nature* **256:** 495–497.

————. 1976. Derivation of specific antibody producing tissue culture and tumor cell lines by cell fusion. *Eur. J. Immunol.* **6:** 511–519.

Kraemer, K.H., H.G. Coon, and J.H. Robbins. 1973. Cell-fusion analysis of different inherited mutations causing defective DNA repair in *Xeroderma pigmentosum* fibroblasts. *J. Cell Biol.* **59:** 176a.

Kraemer, K.H., H.G. Coon, P.A. Petinga, S.F. Barrett, A.E. Rahe, and J.H. Robbins. 1975. Genetic heterogeneity in *Xeroderma pigmentosum*. Complementation groups and their relationship to DNA repair rates. *Proc. Natl. Acad. Sci.* **72:** 59–63.

Krauss, E. 1884. Beiträge zur Riesenzellenbildung in epithelialen Geweben. *Arch. Pathol. Anat.* **95:** 249–272.

Kucherlapati, R.S., R.M. Baker, and F.H. Ruddle. 1975. Ouabain as a selective agent in the isolation of somatic cell hybrids: Human gene mapping 2. *Birth Defects. Orig. Artic. Ser.* **11:** 192–193.

Kunkel, H.G. 1964. Myeloma proteins and antibodies. *Harvey Lect.* **9:** 219–242.

Lambert, R.A. 1912. The production of foreign body giant cells *in vitro. J. Exp. Med.* **15:** 510–515.

Lange, O. 1875. Ueber die Entstehung der blutkörperhaltigen Zellen und die Metamorphosen des Blutes im Lymphsack des Frosches. *Arch. Pathol. Anat.* **65:** 27–35.

Langhans, T. 1868. Ueber Riesenzellen mit wandständigen Kernen in Tuberkeln und die fibröse Form des Tuberkels. *Arch. Pathol. Anat.* **42:** 382–404.

———. 1870. Beobachtungen über Resorption der Extravasate und Pigmentbildung in denselben. *Arch. Pathol. Anat.* **49:** 66–116.

Lewis, W.H. 1927. The formation of giant cells in tissue cultures and their similarity to those in tuberculous lesions. *Am. Rev. Tuberc.* **15:** 616–628.

Littlefield, J.W. 1964. Selection of hybrids from matings of fibroblasts *in vitro* and their presumed recombinants. *Science* **145:** 709–710.

Lucy, J.A., Q.F. Ahkong, F.C. Cramp, D. Fisher, and J.I. Howell. 1971. Cell fusion without viruses. *Biochem. J.* **124:** 46–47.

Luginbühl, D. 1873. Der Mikrococcus der Variola. *Verh. Phys.-Med. Ges. Würzburg* **4:** 97–113.

Lyons, L.B., R.P. Cox, and J. Dancis. 1973. Complementation analysis of maple syrup urine disease in heterokaryons derived from cultured human fibroblasts. *Nature* **243:** 533–535.

Macklin, C.C. 1916. Binucleate cells in tissue culture. *Contr. Embryol.* **13:** 69–106. Carnegie Institution of Washington, D.C.

Marston, R.Q. 1958. Cytopathogenic effects of haemadsorption virus type 1. *Proc. Soc. Exp. Biol. Med.* **98:** 853–856.

Matsuya, Y., H. Green, and C. Basilico. 1968. Properties and uses of mouse-human hybrid cell lines. *Nature* **220:** 1199–1202.

McBride, O.W. and H.L. Ozer. 1973. Transfer of genetic information by purified metaphase chromosomes. *Proc. Natl. Acad. Sci.* **70:** 1258–1262.

McDougall, J.K., R. Kucherlapati, and F.H. Ruddle. 1973. Localization and induction of the human thymidine kinase gene by adenovirus 12. *Nat. New Biol.* **245:** 172–175.

McKusick, V.A. 1978. *Mendelian inheritance in man*, 5th edition (and later editions). Johns Hopkins University Press, Baltimore.

Meera Khan, P. 1971. Enzyme electrophoresis on cellulose acetate gel: Zymogram patterns in man-mouse and man-Chinese hamster somatic cell hybrids. *Arch. Biochem. Biophys.* **145:** 470–483.

Melchers, G. and G. Labib. 1974. Somatic hybridization of plants by fusion of protoplasts. I. Selection of light resistant hybrids of "haploid" light sensitive varieties of tobacco. *Mol. Gen. Genet.* **135:** 277–294.

Melchers, G., M.D. Sacristan, and A.A. Holder. 1978. Somatic hybrid plants of potato and tomato regenerated from fused protoplasts. *Carlsberg Res. Commun.* **43:** 203–218.

Merwin, R.M. and G.H. Algire. 1959. Induction of plasma cell neoplasms and fibrosarcomas in Balb/c mice carrying diffusion chambers. *Proc. Soc. Exp. Biol. Med.* **101:** 437–439.

Metchnikoff, E. 1884. Untersuchungen über die intracelluläre Verdauung bei wirbellosen Thieren. *Arb. Zool. Inst. Univ. Wien* **5:** 141–168.

Michel, W. 1937. Über die experimentelle Fusion pflanzlicher Protoplasten. *Arch. Exp. Zellforsch.* **20:** 230–252.

Migeon, B.R. and C.S. Miller. 1968. Human-mouse somatic cell hybrids with single human chromosome (group E). Link with thymidine kinase activity. *Science* **162:** 1005–1006.

Migeon, B.R., R.A. Norum, and C.M. Corsaro. 1974. Isolation and analysis of somatic hybrids derived from two human diploid cells. *Proc. Natl. Acad. Sci.* **71:** 937–941.

Miller, D.A., O.J. Miller, V.G. Dev, S. Hashmi, R. Tantravi, L. Medrano, and H. Green. 1974. Human chromosome 19 carries a poliovirus receptor gene. *Cell* **1:** 167–173.

Miller, O.J., P.W. Allderdice, D.A. Miller, W.R. Breg, and B.R. Migeon. 1971. Human thymidine kinase gene locus. Assignment to chromosome 17 in a hybrid of man and mouse cells. *Science* **173**: 244–245.

Minna, J.D. and H.G. Coon. 1974. Human x mouse hybrid cells segregating mouse chromosomes and isozymes. *Nature* **252**: 401–404.

Minna, J.D., T.H. Marshall, and P. Shaffer-Berman. 1976. Gene mapping by somatic cell hybridization in species other than man: Human gene mapping 3. *Birth Defects Orig. Artic. Ser.* **12**: 422–426.

Mohit, B. and K. Fan. 1971. Hybrid cell line from a cloned immunoglobulin-producing mouse myeloma and a nonproducing mouse lymphoma. *Science* **171**: 75–77.

Müller, J. 1838. *Ueber den feineren Bau und die Formen der krankhaften Geschwülste*, part I, tables I–IV. Reimer, Berlin.

Nabholz, M., V. Miggiano, and W. Bodmer. 1969. Genetic analysis with human-mouse somatic cell hybrids. *Nature* **223**: 358–363.

Okada, Y. 1958. The fusion of Ehrlich's tumor cells caused by H.V.J. virus *in vitro*. *Biken J.* **1**: 103–110.

———. 1962. Analysis of giant polynuclear cell formation caused by HVJ virus from Ehrlich's ascites tumor cells. *Exp. Cell Res.* **26**: 98–128.

Okada, Y. and F. Murayama. 1965a. Multinucleated giant cell formation by fusion between cells of different strains. *Biken J.* **8**: 7–21.

———. 1965b. Multinucleated giant cell formation by fusion between cells of two different strains. *Exp. Cell Res.* **40**: 154–158.

Okada, Y. and J. Tadokoro. 1962. Analysis of giant polynuclear cell formation caused by HVJ virus from Erlich's tumour cells. II. Quantitative analysis of giant polynuclear cell formation. *Exp. Cell Res.* **26**: 108–118.

———. 1963. The distribution of cell fusion capacity among several cell strains or cells caused by HVJ. *Exp. Cell Res.* **32**: 417–430.

Okada, Y., F. Murayama, and J. Tadokoro. 1965. Cell fusion reaction caused by HJV (haemagglutinating virus of Japan). *Symp. Cell. Chem.* **15**: 159–177.

Palser, H.R. and P.J. McAlpine. 1976. An immunochemical method for the detection of the expression of human gene loci in human-rodent somatic cell hybrids with special reference to the GPI locus. *Biochem. Genet.* **14**: 661–670.

Parkman, R., A. Hagemeier, and E. Merler. 1971. Production of a human gamma-globulin fragment by human thymocyte-mouse fibroblast hybrid cells. *Fed. Proc.* **30**: 530.

Periman, P. 1970. IgG synthesis in hybrid cells from antibody-producing mouse myeloma and an L cell substrain. *Nature* **228**: 1086–1087.

Pernis, B., G. Chippino, A.S. Kelus, and P.G.H. Gell. 1965. Cellular localization of immunoglobulins with different allotypic specificities in rabbit lymphoid tissues. *J. Exp. Med.* **122**: 853–875.

Pettengill, O.S. and G.D. Sorenson. 1967. Murine myeloma cells in suspension culture. *Exp. Cell Res.* **47**: 608–613.

Pontecorvo, G. 1975. Production of mammalian somatic cell hybrids by means of polyethylene glycol treatment. *Somatic Cell Genet.* **1**: 397–400.

Pontecorvo, G., P.N. Riddle, and A. Hales. 1977. Time and mode of fusion of human fibroblasts treated with polyethylene glycol (PEG). *Nature* **265**: 257–258.

Potter, M. and C.R. Boyce. 1962. Induction of plasma-cell neoplasms in strain BALB/c mice with mineral oil and mineral oil adjuvants. *Nature* **193**: 1086–1087.

Potter, M. and M.A. Leon. 1968. Three IgA myeloma immunoglobulins from the Balb/c mouse: Precipitation with pneumococcal C polysaccharide. *Science* **162**: 369–371.

Prescott, D.M., D. Myerson, and J. Wallace. 1972. Enucleation of mammalian cells with cytochalasin B. *Exp. Cell Res.* **71**: 480–485.

Puck, T.T., P. Wuthier, C. Jones, and F.-T. Kao. 1971. Genetics of somatic mammalian cells. Lethal antigens as genetic markers for study of human linkage groups. *Proc. Natl. Acad. Sci.* **68**: 3102–3106.

Rastinejad, F. and H. Blau. 1993. Genetic complementation reveals a novel regulatory role for 3' untranslated regions in growth and differentiation. *Cell* **72**: 903–917.

Ringertz, N.R. and L. Bolund. 1974. Reactivation of chick erythrocyte nuclei by somatic cell hybridization. *Int. Rev. Exp. Pathol.* **8**: 83–116.

Ringertz, N.R. and R.E. Savage. 1976. *Cell hybrids*. Academic Press, New York.

Ringertz, N.R., S.-A. Carlsson, T. Ege, and L. Bolund. 1971. Detection of human and chick nuclear antigens in nuclei of chick erythrocytes during reactivation in heterokaryons with HeLa cells. *Proc. Natl. Acad. Sci.* **68**: 3228–3232.

Robin, C. 1849. Sur l'existence de deux espèces nouvelles d'éléments anatomiques qui se trouvent dans le canal médullaire des os. *C. R. Soc. Biol.* 149–150.

Röhme, D. 1974. Prematurely condensed chromosomes of the Indian muntjac. A model system for the analysis of chromosome condensation and banding. *Hereditas* **76**: 251–258.

Roizman, B. 1962. Polykaryocytosis induced by viruses. *Proc. Natl. Acad. Sci.* **48**: 228–234.

Rokitansky, C. 1855. *Lehrbuch der pathologischen Anatomie*, 3rd edition, vol.1, pp. 294–295. Braumüller, Vienna.

Ruddle, F.H., V.M. Chapman, F. Ricciuti, M. Murnane, R. Klebe, and P. Meera Kahn. 1971. Linkage relationships of seventeen human gene loci as determined by man-mouse somatic cell hybrids. *Nat. New Biol.* **232**: 69–73.

Schneider, J.A. and M.C. Weiss. 1971. Exxpression of differentiated functions in hepatoma cell hybrids. I. Tyrosine aminotransferase in hepatoma-fibroblast hybrids. *Proc. Natl. Acad. Sci.* **68**: 127–131.

Schor, S.L., R.T. Johnson, and C.A. Waldren. 1975. Changes in the organization of chromosomes during the cell cycle: Response to ultraviolet light. *J. Cell Sci.* **17**: 539–566.

Schubert, D., J. Jobe, and M. Cohn. 1968. Mouse myelomas producing precipitory antibody to nucleic acid bases and/or nitrophenyl derivatives. *Nature* **220**: 882–885.

Schwaber, J. and E.P. Cohen. 1973. Human X mouse somatic cell hybrid clone secreting immunoglobulins of both parental types. *Nature* **244**: 445–447.

Schwartz, A.G., P.R. Cook, and H. Harris. 1971. Correction of a genetic defect in a mammalian cell. *Nat. New Biol.* **230**: 5–8.

Shimizu, N., Y. Shimizu, R.S. Kucherlapati, and F.H. Ruddle. 1976. Immunochemical detection of human enzymes in hybrid cells. *Cell* **7**: 123–130.

Silagi, S.G. 1967. Hybridization of a malignant melanoma cell line with L cells *in vitro*. *Cancer Res.* **27**: 1953–1960.

Siniscalco, M., B.B. Knowles, and Z. Steplewski. 1969. Hybridization of human diploid strains carrying X-linked mutants and its potential in studies of somatic cell genetics. *Wistar Inst. Symp. Monogr.* **9**: 117–136.

Sinkovics, J.G. 1982. An interesting early observation concerning specific antibody-producing hybridomas. *J. Infect. Dis.* **145**: 135.

Sinkovics, J.G., B. Drewinko, and E. Thornell. 1970. Immunoresistant tetraploid lymphoma cells. *Lancet* **I**: 139–140.

Sorieul, S. and B. Ephrussi. 1961. Karyological demonstration of hybridization of mammalian cells *in vitro*. *Nature* **190**: 653–654.

Sperling, K. and P.N. Rao. 1974. The phenomenon of premature chromosome condensation. Its relevance to basic and applied research. *Humangenetik* **23**: 235–258.

Steward, F.C., M.O. Mapes, and K. Mears. 1958. Growth and organized development of cultured cells. II. Organization in cultures from freely suspended cells. *Am. J. Bot.* **45**: 705–708.

Szpirer, J., C. Szpirer, and J.C. Wanson. 1980. Control of serum protein production in hepatocyte hybridomas. Immortalization and expression of normal hepatocyte genes. *Proc. Natl. Acad. Sci.* **77**: 6616–6620.

Szybalski, W., E.H. Szybalska, and G. Ragni. 1962. Genetic studies with human cell lines. *Natl. Cancer Inst. Monogr.* **7**: 75–89.

Thompson, E.B. and T.D. Gelehrter. 1971. Expression of tyrosine aminotransferase activity in somatic cell heterokaryons. Evidence for negative control of enzyme expression. *Proc. Natl. Acad. Sci.* **68**: 2589–2593.

Trujillo, J.M., M.J. Ahearn, R.J. Pienta, C. Gott, and J.G. Sinkovics. 1970. Immuno-competence of leukemic murine lymphoblasts: Ultrastructure, virus and globulin production. *Cancer Res.* **30**: 540–545.

Unakul, W., R.T. Johnson, P.N. Rao, and T.C. Hsu. 1973. Giemsa banding in prematurely condensed chromosomes obtained by cell fusion. *Nat. New Biol.* **242**: 106–107.

Unna, P.G. 1896. *The histopathology of the diseases of the skin*, p. 637. Clay, Edinburgh.

Van Someren, A., A. Westerveld, A. Hagemeijer, J.R. Mees, P. Meera Kahn, and O.B. Zaalberg. 1974a. Human antigen and enzyme markers in man-Chinese hamster somatic cell hybrids: Evidence for synteny between HL-A, PGM_3, ME_1, and 1PO-B loci. *Proc. Natl. Acad. Sci.* **71:** 962–965.

Van Someren, H., H. Beijersbergen van Henegouwen, W. Los, E. Wurzer-Figurelli, B. Doppert, M. Verrloet, and P. Meera Kahn. 1974b. Enzyme electrophoresis on cellulose acetate gel II. Zymogram patterns in man-Chinese hamster somatic cell hybrids. *Humangenetik* **25:** 189–201.

Vasil, V. and A.C. Hildebrandt. 1965. Differentiation of tobacco plants from single, isolated cells in microcultures. *Science* **150:** 889–892.

Virchow, R. 1858. Reizung und Reisbarkeit. *Arch. Pathol. Anat.* **14:** 1–63.

Waldren, C.A. and R.T. Johnson. 1974. Analysis of interphase chromosome damage by means of premature chromosome condensation after X- and ultraviolet-irradiation. *Proc. Natl. Acad. Sci.* **71:** 1137–1141.

Warthin, A.S. 1931. Occurrence of numerous large giant cells in the tonsils and pharyngeal mucosa in the prodromal stage of measles. *Arch. Pathol.* **11:** 864–874.

Watkins, J.F. and D.M. Grace. 1967. Studies on the surface antigens of interspecific mammalian cell heterokaryons. *J. Cell Sci.* **2:** 193–204.

Weigert, C. 1874. *Anatomische Beiträge zur Lehre von den Pocken*, p. 40. Breslau. (Quoted by Krauss 1884.)

Weiler, E. 1965. Differential activity of allelic gamma-globulin genes in antibody producing cells. *Proc. Natl. Acad. Sci.* **54:** 1765–1772.

Weiss, M.C. 1992. Contributions of Boris Ephrussi to the development of somatic cell genetics. *BioEssays* **14:** 349–353.

Weiss, M.C. and M. Chaplain. 1971. Expression of differentiation functions in hepatoma cell hybrids: Reappearance of tyrosine aminotransferase inducibility after the loss of chromosomes. *Proc. Natl. Acad. Sci.* **68:** 3026–3030.

Weiss, M.C. and H. Green. 1967. Human-mouse hybrid cell lines containing partial complements of human chromosomes and functioning human genes. *Proc. Natl. Acad. Sci.* **58:** 1104–1111.

Westerveld, A., R.P.L.S. Visser, P.M. Meera Khan, and D. Bootsma. 1971. Loss of human genetic markers in man-Chinese hamster somatic cell hybrids. *Nat. New Biol.* **234:** 20–24.

Willecke, K. and F.H. Ruddle. 1975. Transfer of human gene for hypoxanthine-guanine phosphoribosyl transferase via isolated human metaphase chromosomes into mouse L cells. *Proc. Natl. Acad. Sci.* **72:** 1792–1796.

Williams, A.F., G. Galfré, and C. Milstein. 1977. Analysis of cell surfaces by xenogeneic myeloma-hybrid antibodies. Differentiation antigens of rat lymphocytes. *Cell* **12:** 663–673.

Wullems, G.J., J. van der Horst, and D. Bootsma. 1975. Incorporation of isolated chromosomes and induction of hypoxanthine phosphoribosyltransferase in Chinese hamster cells. *Somatic Cell Genet.* **1:** 137–152.

Wuthier, P., C. Jones, and T.T. Puck. 1973. Surface antigens of mammalian cells as genetic markers. *J. Exp. Med.* **138:** 229–244.

Yerganian, G. and M.B. Nell. 1966. Hybridization of dwarf hamster cells by UV-inactivated Sendai virus. *Proc. Natl. Acad. Sci.* **55:** 1066–1073.

6

SOMATIC CELL GENETICS
AND MOLECULAR BIOLOGY
COME TOGETHER

No attempt can be made here to review the history of modern molecular biology, but there are a number of technical advances in that discipline that bear directly on the further development of somatic cell genetics, and these must be understood if the interaction of molecular and cellular biology over the last two decades is to be sensibly recorded. The essential problem that faced somatic cell geneticists at the end of the 1970s was how to push the genetic analysis of somatic cells beyond the limits that had so far been reached and, ultimately, of course, how to reduce genetic loci to sequences of nucleotides. It was not simply a matter of nucleic acid chemists turning their attention to eukaryotic cells. How the spectacular methodological developments in the structural analysis of nucleic acids could be applied to higher cells was not at first clear, and many important advances in cell biology had to be made before the genes of higher cells became accessible to molecular analysis. The aim of this chapter is to review not only the main elements of the recent dramatic progress in the analysis of nucleic acids, including that branch of the subject now known as recombinant DNA technology, but also to show how parallel advances in the techniques of cell biology were not only contributory, but also indispensable, to the ultimate success of the joint venture.

HYBRIDIZATION OF NUCLEIC ACIDS

At the heart of the technological revolution in nucleic acid manipulation lay a reaction that stemmed from the complementary structure of the two strands of DNA itself. As mentioned in Chapter 3, Doty and his collaborators showed in 1960 that two single strands of DNA having nucleotide sequences that were complementary to each other would, under appropriate conditions, combine to form a stable duplex. This phenomenon, which became known as nucleic acid hybridization, was first demonstrated by heating double-stranded DNA until the two strands separated and then showing that the strands reannealed in a specific manner when the temperature was lowered (Doty [Fig. 40] et al. 1960; Marmur [Fig. 40] and Lane 1960). Furthermore, it was shown that RNA would similarly anneal to DNA with which it was complementary (Hall and Spiegelman 1961), and that, at lower temperatures, annealing could take place between nucleic acids in which complementarity was imperfect (Schildkraut,

FIGURE 40 Paul Doty (1920–) (left) and Julius Marmur (1922–) (right). Doty and Marmur showed in 1960 that two single strands of DNA having nucleotide sequences that were complementary to each other would, under appropriate conditions, combine to form a stable duplex. This reaction, which came to be known as nucleic acid hybridization, was central to the development of methods for the recognition and isolation of genes. This photograph, taken at about the time the discovery was made, shows Marmur holding a large centrifuge tube from which he had just spooled a preparation of DNA. *(Courtesy of Dr. Julius Marmur.)*

Marmur, and Doty 1961). These findings meant that sequences of nucleotides could, in principle, be used to identify and seek out complementary or closely related sequences wherever in the cell they might find themselves.

It will be seen that the principle of annealing by complementarity was exploited at almost every stage in the development of recombinant DNA technology, but, to begin with, nucleic acid hybridization was used to study the composition of nucleic acids in solution. A vast literature was quickly generated in which the kinetics of hybridization in solution were used to explore the properties and relatedness of various nucleic acid preparations. Britten and Kohne (1968) showed that mammalian DNA contained fractions that reannealed much more rapidly than the bulk of the material and concluded that

FIGURE 41   Robert Holley (1922–1993) determined the first complete sequence of a nucleic acid, the alanine transfer RNA of yeast. *(Courtesy of the Nobel Foundation.)*

this complex DNA contained sequences that were to a variable extent reiterated. The fraction that reannealed most rapidly appeared to be composed of relatively short sequences of nucleotides that were closely related if not identical. This fraction, by misappropriation, acquired the sobriquet 'satellite DNA'. Hoyer, McCarthy, and Bolton (1964) showed that these specific annealing reactions could take place when the DNA was suspended in agar. This observation was of great importance from the technical point of view, for the fractionation of nucleic acids on semi-solid substrates formed the basis of many subsequent developments in the analysis of their structure.

DETERMINATION OF NUCLEOTIDE SEQUENCE IN RNA

Because of the unmanageable size of DNA molecules and, despite intensive research, the absence of any reproducible method for achieving their limited scission rather than their random degradation, early work on the determination of nucleotide sequence was limited to relatively small and homogeneous families of RNA. In 1966, Holley (Fig. 41) published the first complete sequence of a nucleic acid, the alanine transfer RNA (4S) of yeast. This feat was achieved by direct chemical fractionation and showed that sequence analysis of nucleic acids was possible, even if only for molecules of rather low molecular weight that could be prepared relatively easily in an intact and homogeneous state. The next step was taken by Brownlee, Sanger, and Barrell (1967, 1968) who determined the complete sequence of the 5S ribosomal RNA from *Escherischia coli*. This represented a sequence of 120 residues, a substantial advance on the 75–85 residues found in transfer RNAs. By 1970, some 17 transfer RNAs had been completely sequenced, and partial sequences had been published for large parts of the major ribosomal RNA components and the small RNA bacteriophages (MS2, R17, f2, Qβ) (Gilham 1970). In 1976, Fiers and his colleagues presented the complete nucleotide sequence of the RNA of MS2 bacteriophage, which harboured three genes coding for three different proteins. Fiers et al. (1976) also established the sequences that terminated transcription of the genes (the stop codons in contemporary jargon) and discovered that the RNA contained long sequences that were not translated. For some years after their discovery, the mode of replication of RNA viruses remained a mystery, for animal cells were not thought to contain any enzyme that could make direct copies of RNA. This mystery was penetrated by Baltimore (1970) and Temin and Mizutani (1970) who showed that the first step in the cycle of replication was the production of a DNA transcript of the RNA by an enzyme that was named reverse transcriptase. It was subsequently found that the transcribed DNA was integrated into the genome of the cell where it could be transcribed into multiple copies of the RNA that had been originally introduced into the cell by the virus particle. This discovery was not only an interesting piece of biology in its own right, it also provided a reagent of great usefulness in the subsequent development of analytical techniques for the study of gene expression, for it was soon found that the reverse transcriptase coded by the RNA viruses could be used under appropriate conditions to make DNA copies (cDNA) from virtually any sequence of RNA nucleotides. The importance of this reaction in determining which genes are actually expressed in any cell type or in any tissue will presently become apparent.

THE DISCOVERY OF RESTRICTION ENZYMES

However, the analysis of nucleotide sequence in DNA remained frustrated by the protracted failure to devise methods for generating reproducible homogeneous fragments of DNA of manageable size. The solution to this problem came from an unexpected quarter. It had been known since the early 1950s that DNA transfected from one strain of bacterium to another was often rapidly degraded in the recipient organism. Linn and Arber (1968) showed that *E. coli* contained an enzyme that methylated certain DNA nucleotide residues and another that could distinguish between methylated and unmethylated DNA, sparing the former but degrading the latter to an assortment of smaller pieces. This discriminating degradative enzyme was termed a 'restriction' nuclease because, by degrading the unmethylated DNA of certain bacteriophages, it restricted their growth in foreign strains of bacteria. Although the early restriction enzymes detected in *E. coli* did recognise specific unmethylated sites in the DNA, they did not cleave the DNA at these sites and did not, in practice, provide the controlled reproducible scission required for sequence analysis. However, in 1970, Smith and his colleagues discovered a restriction enzyme in *Haemophilus influenzae* that discriminated between the DNA of the parent organism and that of *E. coli*. This enzyme, named *Hind*III, cleaved the double-stranded DNA of bacteriophage T7 into about 40 fragments. It was purified and the nucleotide sequence that it recognised was determined (Smith and Wilcox 1970; Kelly and Smith 1970). In the following year, Danna and Nathans (1971) demonstrated that when *Hind*III acted on the circular DNA of simian virus 40, it generated 11 fragments that could be resolved by electrophoresis in an agarose gel. By studying the order in which these fragments were generated as the enzyme digestion proceeded, it was possible to establish the relative positions of the restriction enzyme recognition sites in the simian virus 40 DNA. Other restriction enzymes that recognised different sites in the DNA were soon discovered and, in 1973, Danna, Sack, and Nathans published the first restriction enzyme cleavage map. This was deduced from overlapping fragments produced by the digestion of simian virus 40 DNA by three different restriction enzymes, one from *Haemophilus influenzae*, one from *Haemophilus parainfluenzae*, and one from *E. coli*. This work precipitated an avalanche of work on restriction enzymes that continues to the present day; something close to 200 such enzymes have now been described. The specific sequences recognised by these enzymes ranged from four to eight nucleotides, and since the longer sequences occurred less frequently in DNA than the shorter ones, enzymes recognising the former generated larger fragments than those recognising the latter. Moreover, it was found that whereas some restriction enzymes cut the DNA at the same point in both strands, thus generating what came to be known as 'blunt ends', others made asymmetrical scissions in which the cut in one strand of the DNA was separated by a distance of two or more nucleotides from the cut in the other strand. Such asymmetrical fragments generated scissions with single-stranded termini that were capable of annealing to complementary sequences. Single-stranded termini were dubbed 'cohesive' or 'sticky' ends and, as will be discussed presently, were of great importance in the development of recombinant DNA technology.

DETERMINATION OF NUCLEOTIDE SEQUENCE IN DNA

A review by Salser in 1974 entitled 'DNA sequencing techniques' reveals that there were still at that time essentially no methods for sequencing DNA directly. To establish the nucleotide sequence of a piece of DNA it was necessary first to transcribe it into RNA and then sequence the RNA by the limited and cumbersome methods then available. The advent of restriction enzymes and the realisation that they could be used to generate a range of reproducible fragments of DNA completely transformed the situation. Within two or three years, powerful and relatively simple techniques for sequencing DNA had been devised, and it soon became apparent that the most economical way of sequencing RNA was first to transcribe it into DNA. The methodology of nucleotide sequence determination in DNA is dominated by the name of Frederick Sanger (Fig. 42). In 1975, Sanger and Coulson published for the first time a direct method for sequencing DNA. This was named the 'plus-minus' method because it was based on a polymerization reaction carried out in the absence of one of the four nucleotides required to make DNA and a degradative reaction carried out in the presence of one of the DNA nucleoside triphosphates. In the 'minus' reaction all the oligonucleotide chains formed terminated at the nucleotide preceding the one omitted from the reaction; in the 'plus' reaction degradation stopped at the nucleotide corresponding to the added nucleoside triphosphate because the latter was incorporated into the DNA by an exchange reaction. The denatured oligonucleotide chains, marked by prior labelling with phosphorus-32, were then separated by electrophoresis on gels sensitive enough to discriminate between them. The autoradiographs produced from these gels permitted the sequence of nucleotides in the DNA to be read off. With gels containing eight electrophoretic tracks, the sequence of 50–100 nucleotides could be determined in a single experiment. There were

FIGURE 42   Frederick Sanger (1918–), in collaboration with A.R. Coulson, provided the first direct method for determining the nucleotide sequence of DNA. He and his colleagues then developed an improved procedure based on chain termination, and this remains to the present day the standard method for sequencing DNA. Some 25 years earlier, Sanger had been the first to determine the complete amino-acid sequence of a protein (insulin). *(Courtesy of Dr. Frederick Sanger.)*

some ambiguities in the plus-minus method, and it had the disadvantage that the first 15 nucleotides in the DNA could not be determined. However, the method was used successfully to unravel essentially the complete sequence of the DNA in the bacteriophage ΦX174 (Sanger et al. 1977). This work established the sites at which transcription was initiated and terminated and also revealed that, in the case of two pairs of ΦX174 genes, the same region of DNA coded for two different messages that were transcribed from different reading frames. This was the first indication that the structure of genes might prove to be more complex than envisaged in simple models of co-linearity between gene and protein.

A simpler method than the plus-minus procedure was devised by Maxam and Gilbert (1977). The DNA was terminally labelled with phosphorus-32 and then subjected to four separate chemical reactions. One of these broke the DNA chains preferentially at guanine residues, one preferentially at adenine residues, one with equal efficiency at cytosine and thymine residues, and one at cytosine residues only. The fragments thus generated were again separated by gel electrophoresis and the sequence of nucleotides read off from the resulting autoradiographs. Up to 100 nucleotides from the labelled termini of the DNA could be sequenced in one run. The Maxam and Gilbert procedure, because of its relative simplicity, enjoyed a period of widespread but transient success. It was, however, soon displaced by a more efficient procedure that was applicable to much longer stretches of DNA. This was the chain-termination method devised by Sanger, Nicklen, and Coulson (1977). In this procedure, 2'3'-dideoxynucleoside triphosphates were used to interrupt DNA polymerization. Four separate polymerization reactions were carried out in the presence of a small amount of each of the four dideoxynucleoside triphosphates. Incorporation of the dideoxy derivatives terminated the growth of the DNA polymers at the corresponding nucleotides, and the interrupted chains, pre-labelled with phosphorus-32, were then resolved by electrophoresis on gels that were sensitive enough to discriminate between oligonucleotides that differed in length by only one residue. Sequence could be read directly from autoradiographs of the gels (Fig. 43). The chain-termination procedure of Sanger, Nicklen, and Coulson soon became the standard method for sequencing DNA and, with minor modifications, has remained so. The complete sequence of simian virus 40 DNA was published by two groups in 1978 (Fiers et al. 1978; Reddy et al. 1978), and other complete sequences soon followed: several bacteriophages, mitochondrial DNA, the *lac* operon of *E. coli* and, eventually, even the huge genome of the Epstein-Barr virus that contained some 170,000 bp. During the 1980s, techniques for sequencing DNA based on chain termination became increasingly mechanised, and finally automatic DNA-sequencing machines were marketed.

THE ENZYMOLOGY OF DNA SYNTHESIS AND REPAIR

The development of DNA sequencing methods relied not only on the prior discovery of enzymes that cut DNA at specific sites but also on the availability of enzymes that could synthesize DNA chains. The first of these to be described was the enzyme known as DNA polymerase I (Kornberg 1960). For almost a decade, it was generally assumed that this was the one enzyme responsible for the replication of DNA, but genetic experiments with *E. coli.* showed that cells in which this enzyme was inactivated by a mutation could still replicate their DNA (de Lucia and Cairns 1969). This initiated a search for other enzymes with DNA polymerase activity. It quickly became clear that there were at least three DNA polymerases in *E. coli*, and it appeared likely that DNA polymerase III was the one primarily responsible for DNA replication in that organism. Further investigation brought further complexity, and by 1975 a review of the subject listed, in addition to the three DNA polymerases, half a dozen reasonably well characterised proteins involved in the replication of *E. coli* (Gefter 1975). By 1978, this number had almost doubled (Wickner 1978). The enzymology of DNA replication in animal cells was at that time very obscure and, largely because of the paucity of informative mutants, our understanding of the process is still far from complete. The study of DNA repair yielded a comparable range of enzymatic activities. Enzymes were discovered that excised DNA at sites that had been damaged, others that removed the aberrant nucleotide sequences, and others that correctly filled in the empty spaces. Of crucial importance for the later development of recombinant DNA technology was the discovery of the enzyme DNA ligase which had the ability to rejoin the ends of DNA strands that had been cleaved. That such an enzyme existed was indicated by the prior demonstration that genetic recombination involved the breaking and rejoining of DNA molecules (Meselson and Weigle 1961; Kellenberger, Zichichi, and Weigle 1961). DNA ligase, which was essential for both DNA replication and DNA repair, was discovered more or less simultaneously, and apparently independently, by five different groups (Cozzarelli et al. 1967; Gefter, Becker, and

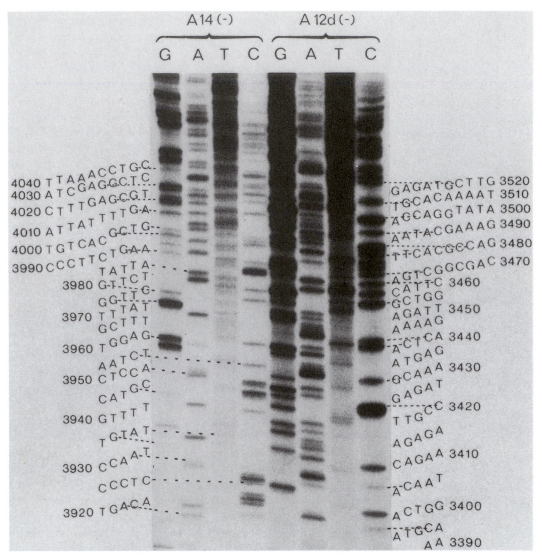

FIGURE 43 Autoradiograph of an acrylamide gel in which the nucleotide sequence of the DNA of the bacteriophage ΦX174 was determined by the method of chain termination. (Reprinted, with permission, from Sanger, Nicklen, and Coulson 1977.)

Hurwitz 1967; Gellert 1967; Olivera and Lehman 1967; Weiss and Richardson 1967).

By the mid-1970s, then, investigators interested in the manipulation or analysis of DNA had at their disposal a substantial armamentarium of enzymes for synthesizing DNA on a template of either DNA or RNA, repairing DNA, cleaving it at specific sites and rejoining the fragments. But progress also required the development of chemical methods for the synthesis of oligonucleotides of any desired nucleotide sequence. These were necessary not only as primers for synthetic reactions, but also as probes for specific sequences that could be detected by complementary strand hybridization. Chemical synthesis of oligonucleotides initially proceeded by the sequential condensation of mononucleotides or dinucleotides blocked at either the 5' or 3' termini. This was a laborious process that reached its limit at oligo-nucleotides containing approximately 20 residues. More rapid and efficient procedures were soon devised that permitted the synthesis of much longer nucleotide sequences (Heyneker et al. 1976; Gait and Sheppard 1977); and eventually the complete chemical synthesis of a gene was achieved (Khorana 1979). Oligonucleotide synthesis, like DNA sequencing, was progressively mechanised during the 1980s, and eventually rapid automatic machines for this purpose became available.

ANALYSIS OF RESTRICTION ENZYME DIGESTS

An important technical innovation based on the hybridization of com-plementary nucleotide sequences was introduced by Southern in 1975. In this procedure, ever since known as the 'Southern blot', DNA cleaved into frag-ments by one or more restriction enzymes was first subjected to electro-phoresis on an agarose gel. The resolved fragments were then transferred by a flow of buffer to a nitrocellulose filter closely apposed to the gel. The pattern of fragments in the gel was found to be faithfully replicated on the nitrocel-lulose filter. If this was then exposed to radioactively labelled probes, either purified nucleic acids or oligonucleotides, under conditions that permitted stable hybridization to take place, autoradiographs revealed the location of the complementary sequences (Fig. 44). The Southern blot has since found the widest application in the identification and purification of genes, in detecting structural changes within them and in revealing evolutionary homologies. With the advent of 'pulsed-field' gel electrophoresis, which permitted the separation of very large tracts of DNA (Schwartz and Cantor 1984), the practi-cal range of the Southern blot was further extended. Southern's methodology was found to be applicable to RNA as well as DNA (Alwine, Kemp, and Stark 1977). In this case, an RNA preparation was subjected to electrophoresis and then transferred by blotting to diazobenzyloxymethyl paper where it could similarly be reacted with labelled probes. The procedure for RNA was given, and has retained, the facetious name 'Northern blot'.

METHODS FOR LINKING TOGETHER DNA FROM DIFFERENT SOURCES: THE BIRTH OF RECOMBINANT DNA TECHNOLOGY

Recombinant DNA technology is based on the fact that it is possible to link stretches of DNA from two different sources to make a single hybrid molecule—the mechanistic equivalent of genetic recombination. It has been noted that some restriction enzymes cut the two strands of DNA symmetrical-ly at the same point, but that others make asymmetric cuts at different points on the two strands. The first of the operationally useful restriction enzymes, *Hin*dIII, was found to cut the DNA symmetrically to produce fragments with blunt ends; but Mertz and Davis (1972) discovered that one of the restriction enzymes of *E. coli* (*Eco*RI) cut asymmetrically and hence produced fragments with single-stranded termini in which the nucleotide sequences were complementary. Mertz (Fig. 45) and Davis realised that such termini were cohesive and would therefore permit the annealing of any fragments of DNA

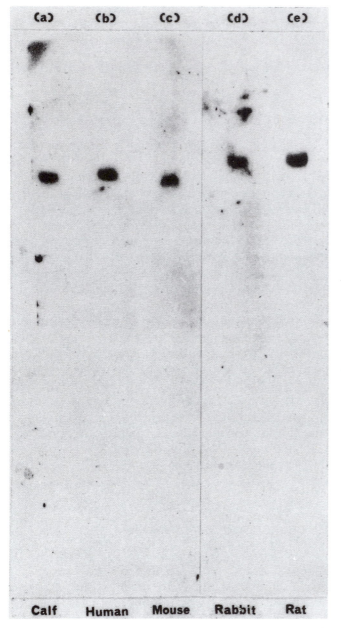

FIGURE 44 A Southern blot. Preparations of DNA from five mammalian species were digested by the restriction enzyme *Eco*RI and hybridized with ribosomal RNA. The ribosomal genes are identified in the autoradiograph. (Reprinted, with permission, from Southern 1975.)

FIGURE 45 Janet Mertz (1949–), in collaboration with R.W. Davis, discovered that one of the restriction enzymes of *Escherichia coli* cut DNA asymmetrically to produce fragments with single-stranded termini in which the nucleotide sequences were complementary. Such termini, being cohesive, permitted the annealing of any fragments of DNA that were cut by this enzyme. This observation can be regarded as the starting point of recombinant DNA technology. *(Courtesy of the Cold Spring Harbor Laboratory Archives.)*

that had been cut by this enzyme. This annealing of cohesive or sticky ends thus provided a general method for producing hybrid molecules from any sources of DNA, provided the DNA contained sites that could be recognised by an enzyme that cut asymmetrically. A year later, Lobban and Kaiser (1973) devised a method for linking together the blunt ends formed by restriction enzymes that cut both strands of DNA at the same point. This was done by adding single-stranded complementary sequences to the ends of the two DNA strands, a reaction catalyzed by an enzyme from calf thymus known as 'terminal transferase'. Initially, complementary homopolymers were added, but with the development of increasingly efficient procedures for oligonucleotide synthesis, oligonucleotide 'linkers' were constructed that could incorporate any desired sequence of nucleotides such as, for example, a recognition site for a restriction enzyme. Jackson, Symons, and Berg (Fig. 46) (1972), using the method of Lobban and Kaiser (1973), ligated genes from the lambda bacteriophage and the galactose operon of *E. coli* into the circular DNA of simian virus 40.

BACTERIAL PLASMIDS AS GENE VECTORS

A critical step in the further development of this technology, and one that was patented, was taken by Cohen et al. (1973; see Fig. 47 [Cohen] and Fig. 48 [Boyer]). These authors introduced fragments of foreign DNA into bacterial plasmids which could then replicate in bacteria and thus form clones of bacterial cells that contained the interpolated DNA fragments. The first plasmid to be used was pSC101 which had only a single site recognised by the *Eco*R1 restriction enzyme so that treatment of the circular DNA with this enzyme simply converted it into a linear form with cohesive ends. DNA from another

FIGURE 46 Paul Berg (1926–) and his collaborators, developing the discovery made by Mertz and Davis, ligated genes from the lambda bacteriophage and the galactose operon of *Escherichia coli* into the circular DNA of simian virus 40. These constructs were the first recombinant DNA molecules to be made. *(Courtesy of the Nobel Foundation.)*

plasmid, and later DNA from other sources, was similarly digested with *Eco*R1 to produce a random assortment of fragments with cohesive ends, and these fragments were then linked to the linearized DNA of pSC101. The provision of general methods for cloning defined stretches of DNA had revolution-

FIGURE 47 Stanley Cohen (1935–), in collaboration with Herbert Boyer (Fig. 48), introduced fragments of foreign DNA into bacterial plasmids which could then replicate in bacteria and thus form clones of bacterial cells that contained the interpolated DNA fragments. These plasmids were the first of a still growing plenitude of gene vectors. *(Courtesy of Dr. Stanley Cohen.)*

FIGURE 48 Herbert Boyer (1936–). *(Courtesy of Dr. Herbert Boyer.)*

ary consequences. The significance of the work was at once recognised, but also the possibility that the hybrid plasmids might constitute a biological hazard. 'Disabled' vectors that could replicate only under certain strictly defined conditions, and safe strains of *E. coli* in which they could be propagated, were therefore produced (Blattner et al. 1977; Curtiss et al. 1977). With these advances, a major industry was generated. Vectors incorporating selectable markers such as antibiotic-resistance genes and markers that permitted clones harbouring a particular gene to be identified soon became available (Bolivar et al. 1977). DNA 'libraries' from human and other sources were constructed by treating the DNA with restriction enzymes and then incorporating the random fragments generated into bacterial plasmids. Colonies grown from bacterial cultures infected with such plasmids could then be screened for the presence of particular genes by hybridization with radioactively labelled probes, either defined nucleic acids (Grunstein and Hogness 1975) or, where the necessary sequence information was available, synthetic oligonucleotides (Suggs et al. 1981). At a later stage, radioactive probes were replaced by equally or more sensitive probes based on fluorescent, chemiluminescent or linked enzyme reactions (Urdea et al. 1988). The first identifiable mammalian gene to be inserted into a plasmid was the gene coding for a rabbit β-globin (Rougeon, Kourilsky, and Mach 1975), and, a year later, Rabbitts (1976) and Maniatis et al. (1976), working with cDNA synthesized *in vitro* from β-globin messenger RNA, cloned a full length copy of this gene in bacteria.

LAMBDA BACTERIOPHAGES, 'COSMIDS' AND YEAST ARTIFICIAL CHROMOSOMES AS GENE VECTORS

As vectors of foreign DNA, bacterial plasmids had two disadvantages. The first was that there was a severe limitation on the size of the DNA molecules that they could accommodate; and the second was that those plasmids that had taken in larger stretches of DNA grew more slowly than those that had taken in smaller pieces, so that longer stretches of DNA were poorly represented in plasmid libraries. These disadvantages prompted a search for more capacious vectors. The first successful extension in this direction was the use of disabled lambda bacteriophages (Blattner et al. 1977; Leder, Tiemeier, and Enquist 1977). Lambda bacteriophages were able to accommodate stretches of DNA up to 15 kb in length. In order to facilitate DNA sequencing, which required the DNA to be melted, filamentous single-stranded DNA phages were also adopted as cloning vectors. These were derivatives of the M13 bacteriophage and gave rise to a widely used series of constructs named pUC (Messing and Vieira 1982; Yanisch-Peron, Vieira, and Messing 1985). During the process of packaging within the phage head, lambda DNA forms concatemers by annealing cohesive single-stranded termini (*cos* ends). By means of these termini, foreign DNA could be interpolated and later excised (Hohn and Murray 1977). Hybrids formed in this way between lambda phages and plasmids were found to be able to accommodate up to 45 kb and were given the name 'cosmids' (Collins and Hohn 1978; Hohn and Collins 1980). Yeast artificial chromosomes (YACs) were a further development designed to permit the cloning of still longer stretches of DNA. YACs were elaborate constructs that combined the replication origins of the yeast chromosome together with centromeric and telomeric sequences (Burke, Carle, and Olsen 1987). These constructs were able to replicate autonomously and had the capacity to accommodate inserts several hundred kb in length. In libraries constructed with YACs, not only full length genes, but also neighbouring regulatory sequences, and, in some cases, even clusters of genes were adequately represented.

ANIMAL VIRUSES AS GENE VECTORS

Animal viruses, too, were used as vectors for foreign DNA. Adenoviruses were introduced by Thummel, Tjian, and Grodzicker (1981) because of the high level of viral protein synthesis that they induced. The vaccinia virus genome was too large for direct insertion of a foreign gene, but this could be achieved indirectly by exploiting recombination within the cell. The vaccinia virus was introduced into the cell together with a bacterial plasmid that contained the gene to be expressed; this was flanked by the initiation site of the vaccinia virus genome and some regulatory sequences (Panicali and Paoletti 1982; Mackett, Smith, and Moss 1982). Since infection with these animal viruses normally killed the host cell, the effect of the transfected gene could be studied only transiently, and such vectors have found their main application in the production of experimental vaccines. It had been observed that infection of insects with pathogens known as baculoviruses often resulted in a massive production of viral coat protein. Baculoviruses were therefore modified to serve as vectors for genes encoding proteins that were required in large amounts (Smith, Summers, and Fraser 1983). For some proteins, production via baculoviruses proved to be the most efficient way to accumulate large amounts of material.

EXPRESSION VECTORS

For a number of experimental, and even commercial, purposes, it was necessary to ensure that the particular mammalian gene, or cDNA, transmitted by a vector to a bacterial cell was expressed there at a high level. Several modifications were therefore made to the range of vectors that have been discussed in order to stimulate the transcription of the intercalated gene and to stabilise the message that it produced. Vectors modified in this way were called 'expression vectors' (Chang et al. 1978; Villa-Komaroff et al. 1978; Guarente et al. 1980). Promoter regions of bacterial, bacteriophage or viral origin were introduced into the construct and so arranged that the gene to be studied was inserted at a site next to the promoter and in the right orientation. When it became known that messenger RNA from animal cells was terminated and perhaps stabilised by the addition of polyadenylic acid sequences (Lim and Canellakis 1970; Edmonds, Vaughan, and Nakazato 1971; Lee, Mendecki, and Brawerman 1971), nucleotide sequences that ensured terminal polyadenylation were also inserted into the vector. In some cases, it was found that if a mammalian gene was fused with a bacterial gene, the resulting fusion protein was produced by the transfected bacterium at a very high level. Expression vectors continued to be modified over the years in order to improve the yield of particular products or to facilitate the detection of productive clones; and this remains a fertile industry. Clones producing defined proteins could be efficiently selected by immunological procedures, at first by the use of radioactively labelled antibodies and later by antibodies coupled to chromogenic reagents of various kinds (Broome and Gilbert 1978; Helfman et al. 1983; Young and Davis 1983).

THE INSERTION OF FOREIGN GENES INTO ANIMAL CELLS

The application of all these technological advances to the somatic cells of animals required the development of methods for the efficient introduction of isolated foreign genes into such cells. Cell fusion and chromosome transfer had shown that foreign genes could be stably maintained by cells in culture when these genes were present in chromosome fragments too small to be detected by standard optical methods. But if anything in the way of genuine fine structure genetics was to be achieved, it was obviously necessary to devise robust and precise techniques for transferring single genes or well defined groups of genes from one cell to another. As has already been mentioned, earlier attempts by Szybalski and his colleagues to do this with naked DNA as the vehicle were judged to be inconclusive. However, in 1973, Graham and van der Eb showed that DNA from human adenovirus 5 could be transferred to cells in culture, with retention of function, if the DNA was precipitated onto the cells by means of calcium phosphate. The particulate complex of DNA and calcium phosphate was apparently taken into the cells by endocytosis, and the DNA was then released in a functional state. Goff and Berg (1976) used simian virus 40 DNA, linked to the origin of replication of lambda phage, to construct hybrid vectors for foreign genes. These constructs were introduced into the cell as naked DNA suspended in a solution containing DEAE-dextran (Mertz and Berg 1974), and the transfected DNA could be continuously propagated as a hybrid virus. In addition to dextrans, polybasic compounds such as spermine and spermidine were also used to facilitate the entry of DNA into the cells, but, for several years, no procedure proved more effective than precipitation with calcium phosphate. Bacchetti and Graham (1977) used calcium phosphate to introduce purified herpes simplex virus DNA into thymidine-kinase-deficient human cells and showed that transfected cells could be selected that produced thymidine kinase with the characteristics of the herpes virus enzyme. Wigler et al. (1977) transferred the herpes simplex thymidine kinase gene to mouse cells within a fragment of herpes DNA produced by digestion with a restriction enzyme. Wigler et al. (1978) extracted the total DNA from a cell line that harboured only a single copy of the herpes simplex thymidine kinase gene and with this material succeeded in transferring the gene to other cells.

In 1978, Schimke and his colleagues showed that when cell lines in culture were exposed to the folic acid antagonist methotrexate, resistant variants could be obtained in which the dihydrofolate reductase gene was selectively amplified, apparently by tandem duplication (Alt et al. 1978; Schimke et al. 1978). In some cases, as much as a 200-fold amplification of the gene was observed. Using this knowledge, Wigler and his colleagues showed that when a selectable gene was transfected into a cell together with a gene that was not subject to selection, both genes were incorporated into the genome of the host cell at the one site; and when selection for the selectable gene was applied, both genes were amplified synchronously (Wigler et al. 1979; Perucho, Hanahan, and Wigler 1980). The selectable gene used in these experiments was again the herpes simplex virus thymidine kinase, and the genes not subject to selection were the rabbit β-globin gene and the genes of a bacteriophage and a plasmid. These experiments represented a major methodological advance because they provided a general method of incorporating into cells markers for which there was no selective system. 'Co-transfection', in which an unselected gene was incorporated together with a selectable gene, usually an antibiotic-resistance marker, quickly became standard practice. Mulligan, Howard, and Berg (1979) showed that monkey kidney cells transfected with a hybrid construct in which simian virus 40 genes were linked to the rabbit β-globin gene synthesized rabbit β-globin.

'SHUTTLE' VECTORS

The first evidence that the genes of bacterial viruses could be stably incorporated and expressed in mammalian cells appears to have been the work of Merril, Geier, and Petricciani (1971). These authors showed that when cells from a congenitally galactosaemic patient were transfected with a lambda phage containing the complete galactose operon of *E. coli*, the missing enzyme activity (α-D-galactose-1-phosphate uridyl transferase) reappeared. A phage construct in which there was a mutation that inactivated the galactose operon failed to restore enzyme activity. The further development of bacteriophages as gene vectors lay in the incorporation of markers that permitted the one vector to be selected in cells of different genera. Such constructs, moveable from bacteria to yeasts or animal cells, were called 'shuttle' vectors. The first of these was a construct made by Mulligan and Berg (1981). This was based on a bacteriophage into which the bacterial gene for xanthine guanine phosphoribosyl transferase was incorporated. This gene, in appropriate media, enabled the phage to be selected in both bacteria and animal cells. The hybrid vector, which also contained the simian virus 40 origin of replication, was able to accommodate long stretches of DNA encompassing complete gene sequences. It appeared to be stably integrated into the genome of the host cell, for it was not lost from the cells when the selection pressure was removed. Robins et al. (1981) provided the decisive evidence that genes transfected in this way were stably integrated. They showed that when a variant gene for human growth hormone was transfected into a line of liver cells, between 50 and 100 copies of it were localised at one site in one particular chromosome. In different experiments integration occurred in other chromosomes, but always at one site. The transfected genes could not be detected in the cytoplasm of the cell. The earliest shuttle vectors, based on defective simian virus 40, required co-transfection with a helper virus carrying genes that complemented the defect in the substituted simian 40 genome; but later, specialised animal cell lines were developed in which the missing simian virus 40 genes were already integrated. One such cell line, COS, harboured an integrated copy of the simian virus 40 T-antigen gene. The protein encoded by this gene was known to induce the replication of simian virus 40 DNA, so that COS cells automatically stimulated the replication of any vector that incorporated the simian virus 40 origin of replication. Numerous shuttle vectors have since been developed containing markers selectable in bacteria, usually ampicillin resistance, coupled with markers selectable in animal cells such as resistance to neomycin or hygromycin.

RETROVIRUSES AS GENE VECTORS

As mentioned previously, recombinant adenovirus and vaccinia virus, although effective expression vectors for foreign genes, had the disadvantage that they killed the host cell and thus had only a transient effect. However, with retroviruses stable integration and continuous replication of the transfected gene could be achieved. This was first done with an avian retrovirus (spleen necrosis virus) containing the herpes simplex thymidine kinase gene (Shimotohno and Temin 1981). The gene to be stably integrated into a recipient cell was first inserted into the cloned cDNA of the retrovirus from which genes essential for replication were removed. This vector was then transfected into a so-called 'packaging' cell. The packaging cell harboured a provirus that contained all the genes necessary for packaging the retrovirus except the nucleotide sequence recognised by the packaging mechanism. The provirus could not replicate itself, but it provided all that was necessary to replicate the DNA of the vector carrying the intercalated gene. This DNA was transcribed into RNA which could then be harvested in the form of infectious RNA particles. When these were introduced into any other susceptible cell, the RNA was transcribed into DNA by reverse transcriptase, and the DNA was integrated into the host genome (Mann, Mulligan, and Baltimore 1983; Cepko, Roberts, and Mulligan 1984). More recently, the stable transfection of YACs into mammalian cells has been achieved with the help of polyethylene glycol.

The YACs accommodated about 450 kb of human DNA and incorporated a gene coding for neomycin resistance that permitted successfully transfected cells to be selected (Pachnis et al. 1990).

GENE TRANSFER BY ELECTROPORATION, LIPOSOMES AND MICROINJECTION

The transfection of these various vectors into somatic cells was not uniformly successful, and methods other than precipitation with calcium phosphate were explored. In some situations, a mixture of polybrene (hexadimethrine bromide) and dimethylsulphoxide was found to give a higher yield of transfected cells than calcium phosphate (Chaney et al. 1986; Aubin, Weinfeld, and Paterson 1988), but a more generally applicable enhancement of transfection was achieved by a process that eventually acquired the name electroporation. This technique was based on earlier work which showed that the application of high electric fields to suspensions of mammalian cells increased membrane permeability and, under appropriate conditions, induced cell fusion (Neumann and Rosenheck 1972, 1973; Zimmermann, Schulz, and Pilwat 1973). Zimmermann devised and marketed a cell fusion machine based on the controlled application of electric fields. Wong, Nicolau, and Hofschneider (1980) appear to have been the first to introduce an isolated gene, bacterial β-lactamase, into mammalian cells by electroporation. Wong and Neumann (1982) and Neumann et al. (1982) transfected the selectable herpes virus thymidine kinase gene into mouse cells lacking thymidine kinase, and Potter, Weir, and Leder (1984) transfected human immunoglobulin genes into mouse lymphocytes by this method. Simpler machines than that devised by Zimmermann soon became commercially available, and transfection of genes by electroporation became a standard laboratory procedure.

Another general method for introducing macromolecules into cells was to encapsulate them in artificial fat globules called liposomes which could fuse with the cell membrane and thus release their contents into the cell cytoplasm. Large unilamellar liposomes capable of carrying macromolecules were first produced by Papahadjopoulos et al. (1975). Using such liposomes, Ostro et al. (1978) inserted rabbit β-globin messenger RNA into a human cell line and provided evidence that this RNA was translated. Dimitriadis (1978) did the same thing with mouse lymphocytes. Fraley et al. (1980) transfected simian virus 40 DNA by means of liposomes, and Schaefer-Ridder, Wang, and Hofschneider (1982) transfected the thymidine kinase gene. Liposome-mediated transfer of genes was largely displaced by other transfection techniques but has recently been resurrected for possible clinical application. In some situations, microinjection of macromolecules into cells was the most direct way of studying their function. Microinjection techniques accurate enough for use with mammalian cells in culture were devised by Diacumakos (1973). Graessmann and Graessmann (1976) introduced the messenger RNA for simian virus T antigen into renal epithelial cells by microinjection and showed that it could induce replication of the cellular DNA. Diacumakos and Gershey (1977) microinjected simian virus 40 directly into the nuclei of cells in culture and showed that the injected virus was uncoated and that the viral genes were expressed. Capecchi (1980) further developed microinjection and converted it into a highly efficient technique for transforming cells. Klein et al. (1987) devised a method for delivering DNA into cells by means of high velocity microprojectiles. Tungsten particles onto which the DNA was adsorbed were shot directly into the cells. Microinjection has since been fully automated under computerised control and can be used in routine experiments involving large numbers of cells.

THE POLYMERASE CHAIN REACTION

A major advance in the identification, isolation and amplification of DNA sequences was the introduction of a process called the polymerase chain reaction (PCR) (Saiki et al. 1985; Mullis and Faloona 1987). By this process, any stretch of DNA for which some sequence information at the two ends was available could be amplified exponentially *in vitro*. This reaction was based on the knowledge that *E. coli* DNA polymerase I copied single-stranded DNA in the 5' to 3' direction but required a double-stranded region as a primer. The two strands of DNA containing the sequence to be amplified were separated by heating, and complementary oligonucleotides were then annealed to the two ends of the sequence on opposite strands. The double-stranded region so formed served as primers for the DNA polymerase which then extended the primers in the 5' to 3' direction thus copying the sequence to be amplified. The double-stranded DNA was again melted, the oligonucleotides annealed to the single strands and the polymerization reaction repeated. With each such cycle, requiring no more than a couple of minutes to perform, the number of copies of the target sequence was doubled. Single-stranded overhangs produced by the DNA polymerase accumulated only in a linear fashion and were rapidly diluted out by the exponential expansion of the sequences between the two oligonucleotide primers. In practice, this expansion fell a little short of the calculated exponential, but for a 110-bp fragment of the human β-globin gene a 200,000-fold amplification was achieved after 20 cycles. This corresponded to 85% of the theoretical yield (Mullis and Faloona 1987).

The *E. coli* DNA polymerase used in the original PCR procedure was inactivated at the temperature required to separate DNA into single strands so that fresh enzyme had to be added for each polymerase cycle. However, in 1976 a new DNA polymerase was discovered in the extreme thermophilic bacterium *Thermus aquaticus* which has its natural habitat in water at 75°C (Chien, Edgar, and Trela 1976). The optimal temperature for the mode of operation of this *Taq* DNA polymerase was found to be 72°C, so that the enzyme was not denatured at the temperature needed to melt DNA and thus did not have to be replenished with each PCR cycle (Saiki et al. 1988). Moreover, at the high temperatures at which the *Taq* polymerase operated, fewer copying errors were made (Eckert and Kunkel 1990). The introduction of PCR, especially with the simplification achieved by the use of the *Taq* enzyme, had dramatic consequences. Simple automatic PCR machines became available and the technique found so many applications that it is difficult to enumerate them. Perhaps the most important was that it was now possible to amplify and hence clone very rare sequences in a complex mixture of DNA molecules, even as few as one or two molecules in a cell. Preparing enough DNA for sequencing became overnight a routine procedure, and the detection of mutations in both experimental and clinical contexts was greatly simplified (Wong et al. 1987). Human DNA in hybrid cells containing predominantly mouse genetic material could be specifically amplified by means of probes that recognised human but not mouse sequences (Nelson et al. 1989). The presence of bacterial or viral DNA in cells or tissues could easily be detected even in paraffin sections (Laure et al. 1988; Ou et al. 1988; Brisson-Noël et al. 1989). With primers made from male-specific sequences on the Y chromosome, the sex of an embryo could be determined from biopsy specimens or even from a single cell (Handyside et al. 1989, 1990; Lo et al. 1989). Virtually every facet of recombinant DNA technology has now found some application for the polymerase chain reaction.

INHIBITION OF GENE ACTION BY 'ANTISENSE' RNA

The ability to introduce and stably integrate virtually any foreign gene into a somatic cell was obviously a major advance in the analysis of gene function. But it was of no less importance to be able to annul the function of a gene or modify it in an interpretable way. Two general approaches were devised for achieving this end. The first was to introduce specific 'antisense' RNA into the cell; the second was to inactivate the gene of interest by mutation. Antisense RNA was simply RNA that was complementary to, and hence capable of complexing with, the messenger RNA produced by the gene one wished to inactivate. There was ample earlier evidence that such complexes could impair function. It was known, for example, that complexes of this kind formed with ribosomal RNA inhibited translation. But the modern development of antisense RNA methodology began with the work of Zamecnik and Stephenson (1978). Zamecnik (Fig. 49) and Stephenson showed that replication of Rous sarcoma virus in tissue culture cells could be inhibited by a deoxynucleotide tridecamer complementary to the terminal nucleotides of the Rous sarcoma virus 35S RNA. Stephenson and Zamecnik (1978) showed that this effect was due to inhibition of the translation of the viral RNA. This work initiated a major effort to develop antisense RNA not only as an experimental tool but also as a possible therapeutic modality. In order to achieve continuous production of antisense RNA in the cell, Izant and Weintraub (1984) introduced a plasmid containing a DNA sequence that produced such RNA. These authors microinjected plasmids incorporating the gene for thymidine kinase together with a 100-fold excess of a plasmid containing this DNA in the reverse orientation in order to produce an excess of thymidine kinase antisense RNA. They found, however, that no more than a transient reduction in the level of thymidine kinase was produced. Numerous constructs incorporating antisense DNA coupled to an efficient promoter of transcription have since been transfected into mammalian cells in culture, but usually with only partial suppression of the action of the target gene. Nonetheless, in some cases where high levels of antisense RNA could be attained, or where the cells were given repeated doses of the antisense construct, complete suppression of the target gene was achieved (Griffin and Harris 1992). In order to use antisense RNA sequences for clinical therapeutic purposes, it was obviously necessary to be able to deliver them in a form that was stable to *in vivo* conditions and that penetrated the cell. Phosphorothioate and phosphoramidate derivatives of antisense oligonucleotides, which are less susceptible to degradation in biological fluids or within the cell, have shown promise in inhibiting the replication of human immunodeficiency virus (Agarwal et al. 1988); and, more recently, antisense oligonucleotides in which the phosphodiester backbone has been replaced by a polyamide (peptide nucleic acids) have been explored (Nielson et al. 1991).

FIGURE 49 Paul Zamecnik (1912–), in collaboration with M.L. Stephenson, showed that 'antisense' oligonucleotides could be used to inhibit the replication of Rous sarcoma virus. Zamecnik and Stephenson discovered transfer RNA in 1956. *(Courtesy of Dr. Paul Zamecnik.)*

INACTIVATION OF GENES BY SITE-DIRECTED MUTATION

Inducing site-directed mutations in somatic cells *in vitro* proved to be difficult. With the advent of recombinant DNA technology, it became a relatively straightforward matter to introduce mutations into DNA *in vitro* and to construct vectors of various kinds bearing these mutations. This could be done by inserting nucleotides (Heffron, So, and McCarthy 1978), by deleting nucleotides (Lai and Nathans 1974; Mertz et al. 1975), by chemical modification of nucleotides (Chu et al. 1979), or, more generally, by replicating error-laden oligonucleotides annealed by complementarity to the target gene (Hutchinson et al. 1978; Wallace et al. 1981; Zoller and Smith 1982). However, although vectors bearing mutated cellular genes could easily be introduced into the cell, these transfected genes were obliged to act against a background of homologous genes that were functioning normally, except in the rare circumstance that the mutated gene happened to inactivate the resident normal gene by homologous recombination. Even so, to produce a null mutation both normal alleles would have had to be involved in homologous recombination events. There had been earlier experiments involving truncated human histocompatibility antigens that were interpreted as evidence of homologous recombination, but these were not subsequently substantiated. The first decisive evidence of homologous recombination taking place within mammalian cells was the work of Smithies et al. (1985). Using neomycin resistance as a selective marker, these workers succeeded in introducing foreign DNA sequences into the human chromosomal β-globin locus. The technique was developed further and made applicable to genes for which there was no selective system by Thomas and Capecchi (1987), Doetschman, Maeda, and Smithies (1988), and Mansour, Thomas, and Capecchi (1988), all of whom induced site-directed mutations in mouse embryonic stem cells. This was a development of great importance for, although only one of the two alleles was inactivated in these cells, they could be used to populate mouse embryos and eventually, by breeding, to produce mice in which all cells were homozygous for the targeted mutation (Zimmer and Gruss 1989). This development, which was named transgenesis, will be the subject of more detailed treatment later in this chapter.

GENES IN PIECES: INTRONS, EXONS AND RNA SPLICING

We have now to consider how the application of these remarkable technological developments advanced our understanding of the structure of genes and of their mode of operation in somatic cells. This was a saga of repeated surprises, of which perhaps the most dramatic was the discovery that genes were not always simple, unbroken sequences of coding nucleotides; in some cases the coding sequences within the one gene were found to be interrupted by sequences that did not appear to code for anything at all. This discovery was made more or less simultaneously by two groups working with the DNA of adenovirus (Berget, Moore, and Sharp [Fig. 50] 1977; Chow, Gelinas, Broker, and Roberts [Fig. 51] 1977). Just how unexpected such a finding was at the time can be gathered from the title of the paper by Chow et al. which read: "An amazing sequence arrangement at the 5′ ends of adenovirus 2 messenger RNA". Electron micrographs of hybrids formed between the messenger RNA of this virus and its DNA showed that there were regions of the DNA that did not hybridize with the completed messenger RNA; the transcripts from these regions had to be spliced out in order to form the continuous sequence of completed messenger RNA (Fig. 52). It was quickly shown that this state of affairs was also to be found in the genes of vertebrates, in chick ovalbumin by Breathnach, Mandel, and Chambon (1977) and in rabbit β-globin by Jeffreys and Flavell (1977). The splicing out of non-coding RNA transcripts and their intranuclear degradation provided at least a partial answer to a puzzle that arose in 1960 when Harris and his colleagues presented evidence, at that time inexplicable, that much of the RNA made in the cell nucleus was actually broken down within it (Harris 1963; Harris et al. 1963). In an article in *Nature*, Gilbert (1978) proposed that the coding regions of the split genes be called exons and the intervening sequences introns, and this nomenclature was adopted. Gilbert also proposed that exons might correspond to functional domains in proteins, and that non-coding sequences might play an evolutionary role in facilitating the emergence of polypeptides with new functions, an idea that had actually been canvassed more than a decade previously (Harris 1965). Blake (1978) provided structural evidence for the proposal that introns marked the boundaries between protein domains and thus gave support to the suggestion that new proteins might evolve as a consequence of exon rearrangement, a process that came to be called 'exon shuffling'. Early et al.

FIGURE 50 Phillip Sharp (1944–). Sharp and Richard Roberts (Fig. 51) independently discovered that genes were not always simple unbroken sequences of coding nucleotides; in some cases the coding sequences within the one gene were found to be interrupted by sequences that did not code for anything at all (split genes). *(Courtesy of the Nobel Foundation.)*

(1980b) showed that, in the case of one of the immunoglobulin genes, alternative modes of splicing the RNA transcript could give rise to two different messenger RNAs, a phenomenon reminiscent of the finding by Sanger et al. (1977) in bacteriophage ΦX174 that two different messages could be transcribed from the one gene by the use of different reading frames. Splice variants of this kind were named isoforms and were later found in many other proteins. Henikoff et al. (1986) showed that in *Drosophila* two unrelated proteins could be encoded by genes located on opposite strands of the DNA at the one site, and this was also shown for two unrelated rat proteins by Lazar et al. (1989). Treisman et al. (1982) appears to have been the first to show that faulty splicing could give rise to a diseased state, one form of thalassaemia.

REITERATED DNA SEQUENCES

With the advent of DNA sequencing, it became apparent that the sequence reiteration that Britten and Kohne (1968) had deduced from nucleic acid hybridization kinetics encompassed a number of very different kinds of repetitive DNA. The satellite DNA that annealed most rapidly and that could easily be separated from the bulk of the genome by ultracentrifugation was found to be composed of short sequences of nucleotides reiterated many times in a tandem fashion. In man, sequences of this kind called 'minisatellites' were found to be composed of a unit of 15–100 bp that was reiterated up to about 50 times. Moreover, it transpired that the degree of polymorphism in minisatellites was such that no two individuals gave the same fingerprint when

FIGURE 51 Richard Roberts (1943–). *(Courtesy of the Nobel Foundation.)*

these components were digested with restriction enzymes and resolved on gels (Jeffreys, Wilson, and Thein 1985). This extreme polymorphism lent itself to the almost unequivocal identification of individuals from samples of their DNA (minute samples after the introduction of the polymerase chain reaction), and this procedure was soon widely accepted for forensic purposes. Other repetitive elements were found to be widely dispersed throughout the genome of mammalian cells but not tandemly reiterated (Jelinek et al. 1980). These were classified into two categories, the short and the long interspersed elements (*sines* and *lines*) (Singer 1982). Their function remains obscure, but, in some cases, evidence was obtained that they were in all probability derived from an RNA intermediate by reverse transcription. An interesting degree of homology was found between one such repetitive sequence and a cytoplasmic 7S RNA that was involved in intracellular protein transport (Weiner 1980). The *Alu* family of repetitive elements (so-called because it contains a recognition sequence for the restriction enzyme *Alu*I) was found to be characteristic of the human genome (Duncan et al. 1981; Schmid and Jelinek 1982). It was subsequently used as a template for the isolation of human nucleotide sequences from interspecific hybrid cells by means of the polymerase chain reaction (*Alu* PCR) (Nelson et al. 1989). The complete sequencing of the *Alu* repeats showed that they were terminated by a polyadenylic acid tail, which provided further support for the view that they were derived at some stage from an RNA precursor.

GENE DUPLICATIONS AND PSEUDOGENES

It had been known since the 1960s that ribosomal genes were amplified, notably in *Xenopus laevis*, and this amplification, as described in Chapter 3, enabled Gall and Pardue (1969) to locate these genes by *in situ* hybridization with ribosomal RNA. Wellauer et al. (1974) showed that the amplified genes

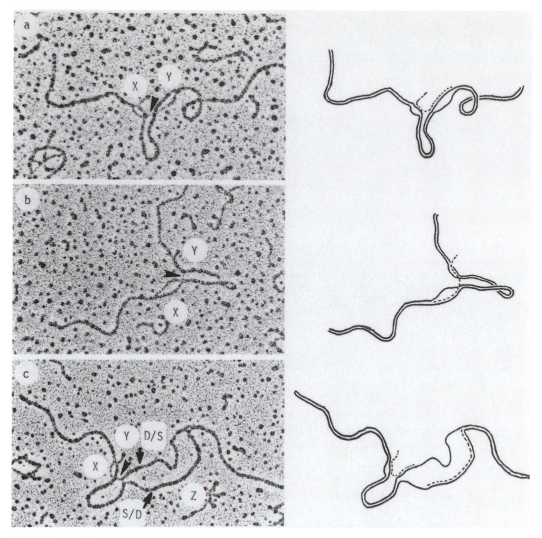

FIGURE 52 Electron micrographs of DNA from adenovirus 2 hybridized with messenger RNA produced by the virus. The DNA contains loops that do not hybridize with the messenger RNA, thus indicating that the gene involved is interrupted by nucleotide sequences that are not represented in the mature message: the first evidence of 'genes in pieces'. (Reprinted, with permission, from Chow et al. 1977 [copyright Cell Press].)

were separated by 'spacer' regions of various lengths, and Arnheim and Southern (1977) showed that this was also true of mammals including man. Smith (1976) argued that repeated DNA sequences would inevitably evolve as a result of unequal crossing over unless restrained by selective pressure. The studies of Fritsch, Lawn, and Maniatis (1980) and Slauer, Shen, and Maniatis (1980) on the human α- and β-globin genes provided evidence that was consistent with the view that clusters of related genes were originally generated by gene duplications that were subsequently modified. Jacq, Miller, and Brownlee (1977) were the first to discover 'pseudogenes', a name that they

FIGURE 53   Barbara McClintock (1902–1992), decades before anyone else had given the matter a moment's thought, provided strong evidence for the view that genes were able to move from one site to another within the genome. *(Courtesy of the Nobel Foundation.)*

conferred on a gene copy that had been rendered inactive by structural modifications. The pseudogene discovered by Jacq, Miller and Brownlee was an inactive copy of the 5S DNA of *Xenopus laevis*; Proudfoot and Maniatis (1980) found a pseudogene in the α-globin gene cluster in man. Numerous pseudogenes have since been found, and, in the case of the rat α-tubulin gene, a pseudogene was generated by the intercalation within the gene of a repetitive element (Lemischka and Sharp 1982). Many evolutionary explanations have been given for the selective advantage that might be conferred by gene duplication. One theory, to which the observation of Lemischka and Sharp lent support, was that duplication would reduce the chance of essential genes being inactivated by the interpolation of moveable parasitic DNA sequences (Southern 1993).

MOVEABLE GENES

The idea that genes might move from one site to another has its origin in the work of McClintock (1957) on maize mutants. McClintock (Fig. 53) began work on these mutants in 1944 and provided a first account of her experiments at the Cold Spring Harbor Symposium in 1951 (McClintock 1952). These mutants were unstable and frequently reverted giving rise to clones of cells visible in the seeds as spots. McClintock was convinced that the inactivation of the responsible gene was due to the attachment of a moveable element, and that reactivation occurred when that element moved elsewhere. This interpretation met with widespread scepticism, and more than two decades were to elapse before McClintock's work began to be appreciated. The turning point was the discovery that in *E. coli* certain mutations were caused by the insertion into the gene of a segment of extraneous DNA. This same segment was soon found to be inserted into many different sites in the genome, and it was therefore difficult to avoid the conclusion that it was a moveable element that inactivated the gene in which it was lodged (Kleckner et al., 1975). These moveable elements in bacteria were named transposons, and the various mechanisms by which they were mobilized, replicated and integrated elsewhere were subjected to detailed study (Reed and Grindley 1981; Bender and Kleckner 1986). Similar elements were discovered in yeast (Cameron, Loh, and Davis 1979; Hicks, Strathern, and Klar 1979) and in *Drosophila* (Rubin and Spradling 1982; Laski, Rio, and Rubin 1986) where one of them, called the P element was adapted for use as a gene vector. There does not appear to be much evidence for the presence of transposons or similar moveable elements still active in the genomes of contemporary mammals, but, as mentioned previously, the characteristics of some of the reiterated sequences seen in these genomes, including that of man, and the presence of pseudogenes harbouring reiterated sequences, strongly suggest that transposons of some kind were involved in the evolutionary history of mammalian genes.

TRANSLOCATION OF DNA IN THE FORMATION OF ANTIBODY GENES

There is, however, another form of gene rearrangement that does take place in mammalian cells and that bears directly on at least one form of cellular differentiation. All antibodies are composed of a region in which the amino acid sequence is constant and a region in which it is highly variable. The discovery of this dramatic fact by Hilschmann and Craig (1965) at once initiated a wave of speculation about the genetic basis of such a huge variety of these curiously hybrid proteins. Among these speculations was the proposal by Dreyer and Bennett (1965) that the constant region of the antibody was coded by a single gene and the variable region by a large number of separate genes, and that the two elements were brought together into a single molecule by somatic recombination within the antibody-forming cell. Because few people then took the idea of moveable genes seriously, this proposal did not commend itself. However, as soon as Southern blotting was devised, its application to the DNA of antibody-forming cells at once revealed that the proposal of Dreyer and Bennett was essentially correct. Hozumi and Tonegawa (Fig. 54) (1976) found that when the fragments generated by a restriction enzyme from the DNA of a myeloma were probed with radioactive messenger RNA, only a single labelled band was detected; but a similar preparation of embryonic DNA revealed two bands. The conclusion was thus inevitable that genes that were separate in the embryo were somehow brought together during the differentiation of the antibody-forming cell. Further analysis showed decisively that the completed immunoglobulin gene was indeed formed by somatic recombination (Brack et al. 1978). Later work revealed that the mechanism of gene translocation was quite complex involving in some cases inversion of one of the genes, in others deletion of the intervening sequences (Davis et al. 1980; Early et al. 1980a). Alternative RNA splicing was also found to contribute to the generation of antibody diversity (Early et al. 1980b). A few years after the discovery of somatic recombination in antibody-forming cells, the cDNA for

FIGURE 54 Susumu Tonegawa (1939–), in collaboration with N. Hozumi, showed that, in the formation of an immunoglobulin molecule, genes that were separated from each other in the embryo were brought into apposition by somatic recombination within the antibody-forming cell. This was the first evidence of moveable gene sequences in animal cells. *(Courtesy of the Nobel Foundation.)*

the T-cell receptor was cloned. The T-cell receptor is a molecule on the surface of a subfamily of lymphocytes involved in executing cellular, as opposed to humoral, immune reactions; its function is to recognise and interact with antigens. When the receptor cDNA was sequenced it was found to have a structure that closely resembled that of immunoglobulins and to have been generated by similar somatic recombination events (Saito et al. 1984; Yanagi et al. 1984). It was, and still is, generally held that the gene translocation seen in the cells of the immune system was a phenomenon limited to this system and driven by the necessity to recognise a virtually inexhaustible number of antigenic configurations. However, translocation of genetic elements was also found to be the basis of antigenic variation in the surface glycoproteins of trypanosomes (Hoeijmakers et al. 1980; Bernards et al. 1981). It remains a possibility that somatic recombination may be involved in other forms of differentiation that are stably inherited at the cellular level.

GENE REGULATION: ENHANCERS, TRANSCRIPTION FACTORS AND DNA METHYLATION

Be that as it may, sequence analysis of DNA revealed complex regulatory mechanisms of a different kind in somatic cells. In addition to promoter regions, which stimulated transcription in a manner comparable to bacterial promoters, regulatory sequences were found at sites other than in close proximity to the 5' terminus of the gene. These regulatory sequences, named 'enhancers', were located at substantial distances from the gene and worked efficiently when present on either side of the gene or even within the gene itself. Enhancers were first detected in the genome of simian virus 40, where a deletion within a tandem duplication at some distance from the gene resulted in a massive reduction in transcription (Benoist and Chambon 1981). Moreover, it was shown that if this region was removed from the simian virus 40 genome and inserted next to a different promoter, it stimulated the transcription of the gene controlled by that promoter (Banerji, Rusconi, and Schaffner 1981). Structural analysis of enhancers showed that they were composed of multiple subunits some of which could be removed without impairing function (Herr and Clarke 1986). Remote enhancers of this kind were soon found associated with the genes of mammalian cells. Some, like the enhancer operative in antibody-forming cells, were tissue-specific and continuously active (Gillies et al. 1983); others were activated by external stimuli (Chandler, Maler, and Yamamoto 1983; Goodbourn, Zinn, and Maniatis 1985). It was, of course, at once assumed that the functioning of enhancers was controlled by proteins that interacted specifically with them, and such proteins were quickly found (Church et al. 1985; Davidson et al. 1986; Sen and Baltimore 1986). They were named 'transcription factors' and, when they were purified and their structure was determined, they were found to have two functional domains, one that interacted with the enhancer and one that stimulated transcription. Based on the structural features of the domains that interacted with the enhancer, transcription factors were found to fall into four general, but not mutually exclusive, classes: 'zinc-finger' proteins (Miller, McLachlan, and Klug 1985); 'leucine-zipper' proteins (Bohmann et al. 1987); 'helix-loop-helix' proteins (Murre et al. 1989); and 'homeodomain' proteins (Kissinger et al. 1990), so called because their structure was similar to proteins that had been found to be involved in the homeotic mutations of *Drosophila*. A detailed description of the structure and function of transcription factors is beyond the scope of this book, but their discovery at once made it clear that they were crucially involved in the expression of at least some differentiated traits.

There were those who held the view that transcription factors provided all that was needed to explain the process of differentiation which, it was generally agreed, must in some way be achieved by the activation of some genes and the inactivation of others. However, it was not immediately obvious how transcription factors could achieve the systematic transmission from one cell generation to the next of the complex differentiated states that characterised individual tissues—the heritable cellular differentiation that classical embryologists called 'determination'. Models based on self-sustaining differential levels of transcription factors were advanced to account for the stability of determination (see, for example, Blau 1992), and such models gained some direct support from observations showing that the extinction of differentiated traits in hybrid cells was in fact accompanied by modification and loss of essential transcription factors (Nitsch, Boshart, and Schütz 1993). These latter-day models involving self-generating or self-sustaining metabolic equilibria are reminiscent of ideas put forward a generation earlier when Novick and Weiner (1957) demonstrated how production of the inducible enzyme β-galactosidase in *E. coli* could be sustained even after the concentration of the inducer in the medium was reduced to a level far below that required to induce the synthesis of the enzyme in the first place. (For a discussion of these earlier models, see Harris 1974.) On the other hand, there was good evidence that stable and selective inhibition of gene activity could be achieved by structural changes in the DNA itself. The most thoroughly investigated of these was the selective methylation of DNA at certain cytosine residues, first described by Hotchkiss in 1948. A substantial body of work during the next three decades established that the methylation of DNA sequences was systematically associated with suppression or reduction of their transcription (Sager and Kitchin 1975; Mandel and Chambon 1979; McGhee and Ginder 1979). With the advent of DNA sequencing techniques, the precise nucleotide sequences recognised by the methylating enzyme (cytosine methylase) were determined (Gruenbaum, Cedar, and Razin 1982). Riggs (1975) and Holliday and Pugh (1975) put forward specific models for the replication of methylation patterns in DNA, and later work confirmed that methylation patterns could indeed be replicated. This appeared to be true not only for special situations such as the inactivation of the X chromosome (Mohandas, Sparkes, and Shapiro 1981; Graves 1982; Jones et al. 1982; Wolf and Migeon 1982) or the parental imprinting of chromosomes where the pattern of activity of the chromosome is stably modified by its parental origin (Cattanach 1986; Reik et al. 1987; Sapienza et al. 1987; Swain, Stewart, and Leder 1987), but also for tissue-specific DNA methylation patterns (Silva and White 1988). Finally, in support of earlier circumstantial evidence, Jackson, McCready, and Cook (1981) and Jackson and Cook (1985) demonstrated that transcription of DNA in eukaryotic cells was associated with elements that reflected a higher order structure in the cell nucleus. It would thus seem reasonable at present to conclude that, despite the attractiveness of self-sustaining metabolic equilibria as determinants of heritable differentiated states, structural modifications of the DNA are not excluded.

FURTHER DEVELOPMENT OF *IN SITU* HYBRIDIZATION

As might be expected, the development of recombinant DNA technology and DNA sequencing greatly enhanced the precision of gene mapping procedures and hence facilitated the identification and isolation of new genes. The direct localisation of genes by hybridization *in situ* with radioactive probes began, as discussed previously, with the localisation of the grossly amplified ribosomal genes in *Xenopus laevis*. Other cellular genes subject to amplification were also localised in this way (Stenman, Anisowicz, and Sager 1988). Using a plasmid containing a human α-globin cDNA labelled to a very high specific activity with iodine-125, Gerhard et al. (1981) succeeded in localising the α-globin gene cluster to chromosome 16. These authors exploited the ability of double-stranded DNA to form networks at the site where it annealed to chromosomal DNA that had been previously denatured with formamide. Harper, Ullrich, and Saunders (1981) were probably the first to localise a unique cellular gene by *in situ* hybridization. They used as a probe a recombinant plasmid containing a fragment of genomic human insulin DNA labelled by enzymatic incorporation of radioactive cytidine, adenosine and thymidine triphosphates. Network formation was encouraged by annealing the probe in the presence of dextran. But locating unique genes by *in situ* hybridization lay at the very limits of resolution of the method. The problem was that the signal to noise ratio against a background of non-specific labelling was often far too low. Zabel et al. (1983) improved the resolution of the technique by applying it to stretched prometaphase chromosomes and succeeded in localising the human amylase gene to chromosome 1p21, the proopiomelanocortin gene to 2p23 and the somatostatin gene to 3q28. Franke et al. (1989) partially overcame the problem of non-specific background labelling by an elaborate statistical treatment of the grain counts, but this procedure was too laborious to be generally adopted. Fan, Davis, and Shows (1990) introduced fluorescent probes, in principle more sensitive than radioactive probes, and Lichter et al. (1990) succeeded in constructing a high resolution map of human chromosome 11 by *in situ* hybridization with cosmid clones. However, locating a gene by *in situ* hybridization was only possible where enough sequence information about the gene was available to permit probes to be constructed. To search for unidentified genes new methods had to be devised. These new methods leant heavily on recombinant DNA technology and were at first collectively referred to as 'reverse genetics', an inept description later replaced by the term 'positional cloning'.

POSITIONAL CLONING: RESTRICTION FRAGMENT LENGTH POLYMORPHISM AND CHROMOSOME 'WALKING'

For the most part, positional cloning was driven by prior cytogenetic information or linkage data that gave an approximate location for the unidentified gene that was being sought. The limit of resolution of cytogenetic localisation was not very different from that given by linkage analysis, something in the region of 10^6–10^8 bp; the results given by *in situ* hybridization and by mapping with radiation hybrids fell within the same limits. Conventional cloning by means of vectors gave a resolution of approximately 10^2–5×10^4 bp, so that there was a very large 'resolution gap' that had to be bridged. If one wished to move from a cytogenetic marker to a particular gene, one was faced with the prospect of systematically analysing very large numbers of clones until a coding DNA sequence was reached that might permit a plausible gene to be isolated and further characterised. This analytic progression along the chromosome was called chromosome 'walking', and because it was exceedingly laborious, it was often, in practice, not feasible to walk the enormous distances (in terms of base pairs) that cytogenetic or somatic cell genetic methods delimited. A major advance was the discovery of restriction fragment length polymorphism (Kan, Golbus, and Dozy 1976). Single base pair changes were known to occur in DNA with great frequency, according to some estimates as frequently as one in every hundred or so base pairs. Such changes sometimes occurred at recognition sites for restriction enzymes; and if only one of the two allelic sites was affected, then this was reflected in Southern blots of the digested DNA by the presence of two bands, one shorter than the other. Kan, Golbus, and Dozy showed that the degree of linkage between the restriction fragment length polymorphism (RFLP) and a particular genetic disease gave information about the proximity of the RFLP to the gene defect determining that disease. And since RFLPs occurred frequently, they provided markers, progressively closer to the gene, from which chromosome walks could begin. Kan, Golbus, and Dozy also showed that RFLPs could be used for diagnostic purposes and to underpin genetic counselling. The very frequency of RFLPs led Botstein et al. (1980) to suggest that it would be possible to construct a complete genetic map in man based entirely on these polymorphisms.

IDENTIFICATION OF THE DUCHENNE MUSCULAR DYSTROPHY GENE

The first successful application of positional cloning was the identification of the gene which, when mutated, determined the X-linked genetic disease Duchenne muscular dystrophy. Limited normally to males, there were, however, some cases of the disease in women, and these were found to have a translocation between the X chromosome and an autosome. The autosome involved varied in different cases, but the breakpoint in the X chromosome was always on the short arm at Xp21 thus indicating that the gene responsible was in all probability located at or near the breakpoint. RFLPs and a probe that mapped to Xp21 confirmed the linkage (Murray et al. 1982). One of these translocations between X and an autosome involved a breakpoint at which ribosomal genes were known to be located. Ribosomal sequences could therefore be used as a marker to monitor the cloning of the genes at the breakpoint, thus providing direct access to the gene determining the abnormality (Worton et al. 1984). Kunkel et al. (1985), by means of a sensitive nucleic acid hybridization procedure, identified sequences on the short arm of the X chromosome that were absent in a case of Duchenne muscular dystrophy. Deletions at this site were then found in other cases of the disease, which made it probable that the crucial gene had been found, but additional evidence was obviously needed to reinforce this conclusion. Two lines of evidence were presented that soon became accepted as appropriate criteria for this kind of investigation. The first was the demonstration that closely homologous DNA sequences were widely represented in the animal kingdom, for it was the general experience that the structure of essential genes tended to be strongly conserved in evolution. Southern blots that scanned a range of animal species were later dubbed 'zoo blots'. The second line of evidence was that the gene was expressed in the tissue affected by the disease, in this case human skeletal muscle. This was done by means of Northern blots and by screening cDNA libraries made from this tissue. The complete gene was eventually cloned and was found to contain 2.5×10^6 nucleotides and to encompass 65 exons (Koenig et al. 1987). Sequence analysis permitted the mutations responsible for the disease to be determined and the amino acid sequence of the encoded protein to be deduced. This protein was named 'dystrophin', and a search of the protein sequence databases revealed a homology with proteins of the cytoskeleton.

POSITIONAL CLONING: CHROMOSOME 'JUMPING'

However, even with the help of cytogenetic data and RFLPs, there was often a prohibitively long walk to the gene, and other methods had to be devised to bridge the 'resolution gap'. Two innovations proved decisive. The first of these, to which reference has already been made, was pulsed-field gel electrophoresis, which enabled the separation and resolution of very large stretches of DNA; and the second was the technique of chromosome 'jumping' (Collins and Weissman 1984). In the latter procedure, the high-molecular-weight DNA preparation was cut with an enzyme that recognised rare restriction sites, for example *Not*I or *Mbo*I. The digest was resolved by pulsed-field gel electrophoresis and fragments in the required size range were separated. These were then circularized by ligation in the presence of an excess of a transfer RNA suppressor gene (*supF*) which was incorporated into the circles at their point of ligation. The circles were next digested with a restriction enzyme such as *Eco*RI, which did not cut the transfer RNA suppressor gene. Fragments were thus generated that contained this gene flanked by stretches of DNA that were separated by the 'jump distance'. These fragments were then cloned in phages with amber mutations in the genes coding for coat proteins. The bacteria on which the phages were plated lacked the transfer RNA suppressor gene, so that only those phages that carried their own suppressor gene could replicate and form plaques. Clones obtained in this way could be used to generate chromosome jump libraries which were then screened with a range of informative probes.

IDENTIFICATION OF THE CYSTIC FIBROSIS GENE

The power of chromosome jumping was demonstrated by the identification and isolation of the gene responsible for the inherited disease cystic fibrosis. An approximate localisation of the gene within human chromosome 7 was provided by the discovery of a close linkage to an RFLP (Knowlton et al. 1985). Two other RFLP markers were found that flanked the gene (Wainwright et al. 1985; White et al. 1985). The whole of the region between these flanking markers was then scanned by chromosome jumping; and further overlapping clones were made in cosmids. Eventually some 500 kb of DNA were completely cloned. It had been shown by Bird (1986) that most genes that were expressed constitutively, and some whose expression was regulated, contained at their 5'ends clusters or islands of CpG residues (cytosine-guanine pairs). These islands were found to be unmethylated when the gene was active and methylated when it was inactive. Among the clones generated by the search for the cystic fibrosis gene, one was found to contain a CpG island, and this provided the first clue that a structural gene had been identified. It was then shown, as in the case of Duchenne muscular dystrophy, that DNA sequences closely homologous to this gene were widely represented in the animal kingdom; and Northern blots established that the gene was expressed in tissue affected by the disease. The RNA in this case was extracted from sweat glands where the cystic fibrosis gene was known to be active because these glands exhibited a defect in chloride transport in individuals with the disease. Eventually the complete gene was isolated and was found to contain 6.1 kb and to harbour 24 exons (Kerem et al. 1989; Riordan et al. 1989; Rommens et al. 1989). This huge gene was then completely sequenced, and it was thus revealed that in 70% of affected individuals there was a deletion of 3 bp coding for phenylanine.

IDENTIFICATION OF OTHER GENES DETERMINING HUMAN GENETIC DISEASES

The methods and criteria used in the isolation of the cystic fibrosis gene were rapidly adopted. Within a year, the gene involved in neurofibromatosis type 1 was identified and a major segment of it bearing a mutation was isolated (Fountain et al. 1989; O'Connell et al. 1989; Cawthorn et al. 1990; Viskochil et al. 1990). In the meantime, further improvements in techniques for identifying and isolating coding sequences were devised. Duyk et al. (1990) introduced a procedure, which they called 'exon trapping', that exploited the splicing of mammalian gene transcripts to isolate the exons. A retrovirus with a selectable marker was introduced into the cell cultures, and this was used to capture exons that were released from the primary gene transcripts by splicing. The selectable marker in the virus permitted the isolation of clones that harboured the spliced exons. Exon trapping was taken a stage further with the introduction of the polymerase chain reaction, as this could be used to amplify directly the exons produced by RNA splicing. This procedure was named 'exon amplification' (Buckler et al. 1991). After 1990, positional cloning, although it remained a laborious procedure, despite the methodological improvements that have been described, fell within the compass of many well-equipped research laboratories, and a number of genes responsible for inherited diseases were soon identified. Verkerk et al. (1991), Kremer et al. (1991), and Oberlé et al. (1991) isolated the gene involved in the fragile X syndrome and showed that the defective gene contained a triplet of one cytosine and two guanine residues (CGG) that was reiterated to a varying degree in different patients. This variable reiteration was thought to account for the inherent variability of the disease. A similarly expandable nucleotide triplet was found in the genes determining X-linked spinal and bulbar muscular atrophy (La Spada et al. 1991), myotonic dystrophy (Brook et al. 1992; Fu et al. 1992; Mahadevan et al. 1992), spino-cerebellar ataxia type 1 (Orr et al. 1993), and Huntington's disease (Huntington's Disease Collaborative Research Group 1993). One of the notable features of the research that led to the identification of these genes was the extent to which it depended on the collaboration of ever larger groups. Fifteen workers were involved in the identification of the cystic fibrosis gene, 24 in one of the teams that identified the mytonic dystrophy gene, and 58 in the Huntington's Disease Collaborative Research Group. It was clear that some areas of modern biology were going the way of experimental physics and would be pursued effectively only in prosperous countries. Other inherited disorders for which the responsible genes have been identified include Menke's disease (Chelly et al. 1992; Mercer et al. 1992; Vulpe et al. 1992), neurofibromatosis type 2 (Rouleau et al. 1993), X-linked adrenoleukodystrophy (Mosser et al. 1993), X-linked agammaglobulinaemia (Vetrie et al. 1993), and Canavan's disease (Kaul et al. 1993). Goodfellow, Lovell-Badge, and their collaborators identified within the sex-determining region of the mouse Y chromosome the long-sought-after gene that determines maleness (Gubbay et al. 1990; Sinclair et al. 1990; Koopman et al. 1991).

SOMATIC CELL GENETICS AND PROGRESS TOWARD THE CONSTRUCTION OF A COMPLETE MAP OF THE HUMAN GENOME

The success of recombinant DNA technology in locating, isolating and sequencing human genes generated in some minds the ambitious project of sequencing the entire human genome. It was argued at the political level that the knowledge that would accrue from this endeavour would be of inestimable human benefit, and these arguments found sufficient favour with influential politicians to release a flow of funds to support an international effort that was expected to achieve this end within a modest number of years. At the same time, in order to shed light on homologous regions in the human genome, and in order to develop further the semi-industrial technology that was required, the genomes of *E. coli*, yeast, the nematode *Caenorhabditis elegans* and the mouse were adopted as interim targets. An account of the current status of the attempt to map the entire human genome does not at present constitute an essential component of a history of somatic cell genetics, but it is of interest to note how techniques developed for the genetic analysis of somatic cells contributed to the human genome project. The first step in any programme to sequence something as immense as the human genome was to partition and simplify the starting materials. To this end the use of hybrid cells containing only a single human chromosome in a rodent genetic background made an important contribution. Such cells were used to check the products of chromosome jump libraries to ensure that ligated fragments were on the same chromosome and had not been formed by spurious cross-ligation. They also served as a preparative source of human DNA limited to a single chromosome. The desired chromosome could be isolated from metaphase cells by cell sorting techniques (Davies et al. 1981), or the human DNA could be amplified directly by the polymerase chain reaction by means of probes that recognized the *Alu* sequences, as previously described (Nelson et al. 1989). Defined segments of chromosomes could also be isolated by microdissection. This was first successfully done with single, identifiable puffs in the giant salivary chromosomes of *Drosophila* (Scalenghe et al. 1981), but the technique was later refined and used to clone specific regions of banded human chromosomes (Bates et al. 1986; Ludecke et al. 1989).

FURTHER DEVELOPMENTS IN RADIATION HYBRID MAPPING

A major topological problem in establishing the complete sequence of even a single human chromosome was to establish the order of cloned sequences and to determine the distances between them. In this respect an advanced application of the Goss-Harris technique of radiation hybrid mapping proved to be of great value. In the decade or more that elapsed between the appearance of the original Goss and Harris papers (1977a,b) and the later resurrection of the technique for fine structure mapping, a plenitude of markers had become available for each of the human chromosomes. It was thus possible to see whether the technique would work for hundreds of markers as it had done for the eight linked markers on chromosome 1 that Goss and Harris had at their disposal. This investigation was mounted by Cox and his colleagues who, in the first instance, used crosses between unirradiated hamster cells and irradiated hamster hybrid cells that contained only one human chromosome, number 4 (Cox et al. 1989). Segregation analysis of a very large number of markers on chromosome 4 was done essentially as described by Goss and Harris, and, with the aid of appropriate computer programmes, a high resolution map of this chromosome was generated (Cox et al. 1990). The validity of this map was reinforced by its correspondence with maps generated by other procedures. More recently, the statistical approach devised by Goss and Harris for unselected markers has been applied to hundreds of markers scattered throughout the whole human genome, and promising preliminary results have been reported (Cox 1994). Mapping by means of radiation-induced segregation has also been applied to isolated DNA preparations. An essentially similar statistical procedure was used, felicitously described as 'happy mapping' (Dear and Cook 1993; Walter et al. 1993).

ANALYSIS OF GENE FUNCTION

Although the isolation of a hitherto unknown determinant of a clinical condition represents the end of one kind of investigation, it also represents the beginning of another. For only very rarely has the identification of a new gene and the mutation that it has undergone provided a satisfactory explanation, in biochemical terms, of how the gene acts or how the mutation produces a deleterious effect in the particular tissue or tissues that are affected by the disease. For this reason, the functional analysis of new genes has assumed increasing importance; and it is not difficult to detect a movement of molecular biologists back to biochemical methods that were largely forsaken in the rush to exploit the astonishing opportunities offered by recombinant DNA technology. The ability to insert genes, both normal and mutated, into cells and to inactivate resident cellular genes has been of decisive importance in the analysis of gene function. In the first instance, it provided a means of testing whether a new gene that was thought to be a 'candidate' for a causal role in some genetic disease actually was the gene being sought. For example, in the case of the cystic fibrosis gene, the decisive evidence that the correct gene had been isolated was the demonstration that the isolated gene, when introduced into the cells of a patient with cystic fibrosis, corrected the defect in chloride transport that was pathognomonic of the disease (Drumm et al. 1990; Rich et al. 1990). Similar confirmations of function were made with several other genes, and where a characteristic biochemical abnormality had been defined for the disease, restitution of normal function was naturally regarded as an essential component of the evidence required to support a candidate gene. It was, of course, obvious that once normal function could be restored in defective cells, transfection of the relevant genes readily lent itself to a detailed analysis of mechanism. Genes in which regulatory or structural sequences had been deleted or changed could be introduced into both normal and defective cells, and the consequences of such genetic modifications could be studied in much the same way as spontaneous mutations, but with a greater degree of control.

CORRECTION OF GENETIC DEFECTS AND MODEST PROGRESS TOWARD 'GENE THERAPY'

Several monogenic defects were shown to be correctable in cell culture by the introduction of an unmutated copy of the appropriate gene, for example, hypoxanthine guanine phosphoribosyl transferase deficiency in cells from patients with Lesch-Nyhan disease (Miller et al. 1983), glucocerebrosidase deficiency in cells from patients with type I Gaucher's disease (Sorge et al. 1987) and adenosine deaminase deficiency in cells from patients with severe combined immunodeficiency (Palmer et al. 1987). These results encouraged the hope that it might be possible to correct or ameliorate such defects in individuals afflicted with monogenic familial diseases by introducing normal genes into their tissues in various ways. This ambition soon generated a programme of optimistic work that acquired the name 'gene therapy'. Dzierzak et al. (1988) introduced the human β-globin gene into mice by reconstituting their bone marrow with stem cells into which the gene had been incorporated. Bone marrow stem cells were also the vehicle that Lim et al. (1989) used to introduce the adenosine deaminase gene into mice. Palmer, Thompson, and Miller (1989) used grafts of fibroblasts to introduce human blood clotting factor IX into animals; Ledley et al. (1987), Wilson et al. (1988), and Anderson et al. (1989) used hepatocyte grafts to restore defective liver functions. Flowers et al. (1990) may have been the first to use grafts of skin keratinocytes as vectors for introducing foreign genes into animals; and Gerrard et al. (1993) showed that when keratinocytes transfected with the gene for clotting factor IX were grafted onto mice, the graft secreted this protein into the bloodstream. These experiments offered some promise that grafts of one sort or another might eventually provide a more stable form of treatment for haemophilia B than repeated blood transfusions. The adenosine deaminase gene was successfully introduced into non-human primates by Kantoff et al. (1987). Clinical trials of this methodology have now been initiated with tranfected bone marrow cells and lymphocytes as the gene vectors. In the case of cystic fibrosis, attempts are being made to provide a transient alleviation of the condition by delivering the normal gene directly to the epithelial cells of the patients' airways. This is being done with preparations of liposomes carrying the gene and with disabled recombinant viruses. So far these approaches have not yielded convincing clinical results in patients with this disease.

TRANSGENESIS: THE INSERTION OF FOREIGN GENES INTO ANIMALS

The development of transgenic animals introduced a new dimension into the study of gene function. Transgenesis has its origins in the experiments of Tarkowski (Fig. 55) (1961), who produced chimaeric mice by fusing cleaving eggs together, and in the work of Gardner (Fig. 56) (1968), who devised a method for producing mouse chimaeras by injecting cells into the developing blastocyst. Tarkowski demonstrated the chimaerism by generating intersexes from the fused eggs and also by the presence of incomplete pigmentation in fusions between the eggs of pigmented and non-pigmented parents. Mintz (1962) extended this work and made a detailed study of the tissue chimaerism that resulted. Gardner used stable genetic markers to trace the fate of the progeny of the foreign cells that he introduced into the blastocyst (Fig. 57). However, in order to produce a mouse in which all the cells carried a particular foreign gene, it was necessary to achieve the integration of this gene into the germ line. Jaenisch (Fig. 58) (1976) was the first to succeed in doing this. He introduced mouse leukaemia virus into embryos and, from the animals that developed, obtained progeny that transmitted the virus in a strictly Mendelian fashion. Gordon and Ruddle (1981) introduced plasmids contain-

FIGURE 55   Krzysztof Tarkowski (1933–) produced the first chimaeric animals by fusing cleaving mouse eggs together. *(Courtesy of Prof. Christopher Graham.)*

ing the herpes thymidine kinase gene or a segment of simian virus 40 DNA into embryos and from the resulting adults obtained progeny that carried these genes. Gordon and Ruddle also achieved germ-line transmission of human leucocyte interferon DNA by injecting it directly into the embryonic pronucleus. The transmission was not entirely Mendelian, but this was thought to be due to technical complications. Costantini and Lacy (1981) successfully transmitted the rabbit β-globin gene via the germ line, and in this case the transmission was Mendelian. The direct injection of DNA was, however, a rather haphazard procedure, and a much more predictable methodology was developed by the use of embryonic stem cells which could be manipulated *in vitro* as required before being introduced into the embryo. Embryonic stem (ES) cells were derived from the inner cell mass of the developing embryo. They were pluripotent in the sense that they could differentiate into a wide range of specialised tissues, and they could be grown for reasonable periods *in vitro* without becoming aneuploid (Evans and Kaufman 1981; Martin 1981). When these cells were introduced into blastocysts, they populated the developing embryo and, via the germ line, could be transmitted to progeny. It was therefore possible to introduce any desired gene into the embryonic stem cell and eventually obtain animals in which all the cells carried the interpolated gene. In the case of animals, as opposed to cells growing *in vitro*, homozygosity for the foreign gene, whether normal or mutated, could be obtained by normal breeding provided that this homozygosity was not lethal.

FIGURE 56 Richard Gardner (1943–) produced chimaeric mice by injecting single, genetically marked cells into the developing blastocyst. *(Courtesy of the Archives of the Sir William Dunn School of Pathology, University of Oxford.)*

The use of transgenic animals rapidly became a world-wide industry, and the functional consequences of introducing genes into animals in this way were eagerly examined. Many candidate genes for known functions were tested for their ability to express these functions in transgenic animals. The final certification of the sex-determining gene on the Y chromosome, for example, was made by demonstrating that this gene in transgenic mice could confer maleness on chromosomally female animals (Koopman et al. 1991). However, it soon transpired that such 'transgenes' often behaved in an unpredictable manner and not as might have been expected from their mode of operation in their normal tissue habitat.

Ectopic expression of the transgene in inappropriate tissues and complex pleiotropic effects were common. Efforts were therefore made to limit the expression of the transgene to its proper tissue and to achieve normal regulation of the gene. Swift et al. (1984) showed that the gene for pancreatic elastase I was expressed only in the pancreas of transgenic animals; and Hanahan (1985), by including 600 bp of DNA proximal to the 5' end of the insulin gene in a recombinant simian virus 40 vector, generated transgenic animals that developed pancreatic tumours composed entirely of β cells. But if transgenic animals were to be used to study the function of genes or clusters of genes in their normal context, it was obvious that means would have to be found to accommodate very long stretches of DNA in the transgene constructs. This was accomplished by Peterson et al. (1993) using yeast artificial chromosomes as vectors. These authors incorporated the human β-globin locus into a yeast artificial chromosome containing 248 kb of DNA and showed that, in the transgenic animal, proper developmental control of the human globin genes was achieved. Schedl et al. (1993) used a yeast artificial chromosome containing a tyrosinase gene and succeeded via transgenesis in restoring normal pigmentation to albino mice. There was scant evidence of any aberrant function of the transgene.

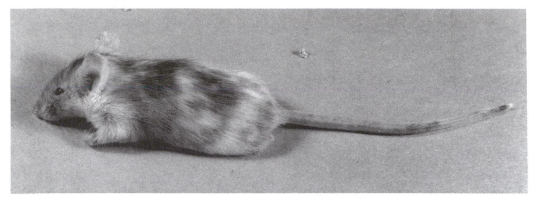

FIGURE 57 A chimaeric mouse produced by injecting foreign cells into the developing blastocyst. Three cells of pigmented genotype were injected into a blastocyst derived from an albino mouse. The resultant animal shows patchy pigmentation of the fur. (From the original series of experiments described in Gardner 1968.) *(Courtesy of Prof. R.L. Gardner.)*

FIGURE 58 Rudolf Jaenisch (1942–) was the first to introduce a foreign gene into the germ line of an animal and to show that the interpolated gene was inherited in a Mendelian fashion. This was the starting-point of what is now known as transgenesis. This photograph shows Rudolf Jaenisch interpolated into a double helix. *(Courtesy of Dr. Rudolf Jaenisch.)*

TRANSGENESIS: THE INACTIVATION OF RESIDENT GENES

In addition to acting as vehicles for intercalated genes, embryonic stem cells could also be used to study the physiological consequences of inactivating specific genes. This could be done by means of homologous recombination, as previously described (Smithies et al. 1985; Mansour, Thomas, and Capecchi 1988); and the ES cells bearing the mutated gene could then be used to generate animals in which all the cells had the mutation, initially in the heterozygous condition but, after breeding, in the homozygous condition also. Transgenic animals thus made it possible, in principle, to generate artificial mutants for any gene that one wished to study. Zijlstra et al. (1989, 1990) found that when β_2-microglobulin, an essential component of the histocompatibility antigen complex, was disrupted in ES cells by homologous recombination, animals homozygous for the defective gene failed to produce specific cytolytic T cells. Chisaka and Capecchi (1991) showed that in transgenic animals homozygous inactivation of the mouse homeobox gene *hox* 1.5 (a mouse homologue of a gene responsible for a homeotic mutation in *Drosophila*) produced specific regional developmental defects. Genes in ES cells could also be inactivated by the insertion of cDNA from retroviruses. Woychik et al. (1985) produced an inherited limb deformity in this way, and Krulewski, Neumann, and Gordon (1989) produced a constitutional degeneration of Purkinje cells in the nervous system. Animals rendered null for particular genes, 'gene knockouts' as they came to be called, soon became the focus of intense interest, and numerous studies on such animals were reported. In addition, gene knockouts proved to be of use in providing approximate animal models for monogenic familial human diseases, for example cystic fibrosis (Dorin et al. 1992; Snouwert et al. 1992). Nonetheless, as in the case of intercalated foreign genes, the results were not always easy to interpret. Bizarre ectopic effects were common, and it sometimes happened that the absence of the gene was, unexpectedly, without obvious effect. Not only genes, but also specific cell lineages could be eliminated from transgenic animals. This was accomplished by controlled intracellular synthesis of a cytolytic bacterial toxin. Palmiter et al. (1987) introduced into transgenic animals a vector in which the elastase gene was coupled to the gene coding for the A chain of diphtheria toxin. Since the elastase gene was expressed only in the pancreas, synthesis of the cytolytic A chain was limited to pancreatic cells or their precursors, and about a third of these transgenic animals failed to develop a pancreas. Borrelli et al. (1988) showed that cytolytic toxin production in the cells of transgenic animals could be made inducible by coupling the toxin gene to the herpes simplex thymidine kinase gene which was activated only when the animals were given exogenous nucleosides. The applications of transgenic animals and the complications involved in their use are not yet exhausted.

THE INSERTION OF FOREIGN GENES INTO PLANTS

The methodology devised for inserting genes into animal cells and for disrupting resident cellular genes was soon applied to plant cells. The first successful experiments of this kind in plants exploited a plasmid carried by *Agrobacterium tumefaciens*, the bacterium responsible for the production of plant crown gall tumours. Van Larebeke et al. (1974) made the fundamental discovery that induction of the tumour involved the transfer of a large plasmid (named the Ti plasmid) from the bacterium to the plant cell. Chilton et al. (1977) showed that, in the crown gall tumour, the plasmid was stably incorporated into the host cell DNA. Subsequent development of the Ti plasmid as a gene vector followed the usual pattern of incorporating foreign genes into it by recombination. Horsch et al. (1984) were apparently the first to demonstrate the inheritance of functional foreign genes in plants. These authors transfected protoplasts of the tobacco plant, *Nicotiana plumbaginifolia*, with a kanamycin-resistance gene, and then co-cultivated the protoplasts with dissociated plant cells capable of regenerating whole plants. De Block et al. (1984), using essentially the same technique, successfully incorporated foreign genes for kanamycin-, chloramphenicol- and methotrexate-resistance into tobacco plants. *Agrobacterium rhizogenes*, which induces the formation of accessory roots, but not undifferentiated tumours, was also found to harbour a transmissible plasmid (Tepler 1982, 1984; David, Chilton, and Tempé 1984). This plasmid, called the Ri plasmid, was developed as a gene vector in much the same way as the Ti plasmid. The technique of gene transfer was simplified by Horsch et al. (1985) who found that the recombinant Ti phage carrying the foreign gene could be transmitted to the plant cells directly by infecting leaf discs with the *Agrobacterium* itself. More robust techniques for incorporating the foreign genes into plants were progressively introduced, much as they had been with animal cells: microprojectiles by Klein et al. (1987) and particle acceleration by McCabe et al. (1988). The stable incorporation of genes into commercial crops was accomplished in soya bean by Hinchee et al. (1988), in rice by Toriyama et al. (1988) and Shimamoto et al. (1989), and in maize by Gordon-Kamm et al. (1990) and Fromm et al. (1990). Efficient transfection procedures have also been developed for the incorporation of commercially important genes such as resistance to viruses, insects and herbicides. Moreover, plants transfected with the appropriate genes have been used for the production of animal proteins such as antibodies (Hiatt, Cafferkey, and Bosdish 1989), encephalins (Vandekerckhove et al. 1989), and serum albumin (Sijmons et al. 1990).

But during this period of explosive growth in nucleic acid technology the central preoccupation of somatic cell geneticists, as distinct from geneticists generally, remained the nature of the genetic changes that rendered cells tumorigenic. This subject is discussed in the next chapter.

REFERENCES

Agarwal, S., J. Goodchild, M.P. Civeira, A.H. Thornton, P.S. Sarin, and P.C. Zamecnik. 1988. Oligodeoxynucleoside phosphoramidates and phosphorothioates as inhibitors of human immunodeficiency virus. *Proc. Natl. Acad. Sci.* **85**: 7079–7083.

Alt, F.W., R.E. Kellems, J.R. Bertino, and R.T. Schimke. 1978. Selective multiplication of dihydrofolate reductase genes in methotrexate-resistant variants of cultured murine cells. *J. Biol. Chem.* **253**: 1357–1370.

Alwine, J.C., D.J. Kemp, and G.R. Stark. 1977. Method for detection of specific RNAs in agarose gels by transfer to diazobenzyloxymethyl-paper and hybridization with DNA probes. *Proc. Natl. Acad. Sci.* **74**: 5350–5354.

Anderson, K.D., J.A. Anderson, J.M. DiPietro, K.T. Montgomery, L.M. Reid, and W.F.

Anderson. 1989. Gene expression in implanted rat hepatocytes following retroviral-mediated gene transfer. *Somatic Cell Mol. Genet.* **15**: 215–217.

Arnheim, N. and E.M. Southern. 1977. Heterogeneity of the ribosomal genes in mice and men. *Cell* **11**: 363–370.

Aubin, R.J., M. Weinfeld, and M.C. Paterson. 1988. Factors influencing efficiency and reproducibility of polybrene-assisted gene transfer. *Somatic Cell Mol. Genet.* **14**: 155–167.

Bacchetti, S. and F.L. Graham. 1977. Transfer of the gene for thymidine kinase to thymidine-kinase deficient human cells by purified herpes simplex virus DNA. *Proc. Natl. Acad. Sci.* **74**: 1590–1594.

Baltimore, D. 1970. Viral RNA-dependent DNA polymerase. *Nature* **226**: 1209–1211.

Banerji, J., S. Rusconi, and W. Schaffner. 1981. Expression of a β-globin gene is enhanced by remote SV40 DNA sequences. *Cell* **27**: 299–308.

Bates, G.P., B.J. Wainwright, R. Williamson, and S.D.M. Brown. 1986. Microdissection of and microcloning from the short arm of human chromosome 2. *Mol. Cell. Biol.* **6**: 3826–3830.

Bender, J. and N. Kleckner. 1986. Genetic evidence that Tn10 transposes by a non-replicative mechanism. *Cell* **45**: 801–815.

Benoist, C. and P. Chambon. 1981. In vivo sequence requirements of the SV40 early promoter region. *Nature* **290**: 304–310.

Berget, S.M., C. Moore, and P. Sharp. 1977. Spliced segments at the 5′ termini of adenovirus-2 late mRNA. *Proc. Natl. Acad. Sci.* **74**: 3171–3175.

Bernards, A., L.H.T.V. de Ploeg, A.C.C. Frasch, P. Borst, J.C. Boothroyd, S. Coleman, and G.A.M. Cross. 1981. Activation of trypanosome surface glycoprotein genes involves a duplication-transposition leading to an altered 3′ end. *Cell* **27**: 497–505.

Bird, A.P. 1986. CpG rich islands and the function of DNA methylation. *Nature* **321**: 209–213.

Blake, C.C.F. 1978. Do genes-in-pieces imply proteins in pieces. *Nature* **273**: 267–268.

Blattner, F.R., B.G. Williams, A.E. Blechl, K. Denniston-Thompson, H.E. Faber, L.-A. Furlong, D.J. Grunwald, D.O. Keifer, D.D. Moore, J.W. Schumm, E.L. Sheldon, and O. Smithies. 1977. Charon phages: Safer derivatives of bacteriophage lambda for DNA cloning. *Science* **196**: 161–169.

Blau, H.M. 1992. Differentiation requires continuous active control. *Annu. Rev. Biochem.* **61**: 1213–1230.

Bohmann, D., T.J. Bos, A. Admon, T. Nishimura, P.K. Vogt, and R. Tjian. 1987. Human proto-oncogene c-*jun* encodes a DNA binding protein with structural and functional properties of transcription factor AP1. *Science* **238**: 1386–1392.

Bolivar, F., R.L. Rodrigues, P.J. Greene, M.C. Betlach, H.L. Heyneker, H.W. Boyer, J. Crosa, and S. Falkow. 1977. Construction and characterization of new cloning vehicles. II. A multi-purpose cloning system. *Gene* **2**: 95–113.

Borrelli, E., R. Heyman, M. Hsi, and R.M. Evans. 1988. Targeting of an inducible toxic phenotype in animal cells. *Proc. Natl. Acad. Sci.* **85**: 7572–7576.

Botstein, D., R. White, M. Skolnick, and R. Davis. 1980. Construction of a genetic linkage map in man using restriction fragment length polymorphisms. *Am. J. Hum. Genet.* **32**: 314–331.

Brack, C.M., R. Hirama, R. Lenard-Schuller, and S. Tonegawa. 1978. A complete immunoglobulin gene is created by somatic recombination. *Cell* **15**: 1–14.

Breathnach, R., J.L. Mandel, and P. Chambon. 1977. Ovalbumin gene is split in chicken DNA. *Nature* **270**: 314–319.

Brisson-Noël, A., D. Lecossier, X. Nassif, B. Gicquel, V. Levy-Frebault, and A.J. Hance. 1989. Rapid diagnosis of tuberculosis by amplification of mycobacterial DNA in clinical samples. *Lancet* **II**: 1069–1071.

Britten, R.J. and D.E. Kohne. 1968. Repeated sequences in DNA. *Science* **161**: 529–540.

Brook, L.J.D., M.E. McCurrach, H.G. Harley, A.J. Buckler, D. Church, H. Aburatani, K. Hunter, V.P. Stanton, J.-P. Thirion, T. Hudson, R. Sohn, B. Zemelman, R.G. Snell, S.A. Rundle, S. Crow, J. Davies, P. Shelborne, J. Buxton, C. Jones, V. Juvonen, K. Johnson, P.S. Harper, D.J. Shaw, and D.E. Housman. 1992. Molecular basis of myotonic dystrophy: Expansion of a trinucleotide (CTG) repeat at the 3′ end of a transcript encoding a protein kinase member. *Cell* **68**: 799–808.

Broome, S. and W. Gilbert. 1978. Immunological screening method to detect specific translation products. *Proc. Natl. Acad. Sci.* **75**: 2746–2749.

Brownlee, G.G., F. Sanger, and B.G. Barrell. 1967. Nucleotide sequence of 5S-ribosomal RNA. *Nature* **215**: 735–736.

———. 1968. The sequences of 5S ribosomal ribonucleic acid. *J. Mol. Biol.* **34**: 379–412.

Buckler, A.J., D.D. Chang, S. Graw, J.D. Brook, D.A. Haber, P.A. Sharp, and D.E. Housman. 1991. Exon amplification: A strategy to isolate mammalian genes based on RNA splicing. *Proc. Natl. Acad. Sci.* **88**: 4005–4009.

Burke, D.T., G.F. Carle, and M.V. Olsen. 1987. Cloning of large segments of exogenous DNA into yeast by means of artificial chromosome vectors. *Science* **236**: 806–812.

Cameron, J.R., E.Y. Loh, and R.W. Davis. 1979. Evidence for transposition of dispersed repetititve DNA families in yeast. *Cell* **16**: 739–751.

Capecchi, M. 1980. High efficiency transformation by direct microinjection into cultured mammalian cells. *Cell* **22**: 479–488.

Cattanach, B.M. 1986. Parental origin effects in mice. *J. Embryol. Exp. Morphol.* (suppl.) **97**: 137–150.

Cawthorn, R.M., R. Weiss, G. Xu, D. Viskochil, M. Culver, J. Stevens, M. Robertson, D. Dunn, R. Gesteland, P. O'Connell, and R. White. 1990. A major segment of the neurofibromatosis type 1 gene: cDNA sequence, genomic structure and point mutations. *Cell* **62**: 193–201.

Cepko, C.L., B.E. Roberts, and R.C. Mulligan. 1984. Construction and applications of a highly transmissible murine retrovirus shuttle vector. *Cell* **37**: 1053–1062.

Chandler, V.L., B.A. Maler, and K.R. Yamamoto. 1983. DNA sequences bound specifically by glucocorticoid receptor in vitro render a heterologous promoter hormone responsive in vivo. *Cell* **33**: 489–499.

Chaney, W.G., D.R. Howard, J.W. Pollard, S. Sallustio, and P. Stanley. 1986. High-frequency transfection of CHO cells using polybrene. *Somatic Cell Mol. Genet.* **12**: 237–244.

Chang, A.C.Y., J.H. Nunberg, R.J. Kaufman, H.A. Erlich, R.T. Schimke, and S.N. Cohen. 1978. Phenotypic expression in *E. coli* of a DNA sequence coding for mouse dihydrofolate reductase. *Nature* **275**: 617–624.

Chelly, J., Z. Tümer, T. Tønnesen, A. Petterson, Y. Ishikawa-Brusk, N. Tommerup, N. Horn, and A.P. Monaco. 1992. Isolation of a candidate gene for Menkes disease that encodes a potential heavy metal binding protein. *Nat. Genet.* **3**: 14–19.

Chien, A., D.B. Edgar, and J.M. Trela. 1976. Deoxyribonucleic acid polymerase from the extreme thermophile *Thermus aquaticus*. J. Bacteriol. **127**: 1550–1557.

Chilton, M.D., M.H. Drummond, D.J. Merlo, D. Sciaky, A.L. Montoya, M.P. Gordon, and E.W. Nester. 1977. Stable incorporation of plasmid DNA into higher plant cells: The molecular basis of crown gall tumorigenesis. *Cell* **11**: 263–271.

Chisaka, O. and M.R. Capecchi. 1991. Regionally restricted developmental defects resulting from targeted disruption of the mouse homeobox gene *hox-1.5*. *Nature* **350**: 473–479.

Chow, L.T., R.E. Gelinas, T.R. Broker, and R.J. Roberts. 1977. An amazing sequence arrangement at the 5' ends of adenovirus 2 messenger RNA. *Cell* **12**: 1–8.

Chu, C.T., D.S. Parris, R.A.F. Dixon, F.E. Farber, and P.A. Schaffer. 1979. Hydroxylamine mutagenesis of HSV DNA and DNA fragments: Introduction of mutations into selected regions of the viral genome. *Virology* **98**: 168–181.

Church, G.M., A. Ephrussi, W. Gilbert, and S. Tonegawa. 1985. Cell-type-specific contacts to immunoglobulin enhancers in nuclei. *Nature* **313**: 798–801.

Cohen, S., A. Chang, H. Boyer, and R. Helling. 1973. Construction of biologically functional bacterial plasmids *in vitro*. *Proc. Natl. Acad. Sci.* **70**: 3240–3244.

Collins, F.S. and S.M. Weissman. 1984. Directional cloning of DNA fragments at a large distance from an initial probe: A circularization method. *Proc. Natl. Acad. Sci.* **81**: 6812–6816.

Collins, J. and B. Hohn. 1978. Cosmids: A type of plasmid gene cloning vector that is packageable in vitro in bacteriphage heads. *Proc. Natl. Acad. Sci.* **75**: 4242–4246.

Costantini, F. and E. Lacy. 1981. Introduction of a rabbit β-globin gene into the mouse germ line. *Nature* **294**: 92–94.

Cox, D.R. 1994. Radiation hybrid mapping: An idea whose time has finally arrived. In

The legacy of cell fusion (ed. S. Gordon), pp. 131–139. Clarendon Press, Oxford.

Cox, D.R., M. Burmeister, E.R. Price, S. Kim, and R.M. Myers. 1990. Radiation hybrid mapping: A somatic cell genetics method for constructing high-resolution maps of mammalian chromosomes. *Science* **250:** 245–250.

Cox, D.R., C.A. Pritchard, E. Uglum, D. Casher, J. Kohori, and R.M. Myers. 1989. Segregation of the Huntington disease region of human chromosome 4 in a somatic cell hybrid. *Genomics* **4:** 397–407.

Cozzarelli, N.R., N.E. Melechen, T.M. Jovin, and A. Kornberg. 1967. Polynucleotide cellulose as a substrate for a polynucleotide ligase induced by phage T4. *Biochem. Biophys. Res. Commun.* **28:** 578–586.

Curtiss, R., III, M. Inoue, D. Pereira, J.C. Hsu, L. Alexander, and L. Rock. 1977. Construction in use of safer bacterial host strains for recombinant DNA research. In *Molecular cloning of recombinant DNA* (ed. W.A. Scott and R. Werner). Proceedings of the Miami Winter Symposia, vol. 13, pp. 99–114. Academic Press, New York.

Danna, K. and D. Nathans. 1971. Specific cleavage of simian virus 40 DNA by restriction endonuclease of *Hemophilus parainfluenzae*. *Proc. Natl. Acad. Sci.* **68:** 2913–2917.

Danna, K.J., G.H. Sack, and D. Nathans. 1973. Studies on simian virus 40 DNA. VII. A cleavage map of the SV40 genome. *J. Mol. Biol.* **78:** 363–376.

David, C., M.D. Chilton, and J. Tempé. 1984. Conservation of T-DNA in plants regenerated from hairy root cultures. *Biotechnology* **2:** 73–76.

Davidson, I., C. Fromental, P. Augereau, A. Wildeman, M. Zenke, and P. Chambon. 1986. Cell-type-specific protein binding to the enhancer of SV40 in nuclear extracts. *Nature* **323:** 544–548.

Davies, K.E., B.D. Young, R.G. Elles, M.E. Hill, and R. Williamson. 1981. Cloning of a representative genomic library of the human X-chromosome after sorting by flow cytometry. *Nature* **293:** 374–376.

Davis, M.M., K. Calame, P.W. Early, P.L. Livant, R. Joho, J.L. Weissman, and L.E. Hood. 1980. An immunoglobulin heavy-chain gene is formed by at least two recombinational events. *Nature* **283:** 733–739.

Dear, P.H. and P.R. Cook. 1993. Happy mapping: Linkage mapping using a physical analogue of meiosis. *Nucleic Acids Res.* **21:** 13–20.

De Block, M., L. Herrera-Estrella, M. Van Montagu, J. Schell, and P. Zambryski. 1984. Expression of foreign genes in regenerated plants and their progeny. *EMBO J.* **3:** 1681–1689.

de Lucia, P. and J. Cairns. 1969. Isolation of an *E. coli* strain with a mutation affecting DNA polymerase. *Nature* **224:** 1164–1166.

Diacumakos, E.G. 1973. Methods of micromanipulation of human somatic cells in culture. *Methods Cell Biol.* **7:** 287–312.

Diacumakos, E.G. and E.L. Gershey. 1977. Uncoating and gene expression of simian virus 40 in CV-1 cell nuclei inoculated by microinjection. *J. Virol.* **24:** 903–906.

Dimitriadis, G.J. 1978. Translation of rabbit globin mRNA introduced by liposomes into mouse lymphocytes. *Nature* **274:** 923–924.

Doetschman, T., N. Maeda, and O. Smithies. 1988. Targeted mutation of the *hprt* gene in mouse embryonic stem cells. *Proc. Natl. Acad. Sci.* **85:** 8583–8587.

Dorin, J.R., P. Dickinson, E.W.F.W. Alton, S.N. Smith, D.M. Geddes, B.J. Stevenson, W.L. Kimber, S. Fleming, A.R. Clarke, M.L. Hooper, L. Anderson, R.S.P. Beddington, and D.J. Porteous. 1992. Cystic fibrosis in the mouse by targeted insertional mutagenesis. *Nature* **359:** 211–215.

Doty, P., J. Marmur, J. Eigner, and C. Schildkraut. 1960. Strand separation and specific recombination in deoxyribonucleic acids: Physical chemical studies. *Proc. Natl. Acad. Sci.* **46:** 461–476.

Dreyer, W.J. and J.D. Bennett. 1965. The molecular basis of antibody formation: A paradox. *Proc. Natl. Acad. Sci.* **54:** 864–869.

Drumm, M.L., H.A. Pope, W.H. Cliff, J.M. Rommens, S.A. Marvin, L.-C. Tsui, F.S. Collins, R.A. Frizzell, and J.M. Wilson. 1990. Correction of the cystic fibrosis defect in vitro by retrovirus-mediated gene transfer. *Cell* **62:** 1227–1233.

Duncan, C.H., P. Jagadeeswaran, R.R.C. Wang, and S.M. Weissman. 1981. Structural analysis of templates and RNA polymerase III transcripts of the Alu family sequences interspersed among the human β-like globin genes. *Gene* **13:** 185–196.

Duyk, G.M., A. Kim, R.M. Myers, and D.R. Cox. 1990. Exon trapping: A genetic screen to identify candidate transcribed sequences in cloned mammalian genomic DNA. *Proc. Natl. Acad. Sci.* **87:** 8995–8999.

Dzierzak, E.A., T. Papayannopoulou, and R.C. Mulligan. 1988. Lineage-expression of a human β-globin gene in murine bone marrow transplant recipients reconstituted with retrovirus-transduced stem cells. *Nature* **331:** 35–41.

Early, P., H. Huang, M. Davis, K. Calame, and L. Hood. 1980a. An immunoglobulin heavy chain variable region gene is generated from three segments of DNA: V_H D and J_H. *Cell* **19:** 981–992.

Early, P., J. Rogers, M. Davis, K. Calame, M. Bond, R. Wall, and L. Hood. 1980b. Two mRNAs can be produced from a single immunoglobulin μ gene by alternative RNA processing pathways. *Cell* **20:** 313–319.

Eckert, K.A. and T.A. Kunkel. 1990. High fidelity DNA synthesis by the *Thermus aquaticus* DNA polymerase. *Nucleic Acids Res.* **18:** 3739–3744.

Edmonds, M., M.H. Vaughan, Jr., and H. Nakazato. 1971. Polyadenylic acid sequences in the heterogeneous nuclear RNA and rapidly-labeled polyribosomal RNA of HeLa cells: Possible evidence for a precursor relationship. *Proc. Natl. Acad. Sci.* **68:** 1336–1340.

Evans, M.J. and M.H. Kaufman. 1981. Establishment in culture of pluripotential cells from mouse embryos. *Nature* **292:** 154–156.

Fan, Y.-S., L.M. Davis, and T.B. Shows. 1990. Mapping small DNA sequences by fluorescence *in situ* hybridization directly on banded metaphase chromosomes. *Proc. Natl. Acad. Sci.* **87:** 6223–6227.

Fiers, W., R. Contreras, G. Haegeman, R. Rogers, A. Van de Voorde, H., Van Heuverswyn, J. Van Herreweghe, G. Volckaert, and M. Ysebaert. 1978. Complete nucleotide sequence of SV40 DNA. *Nature* **273:** 113–120.

Fiers, W., R. Contreras, F. Duerinck, G. Haegeman, D. Iserentant, J. Merregaert, W. Min Jou, F. Molemans, A. Raeymaekers, V. Berghe, G. Volckaert, and M. Ysebaert. 1976. Complete nucleotide sequence of bacteriophage MS2 RNA: Primary and secondary structure of replicase gene. *Nature* **260:** 500–507.

Flowers, M.E.D., M.A.R. Stockschlaeder, F.G. Schuening, D. Niederwieser, R. Hackman, A.D. Miller, and R. Storb. 1990. Long-term transplantation of canine keratinocytes made resistant to G418 through retrovirus-mediated gene transfer. *Proc. Natl. Acad. Sci.* **87:** 2349–2353.

Fountain, J.W., M.R. Wallace, M.A. Bruce, B.R. Seizinger, A.G. Menon, J.F. Gusella, V.V. Michels, M.A. Schmidt, G.W. Dewald, and F.S. Collins. 1989. Physical mapping of a translocation breakpoint in neurofibromatosis. *Science* **244:** 1085–1987,

Fraley, R., S. Subramani, P. Berg, and D. Papahadjopoulos. 1980. Introduction of liposome–encapsulated SV40 DNA into cells. *J. Biol. Chem.* **255:** 10431–10435.

Francke, U., B.T. Darras, N.F. Zander, and M.W. Kilimann. 1989. Assignment of human genes for phosphorylase kinase subunits α *(PHKA)* to Xq12-q13 and β *(PHKB)* to 16q12-q13. *Am. J. Hum. Genet.* **45:** 276–282.

Fritsch, E., R. Lawn, and T. Maniatis. 1980. Molecular cloning and characterization of the human β-like globin gene cluster. *Cell* **19:** 959–972.

Fromm, M.E., F. Morrish, C. Armstrong, R. Williams, J. Thomas, and T.M. Klein. 1990. Inheritance and expression of chimeric genes in the progeny of transgenic maize plants. *Biotechnology* **8:** 833–839.

Fu, Y.-H., A. Pizzuti, R.G. Fenwick, J. King, S. Rajnarayan, P. Dunne, J. Dubel, G.H. Nasser, T. Ashizawa, P. de Jong, B. Wieringa, R. Korneluk, M.B. Perryman, H.F. Epstein, and C.T. Caskey. 1992. An unstable triple repeat in a gene related to myotonic muscular dystrophy. *Science* **255:** 1256–1258.

Gait, M.J. and R.C. Sheppard. 1977. Rapid synthesis of oligodeoxyribonucleotides: A new solid-phase method. *Nucleic Acids Res.* **4:** 1135–1158.

Gall, J.G. and M.L. Pardue. 1969. Formation and detection of RNA-DNA hybrid molecules in cytological preparations. *Proc. Natl. Acad. Sci.* **63:** 378–383.

Gardner, R.L. 1968. Mouse chimaeras obtained by the injection of cells into the blastocyst. *Nature* **220:** 596–597.

Gefter, M.L. 1975. DNA replication. *Annu. Rev. Biochem.* **44:** 45–78.

Gefter, M.L., A. Becker, and J. Hurwitz. 1967. The enzymatic repair of DNA. I. Formation of circular λ DNA. *Proc. Natl. Acad. Sci.* **58:** 240–247.

Gellert, M. 1967. Formation of covalent circles of lambda DNA by *E. coli* extracts. *Proc. Natl. Acad. Sci.* **57:** 148–155.

Gerhard, D.S., E.S. Kawasaki, F.C. Bancroft, and P. Szabo. 1981. Localization of a unique gene by direct hybridization in situ. *Proc. Natl. Acad. Sci.* **78:** 3755–3759.

Gerrard, A.J., D.L. Hudson, G.G. Brownlee, and F.M. Watt. 1993. Towards gene therapy for haemophilia B using primary human keratinocytes. *Nat. Genet.* **3:** 180–183.

Gilbert, W. 1978. Why genes in pieces? *Nature* **271:** 501.

Gilham, P.T. 1970. RNA sequence analysis. *Annu. Rev. Biochem.* **39:** 227–250.

Gillies, S.D., S.L. Morrison, V.T. Oi, and S. Tonegawa. 1983. A tissue-specific transcription enhancer element is located in the major intron of a rearranged immunoglubulin heavy chain gene. *Cell* **33:** 717–728.

Goff, S.P. and P. Berg. 1976. Construction of hybrid viruses containing SV40 and λ phage DNA segments and their propagation in cultured monkey cells. *Cell* **9:** 695–705.

Goodbourn, S., K. Zinn, and T. Maniatis. 1985. Human β-interferon gene expression is regulated by an inducible enhancer element. *Cell* **41:** 509–520.

Gordon, J.W. and F.H. Ruddle. 1981. Integration and stable germ line transmission of genes injected into mouse pronuclei. *Science* **214:** 1244–1246.

Gordon-Kamm, W.J., T.M. Spencer, M.L. Mangano, T.R. Adams, R.J. Daines, W.G. Start, J.V. O'Brien, S.A. Chambers, W.R. Adams, Jr., N.G. Willetts, T.B. Rice, C.J. Mackey, R.W. Krueger, A.P. Kausch, and P.G. Lemaux. 1990. Transformation of maize cells and regeneration of fertile transgenic plants. *Plant Cell* **2:** 603–618.

Goss, S.J. and H. Harris. 1977a. Gene transfer by means of cell fusion. I. Statistical mapping of the human X-chromosome by analysis of radiation-induced gene segregation. *J. Cell Sci.* **25:** 17–37.

———. 1977b. Gene transfer by means of cell fusion. II. The mapping of 8 loci on human chromosome 1 by statistical analysis of gene assortment in somatic cell hybrids. *J. Cell Sci.* **25:** 39–58.

Graessmann, M. and A. Graessmann. 1976. Early simian-virus-40-specific RNA contains information for tumor antigen formation and chromatin replication. *Proc. Natl. Acad. Sci.* **73:** 366–370.

Graham, F.L. and A.J. van der Eb. 1973. A new technique for the assay of infectivity of human adenovirus 5 DNA. *Virology.* **52:** 456–467.

Graves, J.A.M. 1982. 5-azacytidine-induced re-expression of alleles on the inactive X chromosome in a hybrid mouse cell line. *Exp. Cell Res.* **141:** 99–105.

Griffin, E.F. and H. Harris. 1992. Total inhibition of involucrin synthesis by a novel two-step antisense procedure. *J. Cell Sci.* **102:** 799–805.

Gruenbaum, Y., H. Cedar, and A. Razin. 1982. Substrate and sequence specificity of eukaryotic DNA methylase. *Nature* **295:** 620–622.

Grunstein, M. and D.S. Hogness. 1975. Colony hybridization: A method for the isolation of cloned DNAs that contain a specific gene. *Proc. Natl. Acad. Sci.* **72:** 3961–3965.

Guarente, L., G. Lauer, T. Roberts, and M. Ptashne. 1980. Improved methods of maximizing expression of a cloned gene: A bacterium that synthesizes rabbit β-globin. *Cell* **20:** 545–553.

Gubbay, J., J. Collignon, P. Koopman, B. Capel, A. Economon, A. Münsterberg, N. Vivian, P. Goodfellow, and R. Lovell-Badge. 1990. A gene mapping to the sex–determining region of the mouse Y chromosome is a member of a novel family of embryonically expressed genes. *Nature* **346:** 245–250.

Hall, B.D. and S. Spiegelman. 1961. Sequence complementarity of T2-DNA and T2-specific RNA. *Proc. Natl. Acad. Sci.* **47:** 137–146.

Hanahan, D. 1985. Heritable formation of pancreatic β-cell tumours in transgenic mice expressing recombinant insulin/simian virus 40 oncogenes. *Nature* **315:** 115–122.

Handyside, A., E.H. Kontogianni, K. Hardy, and R.M.L. Winston. 1990. Pregnancies from biopsied human preimplantation embryos sexed by Y-specific DNA amplification. *Nature* **344:** 768–770.

Handyside, A.H., J.K. Pattinson, R.J.A. Penketh, J.D.A. Delhanty, R.M.L. Winston, and E.G.D. Tuddenham. 1989. Biopsy of human preimplantation embryos and sexing by DNA amplification. *Lancet* **I:** 347–349.

Harper, M.E., A. Ullrich, and G.F. Saunders. 1981. Localization of the human insulin gene to the distal end of the short arm of chromosome 1. *Proc. Natl. Acad. Sci.* **78:** 4458–4460.

Harris, H. 1963. The breakdown of ribonucleic acid in the cell nucleus. *Proc. R. Soc. Lond. B Biol. Sci.* **158:** 79–87.

———. 1965. The short-lived RNA in the cell nucleus and its possible role in evolution. In *Evolving genes and proteins* (ed. V. Bryson and H.J. Vogel), pp. 469–477. Academic Press, New York.

———. 1974. *Nucleus and cytoplasm,* 3rd edition, p. 155. Clarendon Press, Oxford.

Harris, H., H.W. Fisher, A. Rodgers, T. Spencer, and J.W. Watts. 1963. An examination of the ribonucleic acids in the HeLa cell with special reference to current theory about the transfer of information from nucleus to cytoplasm. *Proc. R. Soc. Lond. B Biol. Sci.* **157:** 177–198.

Heffron, F., M. So, and B.J. McCarthy. 1978. In vitro mutagenesis of a circular DNA molecule using synthetic restriction sites. *Proc. Natl. Acad. Sci.* **75:** 6012–6016.

Helfman, D.M., J.R. Fiddes, G.P. Thomas, and S. Hughes. 1983. Identification of clones that encode chicken tropomyosin by direct immunological screening of a cDNA expression library. *Proc. Natl. Acad. Sci.* **80:** 31–35.

Henikoff, S., M.A. Keene, K. Fechtel, and J.W. Fristron. 1986. Gene within a gene: Nested *Drosophila* genes encode unrelated proteins on opposite DNA strands. *Cell* **44:** 33–42.

Herr, W. and J. Clarke. 1986. The SV40 enhancer is composed of multiple functional elements that can compensate for one another. *Cell* **45:** 461–470.

Heyneker, H.L., J. Shine, H.M. Goodman, H. Boyer, J. Rosenberg, R.E. Dickerson, S.A. Narang, K. Itakura, S. Linn, and A.D. Riggs. 1976. Synthetic *lac* operator is functional *in vivo. Nature* **263:** 748–752.

Hiatt, A., R. Cafferkey, and K. Bosdish. 1989. Production of antibodies in transgenic plants. *Nature* **342:** 76–78.

Hicks, J.B., J.N. Strathern, and A.J.S. Klar. 1979. Transposable mating-type genes in *Saccharomyces cerevisiae. Nature* **282:** 478–483.

Hilschmann, N. and L.C. Craig. 1965. Amino acid sequence studies with Bence-Jones proteins. *Proc. Natl. Acad. Sci.* **53** 1403–1409.

Hinchee, M.A.W., D.V. Connor-Ward, C.A. Newell, R.E. McDonnell, S.J. Sato, C.S. Gasser, D.A. Fischoff, D.B. Re, R.T. Fraley, and R.B. Horsch. 1988. Production of transgenic soybean plants using *Agrobacterium*-mediated DNA transfer. *Biotechnology* **6:** 915–922.

Hoeijmakers, J., A. Frasch, A. Bernards, P. Borst, and G. Cross. 1980. Novel expression-linked copies of the genes for variant surface antigens in trypanosomes. *Nature* **284:** 78–80.

Hohn, B. and J. Collins. 1980. A small cosmid for efficient cloning of large DNA fragments. *Gene* **11:** 291–298.

Hohn, B. and K. Murray. 1977. Packaging recombinant DNA molecules into bacteriophage particles in vitro. *Proc. Natl. Acad. Sci.* **74 :** 3259–3263.

Holley, R.W. 1966. The nucleotide sequence of a nucleic acid. *Sci. Am.* **214(2):** 30–39.

Holliday, R. and J.E. Pugh. 1975. DNA modification mechanisms and gene activity during development. *Science* **187:** 226–232.

Horsch, R.B., R.T. Fraley, S.G. Rogers, P.R. Sanders, A. Lloyd, and N. Hoffmann. 1984. Inheritance of functional foreign genes in plants. *Science* **223:** 496–498.

Horsch, R.B., J.E. Fry, N.L. Hoffmann, D. Eichholtz, S.G. Rogers, and R.T. Fraley. 1985. A simple and general method for transferring genes into plants. *Science* **227:** 1229–1231.

Hotchkiss, R.D. 1948. The quantitative separation of purines, pyrimidines and nucleosides by paper chromatography. *J. Biol. Chem.* **175:** 315–332.

Hoyer, B.H., B.J. McCarthy, and E.T. Bolton. 1964. A molecular approach to the systematics of higher organisms. *Science* **144:** 959–967.

Hozumi, N. and S. Tonegawa. 1976. Evidence for somatic rearrangement of immunoglobulin genes coding for variable and constant region. *Proc. Natl. Acad. Sci.* **73:** 3628–3632.

Huntington's Disease Collaborative Research Group (58 authors). 1993. A novel gene containing a trinucleotide repeat that is expanded and unstable on Huntington's disease chromosomes. *Cell* **72:** 971–983.

Hutchinson, C.A., S. Phillips, M.H. Edgell, S. Gillam, P. Jahnke, and M. Smith. 1978. Mutagenesis at a specific position in a DNA sequence. *J. Biol. Chem.* **253:** 6551–6560.

Izant, J.G. and H. Weintraub. 1984. Inhibition of thymidine kinase gene expression by antisense RNA: A molecular approach to genetic analysis. *Cell* **36:** 1007–1015.

Jackson, D.A. and P.R. Cook. 1985. Transcription occurs at a nucleoskeleton. *EMBO J.* **4:** 919–925.

Jackson, D.A., S.J. McCready, and P.R. Cook. 1981. RNA is synthesized at the nuclear cage. *Nature* **292:** 552–555.

Jackson, D., R. Symons, and P. Berg. 1972. Biochemical method for inserting new genetic information into DNA of simian virus 40. Circular SV40 DNA molecules containing lambda phage genes and the galactose operon of *Escherichia coli. Proc. Natl. Acad. Sci.* **69:** 2904–2909.

Jacq, C., J.R. Miller, and G.G. Brownlee. 1977. A pseudogene structure in 5S DNA of *Xenopus laevis. Cell* **12:** 109–120.

Jaenisch, R. 1976. Germ line integration and Mendelian transmission of the exogenous Moloney leukaemia virus. *Proc. Natl. Acad. Sci.* **73:** 1260–1264.

Jeffreys, A.J. and R.A. Flavell. 1977. The rabbit β-globin gene contains a large insert in the coding sequence. *Cell* **12:** 1097–1108.

Jeffreys, A.J., V. Wilson, and S.C. Thein. 1985. Individual-specific fingerprints of human DNA. *Nature* **316:** 76–78.

Jelinek, W.R., T.P. Toomey, L. Leinwand, C.H. Duncan, P.A. Biro, P.V. Choudary, S.M. Weissman, C.M. Rubin, C.M. Houck, P.L. Deininger, and C.W. Schmid. 1980. Ubiquitous interspersed repeated DNA sequences in mammalian genomes. *Proc. Natl. Acad. Sci.* **77:** 1398–1402.

Jones, P.A., S.M. Taylor, T. Mohandas, and L.J. Shapiro. 1982. Cell cycle-specific reactivation of an inactive X–chromosome locus by 5-azadeoxycytidine. *Proc. Natl. Acad. Sci.* **79:** 1215–1219.

Kan, Y.W., S. Golbus, and A.M. Dozy. 1976. Prenatal diagnosis of alpha–thalassemia: Clinical application of molecular hybridization. *N. Engl. J. Med.* **295:** 1165–1167.

Kantoff, P.W., A.P. Gillio, J.R. McLachlin, C. Bordignon, M.A. Eglitis, N.A. Kernan, R.C. Moen, D.B. Kohn, S.-F. Yu, E. Karson, S. Karlsson, J.A. Zwiebel, E. Gilboa, R.M. Blaese, A. Nienhuis, R.J. O'Reilly, and W.F. Anderson. 1987. Expression of human adenosine deaminase in nonhuman primates after retrovirus-mediated gene transfer. *J. Exp. Med.* **166:** 219–134.

Kaul, R., G.P. Gao, K. Balamurugan, and R. Matalon. 1993. Cloning of the human aspartocyclase cDNA and a common missense mutation in Canavan disease. *Nat. Genet.* **5:** 118–123.

Kellenberger, G.M., M.L. Zichichi, and J.J. Weigle. 1961. Exchange of DNA in the recombination of bacteriophage λ. *Proc. Natl. Acad. Sci.* **47:** 869–878.

Kelly, T.J., Jr. and H.O. Smith. 1970. A restriction enzyme from *Hemophilus influenzae.* II. Base sequence of the recognition site. *J. Mol. Biol.* **51:** 393–409.

Kerem, B.-S., J.M. Rommens, J.A. Buchanan, D. Markiewicz, T.K. Cox, A. Chakravarti, M. Buchwald, and L.-C. Tsui. 1989. Identification of the cystic fibrosis gene: Genetic analysis. *Science* **245:** 1073–1080.

Khorana, H.G. 1979. Total synthesis of a gene. *Science* **203:** 614–625.

Kissinger, C.R., B. Liu, E. Martin-Blanco, T.B. Kornberg, and C.O. Pabo. 1990. Crystal structure of an engrailed homeodomain-DNA complex at 2.8 Å resolution: A framework for understanding homeodomain-DNA interactions. *Cell* **63:** 579–590.

Kleckner, N., R.K. Chan, B.-Y. Tye, and D. Botstein. 1975. Mutagenesis by insertion of a drug-resistance element carrying an inverted repetition. *J. Mol. Biol.* **97:** 561–565.

Klein, T.M., E.D. Wolff, R. Wu, and J.C. Sanford. 1987. High-velocity microprojectiles for delivering nucleic acids into living cells. *Nature* **327:** 70–73.

Knowlton, R.G., O. Cohen-Haguenauer, N.V. Cong, J. Frézal, V.A. Brown, D. Barker, J.C. Braman, J.W. Schumm, L.-C. Tsui, M. Buchwald, and H. Donis-Keller. 1985. A polymorphic DNA marker linked to cystic fibrosis is located on chromosome 7. *Nature* **318:** 380–382.

Koenig, M., E.P. Hoffman, C.J. Bertelson, A.P. Monaco, C. Feener, and L.M. Kunkel.

1987. Complete cloning of the Duchenne muscular dystrophy (DMD) cDNA and preliminary genomic organization of the DMD gene in normal and affected individuals. *Cell* **50:** 509–517.

Koopman, P., J. Gubbay, V. Vivian, P. Goodfellow, and R. Lovell-Badge. 1991. Male development of chromosomally female mice transgenic for *Sry. Nature* **351:** 117–121.

Kornberg, A. 1960. Biological synthesis of deoxyribonucleic acid. *Science* **131:** 1503–1508.

Kremer, E.J., M. Pritchard, M. Lynch, S. Yu, K. Holman, E. Baker, S.T. Warren, D. Schlessinger, G.R. Sutherland, and R.I. Richards. 1991. Mapping of DNA instability at the fragile X to a trinucleotide repeat sequence p(CCG)*n. Science* **252:** 1711–1714.

Krulewski, T.F., P.E. Neumann, and J.W. Gordon. 1989. Insertional mutation in a transgenic mouse allelic with Purkinje cell degeneration. *Proc. Natl. Acad. Sci.* **86:** 3709–3712.

Kunkel, L.M., A.P. Monaco, W. Middlesworth, H.D. Ochs, and S.A. Latt. 1985. Specific cloning of DNA fragments absent from the DNA of a male patient with an X-chromosome deletion. *Proc. Natl. Acad. Sci.* **82:** 4778–4782.

La Spada, A.R., E.M. Wilson, D.B. Lubahn, A.E. Harding, and K.H. Fischbeck. 1991. Androgen receptor gene mutations in X-linked spinal and bulbar muscular atrophy. *Nature* **352:** 77–79.

Lai, C.J. and D. Nathans. 1974. Deletion mutants of SV40 generated by enzymatic excision of DNA segments from the viral genome. *J. Mol. Biol.* **89:** 179–193.

Laski, F.A., D.C. Rio, and G.M. Rubin. 1986. Tissue specificity of *Drosophila* P element transposition is regulated at the level of mRNA splicing. *Cell* **44:** 7–19.

Laure, F., C. Rouzioux, F. Veber, C. Jacomet, V. Courgnard, S. Blanche, M. Burgard, C. Griscelli, and C. Brechot. 1988. Detection of HIV1 in infants and children by means of the polymerase chain reaction. *Lancet* **II:** 538–541.

Lazar, M.A., R.A. Hodin, D.S. Darling, and W.W. Chin. 1989. A novel member of the thyroid/steroid hormone receptor family is encoded by the opposite strand of the rat c-erbAα transcriptional unit. *Mol. Cell. Biol.* **9:** 1128–1136.

Leder, P., D. Tiemeier, and L. Enquist. 1977. EK2 derivatives of bacteriophage lambda useful in the cloning of DNA from higher organisms: The λgt *WES* system. *Science* **196:** 175–177.

Ledley, F.D., G.J. Darlington, T. Hahn, and S.L.C. Woo. 1987. Retroviral gene transfer into primary hepatocytes: Implications for genetic therapy of liver-specific functions. *Proc. Natl. Acad. Sci.* **84:** 5335–5339.

Lee, S.Y., J. Mendecki, and G. Brawerman. 1971. A polynucleotide segment rich in adenylic acid in the rapidly-labeled polyribosomal component of mouse sarcoma 180 ascites cells. *Proc. Natl. Acad. Sci.* **68:** 1331–1335.

Lemischka, I. and P.A. Sharp. 1982. The sequences of an expressed rat α–tubulin gene and a pseudogene with an inserted repetitive element. *Nature* **300:** 330–335.

Lichter, P., C.-J.C. Jang, K. Call, G. Hermanson, G.A. Evans, D. Housman, and D.C. Ward. 1990. High-resolution mapping of human chromosome 11 by in situ hybridization with cosmid clones. *Science* **247:** 64–69.

Lim, B., J.F. Apperley, S.H. Orkin, and D.A. Williams. 1989. Long-term expression of human adenosine deaminase in mice transplanted with retrovirus-infected hematopoietic stem cells. *Proc. Natl. Acad. Sci.* **86:** 8892–8896.

Lim, L. and E.S. Canellakis. 1970. Adenine-rich polymer associated with rabbit reticulocyte messenger RNA. *Nature* **227:** 710–712.

Linn, S. and W. Arber. 1968. Host specificity of DNA produced by *Escherichia coli.* X. In vitro restriction of phage fd replicative form. *Proc. Natl. Acad. Sci.* **59:** 1300–1306.

Lo, Y.-M.D., P. Patel, J.S. Wainscoat, M. Sampietro, M.D.G. Gillmer, and K.A. Fleming. 1989. Prenatal sex determination by DNA amplification from maternal peripheral blood. *Lancet* **II:** 1363–1365.

Lobban, P. and A.D. Kaiser. 1973. Enzymatic end-to-end joining of DNA molecules. *J. Mol. Biol.* **79:** 453–471.

Ludecke, H.-J., G. Senger, U. Claussen, and B. Horsthemke. 1989. Cloning defined regions of the human genome by microdissection of banded chromosomes and enzymatic amplification. *Nature* **338:** 348–350.

Mackett, M., G.L. Smith, and B. Moss. 1982. Vaccinia virus: A selectable eukaryotic cloning and expression vector. *Proc. Natl. Acad. Sci.* **79:** 7415–7419.

Mahadevan, M., C. Tsilfidis, L. Sabourin, G. Shutler, C. Amemiya, G. Jansen, C. Neville, M. Narang, J. Barcelo, K. O'Hoy, C. Leblond, J. Earle–Macdonald, P.J. de Jong, B. Wieringa, and R.G. Korneluk. 1992. Mytotonic dystrophy mutation: An unstable CTG repeat on the 3′ untranslated region of the gene. *Science* **255:** 1253–1255.

Mandel, J.L. and P. Chambon. 1979. DNA methylation: Organ specific variations in the methylation pattern within and around ovalbumin and other chicken genes. *Nucleic Acids Res.* **7:** 2081–2103.

Maniatis, T., S.G. Kee, A. Efstratiadis, and F.C. Kafatos. 1976. Amplification and characterization of a β-globin gene synthesized in vitro. *Cell* **8:** 163–182.

Mann, R., R.C. Mulligan, and D. Baltimore. 1983. Construction of a retrovirus packaging mutant and its use to produce helper-free defective retrovirus. *Cell* **33:** 153–159.

Mansour, S.L., K.R. Thomas, and M.R. Capecchi. 1988. Disruption of the proto-oncogene *int*-2 in mouse embryo-derived stem cells: A general strategy for targeting mutations to non–selectable genes. *Nature* **336:** 348–352.

Marmur, J. and L. Lane. 1960. Strand separation and specific recombination in deoxyribonucleic acids: Biological studies. *Proc. Natl. Acad. Sci.* **46:** 453–661.

Martin, G.R. 1981. Isolation of a pluripotent cell line from early mouse embryos cultured in medium conditioned by teratocarcinoma stem cells. *Proc. Natl. Acad. Sci.* **78:** 7634–7638.

Maxam, A.M. and W. Gilbert. 1977. A new method of sequencing DNA. *Proc. Natl. Acad. Sci.* **74:** 560–564.

McCabe, D.E., W.F. Swain, B.J. Martinell, and P. Cristou. 1988. Stable transformation of soybean *(Glycine max)* by particle acceleration. *Biotechnology* **6:** 923–926.

McClintock, B. 1952. Chromosome organization and genic expression. *Cold Spring Harbor Symp. Quant. Biol.* **16:** 13–47.

————. 1957. Controlling elements and the gene. *Cold Spring Harbor Symp. Quant. Biol.* **21:** 197–216.

McGhee, J.D. and G.D. Ginder. 1979. Specific DNA methylation sites in the vicinity of the chicken β-globin gene. *Nature* **280:** 419–420.

Mercer, J.F.B., J. Livingston, B. Hall, J.A. Paynter, C. Begy, S. Chandrasekharappa, P. Lockhart, A. Grimes, M. Bahve, D. Siemieniak, and T.W. Glover. 1992. Isolation of a partial candidate gene for Menkes disease by positional cloning. *Nat. Genet.* **3:** 20–25.

Merril, C.R., M.R. Geier, and J.C. Petricciani. 1971. Bacterial virus gene expression in human cells. *Nature* **233:** 398–400.

Mertz, J.E. and P. Berg. 1974. Defective simian virus 40 genomes: Isolation and growth of individual clones. *Virology* **62:** 112–114.

Mertz, J.E. and R.W. Davis. 1972. Cleavage of DNA by RI restriction endonuclease generates cohesive end. *Proc. Natl. Acad. Sci.* **69:** 3370–3374.

Mertz, J.E., J. Carbon, M. Herzberg, R.W. Davis, and P. Berg. 1975. Isolation and characterization of individual clones of simian virus 40 mutants containing deletions, duplications and insertions in their DNA. *Cold Spring Harbor Symp. Quant. Biol.* **39:** 69–84.

Meselson, M. and J.J. Weigle. 1961. Chromosome breakage accompanying genetic recombination in bacteriophage. *Proc. Natl. Acad. Sci.* **47:** 857–868.

Messing, J. and J. Vieira. 1982. The pUC plasmids, an M13mp7-derived system for insertion mutagenesis and sequencing with synthetic universal primers. *Gene* **19:** 259–268.

Miller, A.D., D.J. Jolly, T. Friedmann, and I.M. Verma. 1983. A transmissible retrovirus expressing human hypoxanthine phosphori-bosyltransferase (HPRT): Gene transfer into cells obtained from humans deficient in HPRT. *Proc. Natl. Acad. Sci.* **80:** 4709–4713.

Miller, J., A.D. McLachlan, and A. Klug. 1985. Repetitive zinc–binding domains in the protein transcription factor IIIA from *Xenopus* oocytes. *EMBO J.* **4:** 1609–1614.

Mintz, B. 1962. Formation of genotypically mosaic mouse embryos. *Am. Zool.* **2:** 432.

Mohandas, T., R.S. Sparkes, and L.J. Shapiro. 1981. Reactivation of an inactive human X chromosome: Evidence for X inactivation by DNA methylation. *Science* **211:** 393–396.

Mosser, J., H.M. Douar, C.-O. Sarde, P. Kioschis, R. Feil, H. Moser, A.M. Poustka, J.L. Mandel, and P. Aubourg. 1993. Putative X-linked adrenoleukodystrophy gene shares unexpected homology with ABC transporters. *Nature* **361:** 726–730.

Mulligan, R.C. and P. Berg. 1981. Selection for animal cells that express the *Escherichia coli* gene coding for xanthine-guanine phosphori-bosyltransferase. *Proc. Natl. Acad. Sci.* **78:** 2072–2076.

Mulligan, R., B.H. Howard, and P. Berg. 1979. Synthesis of rabbit β-globin in cultured monkey kidney cells following infection with an SV40 β-globin recombinant genome. *Nature* **277:** 108–114.

Mullis, K. and F. Faloona. 1987. Specific synthesis of DNA in vitro via a polymerase catalyzed chain reaction. *Methods Enzymol.* **55:** 335–350.

Murray, J.M., K.E. Davies, P.S. Harper, L. Meredith, C.R. Mueller, and R. Williamson. 1982. Linkage relationship of a cloned DNA sequence on the short arm of the X-chromosome to Duchenne muscular dystrophy. *Nature* **300:** 69–71.

Murre, C., P.S. McCaw, H. Vaessin, M. Caudy, L.Y. Jan, Y.N. Jan, C.V. Cabrera, J.N. Buskin, S.D. Hauschka, A.B. Lassar, H. Weintraub, and D. Baltimore. 1989. Interactions between heterologous helix-loop-helix proteins generate complexes that bind specifically to a common DNA sequence. *Cell* **58:** 537–544.

Nelson, D.L., S.A. Ledbetter, L. Corbo, M.F. Victoria, R. Ramirez-Solis, T.D. Webster, D.H. Ledbetter, and C.T. Caskey. 1989. *Alu* polymerase chain reaction: A method for rapid isolation of human-specific sequences from complex DNA sources. *Proc. Natl. Acad. Sci.* **86:** 6686–6690.

Neumann, E. and K. Rosenheck. 1972. Permeability changes induced by electrical impulses in vesicular membranes. *J. Membr. Biol.* **10:** 279–290.

———. 1973. An alternate explanation for the permeability changes induced by electrical impulses in vesicular membranes. *J. Membr. Biol.* **14:** 194–196.

Neumann, E., M. Schaefer-Ridder, Y. Wang, and P.H. Hofschneider. 1982. Gene transfer into mouse lyoma cells by electroporation in high electric fields. *EMBO J.* **1:** 841–845.

Nielson, P.E., M. Egholm, R.H. Berg, and O. Buchardt. 1991. Sequence-selective recognition of DNA by strand displacement with a thymine–substituted polyamide. *Science* **254:** 1497–1500.

Nitsch, D., M. Boshart, and G. Schütz. 1993. Extinction of tyrosine amino transferase gene activity in somatic cell hybrids involves modification and loss of several essential transcription activators. *Genes Dev.* **7:** 308–319.

Novick, A. and M. Weiner. 1957. Enzyme induction as an all-or-none phenomenon. *Proc. Natl. Acad. Sci.* **43:** 553–566.

Oberlé, I., F. Rousseau, D. Heitz, C. Kretz, D. Devys, A. Hanauer, J. Boué, M.F. Bertheas, and J.L. Mandel. 1991. Instability of a 550-base pair DNA segment and abnormal methylation in fragile X syndrome. *Science* **252:** 1097–1102.

O'Connell, P., R. Leach, R.M. Cawthorn, M. Culver, J. Stevens, D. Viskochil, R.E.K. Fournier, D.C. Rich, D.H. Ledbetter, and R. White. 1989. Two NFI translocations map within a 600 kilobase segment of 17q11.2. *Science* **244:** 1087–1088.

Olivera, B.M. and I.R. Lehman. 1967. Linkage of polynucleotides through phosphodiester bonds by an enzyme from *Escherichia coli*. *Proc. Natl. Acad. Sci.* **57:** 1426–1633.

Orr, H.T., M.-Y. Chung, S. Banji, T.J. Kwiatkowski, A. Servadio, A.L. Beaudet, A.E. McCall, L.A. Duvick, L.P.W. Ranum, and H.Y. Zoghbi. 1993. Expansion of an unstable trinucleotide CAG repeat in spinocerebellar ataxia type 1. *Nat. Genet.* **4:** 221–226.

Ostro, M.J., D. Giacomoni, D. Lavelle, W. Paxton, and S. Dray. 1978. Evidence for translation of rabbit globin mRNA after lysosome-mediated insertion into a human cell line. *Nature* **274:** 921–923.

Ou, C.-Y., S. Kwok, S.W. Mitchell, D.H. Mack, J.J. Sninsky, J.W. Krebs, P. Feorino, D. Warfield, and G. Schochetman. 1988. DNA amplification for the direct detection of HIV-1 in DNA of peripheral blood mononuclear cells. *Science* **239:** 295–297.

Pachnis, V., L. Perry, R. Rothstein, and F. Costantini. 1990. Transfer of a yeast artificial chromosome carrying human DNA from *Saccharomyces cerevisiae* into mammalian cells. *Proc. Natl. Acad. Sci.* **87:** 5109–5113.

Palmer, T.D., A.R. Thompson, and A.D. Miller. 1989. Production of human factor IX in animals by genetically modified skin fibroblasts: Potential for hemophilia B. *Blood* **73:** 438–445.

Palmer, T.D., R.A. Hock, W.R.A. Osborne, and A.D. Miller. 1987. Efficient retrovirus-mediated transfer and expression of a human adenosine deaminase gene in diploid skin fibroblasts from an adenosine deaminase–deficient human. *Proc. Natl. Acad. Sci.* **84:** 1055–1059.

Palmiter, R.D., R.R. Behringer, C.J. Quaife, F. Maxwell, I.H. Maxwell, and R.L. Brinster. 1987. Cell lineage ablation in transgenic mice by cell–specific expression of a toxin gene. *Cell* **50:** 435–444.

Panicali, D. and E. Paoletti. 1982. Construction of poxviruses as cloning vectors: Insertion of the thymidine kinase gene from herpes simplex virus into the DNA of infectious vaccinia virus. *Proc. Natl. Acad. Sci.* **79:** 4927–4931.

Papahadjopoulos, D., W.G. Vail, K. Jacobson, and G. Posle. 1975. Cochleate lipid cylinders: Formation by fusion of unilamellar lipid vesicles. *Biochim. Biophys. Acta* **394:** 483–491.

Perucho, M., D. Hanahan, and M. Wigler. 1980. Genetic and physical linkage of exogenous sequences in transformed cells. *Cell* **22:** 309–317.

Peterson, K.R., C.H. Clegg, C. Huxley, B.M. Josephson, H.S. Haugen, T. Furukawa, and G. Stamatoyannopoulos. 1993. Transgenic mice containing a 248-kb yeast artificial chromosome carrying the human β-globin locus display proper developmental control of human globin genes. *Proc. Natl. Acad. Sci.* **90:** 7593–7597.

Potter, H., L. Weir, and P. Leder. 1984. Enhancer-dependent expression of human K immunoglobulin genes introduced into mouse pre-B lymphocytes by electroporation. *Proc. Natl. Acad. Sci.* **81:** 7161–7165.

Proudfoot, N.J. and T. Maniatis. 1980. The structure of a human α-globin pseudogene and its relationship to α-globin gene duplication. *Cell* **21:** 537–544.

Rabbitts, T.H. 1976. Bacterial cloning of plasmids carrying copies of rabbit globin messenger RNA. *Nature* **260:** 221–225.

Reddy, V.B., B. Thimmappaya, R. Dhar, K.N. Subramanian, B.S. Zain, J. Pan, P.K. Ghosh, M.L. Celma, and S.M. Weissman. 1978. The genome of simian virus 40. *Science* **200:** 494–502.

Reed, R.R. and N.D.F. Grindley. 1981. Transposon-mediated site-specific recombination in vitro: DNA cleavage and protein-DNA linkage at the recombination site. *Cell* **25:** 721–728.

Reik, W., A. Collick, M.L. Norris, S.C. Barton, and M.A.H. Surani. 1987. Genomic imprinting determines methylation of parental alleles in transgenic mice. *Nature* **328:** 248–251.

Rich, D., M.P. Anderson, R.J. Gregory, S.H. Cheng, S. Paul, D.M. Jefferson, J.D. McCann, K.W. Klinger, A.E. Smith, and M.J. Welsh. 1990. Expression of the cystic fibrosis transmembrane conductance regulator corrects defective chloride channel regulation in cystic fibrosis airway epithelial cells. *Nature* **347:** 358–363.

Riggs, A.D. 1975. X-inactivation, differentiation and DNA metyhlation. *Cytogenet. Cell Genet.* **14:** 9–25.

Riordan, J.R., J.M. Rommens, B.-S. Kerem, N. Alon, R. Rozmahel, Z. Grzelczak, J. Zielenski, S. Lok, N. Plavsic, J.-L. Chou, M.L. Drumm, M.C. Iannuzzi, F.S. Collins, and L.-C. Tsui. 1989. Identification of the cystic fibrosis gene: Cloning and characterization of complementary DNA. *Science* **245:** 1066–1073.

Robins, D.M., S. Ripley, A.S. Henderson, and R. Axel. 1981. Transforming DNA integrates into the host chromosome. *Cell* **23:** 29–39.

Rommens, J.M., M.C. Iannuzzi, B.-S. Kerem, M.L. Drumm, G. Melmer, M. Dean, R. Rozmahel, J.L. Cole, D. Kennedy, N. Hidaka, M. Zsiga, M. Buchwald, J.R. Riordan, L.-C. Tsui, and F.S. Collins. 1989. Identification of the cystic fibrosis gene: Chromosome walking and jumping. *Science* **245:** 1059–1065.

Rougeon, F., P. Kourilsky, and B. Mach. 1975. Insertion of the rabbit β-globin gene sequence into *E. coli* plasmid. *Nucleic Acids Res.* **2:** 2365–2378.

Rouleau, G.A., P. Merel, M. Lutchman, M. Sanson, J. Zucman, C. Marineau, K. Hoang-Xuan, S. Demczuk, C. Desmaze, B. Plougastel, S.M. Pulst, G. Lenoir, E. Bijlsma, R. Fashold, J. Dumanski, P. de Jong, D. Parry, R. Eldrige, A. Aurias, O. Delattre, and G. Thomas. 1993. Alteration in a new gene encoding a putative membrane-organizing protein causes neurofibromatosis type 2. *Nature* **363**. 515–521.

Rubin, G.M. and A.C. Spradling. 1982. Genetic transformation of *Drosophila* with transposable element vectors. *Science* **218**: 348–353.

Sager, R. and R. Kitchin. 1975. Selective silencing of eukaryotic DNA. *Science* **189**: 426–433.

Saiki, R.K., S.J. Scharf, F. Faloona, K.B. Mullis, G.T. Horn, H.A. Erlich, and N. Arnheim. 1985. Enzymatic amplification of beta-globin sequences and restriction site analysis for diagnosis of sickle cell anaemia. *Science* **230**: 1350–1354.

Saiki, R.K., D.H. Gelfand, S. Stoffel, S.J. Scharf, R. Higuchi, G.T. Horn, K.B. Mullis, and H.A. Erlich. 1988. Primer-directed enzymatic amplification of DNA with a thermo-stable DNA polymerase. *Science* **239**: 487–491.

Saito, H., D.M. Kranz, Y. Takagaki, A.C. Hayday, H.N. Eisen, and S. Tonegawa. 1984. Complete primary structure of a heterodimeric T-cell receptor deduced from cDNA sequences. *Nature* **309**: 757–762.

Salser, W.A. 1974. DNA sequencing techniques. *Annu. Rev. Biochem.* **43**: 923–965.

Sanger, F. and A.R. Coulson. 1975. A rapid method for determining sequences in DNA by primed synthesis with DNA polymerase. *J. Mol. Biol.* **94**: 444–448.

Sanger, F., S. Nicklen, and A.R. Coulson. 1977. DNA sequencing with chain-terminating inhibitors. *Proc. Natl. Acad. Sci.* **74**: 5463–5467.

Sanger, F., G.M. Air, B.G. Barrell, N.L. Brown, A.R. Coulson, J.C. Fiddes, C.A. Hutchison III, P.M. Slocombe, and M. Smith. 1977. Nucleotide sequence of bacteriophage ΦX174. *Nature* **265**: 678–695.

Sapienza, C., A.C. Peterson, J. Rossant, and R. Balling. 1987. Degree of methylation of transgene is dependent on gamete of origin. *Nature* **328**: 51–54.

Scalenghe, F., E. Turco, J.-E. Edström, V. Pirotta, and M. Melli. 1981. Microdissection and cloning of DNA from specific region of *Drosophila melanogaster* polytene chromosomes. *Chromosoma* **82**: 205–216.

Schaefer-Ridder, M., Y. Wang, and P.H. Hofschneider. 1982. Liposomes as gene carriers. Efficient transformation of mouse L cells by thymidine kinase gene. *Science* **215**: 166–168.

Schedl, A., L. Montolin, G. Kelsey, and G. Schütz. 1993. A yeast artificial chromosome covering the tyrosinase gene confers copy number-dependent expression in transgenic mice. *Nature* **362**: 258–261.

Schildkraut, C.L., J. Marmur, and P. Doty. 1961. The formation of hybrid DNA molecules, and their use in studies of DNA homologies. *J. Mol. Biol.* **3**: 595–617.

Schimke, R.T., R.J. Kaufman, F.W. Alt, and R.F. Kellems. 1978. Gene amplification and drug resistance in cultured murine cells. *Science* **202**: 1051–1055.

Schmid, C.W. and W.R. Jelinek. 1982. The Alu family of dispersed repetitive sequences. *Science* **216**: 1065–1070.

Schwartz, D.C. and C.R. Cantor. 1984. Separation of yeast chromosome-sized DNAs by pulsed field gradient gel electrophoresis. *Cell* **37**: 67–75.

Sen, R. and D. Baltimore. 1986. Multiple nuclear factors interact with the immunoglobulin enhancer sequences. *Cell* **47**: 705–716.

Shimamoto, K., R. Terada, T. Izawa, and H. Fujimoto. 1989. Fertile transgenic rice plants regenerated from transformed protoplasts. *Nature* **338**: 274–276.

Shimotohno, K. and H.M. Temin. 1981. Formation of infectious progeny virus after insertion of herpes simplex thymidine kinase gene into DNA of an avian retrovirus. *Cell* **26**: 67–77.

Sijmons, P.C., B.M.M. Dekker, B. Schrammeijer, T.C. Verwoerd, P.J.M. van den Elzen, and A. Hoekema. 1990. Production of correctly processed human serum albumin in transgenic plants. *Biotechnology* **8**: 217–221.

Silva, A.J. and R. White. 1988. Inheritance of allelic blueprints for methylation patterns. *Cell* **54**: 145–152.

Sinclair, A.H., B. Phillipe, M.S. Palmer, J.R. Hawkins, B.L. Griffiths, M.J. Smith, J.W. Foster, A.M. Frischauf, R. Lovell-Badge, and P.N. Goodfellow. 1990. A gene from the human sex-determining region encodes a protein with homology to a conserved DNA-binding motif. *Nature* **346**: 240–244.

Singer, M.F. 1982. SINEs and LINEs: Highly repeated short and long interspersed sequences in mammalian genomes. *Cell* **28**: 433–434.

Slauer, J., C.-K.J. Shen, and T. Maniatis. 1980. The chromosomal arrangement of human α-like globin genes: Sequence homology and α-globin gene deletions. *Cell* **20**: 119–130.

Smith, G.E., M. Summers, and M.J. Fraser. 1983. Production of human β-interferon in insect cells infected with a baculovirus expression vector. *Mol. Cell. Biol.* **3**: 2156–2165.

Smith, G.P. 1976. Evolution of repeated DNA sequences by unequal crossovers. *Science* **191**: 528–537.

Smith, H.O. and K.W. Wilcox. 1970. A restriction enzyme from *Haemophilus influenzae*. I. Purification and general properties. *J. Mol. Biol.* **51**: 379–391.

Smithies, O., R.G. Gregg, S.S. Boggs, M.A. Koralewski, and R.S. Kucherlapati. 1985. Insertion of DNA sequences into the human chromosomal β-globin locus by homologous recombination. *Nature* **317**: 230–234.

Snouwert, J.N., K.K. Brigman, A.M. Latour, N.N. Malouf, R.C. Boucher, O. Smithies, and B.H. Koller. 1992. An animal model for cystic fibrosis made by gene targeting. *Science* **257**: 1083–1088.

Sorge, J., W. Kuhl, C. West, and E. Beutler. 1987. Complete correction of the enzymatic defect of type I Gaucher disease fibroblasts by retroviral-mediated gene transfer. *Proc. Natl. Acad. Sci.* **84**: 906–909.

Southern, E.M. 1975. Detection of specific sequences among DNA fragments separated by gel electrophoresis. *J. Mol. Biol.* **98**: 503–517.

———. 1993. Physiology and genes. In *The logic of life* (ed. C.A.R. Boyd and D. Noble), pp. 43–62. Oxford University Press, United Kingdom.

Stenman, G., A. Anisowicz, and R. Sager. 1988. Genetic analysis of tumorigenesis. XXXII. Localization of constitutionally amplified k-*ras* sequences to Chinese hamster chromosomes X and Y by in situ hybridization. *Somatic Cell Mol. Genet.* **14**: 639–644.

Stephenson, M.L. and P.C. Zamecnik. 1978. Inhibition of Rous sarcoma virus RNA translation by a specific oligodeoxyribonucleotide. *Proc. Natl. Acad. Sci.* **75**: 285–288.

Suggs, S.V., R.B. Wallace, T. Hirose, E.H. Kawashima, and K. Itakura. 1981. Use of synthetic oligonucleotides as hybridization probes: Isolation of cloned cDNA sequences for human β$_2$-microglobulin. *Proc. Natl. Acad. Sci.* **78**: 6613–6617.

Swain, J.L., T.A. Stewart, and P. Leder. 1987. Parental legacy determines methylation and expression of an autosomal transgene: A molecular mechanism for parental imprinting. *Cell* **50**: 719–727.

Swift, G.H., R.E. Hammer, R.J. MacDonald, and R.L. Brinster. 1984. Tissue-specific expression of the rat pancreatic elastase I gene in transgenic mice. *Cell* **38**: 639–646.

Tarkowski, A.K. 1961. Mouse chimaeras developed from fused eggs. *Nature* **190**: 857–860.

Temin, H.M. and S. Mizutani. 1970. Viral RNA-dependent DNA polymerase. *Nature* **226**: 1211–1213.

Tepler, D. 1982. La transformation génétique de plantes supérieures par *Agrobacterium rhizogenes*. *Colloq. Rech. Fruit.* (Bordeaux) **2**: 47–59.

———. 1984. Transformation of several species of higher plants by *Agrobacterium rhizogenes*: Sexual transmission of the transformed genotype and phenotype. *Cell* **37**: 959–967.

Thomas, K.R. and M.R. Capecchi. 1987. Site-directed mutagenesis by gene targeting in mouse-embryo-derived stem cells. *Cell* **51**: 503–512.

Thummel, C., R. Tjian, and T. Grodzicker. 1981. Expression of SV40 T antigen under control of adenovirus promoters. *Cell* **23**: 825–836.

Toriyama, K., Y. Arimoto, H. Uchimiya, and K. Hinata. 1988. Transgenic rice plants after direct gene transfer into protoplasts. *Biotechnology* **6**: 1072–1074.

Treisman, R., N.J. Proudfoot, M. Shander, and T. Maniatis. 1982. A single-base change at a splice site in a β^0-thalassemic gene causes abnormal RNA splicing. *Cell* **29**: 903–911.

Urdea, M.S., B.D. Warner, J.A. Running, M. Stempien, J. Clyne, and T. Horn. 1988. A comparison of non-radioisotopic hybridization assay methods using fluorescent, chemiluminescent and enzyme labeled synthetic oligodeoxyribonucleotide probes. *Nucleic Acids Res.* **16**: 4937–4956.

Vandekerckhove, J., J. van Damme, M. van Lijsebettens, J. Botterman, M. De Block, M. Vandewiele, A. De Clercq, J. Leemans, M. van Montagu, and E. Krebbers. 1989. Enkephalins produced in transgenic plants using modified 2S seed storage proteins. *Biotechnology* **7**: 929–932.

Van Larebeke, N., G. Engler, M. Holsters, S. Van den Elsacker, I. Zaenen, R.H. Schilperoort, and J. Schell. 1974. Large plasmid in *Agrobacterium tumefaciens* essential for crown gall-inducing ability. *Nature* **252**: 169–170.

Verkerk, A.J.M.H., M. Pieretti, J.S. Sutcliffe, Y.-H. Fu, D.P.A. Kukl, A. Pizzuti, O. Reiner, S. Richards, M.F. Victoria, F. Zhang, B.E. Eussen, G.-J.B. van Ommen, L.A.V. Blonden, G. Riggins, J.L. Chastain, C.B. Kunst, H. Galjaard, C.T. Caskey, D.L. Nelson, B.A. Oostra, and S.T. Warren. 1991. Identification of a gene (FMR-1) containing a CGG repeat coincident with a breakpoint cluster region exhibiting length variation in fragile X syndrome. *Cell* **65**: 905–914.

Vetrie, D., I. Vorechovsky, P. Sideras, J. Holland, A. Davies, F. Flinter, L. Hammarström, C. Kinnon, R. Levinsky, M. Bobrow, C.I.E. Smith, and D.R. Bentley. 1993. The gene involved in X-linked agammaglobulinaemia is a member of the src family of protein kinases. *Nature* **361**: 226–233.

Villa–Komaroff, L., A. Efstratiadis, S. Broome, P. Lomedica, R. Tizard, S.P. Nabet, W.L. Chick, and W. Gilbert. 1978. A bacterial clone synthesizing proinsulin. *Proc. Natl. Acad. Sci.* **75**: 3727–3731.

Viskochil, D., A.M. Buchberg, G. Xu, R.M. Cawthorn, J. Stevens, R.K. Wolff, M. Culver, J.C. Carey, N.G. Copeland, and N.A. Jenkins. 1990. Deletions and a translocation interrupt a cloned gene at the neurofibromatosis type 1 locus. *Cell* **62**: 187–192.

Vulpe, C., B. Levinson, S. Whitney, S. Packman, and J. Gitschier. 1992. Isolation of a candidate gene for Menkes disease and evidence that it encodes a copper-transporting ATPase. *Nat. Genet.* **3**: 7–13.

Wainwright, B.J., P.J. Scambler, J. Schmidtke, E.A. Watson, H.-Y. Law, M. Farrall, H.J. Cooke, H. Eiberg, and R. Williamson. 1985. Localization of cystic fibrosis locus to human chromosome 7 cen-q22. *Nature* **318**: 384–385.

Wallace, R.B., M. Schold, M.J. Johnson, P. Dembek, and K. Itakura. 1981. Oligonucleotide-directed mutagenesis of the human β-globin gene: A general method for producing specific point mutations in cloned DNA. *Nucleic Acids Res.* **9**: 3642–3656.

Walter, G., I.M. Tomlinson, G.P. Cook, G. Winter, T.H. Rabbits, and P.H. Dear. 1993. Happy mapping of a YAC reveals alternative haplotypes in the human immunoglobulin VH locus. *Nucleic Acids Res.* **21**: 4524–4529.

Weiner, A. 1980. An abundant cytoplasmic 7S RNA is partially complementary to the dominant interspersed middle repetitive DNA sequence family in the human genome. *Cell* **22**: 209–218.

Weiss, B. and C.C. Richardson. 1967. Enzymatic breakage and joining of deoxyribonucleic acid. I. Repair of single-strand breaks in DNA by an enzyme system from *Escherichia coli* infected with T4 bacteriophage. *Proc. Natl. Acad. Sci.* **57**: 1021–1028.

Wellauer, P.K., R.H. Reeder, D. Carrol, D.D. Brown, A. Deutch, T. Higashinakagawa, and I.B. Dawid. 1974. Amplified ribosomal DNA from *Xenopus laevis* has heterogeneous spacer lengths. *Proc. Natl. Acad. Sci.* **71**: 2823–2871.

White, R., S. Woodward, M. Leppert, P. O'Connell, M. Hoff, J. Herbst, J.-M. Lalouel, M. Dean, and G. Vande Woude. 1985. A closely linked genetic marker for cystic fibrosis. *Nature* **318**: 382–384.

Wickner, S.H. 1978. DNA replication proteins of *Escherichia coli*. *Annu. Rev. Biochem.* **47**: 1163–1191.

Wigler, M., A. Pellicer, S. Silverstein, and R. Axel. 1978. Biochemical transfer of single-copy eucaryotic genes using total cellular DNA as donor. *Cell* **14**: 725–731.

Wigler, M., S. Silverstein, L.-S. Lee, A. Pellicer, Y.-C. Cheng, and R. Axel. 1977. Transfer of purified herpes virus thymidine kinase gene to cultured mouse cells. *Cell* **11**: 223–232.

Wigler, M., R. Sweet, G.K. Sim, B. Wold, A. Pellicer, E. Lacy, T. Maniatis, S. Silverstein, and R. Axel. 1979. Transformation of mammalian cells with genes from prokaryotes and eukaryotes. *Cell* **16**: 777–785.

Wilson, J.M., D.M. Jefferson, J.R. Chowdhury, P.M. Novikoff, D.E. Johnston, and R.C. Mulligan. 1988. Retrovirus-mediated transduction of adult hepatocytes. *Proc. Natl. Acad. Sci.*. **85:** 3014–3018,

Wolf, S.F. and B.R. Migeon. 1982. Studies of X chromosome DNA methylation in normal human cells. *Nature* **295:** 667–671.

Wong, C., C.E. Dowling, R.K. Saiki, R.G. Higuchi, H.A. Erlich, and H.H. Kazazian. 1987. Characterization of β-thalassemia mutations using direct genomic sequencing of amplified single copy DNA. *Nature* **330:** 384–386.

Wong, T.-K. and E. Neumann. 1982. Electric field mediated gene transfer. *Biochem. Biophys. Res. Commun.* **107:** 584–587.

Wong, T.-K., C. Nicolau, and P.H. Hofschneider. 1980. Appearance of β-lactamase activity in animal cells upon liposome-mediated gene transfer. *Gene* **10:** 87–94.

Worton, R.G., C. Duff, J.E. Sylvester, R.D. Schmickel, and H.F. Willard. 1984. Duchenne muscular dystrophy involving translocation of the *dmd* gene next to ribosomal RNA genes. *Science* **224:** 1447–1449.

Woychik, R.P., T.A. Stewart, L.G. Davis, P. D'Eustachio, and P. Leder. 1985. An inherited limb deformity created by insertional mutagenesis in a transgenic mouse. *Nature* **318:** 36–40.

Yanagi, Y., Y. Yoshikai, K. Leggett, S.P. Clark, I. Aleksander, and T.W. Mak. 1984. A human T-cell-specific cDNA clone encodes a protein having extensive homology to immunoglobulin chains. *Nature* **308:** 145–149.

Yanisch-Peron, C., J. Vieira, and J. Messing. 1985. Improved M13 phage cloning vectors and host strains: Nucleotide sequences of the M13mp18 and pUC19 vectors. *Gene* **33:** 103–119.

Young, R.A. and R.W. Davis. 1983. Efficient isolation of genes by using antibody probes. *Proc. Natl. Acad. Sci.* **80:** 1194–1198.

Zabel, B.U., S.L. Naylor, A.Y. Sakaguchi, G.I. Bell, and T.B. Shows. 1983. High resolution chromosomal localization of human genes for amylase, proopiomelanocortin, somatostatin and a DNA fragment (D3S1) by in situ hybridization. *Proc. Natl. Acad. Sci.* **80:** 6932–6936.

Zamecnik, P.C. and M.L. Stephenson. 1978. Inhibition of Rous sarcoma virus replication and cell transformation by a specific oligodeoxynucleotide. *Proc. Natl. Acad. Sci.* **75:** 280–284.

Zijlstra, M., E. Li, F. Sajjadi, S. Subramani, and R. Jaenisch. 1989. Germ-line transmission of a disrupted β_2-microglobulin gene produced by homologous recombination in embryonic stem cells. *Nature* **342:** 435–438.

Zijlstra, M., M. Bix, N.E. Simister, J.M. Loring, D.H. Raulet, and R. Jaenisch. 1990. β_2-Microglobulin deficient mice lack CD4$^-$8$^+$ cytolytic T cells. *Nature* **344:** 742–746.

Zimmer, A. and P. Gruss. 1989. Production of chimaeric mice containing embryonic stem (ES) cells carrying a homeobox Hox 1.1 allele mutated by homologous recombination. *Nature* **338:** 150–153.

Zimmermann, U., J. Schulz, and G. Pilwat. 1973. Transcellular ion flow in *Escherichia coli* B and electrical sizing of bacterias. Biophys. J. **13:** 1005–1013.

Zoller, M.J. and M. Smith. 1982. Oligonucleotide-directed mutagenesis using M13-derived vectors: An efficient general procedure for production of point mutation in any fragment of DNA. *Nucleic Acids Res.* **10:** 6487–6500.

7
ANALYSIS OF MALIGNANCY

THE GENES OF ONCOGENIC DNA VIRUSES

In Chapter 4, the experiments that implicated DNA viruses in the genesis of tumours were briefly reviewed as was the evidence for the conclusion that the role played by DNA viruses in this process was an indirect one. The developments in nucleic acid biotechnology described in Chapter 6 enabled the mode of action of these viruses to be dissected in terms of the structure and function of specific transforming genes. In the case of polyoma virus, three genes were found to determine nuclear proteins designated large (100 kD), middle (55 kD) and small (22 kD) T antigens. Rassoulzadegan et al. (1982, 1983) showed that the large T antigen was responsible for establishing continuous growth of transfected cultures and for diminishing their serum requirement, and middle T appeared to be involved in determining other elements of the transformed phenotype. No particular role was found for small T in the transformation process. The large T antigen of simian virus 40 combined the functions of both the large and the middle T antigens of polyoma virus and was thus able to achieve transformation alone (Kriegler et al. 1984). Again, the role of the small T antigen in simian virus 40 remained unclear, but there was some indirect evidence that it might produce alterations in the cytoskeleton of the cell. However, the evidence indicating only an indirect role for these viruses in producing tumours and the fact that they did not produce tumours in their natural hosts tended to remove them from the centre of interest. Their place was soon taken by another, long neglected, member of this family, the papilloma virus. Dürst et al. (1983) showed that papilloma virus could transform cells *in vitro*, and substantial evidence was soon accumulated that papilloma virus types 16 and 18 were closely associated with ano-genital cancer in man (zur Hausen 1991). The transforming genes of bovine papilloma virus were mapped and revealed the presence of two domains, one that contained four complete open reading frames and one that contained only one such frame, which was named E6 (Schiller, Vass, and Lowy 1984; Yang, Okayama, and Howley 1985). However, Schwarz et al. (1985) found that in some tumours the messenger RNA from only E6 was present, which made it appear probable that it was this gene that was critically involved in the transformation process. Subsequent experiments revealed that a second gene, E7, was also strongly implicated. Nonetheless, as had previously been shown for polyoma virus, fusion of cells transformed by papilloma virus with non-transformed cells resulted in suppression of the transformed phenotype and inhibition of the expression of the E6 and E7 genes. This indicated that, in this system also, the viral genes could induce transformation only if certain cellular genes were put out of action (Bosch et al. 1990). In the case of the adenoviruses, two genes, named E1A and E1B, were initially defined as the elements responsible for the transformation of cells. Later work showed that E1B was not involved, but E1A was confirmed as an essential component not only of transformation *in vitro* but also of adenovirus-induced tumorigenesis in experimental animals. There was, however, little evidence that adenoviruses were tumorigenic in man (van der Elsen, Houweling, and van der Eb 1983; van der Eb and Bernards 1984). Reference has already been made to the experiments of Galloway and McDougall (1983) which indicated that herpes simplex virus induced transformation by a 'hit-and-run' mechanism that made all the viral genes dispensable once certain stable genetic changes had been inflicted on the cell. Minson (1984) made similar observations with both herpes simplex virus and human cytomegalovirus. As there was no decisive evidence that these herpes simplex viruses, any more than the adenoviruses, were important aetiological factors in the genesis of human cancers, the search for herpes genes that might act as direct carcinogens soon lost its attraction. But there was a resurgence of interest in herpes viruses when it was found that a causative agent in the genesis of Burkitt's lymphoma was a member of the herpes family (Epstein, Achong, and Barr 1964). The Epstein-Barr virus was found to be able to 'transform' B lymphocytes in the sense that some of the cells infected with the virus generated progeny capable of indefinite multiplication *in vitro*; and the related herpes saimiri virus induced an essentially similar transformation of T lymphocytes. In the case of the latter, a 2-kb region of the viral DNA was isolated that appeared to be essential for both transformation and tumorigenicity (Desrosiers et al. 1985). A nuclear antigen produced by the Epstein-Barr virus (EBNA) seemed at one point to be a likely candidate for the essential transforming gene of that virus, but Yates, Warren, and Sugden (1985) showed that this antigen was required for the replication of the viral DNA when this was present in the cell as an episome; it therefore seemed unlikely that EBNA was involved specifically in the process of transformation. But the decisive evidence that the role of these herpes viruses in generating tumours was, at best, indirect, came from the observation that all Burkitt lymphomas were clonal populations. It was thus clear that only a rare cell in the vast number infected by the virus underwent the additional genetic changes that had to take place before a malignant tumour emerged.

ONCOGENES AND ONCOGENIC RNA VIRUSES

In 1969, a paper by Huebner and Todaro, although it proved to be factually incorrect, presented an idea (and a terminology) that largely turned attention away from the DNA-containing tumour viruses to the RNA-containing retroviruses. Huebner and Todaro sought an explanation for the vertical transmission of leukaemia in mice and suggested that some part of the viral genome was present in the germ line of the animal. They proposed that this genetic component, which they named an 'oncogene', was normally inactive, but that, under the influence of carcinogenic agents such as X rays, or even spontaneously as a consequence of ageing, the gene was turned on with the result that complete virus was then produced and the cell became cancerous. Later work showed that murine leukaemia viruses did not have oncogenes in the sense that was subsequently adopted for the use of that term, although it must be said that eventually the label 'oncogene' came to be used to describe virtually any gene that had some role to play in cancer, no matter how peripheral. In a review written in 1971, Temin pointed out that several strains of RNA tumour viruses could induce 'transformation' of the host cell, and Martin (1970), by exposing Rous sarcoma virus to a chemical mutagen, obtained conditional mutants for a viral gene that was essential for the transformation process. This gene, subsequently named the *src* gene, was analysed further by Kawai and Hanafusa (1971) and by Bader (1972) and soon became the object of intense investigation. Using deletion mutants segregated during the preparation of clonal populations of avian sarcoma viruses, Stéhelin (Fig. 59), Guntala, Varmus (Fig. 60), and Bishop (Fig. 61) (1976) purified DNA complementary to the nucleotide sequences that were required for the transformation of fibroblasts *in vitro*; and this permitted the observation to be made that the normal avian genome contained DNA that was homologous to the transforming sequences of avian sarcoma virus (Stéhelin, Varmus, Bishop, and Vogt 1976). It was this observation that launched the decade of the oncogene. Spector, Varmus, and Bishop (1978) showed that sequences related to the avian *src* gene were also present in the genomes of other vertebrates including man. Czernilofsky et al. (1980) determined the nucleotide sequence of the *src* gene and deduced an amino acid sequence for the gene product. Also in 1980, Sheiness et al. discovered a vertebrate homologue of the putative transforming gene of avian myelocytomatosis virus (named *myc*) and characterised both the DNA of this genomic locus and the RNA transcribed from it. From these findings the conclusion was drawn that the genes of the oncogenic retroviruses were originally derived from cellular genes taken into the virus by some form of recombination and subsequently modified by mutational events which were consolidated by evolutionary pressures.

This idea was enormously influential and gave rise not only to a new conception of the role that these cellular homologues of retroviral genes might play in the generation of tumours, but also to an elaborate symbolic nomenclature based on sequence homology. The transforming genes in the viruses themselves were, by general consent, allotted the name 'oncogenes' and given the prefix 'v-'; their genomic homologues were named 'proto-oncogenes' and given the prefix 'c-'. The shorthand designations adopted for the individual oncogens or proto-oncogenes were acronyms or contractions of the name of the virus in which they were found. Thus, the shorthand for the oncogene of avian myeloblastosis virus was *myb*; for that of Moloney murine sarcoma virus, *mos*; for that of avian myelocytomatosis virus, *myc*; for that of Abelson murine leukaemia virus, *abl*; and so on. In 1983, a review by Bishop listed 17 retroviral oncogenes that had by that time been identified. Eventually, the count rose to well over 100. Given that cellular proto-oncogenes captured by viruses could be modified to produce genes capable of inducing transformation in cells, it was a small step to conclude that mutations in proto-oncogenes within the genome might also convert them into active oncogenes that could induce transformation and thus contribute to the production of tumours. This idea met with widespread enthusiasm and at once became the focus of numerous investigations. But as early as 1981, Payne et al. showed that in the case of bursal tumours induced by avian leukosis virus, expression of the viral genes was not required for the maintenance of tumorous growth. And in the

FIGURE 59 Dominique Stéhelin (1943–).
(Courtesy of Dr. Dominique Stéhelin.)

FIGURE 60 Harold Varmus (1939–).
(Courtesy of the Nobel Foundation.)

FIGURE 61 J. Michael Bishop (1936–).
(Courtesy of the Nobel Foundation.)

Stéhelin, Varmus, Bishop, and Vogt showed that DNA nucleotide sequences homologous to the transforming sequences of avian sarcoma virus were present in the normal avian genome. It quickly became apparent that many vertebrates, including man, harboured genes that were closely related to the genes of oncogenic RNA viruses. This family of cellular genes, when mutated or inappropriately expressed, were collectively named 'oncogenes' although this term was originally used to describe a different concept.

case of lymphomas produced by Abelson virus, Grunwald et al. (1982) showed that there was actually selection against the Abelson viral genes during the progressive growth of the tumour. It thus appeared that, at least for some retroviral oncogenes, their role in generating tumours was no more direct than the transforming genes of the DNA viruses. The retroviral oncogenes clearly did produce in some susceptible cells changes that greatly increased the probability of their sustaining further genetic modifications that might eventually lead to malignancy; but once this had been established, the retroviral oncogenes seemed to be dispensable.

ONCOGENES DETECTED BY TRANSFECTION OF DNA

Another method for detecting and isolating oncogenes was developed by C. Shih et al. (1979). These authors transfected into NIH 3T3 cells DNA and chromatin from cells that had been transformed by chemical agents and showed that the transformed phenotype could be transmitted in this way. Shih et al. claimed that DNA from untransformed cells was ineffective, but Cooper, Okenquist, and Silverman (1980) found that DNA from normal cells did produce some transformed colonies in transfected populations of NIH 3T3 cells. In fact, it was soon established that the NIH 3T3 mouse cell line, although it normally had a flat, untransformed growth habit, did spontaneously generate transformed colonies, especially at high population densities. This finding provoked some criticism of the NIH 3T3 transfection assay, but the frequency of spontaneous transformation was low compared with the frequencies that could be obtained with DNA from some transformed or tumorigenic cells. The assay proved, in the event, to be robust enough to permit interesting genes to be identified. Krontiris and Cooper (1981) tested DNA preparations from 26 human tumours and tumour cell lines, but found transforming activity in only two lines derived from bladder carcinomas. The first transforming sequence to be isolated by transfection of DNA was also derived from the genome of a human bladder carcinoma cell line (Shih and Weinberg 1982). This sequence turned out to be a homologue of the Harvey murine sarcoma virus *ras* gene (Der, Krontiris, and Cooper 1982; Parada et al. 1982; Santos et al. 1982). The cellular transforming gene (c-Ha-*ras*) was soon cloned and partially characterised (Goldfarb et al. 1982; Pulciani et al. 1982); and Reddy et al. (1982) showed that its ability to transform cells was conferred by a single point mutation that resulted in the substitution of valine for glycine at position 12 in the polypeptide chain. Der, Krontiris, and Cooper (1982) found in a human lung carcinoma a transforming DNA sequence that was homologous to the *ras* gene of Kirsten murine sarcoma virus. This gene became c-Ki-*ras*. A third member of the *ras* family, designated N-*ras*, was identified first in human sarcoma cell lines (Marshall, Hall, and Weiss 1982; Hall et al. 1983) and then in a human neuroblastoma cell line (Shimizu et al. 1983). Vousden and Marshall (1984) and Paterson et al. (1987) presented strong evidence that it was indeed the mutated N-*ras* gene that induced the transformed phenotype in human sarcoma cells. Smith et al. (1982) showed that the transformed phenotype could also be transmitted to Chinese hamster embryo fibroblasts by DNA transfection; but human fibroblasts were found to be completely refractory to transformation by the v-*src* oncogene that transformed embryonic rodent fibroblasts efficiently (Hjelle, Liu, and Bishop 1988).

The proteins coded by the *ras* genes were found to have an estimated molecular weight of 21,000, and were given the abbreviated designation p21. p21 appeared to be the only gene product of murine sarcoma viruses that was necessary for transformation. The normal cellular homologue was present at low concentrations in the cells of many vertebrates, but relatively high levels of p21 were found in virus-transformed cells (T.Y. Shih et al. 1979a; Langbeheim, Shih, and Scolnick 1980). Analysis of the Harvey and Kirsten ras p21 proteins led Ellis et al. (1981) to conclude that they were divergent members of a family of normal vertebrate genes. Dhar et al. (1982) determined the nucleotide sequence of the Ha-*ras* gene, and Tsuchida, Ryder, and Ohtsubo (1982) determined the sequence of the Ki-*ras* gene. That the mutated ras p21 protein was the key element in producing cell transformation was confirmed by Bar-Sagi and Feramisco (1985, 1986), who demonstrated that morphological changes associated with transformation could be produced by direct microinjection of the protein into the cell. Feramisco et al. (1985) showed that transformation induced by the *ras* oncogene could be reversed by antibodies specific for the ras protein carrying the amino acid substitution in position 12.

INSERTIONAL MUTAGENESIS

The study of avian leukosis viruses revealed that aberrant function of cellular proto-oncogenes could also be produced by insertional mutagenesis at a nearby site. These viruses induced B-cell lymphomas but, as mentioned previously, they did not appear to contain an oncogene as that term now came to be defined. However, Fung et al. (1981), Neel et al. (1981), and Payne et al. (1981) found that nearly all lymphomas produced by avian leukosis virus contained viral sequences integrated at a common site in the host genome. It appeared that this integration site was very close to the normal c-*myc* gene in the host genome, and this was confirmed for avian bursal lymphomas by Noori-Daloii et al. (1981) and by Payne, Bishop, and Varmus (1982). Nusse and Varmus (1982) showed that tumours induced by mammary tumour virus also contained viral sequences integrated into the host genome at a common site. It thus appeared likely that insertional mutagenesis was, in some cases, responsible for alterations in proto-oncogene function, even though the proto-oncogene involved had not sustained any mutation. Even so, as will be seen presently, regulation of the *myc* oncogene turned out to be a very complicated process.

BIOCHEMICAL FUNCTIONS OF ONCOGENES

The very large number of oncogenes identified by homology with retroviral genes or by transfection of DNA naturally exhibited a wide range of different functions. Intensive and protracted analysis revealed, however, that these functions fell into five broad classes: growth factors; receptors for growth factors and cytokines; components of systems that transmitted signals to or within the cell; protein kinases; and nuclear proteins involved in the transcription or replication of DNA. While it is altogether probable that other families of genes had also been captured by retroviruses, it was not at all easy to see how these might be identified; and although the genes captured by the oncogenic viruses were heterogeneous enough, it seemed that they all had something to do with the regulation of cell growth and cell differentiation. The first oncogene product to be identified, a 60-kD polypeptide produced by the avian sarcoma *src* gene, turned out to be a protein kinase (Brugge and Erikson 1977; Collett and Erikson 1978; Levinson et al. 1978). Hunter and Cooper (1985) showed that the phosphorylation mediated by the *src* gene product took place at tyrosine, rather than the usual serine, residues; and it was soon discovered that this property was shared by several other protein kinases, for example *fes* (Snyder-Theilen feline sarcoma virus), *abl* (Abelson murine leukaemia virus), *fms* (McDonough feline sarcoma virus), and also by some normal cellular proteins. All of these tyrosine kinases were found to have a common or closely homologous catalytic domain of approximately 30 kD, and they fell into one of two classes, transmembrane receptors or cytoplasmic proteins that were associated with membranes. The normal cellular transmembrane receptors for epidermal growth factor, platelet-derived growth factor, colony-stimulating factor and insulin all proved to be tyrosine kinases.

Doolittle et al. (1983) and Waterfield et al. (1983) discovered that the v-*sis* (simian sarcoma virus) oncogene product had an 88% amino acid sequence identity with the β chain of platelet-derived growth factor; and Downward et al. (1984) drew attention to the fact that there was a close amino acid sequence similarity between the v-*erb*B (avian erythroblastosis virus) oncogene product and the epidermal growth factor receptor. Ullrich et al. (1984) showed that the gene coding for the epidermal growth factor receptor was amplified and expressed aberrantly in a line of human epidermoid carcinoma cells; and Sherr et al. (1985) showed that the product of the v-*fms* oncogene was homologous with the cellular transmembrane receptor for macrophage colony-stimulating factor. These findings suggested models for tumorigenicity based on continuous stimulation of cell multiplication by aberrant or amplified receptors for growth factors, or by continuous overproduction of the growth factors themselves. Some exemplary, but rather artificial, cell systems were later discovered in which mechanisms of this sort did appear to play a key role in maintaining continuous cell multiplication. The products of the *src*, *abl* and *fes* oncogenes were found to be cytoplasmic tyrosine kinases, but their precise role in the regulatory mechanisms of the cell remained unclear. *src* was originally thought to be bound to the inner surface of the plasma membrane, but was later shown to be associated with the Golgi apparatus.

It took several years for the functional connections of the ras p21 protein to be established. Scolnick and his colleagues showed in 1979 that p21 was phosphorylated and that it formed complexes with guanine nucleotides (Scolnick, Papageorge, and Shih 1979; T.Y. Shih et al. 1979b). Shih et al. (1980) showed further that purified p21, in addition to having guanine nucleotide-binding activity, underwent autophosphorylation at a threonine residue when guanosine tri- or diphosphate, but not adenosine tri- or diphosphate, were used as phosphoryl donors. Willingham et al. (1980) demonstrated by electron microscopic immunochemistry that the viral p21 was located on the inner surface of the plasma membrane of the cell. The first indication that p21 was involved in some way in transmitting signals to or within the cell was the observation by Mulcahy, Smith, and Stacey (1985) that the protein was essential for the growth response induced in NIH 3T3 cells by the addition of serum to the medium. These authors showed that the response to serum was blocked if a monoclonal antibody specific for the ras protein was microinjected into the cells. Similarly, Smith, De Gudicibus, and Stacey (1986) showed that micro-injection of this antibody blocked transformation by a variety of oncogenes. Homologues of the ras p21 proteins were detected in yeast cells where they were found to act as controlling elements of the adenylate cyclase regulatory system (Toda et al. 1985); but this was not the case in vertebrate cells (DeFeo-Jones et al. 1985). It eventually transpired that the interaction of p21 with the guanosine tri- and diphosphates was an essential part of the mechanism that enabled the molecule to act as a signal transmitter. When bound to the diphosphate, p21 was shown to be inactive, but when, in response to an appropriate signal, it shed the diphosphate and bound, in its place, the triphosphate, signal transmission occurred. The ras proteins were subsequently found to be involved in a wide range of differentiation processes: mating, meiosis, sporulation and control of cell shape in the fission yeast *Saccharomyces pombe* (Fukui et al. 1986); differentiation of complex terminal structures, such as the eye, in *Drosophila* (Greenwald and Rubin 1992; Perrimon 1993); and development of the vulva in the nematode *Caenorhabditis elegans* (Horvitz and Sternberg 1991). Egan and Weinberg (1993) have argued that ras proteins play a central role in regulating the transmission of signals, and hence differentiation, within the cell.

TRANSLOCATION OF ONCOGENES

As mentioned in Chapter 3, oncogenes were thought to contribute to the production of malignancy not only when they were mutated, but also when they were translocated to an inappropriate site. The type cases for this form of aberrant proto-oncogene function were the systematic translocations seen in Burkitt's lymphoma and in chronic myeloid leukaemia. In the case of the (8;14) translocation in Burkitt's lymphoma and the (15;12) or (15;6) translocations in mouse plasmacytomas, Klein (1981) had proposed that it was the *myc* proto-oncogene that was translocated to a new site in close proximity to an immunoglobulin locus. Cory, Gerondakis, and Adams (1983) confirmed that in mouse plasmacytomas the *myc* gene was indeed moved to the enhancer region of an immunoglobulin locus and showed that the translocation was produced by a reciprocal exchange. Adams et al. (1983) demonstrated that this was also the case for Burkitt's lymphoma, and Bernard et al. (1983) proved by sequence analysis that the translocated proto-oncogene had not undergone any structural mutation. Although the precise molecular function of the myc protein remains unclear to the present day, *myc* was found to be a member of the family of oncogenes that coded for nuclear proteins involved in the replication or transcription of DNA. Eventually three *myc* proto-oncogenes were detected: c-*myc*, N-*myc* and L-*myc*. Other members of this family of oncogene nuclear proteins were *myb* (avian myeloblastosis virus), *fos* (FBJ osteosarcoma virus), *ski* (avian SKV770 virus) and p53. Some years after the discovery of the translocated *myc* gene in B-cell tumours, it was found that a similar type of translocation was associated with T-cell malignancies. Boehm et al. (1988) showed that an (11;14) translocation found in a T-cell tumour involved the translocation of a transcribed gene to the locus coding for the T-cell receptor, a member of a family of proteins having domains homologous with those seen in immunoglobulins (the immunoglobulin superfamily). McGuire et al. (1989) revealed that the region translocated to the T-cell receptor locus included a gene (*Ttg*-1) that coded for a zinc finger protein that was presumed to interact with DNA. Boehm et al. (1991) found that the product of this gene was a member of a structurally related group of proteins of which different members could be involved in the translocations that characterised T-cell tumours.

Further molecular analysis of the (9;22) translocation in chronic myeloid leukaemia revealed that the *abl* proto-oncogene on chromosome 9 was translocated to a small region on chromosome 22 that was named *bcr* (breakpoint cluster) (Heisterkamp et al. 1983; Groffen et al. 1984). This resulted in the synthesis of a fusion protein (p210) coded by the hybrid *bcr/abl* gene (Ben-Neriah et al. 1986). Hariharan and Adams (1987) determined the nucleotide sequence of *bcr*, but the function of the gene was not thereby elucidated. Because of the ease with which good chromosome preparations could be made with blood cells, the analysis of translocations made faster progress in haematological malignancies than in solid tumours. By 1991, Solomon, Borrow, and Goddard were able to list 19 such translocations that had been completely characterised in molecular terms. Five of these involved transposition of an oncogene to immunoglobulin loci, seven to the T-cell receptor locus, and two to loci whose function was not known. In addition, fusion proteins similar to the p210 of chronic myeloid leukaemia were found in five other haematological malignancies. Solomon, Borrow, and Goddard also listed 22 recurrent translocations that had been detected in solid tumours (14 different types) and observed that, in all, more than 100 recurrent translocations extracted from 14,000 neoplasms had been reported.

ROLE OF ONCOGENES IN TUMORIGENESIS

Although oncogenes revealed by homology with retroviral genes, transfection of DNA and analysis of translocations proved to be a treasure trove of interesting and hitherto unsuspected biological regulators, their role in generating tumours was not obvious. Because the introduction of viruses or preparations of DNA into the cell constituted an addition of genetic information, and because the adventitious DNA produced a phenotypic change in the host cell, it was generally assumed, and in some cases strongly argued (see, for example, Weinberg 1989) that oncogenes acted in a genetically dominant manner. The experiments of Murray et al. (1983) on cells transformed by the Ha-*ras* oncogene appeared to indicate that continued presence of the oncogene was required to maintain the transformed phenotype. But when it came to the formation of tumours by *ras*-transformed cells, Gilbert and Harris (1988) showed not only that the oncogene was dispensable once the cells had become tumorigenic, but also that the tumours were formed not by the unselected growth of the Ha-*ras*-transformed cells, but by selective overgrowth of minority subpopulations with chromosome constitutions markedly different from that of the transformed cell population as a whole. Moreover, Marshall (1980) and Dyson, Quade, and Wyke (1982) had shown that when cells transformed by the viral *src* gene were fused with untransformed cells, the resulting hybrids were not transformed whether the oncogene was expressed or not. Craig and Sager (1985) and Geiser et al. (1986) showed that this was also true of cells transformed by Ha-*ras*. Tolsma et al. (1993) found that transformation of NIH 3T3 cells by the Ha-*ras* oncogene involved the loss of some genetic component that, under normal conditions, suppressed transformation in hybrid cells. These findings indicated that the retroviral oncogenes did not behave as simple dominants in the presence of a normal genome, but that, as with the DNA viruses, their mode of action was complex. In the case of malignant human tumours carrying the Ki-*ras* oncogene (colon, bladder and lung), Capon et al. (1983) and Santos et al. (1984) found that in each case the unmutated c-Ki-*ras* gene had been eliminated; and Bremner and Balmain (1990) observed that in mouse skin cancers, the presence of the mutant *ras* gene was regularly associated with a loss of heterozygosity on mouse chromosome 7. Bailleul et al. (1990), studying the effect of the Ha-*ras* oncogene in transgenic mice, found that when the activity of this gene was governed by a specific keratin promoter that ensured the expression of the mutated gene in the appropriate layers of the skin, hyperkeratoses and papillomas did occur, but not malignant tumours.

The structural basis of translocations involving the *myc* gene had been elucidated in molecular terms by 1983, but the functional consequences of these translocations remained, and still remain, unclear. It was originally proposed that the *myc* gene, brought under the influence of a strong promoter or, later, enhancer of the immunoglobulin gene, would be transcribed at a higher rate than normal and would thus force inappropriate cell multiplication. But Hann, Thompson, and Eisenman (1985) showed that neither the level, nor the rate of synthesis, nor the rate of turnover of the myc protein was any different in cells bearing the *myc* translocation than in cells with the *myc* gene in its normal location. Transgenic mice into which a *myc* gene driven by an immunoglobulin enhancer had been introduced did produce lymphoid tumours, but these developed only after a lag of some five months, and, when examined, they were found to be clonal in origin (Adams et al. 1985; Leder et al. 1986). This indicated that the *myc* translocation was compatible with perfectly normal development in all tissues, and that some other stochastic event or events had to occur before a tumour could be generated. It became clear that the role of the *bcr/abl* translocation in chronic myeloid leukaemia could similarly be no more than a contributory factor in the genesis of the disease when Bartram et al. (1986) showed that the leukaemia persisted even after the *bcr/abl* sequences had been eliminated. This was confirmed by the studies of Hariharan et al. (1989) and Elefanty, Hariharan, and Cory (1990) on transgenic mice into which the *bcr/abl* fusion gene had been introduced. Multiple haemopoietic malignancies did indeed arise in these animals but, as in the case of *myc* translocations, only in a stochastic fashion.

COOPERATION OF ONCOGENES

Although the NIH 3T3 cell line was readily transformable by transfection with the *ras* oncogene, this was not found to be the case for diploid embryonic fibroblasts. However, Land, Parada, and Weinberg (1983) showed that embryonic rat fibroblasts could be transformed if the *ras* gene was transfected together with a viral or cellular *myc* gene or with the gene coding for the polyoma T antigen. The cooperation of the two oncogenes also increased the tumorigenicity of the transfected cells. This was confirmed by Compere et al. (1989) who showed that the incidence of tumours was substantially increased when *ras* and *myc* were introduced together into mid-gestation mouse embryos by means of retroviral vectors. However, Oshimura et al. (1988) found that tumours induced in Syrian hamsters by cells transfected with *ras* and *myc* together showed substantial losses of chromosomes, indicating that, even with the combination of oncogenes, the tumours were formed, as observed by Gilbert and Harris (1988) with cells transformed by *ras* alone, by the selective overgrowth of minority cell populations in which other genetic events had occurred. Cooperative effects enhancing tumorigenicity were described for a number of other combinations of oncogenes, but even the most powerful synergy, as for example that between *myc* and v-Ha-*ras*, driven by mouse mammary tumour virus promoters, produced no more than an acceleration of mammary tumour formation; and the tumours once again arose in a stochastic manner (Sinn et al. 1987).

AMPLIFICATION OF ONCOGENES

The discovery by Collins and Groudine (1982) that the *myc* oncogene had undergone a 30–50-fold amplification in a human myeloid leukaemia cell line prompted an eager search for other examples of oncogene amplification. The work of Collins and Groudine was confirmed and extended by Dalla-Favera, Wong-Staal, and Gallo (1982). Amplification of the *myc* gene was found in breast carcinoma by Capon et al. (1983) and Kozbor and Croce (1984); in colon carcinoma by Alitalo et al. (1983); in neuroblastoma by Schwab et al. (1983b); and in retinoblastoma by Lee, Murphree, and Benedict (1984). Ki-*ras* was found to be amplified 3–5 times in carcinoma of the colon and lung (McCoy et al. 1983) and up to 60 times in a mouse adrenocortical tumour (Schwab et al. 1983a). The many subsequent reports of oncogene amplification in tumours included the Ha-*ras* gene in human bladder carcinoma and the N-*myc* gene in neuroblastoma. Little et al. (1983) reported that some 20% of human lung cancer cell lines showed amplification of either the c-*myc* or N-*myc*. However, none of these studies provided any evidence that the observed oncogene amplification played a causative role in the genesis of the tumour or that it was necessary for the maintenance of tumorigenicity. Wright et al. (1990) showed that gene amplification in response to drugs, as originally described by Schimke and his colleagues (Schimke et al. 1978), did not take place in normal diploid cells, which made it likely that gene amplification in tumour cells took place only after aneuploidy and other forms of genome destabilisation had already supervened. On the other hand, Srivastava et al. (1985) noticed that spontaneous (that is, not drug-induced) amplification of the c-Ha-*ras* proto-oncogene could take place in cultures of normal fibroblasts when the cells began to senesce.

An exhaustive study of oncogene amplification in non-small cell lung carcinoma was undertaken by Slebos et al. (1989). These authors examined all three *ras* genes, all three *myc* genes and a number of other oncogenes in 21 malignant tumours. In two adenocarcinomas c-*myc* was amplified 5–7 times, and in one Ha-*ras* was amplified 3–5 times. Some amplification of Ki-*ras* was found in lung metastases from a colorectal carcinoma, and some amplification of *neu* (an oncogene homologous with the *erb*B-2 gene of avian erythroblastosis virus) was found in metastases from a breast carcinoma. But no amplification was observed in any of the other tumours. These results made it clear that amplification of oncogenes could not be an essential element in the genesis of these tumours. Slebos et al. suggested further that the amplification that they did detect might have been related to drug therapy administered to the patients before their tumours were removed. Finally, Tlsty, White, and Sanchez (1992) showed that the ability of tumour cells to amplify genes in response to drugs was abolished when the tumour cells were fused with normal cells. This provided further evidence in support of the view that oncogene amplification took place in tumours only after destabilisation of the genome had occurred. Tlsty, White, and Sanchez also found that when chromosome loss generated segregants in their hybrid cell populations, the ability to amplify genes and tumorigenicity segregated independently. The weight of evidence thus appeared strongly in favour of the conclusion that amplification of oncogenes was a secondary phenomenon exhibited by some tumours, probably in response to selective pressures operating *in vivo*.

Looking back on the two decades of work that stemmed from the initial formulation of the oncogene concept, it seems reasonable to draw the following conclusions:

- A wide variety of oncogenes with different functions in different parts of the cell can produce the phenotypic changes that we generically call transformation.

- They do this by mechanisms that are more complex than is implied by the term genetic dominance. Where the question has been specifically investigated, it appears that cell transformation by oncogenes involves the inactivation of some normal genetic function or functions that act to suppress the various elements of the transformed phenotype.

- No single oncogene and no combination of oncogenes is enough in itself to induce the formation of a tumour. Experiments with transgenic animals are unanimous in their demonstration that oncogenes do not produce tumours directly, but merely establish a predisposition to tumour formation that ultimately requires other genetic changes which occur in a stochastic fashion.

- Once the tumour has been established, the oncogene, whether mutated or translocated, is dispensable.

SUPPRESSION OF MALIGNANCY

The idea that malignancy was determined by recessive, and not dominant, mutations, appears to have had its origin in cell fusion experiments done by Harris et al. in 1969. The first attempt to analyse malignancy by somatic cell hybridization was made by Barski and Cornefert (1962). They examined the tumorigenicity of hybrids between two established mouse cell lines, one highly malignant and one much less so, and found that these hybrids more closely resembled the highly malignant parent cell in their ability to produce tumours. They therefore concluded that the genetic determinants of malignancy acted in a dominant fashion. Harris and Miller (Fig. 62), reconsidering these findings in the light of some experiments of their own, noted in 1969 that the malignant hybrids isolated by Barski and Cornefert had lost a substantial number of chromosomes relative to what was to be expected from the sum of the two parental chromosome sets (Harris 1993). This loss of chromosomes in the malignant hybrids raised the possibility that the experiments of Barski and

Cornefert might not necessarily have demonstrated that malignancy was a dominant characteristic. It was possible that if karyotypically complete hybrids had been isolated, these might not have been malignant; the malignancy, initially suppressed, might have reappeared when certain chromosomes donated to the hybrid by the non-malignant parent cell were eliminated (Harris and Klein 1969). This idea was explored by Harris, Klein (Fig. 63), and their associates in a series of investigations that extended over several years. These investigations established that when malignant mouse cells were fused with non-malignant ones or with normal diploid cells, malignancy was initially suppressed in the resultant hybrids and reappeared only after certain specific chromosomes derived from the normal cell were eliminated. This was found to be true for a wide range of experimental mouse tumours including tumours induced by chemical carcinogens or oncogenic viruses and tumours that arose spontaneously (Klein et al. 1971; Bregula, Klein, and Harris 1971; Wiener, Klein, and Harris 1971, 1973, 1974). The conclusion drawn from these experiments was that normal cells harboured genes that had the ability to suppress malignancy or hold it in check, and that cells became malignant when these suppressor genes were in some way inactivated or impaired (Harris 1971). It followed, therefore, that the genetic determinants of malignancy, whatever the aetiology, were, in formal terms, recessive to the wild type.

Since the results obtained with hybrids between malignant and normal cells indicated that the reappearance of malignancy required the loss of at least one specific chromosome derived from the normal cell, a systematic attempt was made to identify the chromosome by the then standard technique of establishing synteny between the retention or loss of particular chromosomes and the suppression or reappearance of the malignant phenotype. It was extremely fortunate that chromosome banding techniques were introduced at just that time, for, with the poorly differentiated mouse karyotype available before chromosome banding, such an investigation would have been impossible. It proved complex enough, even with the help of banding and some useful enzyme polymorphisms. Eventually, however, Jonasson, Povey, and Harris (1977) established in crosses between mouse melanoma cells and normal fibroblasts that one normal locus that suppressed tumorigenicity was located on mouse chromosome 4. An informative translocation involving chromosome 4 permitted a regional assignment of the gene to the lower part of the upper half of this chromosome. This assignment was confirmed in a different set of hybrid cells by Evans et al. (1982) who also demonstrated that the suppression of tumorigenicity by this locus was dependent on gene dosage. Eight years later, a suppressor gene was located in the genetically homologous region on rat chromosome 5 (Szpirer et al. 1990), and, a decade later, a gene that suppressed tumorigenicity in human melanoma cells was identified in a similarly homologous region on human chromosome 9 (band 9p21) (Fountain et al. 1992).

The study of tumour suppression in human hybrid cells was initiated by Stanbridge (1976) who found these hybrids more stable with respect to chromosome constitution than the mouse cell hybrids studied by Harris and his colleagues, and hence less difficult to analyse from the karyological point of view. Again, malignancy was found to be recessive to the wild type when malignant cells were fused with normal ones. Stanbridge and Wilkinson

FIGURE 62 Orlando J. Miller (1927–).
(Courtesy of the Archives of the Sir William
Dunn School of Pathology, University of
Oxford.)

FIGURE 63 George Klein (1925–).
(Courtesy of Dr. George Klein.)

Henry Harris (Fig. 30) and O.J. Miller, in collaboration with George Klein and his colleagues, showed that when malignant cells were fused with non-malignant ones, malignancy was initially suppressed in the resulting hybrid cells, but it reappeared when certain normal chromosomes were eliminated from the cell. This was the first indication that there were normal cellular genes that had the ability to suppress tumour formation. Such genes are now known as tumour suppressor genes.

(1978) showed that in such hybrids the transformed phenotype and tumorigenicity segregated independently, and this was confirmed by Klinger (1980). By analysing the synteny relationships between chromosome loss and the reappearance of tumorigenicity in hybrids between malignant and normal human cells, Srivatsan, Benedict, and Stanbridge (1986) and Kaelbling and Klinger (1986) located a suppressor gene on human chromosome 11. Saxon, Srivatsan, and Stanbridge (1986) showed that the malignant phenotype could be suppressed in human tumour cells when a single normal human chromosome 11, unaccompanied by any other chromosome, was introduced into the cells by the technique of microcell transfer, as described in Chapter 5.

TUMOUR SUPPRESSOR GENES

Two years after Harris et al. (1969) had demonstrated the suppression of malignancy in hybrid cells, Ohno (1971) proposed a general model for the genesis of cancers based on recessive genetic lesions, and Knudson (Fig. 64) (1971) proposed the specific model for retinoblastoma discussed cursorily in Chapter 3. Knudson's argument was that both the familial and the sporadic forms of this cancer were determined by recessive mutations at the same

FIGURE 64 Alfred Knudson (1922–) proposed that both the familial and the sporadic forms of the malignant childhood cancer, retinoblastoma, were determined by recessive mutations at the same locus. Knudson argued that in the familial form of this disease one of the alleles was already mutated or deleted in the germ line. Homozygous recessive genetic lesions entailing losses of cellular function have since been found to be important determinants in many different tumours. *(Courtesy of Dr. Alfred Knudson.)*

locus, but that in the familial form one of the alleles was already mutated or deleted in the germ line. If this were so, then it was to be expected that there would be a very high probability of the heterozygous individual developing a tumour because only a single event would be required to put the other allele out of action, whereas, in the sporadic form of the tumour occurring in individuals with no such lesion in the germ line, two mutational events at the one locus would be required. This proposal, which became known as the 'two-hit model', appeared to fit the epidemiological data reasonably well and was soon extended to account for the data on Wilms' tumour of the kidney, another paediatric malignancy (Knudson and Strong 1972). Although Knudson's model was based on the study of familial childhood cancers, Knudson observed that a cryptic genetic component appeared to be involved in many different tumours, and he therefore proposed that the reduction of recessive mutations to homozygosity might be a quite general precipitating factor in the genesis of malignancy (Knudson 1985). So strongly held was the assumption that cancer was caused by dominant mutations that the results obtained with hybrid cells and Knudson's proposal were largely ignored for several years.

In 1976, Francke, as mentioned in Chapter 3, described recurrent abnormalities involving chromosome 13 in retinoblastomas, and Knudson et al. (1976) pointed out the relevance of chromosomal deletions to the two-hit aetiological model that he had proposed for these tumours. But the starting point of analysis at the molecular level was the discovery by Yunis and Ramsay (1978) of interstitial deletions in a number of retinoblastoma specimens at band q14 on chromosome 13. This region was examined in detail by several groups, and, by the analysis of closely linked markers, it was established that there was indeed a reduction to homozygosity, or loss of hetorozygosity (LOH) as it was subsequently named, at this locus in retinoblastomas (Benedict et al. 1983; Cavenee et al. 1983, 1985; Godbout et al. 1983; Sparkes et al. 1983). The deletions that occurred at band q14 were defined in molecular terms by Dryja et al. (1986) and, using the techniques of positional cloning described in Chapter 6, Friend et al. (1986) succeeded in identifying a DNA segment that had the properties to be expected for the gene determining predisposition to retinoblastoma. The complete gene was cloned and sequenced by Lee et al. (1987), and Fung et al. (1987) provided further structural evidence that the gene was indeed the authentic genetic determinant of retinoblastoma. This gene, called *Rb1*, was the first member to be isolated from a family of genes that contributed to the genesis of malignancy only when put out of action. There was for some time indecision about what these genes were to be called. Knudson suggested 'anti-oncogenes', but Stanbridge (1990) pointed out that this term was misleading because genes like *Rb1* did not act to neutralise the effect of oncogenes. The term 'recessive oncogenes' was also used (see, for example, Cavenee, Hastie, and Stanbridge 1989), but this implied that there was another family of oncogenes that acted to produce cancer in a genetically dominant fashion, and that, as already discussed, was open to question. Todaro (1988) suggested 'emerogenes' (from the Greek: to tame or domesticate), but this suggestion attracted few followers. Eventually the term 'tumour suppressor genes' was adopted, although clearly their essential biological function was not to suppress tumours.

THE RETINOBLASTOMA GENE

The product of the *Rb1* gene was found to be a nuclear phosphoprotein with a molecular weight of about 110,000, but its biochemical activities turned out to be very complex and remain incompletely resolved to the present day. Huang et al. (1988) showed that when a normal *Rb1* gene was introduced into a malignant human cell line that lacked functional *Rb1* genes (Saos 2), cell division was blocked and polyploid cells were generated. Eventually these cultures produced a new cell line that was not tumorigenic in nude mice. However, this growth suppressive effect was later shown to be due to the fact that Saos 2 cells were especially sensitive to the Rb1 gene product. Xu et al. (1991) showed that retinoblastoma cells into which a normal *Rb1* gene had been inserted continued to grow within the eye, and Muncaster et al. (1992) reported that they had incorporated a normal *Rb1* gene into many retinoblastoma cell lines without arresting growth or suppressing tumorigenicity. Buchkovich, Duffy, and Harlow (1989) and Mihara et al. (1989) showed that the extent of phosphorylation of the Rb1 gene product varied during the cell cycle. There was very little phosphorylation in the G_1 phase, but at the end of G_1, phosphorylation occurred at multiple sites and was maintained until mitosis, during which dephosphorylation occurred. The Rb1 protein was found to bind specifically to the products of certain viral genes: the E1A protein of adenovirus (Whyte et al. 1988), the large T antigen of simian virus 40 (De Caprio et al. 1988) and of JC virus (Dyson et al. 1989a), and the E7 protein of human papilloma virus (Dyson et al. 1989b). Since these viral genes were able to transform cells *in vitro* and appeared to act in some way as regulators of DNA replication or transcription, it was proposed that the *Rb1* gene suppressed the formation of tumours by impeding the action of these transforming genes or their cellular homologues. However, it was soon found that the Rb1 protein bound to several cellular proteins, and it became obvious that its behaviour was to be explained only in combinatorial terms.

Some clarification of the position was achieved by Chellappan et al. (1991) and Bagchi, Weinmann, and Raychaudhuri (1991) who showed that the Rb1 protein in its hypophosphorylated state bound specifically to the transcription factor E2F. When complexed with the Rb1 protein, E2F was inactive, but when the Rb1 protein was phosphorylated, E2F was displaced from the complex and became active again. E1A and other viral oncogene products were also found to bind to the Rb1 protein only when the latter was hypophosphorylated. Although these results provided an attractive picture of the Rb1 protein as a cyclically regulated inhibitor of transcription, they provided no answer at all to the primary observation that individuals bearing a homozygous defect at the *Rb1* locus in all their cells developed only retinoblastomas, secondary osteosarcomas, and a very limited range of other tumours. Transgenic mice in which both alleles of the *Rb1* gene had been inactivated were found to develop normally until the 12th day of gestation, thus indicating that the *Rb1* gene was not essential for normal development or for normal regulation of cell multiplication in most tissues. On the 13th day of gestation, abnormalities did begin to show themselves, but only in two tissues, the central nervous system and the haemopoietic system, where increased mitotic activity and cell death were observed (Clarke et al. 1992; Jacks et al. 1992; Lee et al. 1992). It was thus clear that the *Rb1* gene did not act as a general regulator of DNA replication or transcription, but was essential for normal regulation of these processes only at certain specific stages in the differentiation of particular organs. Gu et al. (1993) showed decisively that induction of myogenic differentiation by the *myoD* gene required the presence of the Rb1 protein, but we still know too little about the biochemical basis of differentiation in the retina to guess at what the role of the *Rb1* gene might be in generating retinoblastomas. It has in any case now become apparent that inactivation of the *Rb1* locus alone is not enough to generate the fully malignant tumour. As pointed out by Hamel et al. (1993), all retinoblastomas are aneuploid, which in itself indicates that events other than the homozygous inactivation of the *Rb1* gene have to occur before a fully malignant tumour can arise. As early as 1976, Bonaïti-Pellie et al., in an extensive epidemiological study of retinoblastoma in France, noted that their data was more readily accommodated by a 'three-hit' model than a 'two-hit' one. Recent observations have revealed, in individuals with a predisposition to retinoblastoma, the earlier presence of small benign proliferations in the retina. Hamel et al. (1993) have suggested that these growths, called 'retinomas', might be the direct products of the homozygous inactivation of the *Rb1* gene, and that subsequent events in these benign retinoma cells might then determine the emergence of malignant retinoblastomas.

TUMOUR SUPPRESSOR GENES IN *DROSOPHILA*

That tumour suppressor genes were of importance only at critical stages in the differentiation of particular organs was demonstrated conclusively by the analysis of certain recessive mutations that gave rise to tumours in *Drosophila*. Gateff and Schneiderman (1967) discovered that one such mutation mapped to the lethal-(2) giant larvae (*l[2]gl*) locus first described by Bridges (Bridges and Brehme 1944). This mutation gave rise to malignant tumours of the nervous system, but some years elapsed before a sceptical readership was convinced of this fact, because it was widely held at the time that tumours did not occur in insects. Gateff and Schneiderman (1969) showed that these tumours of the nervous system arose only when the mutation was present in the homozygous condition, thus indicating that it was recessive. By 1989, some 16 homozygous recessive mutations had been described that produced tumours in a range of different organs in *Drosophila* (Gateff and Mechler 1989). Mechler, McGinnis, and Gehring (1985) cloned the *l(2)gl* gene and Opper, Schuler, and Mechler (1987) showed that the wild-type gene could suppress the formation of tumours and restore hereditary normality when it was introduced into homozygous *l(2)gl* mutants. Jacob et al. (1987) determined the complete nucleotide sequence of the gene. This was not in itself informative, but it enabled the biological function of a tumour suppressor gene to be studied in a higher organism that was more amenable than any other to genetic manipulation.

Mechler et al. (1989) showed that there were two stages in development at which the product of the *l(2)gl* gene was normally synthesized. During the early development of the embryo, all cells synthesized this product, but during the larval period it was found only in the mid-gut, the salivary glands and the axonal projections of the nervous system, tissues in which tumours did not occur. Second, by the use of genetic mosaics in which the gene was eliminated at different stages of development, they established that tumours were produced only when the gene product was absent during early embryonic development. Its absence at later stages was not tumorigenic. And third, they found that the homozygous mutation produced not only tumours of the nervous system, but also non-tumorigenic abnormalities of terminal differentiation in other tissues. The wild-type product of the *l(2)gl* gene was obviously not a general repressor of transcription or cell multiplication; its essential function in the normal insect was to regulate certain forms of terminal differentiation and to ensure that specific cell lineages achieved the fate to which they were committed. No vertebrate tumour suppressor gene has been analysed *in vivo* with this degree of precision. The essential role of tumour suppressor genes as regulators of differentiation was confirmed by the analysis of two further oncogenic mutations in *Drosophila*. It had been noted that recessive lethal mutations in the *fat* gene produced hyperplastic overgrowths or tumours in the larval imaginal discs. Mahoney et al. (1991) isolated and characterised the *fat* gene and showed that it encoded a transmembrane protein containing approximately 5000 amino acids and encompassing 34 tandemly repeated domains that were characteristic of the cadherin family of adhesion factors. The cadherins were known to be of importance in determining the appropriate apposition of cells and hence in ensuring normal tissue architecture. Willott et al. (1993) determined the structure of the lethal(1)discs-large-1 (*dlg*) locus. Homozygous recessive mutations at this locus resulted in a loss of cellular polarity and also generated neoplastic growths in the imaginal discs. The gene product was found to be a protein with a predicted content of 1736 amino acids and to be closely homologous to the human ZO-1 protein which, like the product of the *fat* gene, was involved in cell adhesion.

THE WILMS' TUMOUR GENE

The next human tumour suppressor gene to be isolated was one of the genes involved in the production of Wilms' tumour. As already mentioned, Knudson and Strong (1972) had found that the epidemiological data on the familial and sporadic forms of this malignant tumour were also consistent with the presence of a predisposing recessive mutation in the germ line and its subsequent reduction to homozygosity in a somatic cell. Cytogenetic data supporting Knudson's thesis in this case were provided by Koufos et al. (1984), Orkin, Goldman, and Sallan (1984), and Fearon, Vogelstein, and Feinberg (1984). All three groups found on chromosome 11 at band p13 a germ-line deletion that was reduced to homozygosity in the cells of the tumour. The widespread adoption of the techniques of positional cloning enabled three groups, within the one year, to identify and characterise the gene involved (Bonetta et al. 1990; Call et al. 1990; Gessler et al. 1990). The gene, called *WT1*, encompassed 50 kb of DNA and 10 exons. The protein that it specified had an estimated molecular mass of 47–49 kD and contained four zinc finger domains. Variant isoforms of the protein could be generated by alternative splicing, and at least some of them acted as repressors of transcription (Madden et al. 1991). One of the genes repressed by the WT1 protein was the gene coding for insulin-like growth factor 2 (Drummond et al. 1992). In rodents, the *WT1* gene was found to be expressed largely in pronephric and metanephric structures, but also in the mesothelial lining of all organs. In developing human embryos, it was expressed in the kidney, gonads, uterus and spleen. Higher levels of expression were found in foetal than in adult kidney.

The decisive evidence that the function of the *WT1* gene was to regulate a specific programme of differentiation was the discovery that germ-line mutations in this gene were present in a genetic disease known as the Denys-Drash syndrome (Huff et al. 1991; Pelletier et al. 1991). This syndrome is characterised by intersex disorders such as ambiguous genitalia, sclerotic changes in the kidneys and the eventual appearance of Wilms' tumours. The existence of this syndrome made it clear that complete absence of the WT1 gene product in man was not an impediment to normal development generally, but only to development in the particular cell lineage destined to produce the kidneys, genitalia and associated structures. This was confirmed in transgenic mice. Embryos in which there was homozygous inactivation of the *WT1* gene grew normally for 10 days, but on the 11th day the metanephric blastema was destroyed so that neither kidneys nor gonads were formed (Kreidberg et al. 1993). As in the case of retinoblastoma, it seems unlikely that homozygous inactivation of the *WT1* locus is itself sufficient to generate the malignant Wilms' tumour. Coppes et al. (1993) have pointed out that the two-hit model proposed by Knudson and Strong (1972) would predict that the familial form of the Wilms' tumour should constitute about 30% of all cases, whereas in fact it constitutes only 1–2%; and bilateral tumours appear in only 20% of familial cases, whereas the two-hit model would predict a much higher figure. In fact it now appears probable that *WT1* is not the only gene on chromosome 11 involved in the genesis of Wilms' tumour. A second locus at chromosome 11 p15 has been shown to be reduced to homozygosity in some sporadic cases of Wilms' tumour and also in familial adrenocortical carcinomas (Henry et al.

1989; Reeve et al. 1989). It is not clear whether the genes at 11p13 and 11p15 contribute to the formation of Wilms' tumour in different ways or whether their effect is cooperative (Stanbridge 1990). What has traditionally been classified as Wilms' tumour might, of course, be a family of related, but different, tumours.

THE NEUROFIBROMATOSIS GENES

By the end of 1993, four other tumour suppressor genes involved in familial cancers had been cloned and characterised: the neurofibromatosis type I and neurofibromatosis type 2 genes of von Recklinghausen's disease, the familial adenomatous polyposis coli gene (known as *APC*) and the p53 gene. Neurofibromatosis is a condition in which multiple benign tumours arise in association with peripheral nerves. The predisposition to form these tumours is inherited as an autosomal dominant, but cytogenetic evidence eventually revealed that, in this case also, the production of the tumour was characterised by a reduction to homozygosity of a germ-line defect. The locus involved mapped to chromosome 17q11. The determinant gene (*NF1*) was identified and its structure determined by Cawthorn et al. (1990), Fountain et al. (1989), O'Connell et al. (1989), and Viskochil et al. (1990). It showed sequence homology with the *IRA1* and *IRA2* genes which were negative regulators of the *ras*-cyclic adenosine monophosphate system in yeast. The *NF1* gene was able to complement IRA⁻ mutants and the catalytic domain of the NF1 protein was found to stimulate the guanosine triphosphatase associated with ras. This suggested that NF1 might be functionally related to the family known as the guanosine triphosphatase activator proteins (GAP) (Ballester et al. 1990; Buchberg et al. 1990). De Clue et al. (1992) showed that the p21 ras protein was regulated abnormally in neurofibromatosis type 1 tumour cells. A gene implicated in neurofibromatosis type 2 was found to be located on chromosome 22; it was identified and sequenced by Rouleau et al. (1993) and Trofatter et al. (1993). The product of this gene, named merlin or schwannomin, was strikingly similar to moesin, ezrin and radixin, proteins thought to be involved in forming linkages between integral membrane proteins and the cytoskeleton.

THE FAMILIAL ADENOMATOUS POLYPOSIS COLI GENE

The gene predisposing to familial adenomatous polyposis coli (*APC*) was localised to chromosome 5q21 by Solomon and her colleagues (Bodmer et al. 1987; Solomon et al. 1987) and identified by Groden et al. (1991), Joslyn et al. (1991), Kinzler et al. (1991), and Nishisho et al. (1991). The gene product was found to bind to the α and β catenins, molecules that interact with the cell adhesion protein E-cadherin (Rubinfeld et al. 1994; Su, Vogelstein, and Kinzler 1994). The *APC* gene, like the neurofibromatosis 2 gene and the *fat* and *dlg* genes in *Drosophila*, thus appears to be involved in some way in establishing normal cell apposition. As in the case of the neurofibromatosis genes and possibly the retinoblastoma gene, homozygous inactivation of the *APC* gene produces only benign tumours which appear in the colon as polyps. At a much later stage, malignant changes may take place in one or more of these polyps and frank carcinomas may then emerge. In terms of cell biology, rather than symptomatology, the pattern of development of all these familial tumours appeared to be very similar. Vogelstein and his co-workers have proposed that the progression to malignancy is driven by a sequence of other mutational events, some of which they have perhaps defined (Fearon and Vogelstein 1990). Fearon et al. (1990) discovered a gene located on chromosome 18q that was frequently deleted in colon carcinoma and was hence named *DCC*. Other genetic changes detected by Vogelstein and his colleagues included mutation of the Ki-*ras* gene and loss of the p53 gene, which will be discussed in more detail presently. Although these mutations often occurred in a defined order, as adenomas progressed to carcinomas, Fearon and Vogelstein concluded from their study that it was not the order of events that was decisive, but their cumulative effect.

However, the significance of these particular genes in the progression to malignancy has recently been called into question by experiments with transgenic mice (Kim et al. 1993). The gene coding for the simian virus 40 T antigen, the Ki-*ras* gene and the p53 gene, both of the latter carrying transforming mutations, were introduced into these animals singly and in all combinations. The transgenes were expressed in intestinal cells from the duodenum down to the colon, but no malignant tumours arose. Each of the genes alone produced no phenotypic abnormalities, but Ki-*ras* together with simian virus 40 T generated marked proliferative and dysplastic changes in the intestinal epithelium. These did not, however, progress to adenomas or to adenocarcinomas in the 12 month period of observation. Adding the mutated p53 to this combination produced no further changes. In order to mimic more closely the supervention of the secondary mutations on a genetic background already lacking the *APC* gene, the transgenic mice carrying one, two or all three of these transgenes were crossed with mice bearing the *min* mutation. This mutation is a fully penetrant dominant mutation affecting the mouse equivalent of the human *APC* gene. The mutant animals, like humans with familial adenomatous polyposis coli, develop multiple small benign intestinal adenomas. Simian virus 40 T antigen alone or together with mutated Ki-*ras* or with both mutated Ki-*ras* and mutated p53, produced a 2–5-fold increase in the number of tumours generated, but the histological features of the adenomas were not altered, and there were no changes in the rest of the intestinal epithelium. While the mutations detected by Vogelstein and his colleagues in the progression from colonic adenoma to colonic carcinoma remain of great interest, the results obtained with transgenic animals have inevitably raised doubts about the role proposed for these particular mutations in driving the progression to malignancy.

THE P53 GENE

The p53 gene has had a chequered but fascinating history. The gene product, with a molecular weight of approximately 53,000, was discovered by Lane and Crawford (1979) in cells transformed by simian virus 40. The discovery was made because the p53 protein in the cell was found to be associated with the simian virus 40 T antigen. It was later found that the p53 protein was a nuclear phosphoprotein and that it was present in a number of tumours. Normal cells appeared to contain only very low concentrations of p53 (Crawford et al. 1981). A genomic p53 clone and a number of p53 cDNAs were found to transform normal rodent cells when they were transfected into the cells together with a mutated *ras* gene. Moreover, there was evidence that expression of the p53 gene could enhance tumour growth *in vivo*. p53 was therefore classified as a nuclear oncogene in the same category as *myc*, *myb* and *fos* (Lane and Benchimol 1990). This view of the gene collapsed when it was found that the genomic clone used in the transfection experiments was in fact mutated; an unmutated genomic clone not only failed to transform in the presence of a mutated *ras* gene, but actually suppressed the transformation produced by the mutated p53 gene (Finlay, Hinds, and Levine 1989). Normal genomic p53 was therefore reclassified: it ceased to be an oncogene and became a tumour suppressor gene, which remains its current status. Mutations and deletions in the p53 gene were found to be extremely common in human malignancies; they were found in 40% of mammary carcinomas and in 30% of colorectal carcinomas. In the case of colorectal carcinoma, both alleles of p53 were commonly affected (Baker et al. 1989). Some compilations of data suggest that mutant p53 is found in some 70% of all human cancers. It was shown by Malkin et al. (1990) and Srivastava et al. (1990) that individuals afflicted with the Li-Fraumeni syndrome carried a p53 mutation in the germ line. The Li-Fraumeni syndrome is a familial disease in which there is a predisposition to form multiple cancers at different sites. Srivastava et al. (1992) and Iavarone et al. (1992) showed that in the tumours that arose in cases of the Li-Fraumeni syndrome, the p53 mutation was reduced to homozygosity. In this respect, therefore, the p53 gene resembles the other tumour suppressor genes that have been discussed. But, unlike the latter, the p53 gene does not appear to be directly involved in regulating a specific programme of differentiation.

The p53 phosphoprotein was shown by Steinmeyer and Deppert (1988) to bind to DNA, and Kern et al. (1991) demonstrated that the binding was sequence-specific. The wild-type protein was able to act as an inhibitor of transcription, dampening the activity of various cellular promotors (Ginsberg et al. 1991). A number of viral oncogene products, in addition to the simian virus 40 T antigen, were found to bind to the p53 protein: E1B (a 55-kD protein produced by adenovirus type 15), the E6 protein of human papilloma virus types 16 and 18, and the *mdm*-2 (murine double minute) oncogene product. Finlay (1993) showed that the *mdm*-2 oncogene could overcome the suppressive effect of wild-type p53 on cell transformation; and Wu et al. (1993) proposed that the interaction of p53 with the *mdm*-2 product constituted an 'autoregulatory feedback loop'. Pietenpol and Vogelstein (1993) list eight proteins that have been shown to interact with p53, which makes it unlikely that the precise significance of these interactions will be easily unravelled. One biological function of the p53 protein, and perhaps its principal function, was brought to light by Livingstone et al. (1992) and Yin et al. (1992). It was known that when cells were exposed to agents that damaged their DNA, progression through the cell cycle was normally arrested in the G_1 phase. This permitted the DNA damage to be repaired before it was replicated, so that mutation and genome destabilisation were reduced to a minimum. Livingstone et al. and Yin et al. showed that in mouse embryo fibroblasts homozygous for a deletion of the p53 gene, the arrest of the cell cycle that was normally provoked by DNA damage did not take place. The normal response could, however, be restored to the cells by the introduction of the wild-type p53 gene. Moreover, cells devoid of the p53 gene product, unlike normal cells, had the ability to amplify genes. This, too, was abolished by the introduction of the wild-type gene. In the light of these experiments, the view came to be adopted that the normal biological function of the p53 gene was to shield the genome from perturbation, a view epitomised by Lane (1992) in an article entitled "p53, guardian of the genome". If this idea is substantially correct, then the role of p53 as a tumour suppressor gene would appear to be both less direct and less specific than that of the other tumour suppressor genes that have so far been described. Wild-type p53, in this view, would not act to prevent the occurrence of a particular tumour, as is the case with other tumour suppressor genes, but would serve as a general suppressor of tumorigenesis by increasing the likelihood that genetic damage more closely involved in tumour formation would be repaired before it was stabilised by DNA replication. This interpretation received some support from experiments with transgenic mice bearing non-functional p53 genes. Such animals were found to develop normally, thus indicating that the p53 gene was not essential for any cellular function, but they did eventually generate a wide variety of tumours at different sites (Donehower et al. 1992).

MALIGNANCY AND DIFFERENTIATION

All the human tumour suppressor genes that have so far been isolated and characterised have involved tumours for which a predisposition can be inherited in a simple Mendelian fashion. In all cases, the hallmark of the tumour suppressor gene has been the presence of a germ-line mutation in the susceptible individual and its reduction to homozygosity in the tumour. But loss of heterozygosity at specific loci is not limited to familial cancers. A review by Cavenee (1994) lists some 25 different tumours in which the loss of heterozygosity has been systematically found at specific chromosomal loci. These loci map to 11 different chromosomes (1p, 2, 3p, 5q, 10, 11p, 11q, 13q, 14q, 17p, 18q, 22). It therefore seems very likely that genetic events producing a loss of cell function will prove to be critical determinants in many, if not most, or even all, malignant tumours. These 'loss of function' mutations may initiate unscheduled growth, as appears to be the case with the familial cancers, but they may also contribute to the progression of the tumour (Stoler, Stenbach, and Balmain 1993; Cavenee 1994). Except in the case of p53, all the tumour suppressor genes so far characterised control critical steps in differentiation pathways. Loss or inactivation of these genes results in failure to complete a scheduled programme of differentiation. The question then arises whether the huge family of genes now included in the term 'oncogene' behave in a categorically different way. A good case can be made for the view that they do not. There is ample evidence that transfection of oncogenes into cells in culture prevents them from executing specific patterns of differentiation. Arbogast et al. (1977) and Vaheri et al. (1978) showed that transfection of Rous sarcoma virus 40 into fibroblasts impaired the synthesis of a normal extracellular matrix. Krieg et al. (1980) and Trüeb, Lewis, and Carter (1985) showed that this was also true for simian virus 40. Liau, Yamada, and de Crombrugghe (1985) and Schmidt, Setoyama, and de Crombrugghe (1985) demonstrated formally that the synthesis of specific components of the extracellular matrix in fibroblasts was inhibited by transfection of isolated Ha-*ras* or v-*mos* oncogenes. When the Ha-*ras* oncogene was transfected into epithelial cells, squamous differentiation was inhibited (Yoakum et al. 1985); and when it was transfected into myoblasts, myogenic differentiation was inhibited (Falcone, Tato, and Alemà 1985).

In most cases, we are still far from understanding in precise molecular terms how this inhibition of differentiation is achieved. However, in one case, the v-*erb*A gene, some clarity has begun to emerge. This gene induces erythroleukaemia in birds and also generates sarcomas. It was shown by Sap et al. (1986) and by Weinberger et al. (1986) that the c-*erb*A gene was a member of a family of nucleoproteins that acted as receptors for the thyroid hormone. The normal function of this gene was to regulate the synthesis of essential components in the differentiation of the erythrocyte. The viral oncogene v-*erb*A was found to suppress the transcription of several genes coding for erythrocyte proteins (Zenke et al. 1988; Schroeder et al. 1990). Zenke et al. (1990) and Disela et al. (1991) showed that v-*erb*A exerted its effect by extinguishing, in a dose-dependent manner, the activity of the c-*erb*A gene. This interaction between the v-*erb*A oncogene and the c-*erb*A cellular gene is, of course, reminiscent of the interaction of the viral oncogenes E1A, E6 and simian virus 40 T with the retinoblastoma tumour suppressor gene *Rb1*. In both cases it appears that the oncogene exerts its effect by producing the physiological equivalent of a 'loss-of-function' mutation. It now seems altogether possible that many oncogenes may exert their effects by inducing losses of function, and that the categorical distinction between oncogenes and tumour suppressor genes may not be as fundamental as it at first appeared.

Experiments with hybrid cells also support the view that the key element in the genesis of malignancy is a constitutional block to differentiation. Peehl and Stanbridge (1982) observed that when malignancy was suppressed in hybrids between human epithelial carcinoma cells and normal keratinocytes, the terminal differentiation pattern of the keratinocyte was imposed on the hybrid cells *in vivo*, and cell multiplication was brought to a stop. But when, as a result of chromosome loss, malignant segregants arose in the hybrid cell population, these cells failed to execute the keratinocyte differentiation programme and multiplied progressively *in vivo*. Harris and Bramwell (1987) showed that where malignancy was suppressed in such hybrids, involucrin, a specific marker of terminal differentiation in the keratinocyte, was synthesized; but no synthesis of involucrin took place in the malignant segregants. Harris (1985) found that suppression of malignancy in hybrids between tumour cells and normal fibroblasts was similarly associated with the imposition of the fibroblast differentiation programme. Non-malignant hybrids produced an organised extracellular matrix *in vivo*, but malignant segregants failed to do so.

As things now stand, it appears that the key cellular events determining malignancy are heritable losses of function and, in particular, loss of the ability to complete specific patterns of differentiation. This may well be true not only for genetic lesions involving tumour suppressor genes, where the evidence is in some cases compelling, but also for mutated oncogenes. The two great peaks that somatic cell geneticists have long been attempting to scale, cancer and differentiation, seem to have merged into one.

REFERENCES

Adams, J.M., S. Gerondakis, E. Webb, L.M. Corcoran, and S. Cory. 1983. Cellular *myc* oncogene is altered by chromosome translocation to an immunoglobulin locus in murine plasmacytomas and is rearranged similarly in human Burkitt lymphomas. *Proc. Natl. Acad. Sci.* **80:** 1982–1986.

Adams, J.M., A.W. Harris, C.A. Pinkert, L.M. Corcoran, W.S. Alexander, S. Cory, R.D. Palmiter, and R.L. Brinster. 1985. The c-*myc* oncogene driven by immunoglobulin enhancers induces lymphoid malignancy in transgenic mice. *Nature* **318:** 533–538.

Alitalo, K., M. Schwab, C.C. Lin, H.E. Varmus, and J.M. Bishop. 1983. Homogeneously staining chromosomal regions contain amplified copies of an abundantly expressed cellular oncogene (c-*myc*) in malignant neuroendocrine cells from a human colon carcinoma. *Proc. Natl. Acad. Sci.* **80:** 1707–1711.

Arbogast, B.W., M. Yoshimura, N.A. Kefalides, H. Holtzer, and A. Kaji. 1977. Failure of cultured chick embryo fibroblasts to incorporate collagen into their extracellular matrix when transformed by Rous sarcoma virus. *J. Biol. Chem.* **252:** 8863–8868.

Bader, J.P. 1972. Temperature-dependent transformation of cells infected with a mutant of Bryan Rous sarcoma virus. *J. Virol.* **10:** 267–276.

Bagchi, S., R. Weinmann, and P. Raychaudhuri. 1991. The retinoblastoma protein copurifies with E2F1, an E1A regulated inhibitor of the transcription factor E2F. *Cell* **65:** 1063–1072.

Bailleul, B., M.A. Kurani, S. White, S.C. Barton, K. Brown, M. Blessing, J. Jorcano, and A. Balmain. 1990. Skin hyperkeratosis and papilloma formation in transgenic mice expressing a *ras* oncogene from a suprabasal keratin promoter. *Cell* **62:** 697–708.

Baker, S.J., E.R. Fearon, J.M. Nigro, S.R. Hamilton, A.C. Preisinger, J.M. Jessup, P. van Tuinen, D.H. Ledbetter, D.F. Barker, Y. Nakamura, R. White, and B. Vogelstein. 1989. Chromosome 17 deletions and p53 mutations in colorectal carcinomas. *Science* **244:** 217–221.

Ballester, R., D. Marchuk, M. Boguski, A. Saulino, R. Letcher, M. Wigler, and F. Collins. 1990. The NFI locus encodes a protein functionally related to mammalian GAP and yeast IRA proteins. *Cell* **63:** 851–859.

Bar-Sagi, D. and J.R. Feramisco. 1985. Microinjection of the *ras* oncogene protein into PC12 cells induces morphological differentiation. *Cell* **42:** 841–848.

————. 1986. Induction of membrane ruffling and fluid-phase pinocytosis in quiescent fibroblasts by *ras* proteins. *Science* **233:** 1061–1068.

Barski, G. and F. Cornefert. 1962. Characteristics of "hybrid"-type clonal cell lines obtained from mixed cultures in vitro. *J. Natl. Cancer Inst.* **28:** 801–821.

Bartram, C.R., J.W.G. Janssen, R. Becker, A. de Klein, and G. Grosveld. 1986. Persistence of chronic myelocytic leukaemia despite deletion of rearranged bcr/c-*abl* sequences in blast crisis. *J. Exp. Med.* **164:** 1389–1396.

Benedict, W.F., A.L. Murphree, A. Banerjee, C.A. Spina, M.C. Sparkes, and R. Sparkes. 1983. Patient with 13 chromosome deletion: Evidence that the retinoblastoma gene is a recessive cancer gene. *Science* **219:** 973–975.

Ben-Neriah, Y., G.Q. Daley, A.-M. Mes-Masson, O.N. Witte, and D. Baltimore. 1986. The chronic myelogenous leukemia-specific P210 protein is the product of the bcr/abl hybrid gene. *Science* **233:** 212–214.

Bernard, O., S. Cory, S. Gerondakis, E. Webb, and J.M. Adams. 1983. Sequence of the murine and human cellular *myc* oncogenes and two modes of *myc* transcription resulting from chromosome translocation in B lymphoid tumours. *EMBO J.* **2:** 2375–2383.

Bishop, J.M. 1983. Cellular oncogenes and retroviruses. *Annu. Rev. Biochem.* **52:** 301–354.

Bodmer, W.F., C.J. Bailey, J. Bodmer, H.J.R. Bussey, A. Ellis, P. Gorman, F.C. Lucibello, V.A. Murday, S.H. Rider, P. Scambler, D. Sheer, E. Solomon, and N.K. Spurr. 1987. Localization of the gene for familial adenomatous polyposis on chromosome 5. *Nature* **328:** 614–616.

Boehm, T., L. Foroni, Y. Kaneko, M.F. Perutz, and T.H. Rabbitts. 1991. The rhombotic family of cysteine-rich LIM-domain oncogenes: Distinct members are involved in T-cell translocations to human chromosomes 11p15 and 11p13. *Proc. Natl. Acad. Sci.* **88:** 4367–4371.

Boehm, T., R. Baer, I. Lavenir, A. Forster, J.J. Waters, E. Nacheva, and T.H. Rabbitts. 1988. The mechanism of chromosomal translocation t(11;14) involving the T-cell receptor Cδ locus on human chromosome 14q11 and a transcribed region on chromosome 11p15. *EMBO J.* **7:** 385–394.

Bonaïti-Pellie, C., M.L. Briard-Guillemot, J. Feingold, and J. Frezal. 1976. Mutation theory of carcinogenesis in retinoblastoma. *J. Natl. Cancer Inst.* **57:** 269–276.

Bonetta, L., S.E. Kuehn, A. Huang, D.J. Law, L.M. Kalikin, M. Koi, A.E. Reeve, B.H. Brownstein, H. Yeger, and B.R.G. Williams. 1990. Wilms' tumor locus on 11p13 defined by multiple CpG island-associated transcripts. *Science* **250:** 994–997.

Bosch, F.X., E. Schwarz, P. Boukamp, N.E. Fusenig, D. Bartsch, and H. zur Hausen. 1990. Suppression *in vivo* of human papillomavirus type 18 E6-E7 gene expression in non tumorigenic HeLa-fibroblast hybrid cells. *J. Virol.* **64:** 4743–4754.

Bregula, U., G. Klein, and H. Harris. 1971. The analysis of malignancy by cell fusion. II. Hybrids between Ehrlich cells and normal diploid cells. *J. Cell Sci.* **8:** 673–680.

Bremner, R. and A. Balmain. 1990. Genetic changes in skin tumor progression: Correlation between presence of a mutant *ras* gene and loss of heterozygosity on mouse chromosome 7. *Cell* **61:** 407–417.

Bridges, C.B. and K.F. Brehme. 1944. The mutations of *Drosophila melanogaster. Carnegie Inst. Washington Publ. No.* **552.**

Brugge, J.S. and R.L. Erikson. 1977. Identification of a transformation-specific antigen induced by an avian sarcoma virus. *Nature* **269:** 346–347.

Buchberg, A.M., L.S. Cleveland, N.A. Jenkins, and N.G. Copeland. 1990. Sequence homology shared by neurofibromatosis type-1 gene and IRA-I and IRA-2 negative regulators of the *RAS* cyclic AMP pathway. *Nature* **347:** 291–294.

Buchkovich, K., L.A. Duffy, and E. Harlow. 1989. The retinoblastoma protein is phosphorylated during specific phases of the cell cycle. *Cell* **58:** 1097–1105.

Call, K.M., T. Glaser, C.Y. Ito, A.J. Buckler, J. Pelletier, D.A. Haber, E.A. Rose, A. Kral, H. Yeger, W.H. Lewis, C. Jones, and D.E. Housman. 1990. Isolation and characterization of a zinc finger polypeptide gene at the human chromosome 11 Wilms' locus. *Cell* **60:** 509–520.

Capon, D.J., P.H. Seeburg, J.P. McGrath, J.S. Hayflick, U. Edman, A.D. Levinson, and D.V. Goeddel. 1983. Activation of Ki-*ras* 2 gene in human colon and lung carcinomas by two different point mutations. *Nature* **304:** 507–513.

Cavenee, W.K. 1994. Loss of function mutations in human cancer. In *The legacy of cell fusion* (ed. S. Gordon), pp. 215–226. Clarendon Press, Oxford.

Cavenee, W., N. Hastie, and E.J. Stanbridge, eds. 1989. *Current communications in molecular biology: Recessive oncogenes and tumor suppression.* Cold Spring Harbor Laboratory Press, Cold Spring Harbor, New York.

Cavenee, W.K., M.F. Hansen, M. Nordenskjold, E. Kock, I. Maumenee, J.A. Squire, R.A. Phillips, and B.L. Gallie. 1985. Genetic origin of mutations predisposing to retinoblastoma. *Science* **228:** 501–503.

Cavenee, W.K., T.P. Dryja, R.A. Phillips, W.F. Benedict, R. Godbout, B.L. Gallie, A.L. Murphree, L.C. Strong, and R.L. White. 1983. Expression of recessive alleles by chromosomal mechanisms in retinoblastoma. *Nature* **305:** 779–784.

Cawthorn, R.M., R. Weiss, G. Xu, D. Viskochil, M. Culver, J. Stevens, M. Robertson, D. Dunn, R. Gesteland, P. O'Connell, and R. White. 1990. A major segment of the neurofibromatosis type 1 gene: cDNA sequence, genomic structure and point mutations. *Cell* **62:** 193–201.

Chellappan, S.P., S. Hiebert, M. Mudryj, J.M. Horowitz, and J.R. Nevins. 1991. The E2F transcription factor is a cellular target for the RB protein. *Cell* **65:** 1053–1061.

Clarke, A.R., E.R. Maandag, M. Van Roon, N.M.T. Van der Lugt, M. Van der Valk, M.L. Hooper, A. Berns, and H. Te Riele. 1992. Requirement for a functional *Rb-1* gene in murine development. *Nature* **359:** 328–330.

Collett, M.S. and R.L. Erikson. 1978. Protein kinase activity associated with the avian sarcoma virus *src* gene product. *Proc. Natl. Acad. Sci.* **75:** 2021–2024.

Collins, S.J. and M. Groudine. 1982. Amplification of endogenous *myc*-related sequences in a human myeloid leukaemia cell line. *Nature* **298:** 679–681.

Compere, S.J., P. Baldacci, A.H. Sharpe T. Thompson, H. Land, and R. Jaenisch. 1989. The *ras* and *myc* oncogenes cooperate in tumor induction in many tissues when introduced into midgestation mouse embryos by retroviral vectors. *Proc. Natl. Acad. Sci.* **86:** 2224–2228.

Cooper, G.M., S. Okenquist, and L. Silverman. 1980. Transforming activity of DNA of chemically transformed and normal cells. *Nature* **284:** 418–421.

Coppes, M.J., C.E. Campbell, and B.R.G. Williams. 1993. The role of *WT1* in Wilms tumorigenesis. *FASEB J.* **7:** 886–895.

Cory, S., S. Gerondakis, and J.M. Adams. 1983. Interchromosomal recombination of the cellular oncogene c-*myc* with the plasmacytomas is a reciprocal exchange. *EMBO J.* **2:** 697–703.

Craig, R.W. and R. Sager. 1985. Suppression of tumorigenicity in hybrids of normal and oncogene-transformed CHEF cells. *Proc. Natl. Acad. Sci.* **82:** 2062–2066.

Crawford, L.V., D.C. Pim, E.G. Gurney, P. Goodfellow, and J. Taylor-Papadimitriou. 1981. Detection of a common feature in several human tumor cell lines–A 53,000-dalton protein. *Proc. Natl. Acad. Sci.* **78:** 41–45.

Czernilofsky, A.P., A.P. Levinson, H.E. Varmus, J.M. Bishop, E. Tischer, and H.M. Goodman. 1980. Nucleotide sequence of an avian sarcoma virus oncogene (*src*) and proposed amino acid sequence for gene product. *Nature* **287:** 198–203.

Dalla-Favera, R., F. Wong-Staal, and R.C. Gallo. 1982. *onc* gene amplification in promyelocytic leukaemia cell line HL-60 and primary leukaemic cells of the same patient. *Nature* **299:** 61–63.

DeCaprio, J.A., J.W. Ludlow, J. Figge, J.-Y. Shew, C.-M. Huang, W.-H. Lee, E. Marsilio, E. Paucha, and D.M. Livingston. 1988. SV40 large tumor antigen forms a specific complex with the product of the retinoblastoma susceptibility gene. *Cell* **54:** 275–283.

De Clue, J.E., A.G. Papageorge, J.A. Fletcher, S.R. Diehl, N. Ratner, W.C. Vass, and D.R. Lowy. 1992. Abnormal regulation of mammalian p21^{ras} contributes to malignant tumor growth in von Recklinghausen (type 1) neurofibromatosis. *Cell* **69:** 265–273.

DeFeo-Jones, D., K. Tatchell, L.C. Robinson, J.S. Sigal, W.C. Vass, D.R. Lowy, and E.M. Scolnick. 1985. Mammalian and yeast *ras* gene products: Biological function in their heterologous systems. *Science* **228:** 179–184.

Der, C.J., T.G. Krontiris, and G.M. Cooper. 1982. Transforming genes of human bladder and lung carcinoma cell lines are homologues to the *ras* genes of Harvey and Kirsten sarcoma viruses. *Proc. Natl. Acad. Sci.* **79:** 3637–3640.

Desrosiers, R.C., A. Bakker, J. Kamine, L.A. Falk, R.D. Hunt, and N.W. King. 1985. A region of the *Herpesvirus saimiri* genome required for oncogenicity. *Science* **228:** 184–187.

Dhar, R., R.W. Ellis, T.Y. Shih, S. Oroszlan, B. Shapiro, J. Maizel, D. Lowy, and E. Scolnick. 1982. Nucleotide sequence of the p21 transforming protein of Harvey murine sarcoma virus. *Science* **217:** 934–936.

Disela, C., C. Glineur, T. Bugge, J. Sap, G. Stengl, J. Dodgson, H. Stunnenberg, H. Beug, and M. Zenke. 1991. v-*erbA* overexpression is required to extinguish c-*erbA* function in erythroid cell differentiation and regulation of the *erbA* target gene CAII. *Genes Dev.* **5:** 2033–2047.

Donehower, L.A., M. Harvey, B.L. Slagle, M.J. McArthur, C.A. Montgomery, Jr., J.S. Butel, and A. Bradley. 1992. Mice deficient for p53 are developmentally normal but susceptible to spontaneous tumours. *Nature* **356:** 215–221.

Doolittle, R.F., M.W. Hunkapiller, L.E. Hood, S.G. DeVare, K.C. Robbins, S.A. Aaronson, and H.N. Antoniades. 1983. Simian sarcoma virus *onc* gene, v-*sis*, is derived from the gene (or genes) encoding a platelet-derived growth factor. *Science* **221:** 275–276.

Downward, J., Y. Yarden, E. Mayes, G. Scrace, N. Totty, P. Stockwell, A. Ullrich, J. Schlessinger, and M.D. Waterfield. 1984. Close similarity of epidermal growth factor receptor and v-*erb*-B oncogene protein sequences. *Nature* **307:** 521–527.

Drummond, I.A., S.L. Madden, P. Rohwer-Nutter, G.I. Bell, V.P. Sukhatme, and F.J. Rauscher III. 1992. Repression of the insulin-like growth factor II gene by the Wilms' tumor suppressor *WT1*. *Science* **257:** 674–678.

Dryja, T.P., J.M. Rapaport, J.M. Joyce, and R.A. Petersen. 1986. Molecular detection of deletions involving band q14 of chromosome 13 in retinoblastomas. *Proc. Natl. Acad. Sci.* **83:** 7391–7394.

Dürst, M., L. Gissmann, H. Ikenberg, and H. zur Hausen. 1983. A papilloma-virus

DNA from a cervical carcinoma and its prevalence in cancer biopsy samples from different geographic regions. *Proc. Natl. Acad. Sci.* **80:** 3812–3815.

Dyson, N., K. Buchkovich, P. Whyte, and E. Harlow. 1989a. The cellular 107K protein that binds to adenovirus E1A also associates with the large T antigens of SV40 and JC virus. *Cell* **58:** 249–255.

Dyson, N., P. Howley, K. Munger, and E. Harlow. 1989b. The human papilloma virus-16 E7 oncoprotein is able to bind to the retinoblastoma gene product. *Science* **243:** 934–937.

Dyson, P.J., K. Quade, and J.A. Wyke. 1982. Expression of the ASV *src* gene in hybrids between normal and virally transformed cells: Specific suppression occurs in some hybrids but not others. *Cell* **30:** 491–498.

Egan, S.E. and R.A. Weinberg. 1993. The pathway to signal achievement. *Nature* **365:** 781–783.

Elefanty, A.G., J.K. Hariharan, and S. Cory. 1990. *bcr-abl:* The hallmark of chronic myeloid leukaemia in man, induces multiple haemopoietic neoplasms in mice. *EMBO J.* **9:** 1069–1078.

Ellis, R.W., D. DeFeo, T.Y. Shih, M.A. Gonda, H.A. Young, N. Tsuchida, D.R. Lowy, and E.M. Scolnick. 1981. The p21 *src* genes of Harvey and Kirsten sarcoma viruses originate from divergent members of a family of normal vertebrate genes. *Nature* **292:** 506–511.

Epstein, M.A., B. Achong, and Y. Barr. 1964. Virus particles in cultured lymphoblasts from Burkitt's lymphoma. *Lancet* **I:** 702–703.

Evans, E.P., M.D. Burtenshaw, B.B. Brown, R. Hennion, and H. Harris. 1982. The analysis of malignancy by cell fusion. IX. Re-examination and clarification of the cytogenetic problem. *J. Cell Sci.* **56:** 113–130.

Falcone, G., F. Tato, and S. Alemà. 1985. Distinctive effects of the viral oncogenes *myc*, *erb*, *fps* and *src* on the differentiation program of quail myogenic cells. *Proc. Natl. Acad. Sci.* **82:** 426–430.

Fearon, E.R. and B. Vogelstein. 1990. A genetic model for colorectal tumorigenesis. *Cell* **61:** 759–767.

Fearon, E.R., B. Vogelstein, and A.P. Feinberg. 1984. Somatic deletion and duplication of genes on chromosome 11 in Wilms' tumours. *Nature* **309:** 176–178.

Fearon, E.R., K.R. Cho, J.M. Nigro, S.E. Kern, J.W. Simons, J.M. Ruppert, S.R. Hamilton, A.C. Preisinger, G. Thomas, K.W. Kinzler, and B. Vogelstein. 1990. Identification of a chromosome 18q gene that is altered in colorectal cancers. *Science* **247:** 49–56.

Feramisco, J.R., R. Clark, G. Wong, N. Arnheim, R. Milley, and F. McCormick. 1985. Transient reversion of *ras* oncogene-induced cell transformation by antibodies specific for amino acid 12 of *ras* protein. *Nature* **314:** 639–642.

Finlay, C. 1993. The *mdm-2* oncogene can overcome wild-type p53 suppression of transformed cell growth. *Mol. Cell. Biol.* **13:** 301–306.

Finlay, C.A., P.W. Hinds, and A.J. Levine. 1989. The p53 proto-oncogene can act as a suppressor of transformation. *Cell* **57:** 1083–1093.

Fountain, J.W., M.R. Wallace, M.A. Bruce, B.R. Seizinger, A.G. Menon, J.F. Gusella, V.V. Michels, M.A. Schmidt, G.W. Dewald, and F.S. Collins. 1989. Physical mapping of a translocation breakpoint in neurofibromatosis. *Science* **244:** 1085–1087.

Fountain, J.W., M. Karayiorgou, M.S. Ernstoff, J.M. Kirkwood, D.R. Vlock, L. Titus-Ernstoff, B. Bouchard, S. Vijayasaradhi, A.N. Houghton, J. Lahti, V.J. Kidd, D.E. Housman, and N.C. Dracopoli. 1992. Homozygous deletions within human chromosome band 9p21 in melanoma. *Proc. Natl. Acad. Sci.* **89:** 10557–10561.

Francke, U. 1976. Retinoblastoma and chromosome 13. *Cytogenet. Cell Genet.* **16:** 131–134.

Friend, S.H., R. Bernards, S. Rogelj, R.A. Weinberg, J. Rapaport, D. Albert, and T.P. Dryja. 1986. A human DNA segment with properties of the gene that predisposes to retinoblastoma and osteosarcoma. *Nature* **323:** 643–646.

Fukui, Y., T. Kozasa, Y. Kaziro, T. Takeda, and M. Yamamoto. 1986. Role of *ras* homologue in the life cycle of *Schizosaccharomyces pombe*. *Cell* **44:** 329–336.

Fung, T.-K.T., A.L. Murphree, A. T'Ang, J. Qian, S.H. Hinrichs, and W.F. Benedict. 1987. Structural evidence for the authenticity of the retinoblastoma gene. *Science* **236:** 1657–1661.

Fung, Y.-K., A.M. Fadly, L.B. Crittenden, and H.-J. Kung. 1981. On the mechanism of retrovirus-induced avian lymphoid leukosis: Deletion and integration of the proviruses. *Proc. Natl. Acad. Sci.* **78:** 3418–3422.

Galloway, D.A. and J.K. McDougall. 1983. The oncogenic potential of herpes simplex viruses: Evidence for a "hit-and-run" mechanism. *Nature* **302:** 21–24.

Gateff, E. and B.M. Mechler. 1989. Tumor-suppressor genes of *Drosophila melanogaster*. *CRC Crit. Rev. Oncogenesis* **1:** 221–245.

Gateff, E. and H.A. Schneiderman. 1967. Developmental studies of a new mutant of *Drosphila melanogaster:* Lethal malignant brain tumor. *J. Am. Soc. Zool.* **7:** 760.

———. 1969. Neoplasms in mutant and cultured wild-type tissues of *Drosophila. Natl. Cancer Inst. Monogr.* **31:** 365–397.

Geiser, A.G., C.J. Der, C.J. Marshall, and E.J. Stanbridge. 1986. Suppression of tumorigenicity with continued expression of the c-Ha-*ras* oncogene in EJ bladder carcinoma-human fibroblast hybrid cells. *Proc. Natl. Acad. Sci.* **83:** 5209–5213.

Gessler, M., A. Poustka, W. Cavenee, R.L. Neve, S.H. Orkin, and G.A. Bruns. 1990. Homozygous deletion in Wilms' tumours of a zinc-finger gene identified by chromosome jumping. *Nature* **343:** 774–778.

Gilbert, P.X. and H. Harris. 1988. The role of the *ras* oncogene in the formation of tumours. *J. Cell Sci.* **90:** 433–446.

Ginsberg, D., F. Mechta, M. Yaniv, and M. Oren. 1991. Wild-type p53 can down-modulate the activity of various promoters. *Proc. Natl. Acad. Sci.* **88:** 9979–9983.

Godbout, R., T.P. Dryja, J. Squire, B.L. Gallie, and R.A. Phillips. 1983. Somatic inactivation of genes on chromosome 13 is a common event in retinoblastoma. *Nature* **304:** 451–453.

Goldfarb, M., K. Shimizu, M. Perucho, and M. Wigler. 1982. Isolation and preliminary characterization of a human transforming gene from T_{24} bladder carcinoma cells. *Nature* **296:** 404–409.

Greenwald, J. and G.M. Rubin. 1992. Making a difference: The role of cell-cell interations in establishing separate identities for equivalent cells. *Cell* **68:** 271–272.

Groden, J., A. Thliveris, W. Samowitz, M. Carlson, L. Gelbert, H. Albertson, G. Joslyn, J. Stevens, L. Spirio, M. Robertson, L. Sargeant, K. Krapcho, E. Wolff, R. Burt, J.P. Hughes, J. Warrington, J. McPherson, J. Wasmuth, D. Le Paslier, H. Abderrahim, D. Cohen, M. Leppert, and R. White. 1991. Identification and characterization of the familial adenomatous polyposis coli gene. *Cell* **66:** 589–600.

Groffen, J., J.R. Stephenson, N. Heisterkamp, A. de Klein, C.R. Bartram, and G. Grosfeld. 1984. Philadelphia chromosomal breakpoints are clustered within a limited region *bcr* on chromosome 22. *Cell* **36:** 93–99.

Grunwald, D.J., B. Dale, J. Dudley, W. Lamph, W. Sugden, B. Ozanne, and R. Risser. 1982. Loss of viral gene expression and retention of tumorigenicity by Abelson lymphoma cells. *J. Virol.* **43:** 92–103.

Gu, W., J.W. Schneider, G. Condorelli, S. Klaushal, V. Mahdavi, and B. Nadal-Ginard. 1993. Interaction of myogenic factors and the retinoblastoma protein mediates muscle cell commitment and differentiation. *Cell* **72:** 309–324.

Hall, A., C.J. Marshall, N.K. Spurr, and R.A. Weiss. 1983. Identification of transforming gene in two human sarcoma cell lines as a new member of the *ras* gene family located on chromosome 1. *Nature* **303:** 396–400.

Hamel, P.A., R.A. Phillips, M. Muncaster, and B.L. Gallie. 1993. Speculations on the roles of *RB1* in tissue-specific differentiation, tumor initiation and tumor progression. *FASEB J.* **7:** 846–854.

Hann, S.R., C.B. Thompson, and N.R. Eisenman. 1985. c-*myc* oncogene protein synthesis is independent of the cell cycle in human and avian cells. *Nature* **314:** 366–369.

Hariharan, J.K. and J.M. Adams. 1987. cDNA sequence for human *bcr*: The gene that translocates to the *abl* oncogene in chronic myeloid leukaemia. *EMBO J.* **6:** 115–119.

Hariharan, J.K., A.W. Harris, M. Crawford, H. Abud, E. Webb, S. Cory, and J.M. Adams. 1989. A *bcr-v-abl* oncogene induces lymphomas in transgenic mice. *Mol. Cell. Biol.* **9:** 2798–2805.

Harris, H. 1971. Cell fusion and the analysis of malignancy: The Croonian Lecture. *Proc. R. Soc. Lond. B* **179:** 1–20.

————. 1985. Suppression of malignancy in hybrid cells: The mechanism. *J. Cell Sci.* **79:** 83–94.

————. 1993. How tumour suppressor genes were discovered. *FASEB J.* **7:** 978–979.

Harris, H. and M.E. Bramwell. 1987. The suppression of malignancy by terminal differentiation: Evidence from hybrids between tumour cells and keratinocytes. *J. Cell Sci.* **87:** 383–388.

Harris, H. and G. Klein. 1969. Malignancy of somatic cell hybrids. *Nature* **224:** 1314–1316.

Harris, H., O.J. Miller, G. Klein, P. Worst, and T. Tachibana. 1969. Suppression of malignancy by cell fusion. *Nature* **223:** 363–368.

Heisterkamp, N., J.R. Stephenson, J. Groffen, P.F. Hansen, A. de Klein, C.R. Bartram, and G. Grosfeld. 1983. Localization of the c-*abl* oncogene adjacent to a translocation point in chronic myelocytotic leukemia. *Nature* **306:** 239–242.

Henry, J., S. Grandjouan, P. Couillin, F. Barichard, C. Huerre-Jeanpierre, T. Glaser, T. Philip, G. Lenoir, J.L. Chaussain, and C. Junien. 1989. Tumor-specific loss of 11p15.5 alleles in del 11p13 Wilms tumor and in familial adrenocortical carcinoma. *Proc. Natl. Acad. Sci.* **86:** 3247–3251.

Hjelle, B., E. Liu, and J.M. Bishop. 1988. Oncogene v-*src* transforms and establishes embryonic rodent fibroblasts but not diploid human fibroblasts. *Proc. Natl. Acad. Sci.* **85:** 4355–4359.

Horvitz, H.R. and P.W. Sternberg. 1991. Multiple intercellular signalling systems control the development of the *Caenorhabditis elegans* vulva. *Nature* **351:** 535–541.

Huang, H., J.K. Yee, J.Y. Shew, P.L. Chen, R. Bookstein, T. Friedmann, E.Y. Lee, and W.-H. Lee. 1988. Suppression of the neoplastic phenotype by replacement of the RB gene in human cancer cells. *Science* **242:** 1563–1566.

Huebner, R.J. and G.J. Todaro. 1969. Oncogenes of RNA tumor viruses as determinants of cancer. *Proc. Natl. Acad. Sci.* **64:** 1087–1094.

Huff, V., F. Villalba, L.C. Strong, and G.F. Saunders. 1991. Alterations of the *WT1* gene in patients with Wilms' tumor and genitourinary anomalies. *Am. J. Hum. Genet.* **49:** 44.

Hunter, T. and J.A. Cooper. 1985. Protein-tyrosine kinases. *Annu. Rev. Biochem.* **54:** 897–930.

Iavarone, A., K.K. Matthay, T.M. Steinkirchner, and M.A. Israel. 1992. Germ line and somatic sarcoma. *Proc. Natl. Acad. Sci.* **89:** 4207–4209.

Jacks, T., A. Fazeli, E.M. Schmitt, R.T. Bronson, M.A. Goodell, and R.A. Weinberg. 1992. Effects of an *Rb* mutation in the mouse. *Nature* **359:** 295–300.

Jacob, L., M. Opper, B. Metzroth, B. Phannavong, and B.M. Mechler. 1987. Structure of the *l(2)gl* gene of *Drosophila* and delimitation of its tumor suppressor domain. *Cell* **50:** 215–225.

Jonasson, J., S. Povey, and H. Harris. 1977. The analysis of malignancy by cell fusion. VII. Cytogenetic analysis of hybrids between malignant and diploid cells and of tumours derived from them. *J. Cell Sci.* **24:** 217–254.

Joslyn, G., M. Carlson, A. Thliveris, H. Albertsen, L. Gelbert, W. Samowitz, J. Groden, J. Stevens, L. Spirio, M. Robertson, L. Sargeant, K. Krapcho, E. Wolff, R. Burt, J.P. Hughes, J. Warrington, J. McPherson, J. Wasmuth, D. Le Paslier, H. Abderrahim, D. Cohen, M. Leppert, and R. White. 1991. Identification of deletion mutations and three new genes at the familial polyposis locus. *Cell* **66:** 601–613.

Kaelbling, M. and H.P. Klinger. 1986. Suppression of tumorigenicity in somatic cell hybrids. III. Cosegregation of human chromosome 11 of a normal cell and suppression of tumorigenicity in intraspecies hybrids of normal diploid X malignant cells. *Cytogenet. Cell Genet.* **41:** 65–70.

Kawai, S. and H. Hanafusa. 1971. The effects of reciprocal changes in temperature on the transformed state of cells infected with a Rous sarcoma virus mutant. *Virology* **46:** 470–479.

Kern, S.E., K.W. Kinzler, A. Bruskin, D. Jarosz, P. Friedman, C. Prives, and B. Vogelstein. 1991. Identification of p53 as a sequence-specific DNA-binding protein. *Science* **252:** 1708–1711.

Kim, S.H., K.A. Roth, A.R. Moser, and J.J. Gordon. 1993. Transgenic mouse models that explore the multistep hypothesis of intestinal neoplasia. *J. Cell Biol.* **123:** 877–893.

Kinzler, K.W., M.C. Nilbert, L.-K. Su, B. Vogelstein, T.M. Bryan, D.B. Levy, K.J. Smith, A.C. Preisinger, P. Hedge, D. McKechnie, R. Finniear, A. Markham, J. Groffen, M.S. Boguski, S.F. Altschul, A. Horii, H. Ando, Y. Iyoshi, Y. Miki, I. Nishisho, and Y. Nakamura. 1991. Identification of FAP locus genes from chromosome 5q21. *Science* **253:** 661–665.

Klein, G. 1981. The role of gene dosage and genetic transpositions in carcinogenesis. *Nature* **294:** 313–318.

Klein, G., U. Bregula, F. Wiener, and H. Harris. 1971. The analysis of malignancy by cell fusion. I. Hybrids between tumour cells and L cell derivatives. *J. Cell Sci.* **8:** 659–672.

Klinger, H.P. 1980. Suppression of tumorigenicity in somatic cell hybrids. I. Suppression and re-expression of tumorigenicity in diploid human X D98 AH₂ hybrids and independent segregation of tumorigenicity from other cell phenotypes. *Cytogenet. Cell Genet.* **27:** 254–266.

Knudson, A.G. 1971. Mutation and cancer: Statistical study of retinoblastoma. *Proc. Natl. Acad. Sci.* **68:** 820–823.

———. 1985. Hereditary cancer, oncogenes and antioncogenes. *Cancer Res.* **45:** 1437–1443.

Knudson, A.G. and L.C. Strong. 1972. Mutation and cancer: A model for Wilms' tumour of the kidney. *J. Natl. Cancer Inst.* **48:** 313–324.

Knudson, A.G., A.T. Meadows, W.W. Nichols, and R. Hill. 1976. Chromosomal deletion and retinoblastoma. *N. Engl. J. Med.* **295:** 1120–1123.

Koufos, A., M.F. Hansen, B.C. Lampkin, M.L. Workman, N.G. Copeland, N.A. Jenkins, and W.K. Cavenee. 1984. Loss of alleles at loci on human chromosome 11 during genesis of Wilms' tumour. *Nature* **309:** 170–172.

Kozbor, D. and C.M. Croce. 1984. Amplification of the c-*myc* oncogene in one of five human breast carcinoma cell lines. *Cancer Res.* **44:** 438–441.

Kreidberg, J.A., H. Sariola, J.M. Loring, M. Maeda, J. Pelletier, D. Housman, and R. Jaenisch. 1993. WT-1 is required for kidney development. *Cell* **74:** 679–691.

Krieg, T., M. Aumailley, W. Dessau, M. Wiestner, and P. Müller. 1980. Synthesis of collagen by human fibroblasts and their SV40 transformants. *Exp. Cell Res.* **125:** 23–30.

Kriegler, M., C.F. Perez, C. Hardy, and M. Botchan. 1984. Transformation mediated by the SV40 T antigens: Separation of the overlapping SV40 early genes with a retroviral vector. *Cell* **38:** 483–491.

Krontiris, T.G. and G.M. Cooper. 1981. Transforming activity of human tumor DNAs. *Proc. Natl. Acad. Sci.* **78:** 1181–1184.

Land, H., L.F. Parada, and R.A. Weinberg. 1983. Tumorigenic conversion of primary embryo fibroblasts requires at least two cooperating oncogenes. *Nature* **304:** 596–602.

Lane, D.P. 1992. p53, guardian of the genome. *Nature* **358:** 15–16.

Lane, D.P. and S. Benchimol. 1990. p53: Oncogene or anti-oncogene? *Genes Dev.* **4:** 1–8.

Lane, D.P and L.V. Crawford. 1979. T antigen is bound to a host protein in SV40-transformed cells. *Nature* **278:** 261–263.

Langbeheim, H., T.Y. Shih, and E.M. Scolnick. 1980. Identification of a normal vertebrate cell protein related to the p21 *src* of Harvey murine sarcoma virus. *Virology* **106:** 292–300.

Leder, A., P.K. Pattengale, A. Juo, T.A. Stewart, and P. Leder. 1986. Consequences of widespread deregulation of the c-*myc* gene in transgenic mice: Multiple neoplasms and normal development. *Cell* **45:** 485–495.

Lee, E.Y-.H.P., C.-Y. Chang, N. Hu, Y.-C. Wang, C.-C. Lai, K. Herrup, W.-H. Lee, and A. Bradley. 1992. Mice deficient for Rb are non-viable and show defects in neurogenesis and haematopoiesis. *Nature* **359:** 288–294.

Lee, W.-H., A.L. Murphree, and W.F. Benedict. 1984. Expression and amplification of the N-*myc* gene in primary retinoblastoma. *Nature* **309:** 458–460.

Lee, W.-H., R. Bookstein, F. Hong, Z.-J. Young, J.-Y. Shew, and E.Y.-H.P. Lee. 1987. Human retinoblastoma susceptibility gene: Cloning, identification and sequence. *Science* **235:** 1394–1399.

Levinson, A.D., H. Oppermann, L. Levintow, H.E. Varmus, and J.M. Bishop. 1978. Evidence that the transforming gene of avian sarcoma virus encodes a protein kinase associated with a phosphoprotein. *Cell* **15**: 561–572.

Liau, G., Y. Yamada, and B. de Crombrugghe. 1985. Coordinate regulation of the levels of type III and type I collagen mRNA in most but not all mouse fibroblasts. *J. Biol. Chem.* **260**: 531–536.

Little, C.D., M.M. Nau, D.N. Carney, A.F. Gazdar, and J.D. Minna. 1983. Amplification and expression of the c-*myc* oncogene in human lung cancer cell lines. *Nature* **306**: 194–195.

Livingstone, L.R., A. White, J. Sprouse, E. Livanos, T. Jacks, and T. Tlsty. 1992. Altered cell cycle arrest and gene amplification potential accompanying loss of wild-type p53. *Cell* **70**: 923–935.

Madden, S.L., D.M. Cook, J.F. Morris, A. Gashler, U.K. Sukhatme, and F.J. Rauscher III. 1991. Transcriptional repression mediated by the WT1 tumor gene product. *Science* **253**: 1550–1553.

Mahoney, P.A., U. Weber, P. Onofrechuk, H. Biessmann, P.J. Bryant, and C.S. Goodman. 1991. The *fat* tumor suppressor gene in *Drosophila* encodes a novel member of the cadherin gene superfamily. *Cell* **67**: 853–868.

Malkin, D., F.P. Li, L.C. Strong, J.F. Fraumeni, C.E. Nelson, D. Kim, J. Kassel, M.A. Gryka, F.Z. Bischoff, M.A. Tainsky, and S.H. Friend. 1990. Germ line p53 mutations in a familial syndrome of breast cancer, sarcomas and other neoplasms. *Science* **250**: 1233–1238.

Marshall, C.J. 1980. Suppression of the transformed phenotype with retention of the viral '*src*' gene in cell hybrids between Rous sarcoma virus-transformed rat cells and untransformed mouse cells. *Exp. Cell Res.* **127**: 373–384.

Marshall, C.J., A. Hall, and R.A. Weiss. 1982. A transforming gene present in human sarcoma lines. *Nature* **299**: 171–173.

Martin, G.S. 1970. Rous sarcoma virus: A function required for the maintenance of the transformed state. *Nature* **227**: 1021–1023.

McCoy, M.S., J.J. Toole, J.M. Cunningham, E.H. Chang, D. Lowy, and R.A. Weinberg. 1983. Characterization of a human colon/lung carcinoma oncogene. *Nature* **302**: 79–81.

McGuire, E.A., R.D. Hockett, K.M. Pollock, M.F. Bartholdi, S.J. O'Brien, and S.J. Korsmeyer. 1989. The t(11;14)(p15;q11) in a T-cell acute lymphoblastic leukemia cell line activates multiple transcripts, including *Ttg-1*, a gene encoding a potential zinc finger protein. *Mol. Cell. Biol.* **9**: 2124–2132.

Mechler, B.M., W. McGinnis, and W.J. Gehring. 1985. Molecular cloning of *lethal(2) giant larvae*: A recessive oncogene of *Drosophila melangaster*. *EMBO J.* **4**: 1551–1557.

Mechler, B.M., I. Torok, M. Schmidt, M. Opper, A. Kuhn, R. Merz, and U. Protin. 1989. Molecular basis for the regulation of cell fate by the *lethal(2) giant larvae* tumour suppression gene of *Drosophila melanogaster*. *Ciba Found. Symp.* **142**: 166–178.

Mihara, K., X.R. Cao, A. Yen, S. Chandler, B. Driscoll, A.L. Murphree, A. T'Ang, and Y.K. Fung. 1989. Cell cycle dependent regulation of phosphorylation of the human retinoblastoma gene product. *Science* **246**: 1300–1303.

Minson, A.C. 1984. Cell transformation and oncogenesis by herpes simplex virus and human cytomegalovirus. *Cancer Surv.* **3**: 91–112.

Mulcahy, L.S., M.R. Smith, and D.W. Stacey. 1985. Requirement for *ras* proto-oncogene function during serum-stimulated growth of NIH 3T3 cells. *Nature* **313**: 241–243.

Muncaster, M., B. Cohen, R.A. Phillips, and B.L. Gallie. 1992. Failure of *RB1* to reverse the malignant phenotype of human tumour cell lines. *Cancer Res.* **52**: 654–661.

Murray, M.J., J.M. Cunningham, L.F. Parada, F. Dautry, P. Lebowitz, and R.A. Weinberg. 1983. The HL-60 transforming sequence: A *ras* oncogene coexisting with altered *myc* genes in hematopoietic tumors. *Cell* **33**: 749–757.

Neel, B.G., W.S. Hayward, H.L. Robinson, J. Fang, and S.M. Astrin. 1981. Avian leukosis virus-induced tumors have common proviral integration sites and synthesize discrete new RNAs: Oncogenesis by promoter insertion. *Cell* **23**: 323–334.

Nishisho, I., Y. Nakamura, Y. Miyoshi, Y. Miki, H. Ando, A. Horii, K. Koyama, J. Utsunomija, S. Baba, P. Hedge, A. Markham, A.J. Krush, G. Petersen, S.R. Hamilton, M.C. Nilbert, D.B. Levy, T.M. Bryan, A.C. Preisinger, K.J. Smith, K.-K. Su, K.W. Kinzler, and B. Vogelstein. 1991. Mutations of chromosome 5q21 genes in FAP and colorectal cancer patients. *Science* **253**: 665–669.

Noori-Daloii, M.R., R.A. Swift, H.-J. Kung, L.B. Crittenden, and R.L. Witter. 1981. Specific integration of REV proviruses in avian bursal lymphomas. *Nature* **294:** 574–576.

Nusse, R. and H.E. Varmus. 1982. Many tumors induced by the mouse mammary tumor virus contain a provirus integrated in the same region of the host genome. *Cell* **31:** 99–109.

O'Connell, P., R. Leach, R.M. Cawthorn, M. Culver, J. Stevens, D. Viskochil, R.E.K. Fournier, D.C. Rich, D.H. Ledbetter, and R. White. 1989. Two NFI translocations map within a 600 kilobase segment of 17q11.2. *Science* **244:** 1087–1088.

Ohno, S. 1971. Genetic implication of karyological instability of malignant somatic cells. *Physiol. Rev.* **51:** 496–526.

Opper, M., G. Schuler, and B.M. Mechler. 1987. Hereditary suppression of *lethal(2) giant larvae* malignant tumor development in *Drosophila* by gene transfer. *Oncogene* **1:** 91–96.

Orkin, S.H., D.S. Goldman, and S.E. Sallan. 1984. Development of homozygosity for chromosome 11p markers in Wilms' tumour. *Nature* **309:** 172–174.

Oshimura, M., M. Koi, N. Ozawa, O. Sugawara, P.W. Lamb, and J.C. Barrett. 1988. Role of chromosome loss in *ras/myc*-induced Syrian hamster tumors. *Cancer Res.* **48:** 1623–1632.

Parada, L.F., C.J. Tabin, C. Shih, and R.A. Weinberg. 1982. Human EJ bladder carcinoma oncogene is homologue of Harvey sarcoma virus *ras* gene. *Nature* **297:** 474–478.

Paterson, H., B. Reeves, R. Brown, A. Hall, A. Furth, J. Boz, P. Jones, and C. Marshall. 1987. Activated N-*ras* controls the transformed phenotype of HT1080 human fibrosarcoma cells. *Cell* **51:** 803–812.

Payne, G.S., J.M. Bishop, and H.E. Varmus. 1982. Multiple arrangements of viral DNA and an activated host oncogene in bursal lymphomas. *Nature* **295:** 209–214.

Payne, G.S., S.A. Courtneidge, L.B. Crittenden, A.M. Fadly, J.M. Bishop, and H.E. Varmus. 1981. Analysis of avian leukosis virus DNA and RNA in bursal tumors: Viral gene expression is not required for maintenance of the tumor state. *Cell* **23:** 311–322.

Peehl, D.M. and E.J. Stanbridge. 1982. The role of differentiation in the suppression of tumorigenicity in human hybrid cells. *Int. J. Cancer* **30:** 113–120.

Pelletier, J., W. Bruening, C.E. Kashtan, S.M. Mauer, J.C. Manivel, J.E. Striegel, D.C. Houghton, C. Junien, R. Habib, L. Fouser, R.N. Fine, B.L. Silverman, D.A. Haber, and D. Housman. 1991. Germline mutations in the Wilms' tumor suppressor gene are associated with abnormal urogenital development in Denys-Drash syndrome. *Cell* **67:** 437–447.

Perrimon, N. 1993. The torso receptor protein-tyrosine kinase signalling pathway: An endless story. *Cell* **74:** 219–222.

Pietenpol, J.A. and B. Vogelstein. 1993. No room at the p53 inn. *Nature* **365:** 17–18.

Pulciani, S., E. Santos, A.V. Lauver, L.K. Long, K.C. Robbins, and M. Barbacid. 1982. Oncogenes in human bladder tumor cell lines: Molecular cloning of a transforming gene from human bladder carcinoma cells. *Proc. Natl. Acad. Sci.* **79:** 2845–2849.

Rassoulzadegan, M., A. Cowie, A. Carr, N. Glaichenhous, and R. Kamen. 1982. The role of individual polyoma virus early proteins in oncogenic transformation. *Nature* **300:** 713–718.

Rassoulzadegan, M., Z. Naghashfar, A. Cowie, A. Carr, M. Grisoni, R. Kamen, and F. Cuzin. 1983. Expression of the large T protein of polyoma virus promotes the establishment in culture of "normal" rodent fibroblast cell lines. *Proc. Natl. Acad. Sci.* **80:** 4354–4358.

Reddy, E.P., R.K. Reynolds. E. Santos, and M. Barbacid. 1982. A point mutation is responsible for the acquisition of transforming properties by the T_{24} human bladder carcinoma oncogene. *Nature* **300:** 149–152.

Reeve, A.E., S.A. Sih, A.M. Raizis, and A.P. Feinberg. 1989. Loss of allelic heterozygosity at a second locus on chromosome 11 in sporadic Wilms' tumor cells. *Mol. Cell. Biol.* **9:** 1799–1803.

Rouleau, G.A., P. Merel, M. Lutchman, M. Sanson, J. Zucman, C. Marineau, K. Hoang-Xuan, S. Demczuk, C. Desmaze, B. Plougastel, S.M. Pulst, G. Lenoir, E. Bijlsma, R.

Fashold, J. Dumanski, P. de Jong, D. Parry, R. Eldrige, A. Aurias, O. Delattre, and G. Thomas. 1993. Alteration in a new gene encoding a putative membrane-organizing protein causes neurofibromatosis type 2. *Nature* **363**. 515–521.

Rubinfeld, B., B. Souza, J. Albert, O. Müller, S.H. Chamberlain, F.R. Masiarz, S. Munemitzu, and P. Polakis. 1994. Association of the APC gene product with β-catenin. *Science* **262**: 1731–1734.

Santos, E., S.K. Tronick, S.A. Aaronson, S. Pulciani, and M. Barbacid. 1982. T$_{24}$ human bladder carcinoma oncogene is an activated form of the normal human homologue of BALB and Harvey-MSV transforming genes. *Nature* **298**: 343–347.

Santos, E., D. Martin-Zanca, E.P. Reddy, M.A. Pierotti, G. Della Porta, and M. Barbacid. 1984. Malignant activation of a K-*ras* oncogene in lung carcinoma but not in normal tissue of the same patient. *Science* **223**: 661–664.

Sap, J., A. Muñoz, K. Damin, Y. Goldberg, J. Ghysdael, A. Leutz, H. Beug, and B. Vennström. 1986. The c-*erb* A protein is a high-affinity receptor for thyroid hormone. *Nature* **324**: 635–640.

Saxon, P.J., E.S. Srivatsan, and E.G. Stanbridge. 1986. Introduction of chromosome 11 via microcell transfer controls tumorigenic expression of HeLa cells. *EMBO J.* **5**: 3461–3466.

Schiller, J.T., W.C. Vass, and D.R. Lowy. 1984. Identification of a second transforming region in bovine papillomavirus DNA. *Proc. Natl. Acad. Sci.* **81**: 7880–7884.

Schimke, R.T., R.J. Kaufman, F.W. Alt, and R.F. Kellems. 1978. Gene amplification and drug resistance in cultured murine cells. *Science* **202**: 1051–1055.

Schmidt, A., C. Setoyama, and B. de Crombrugghe. 1985. Regulation of a collagen gene promoter by the product of viral *mos* oncogene. *Nature* **314**: 286–289.

Schroeder, C., C. Raynoschek, U. Fuhrmann, K. Damm, B. Vennström, and H. Beug. 1990. The v-*erb* A oncogene causes repression of erythrocyte-specific genes and an immature, aberrant differentiation phenotype in normal erythroid progenitors. *Oncogene* **5**: 1445–1453.

Schwab, M., K. Alitalo, H.E. Varmus, J.M. Bishop, and D. George. 1983a. A cellular oncogene (c-Ki-*ras*) is amplified, overexpressed, and located within karyotypic abnormalities in mouse adrenocortical tumour cells. *Nature* **303**: 497–501.

Schwab, M., K. Alitalo, K.-H. Klempnauer, H.E. Varmus, J.M. Bishop, F. Gilbert, G. Brodeur, M. Goldstein, and J. Trent. 1983b. Amplified DNA with limited homology to *myc* cellular oncogene is shared by human neuroblastoma cell lines and a neuroblastoma tumour. *Nature* **305**: 245–249.

Schwarz, E., U.K. Freese, L. Gissmann, W. Mayer, B. Roggenbuck, A. Stremlau, and H. zur Hausen. 1985. Structure and transcription of human papillomavirus sequences in cervical carcinoma cells. *Nature* **314**: 111–115.

Scolnick, E.M., A.G. Papageorge, and T.Y. Shih. 1979. Guanine nucleotide-binding as an assay for *src* protein of rat-derived murine sarcoma viruses. *Proc. Natl. Acad. Sci.* **76**: 5355–5359.

Sheiness, D.K., S.H. Hughes, H.E. Varmus, E. Stubblefield, and J.M. Bishop. 1980. The vertebrate homolog of the putative transforming gene of avian myelocytomatosis virus: Characteristics of the DNA locus and its RNA transcript. *Virology* **105**: 415–424.

Sherr, C.J., C.W. Rettenmier, R. Sacca, M.F. Roussel, A.T. Look, and E.R. Stanley. 1985. The c-*fms* protooncogene product is related to the receptor for the mononuclear phagocyte growth factor CSF-1. *Cell* **41**: 665–676.

Shih, C. and R.A. Weinberg. 1982. Isolation of a transforming sequence from a human bladder carcinoma cell line. *Cell* **29**: 161–169.

Shih, C., B.Z. Shilo, M.P. Goldfarb, A. Dannenberg, and R.A. Weinberg. 1979. Passage of phenotypes of chemically transformed cells via transfection of DNA and chromatin. *Proc. Natl. Acad. Sci.* **76**: 5714–5718.

Shih, T.Y., M.O. Weeks, H.A. Young, and E.M. Scolnick. 1979a. p21 of Kirsten murine sarcoma virus is thermolabile in a viral mutant temperature sensitive for the maintenance of transformation. *J. Virol.* **31**: 546–556.

———. 1979b. Identification of a sarcoma virus-coded phosphoprotein in nonproducer cells transformed by Kirsten or Harvey murine sarcoma virus. *Virology* **96**: 64–79.

Shih, T.Y., A.G. Papageorge, P.E. Stokes, M.O. Weeks, and E.M. Scolnick. 1980.

Guanine nucleotide-binding and autophosphorylating activities associated with the p21[src] protein of Harvey murine sarcoma virus. *Nature* **287**: 686–691.

Shimizu, K., M. Goldfarb, M. Perucho, and M. Wigler. 1983. Isolation and preliminary characterization of the transforming gene of a human neuroblastoma cell line. *Proc. Natl. Acad. Sci.* **80**: 383–387.

Sinn, E., W. Muller, P. Pattengale, J. Tepler, R. Wallace, and P. Leder. 1987. Coexpression of MMTV/v-Ha-*ras* and MMTV/c-*myc* genes in transgenic mice: Synergistic action of oncogenes *in vivo*. *Cell* **49**: 465–475.

Slebos, R.J.C., S.G. Evers, S.S. Wagenaar, and S. Rodenhuis. 1989. Cellular protooncogenes are infrequently amplified in untreated non-small cell lung cancer. *Br. J. Cancer* **39**: 76–80.

Smith, B.L., A. Anisowicz, L.A. Chodosh, and R. Sager. 1982. DNA transfer of focus- and tumor-forming ability into non-tumorigenic CHEF cells. *Proc. Natl. Acad. Sci.* **79**: 1964–1968.

Smith, M.R., S.J. De Gudicibus, and D.W. Stacey. 1986. Requirement for c-*ras* proteins during viral oncogene transformation. *Nature* **320**: 540–543.

Solomon, E., J. Borrow, and A.D. Goddard. 1991. Chromosome aberrations and cancer. *Science* **254**: 1153–1160.

Solomon, E., R. Voss, V. Hall, W.F. Bodmer, J.R. Jass, A.J. Jeffreys, F.C. Lucibello, I. Patel, and S.H. Rider. 1987. Chromosome 5 allele loss in human colorectal carcinomas. *Nature* **328**: 616–619.

Sparkes, R.S., A.L. Murphree, R.W. Lingua, M.C. Sparkes, L.L. Field, S.J. Funderburk, and W.F. Benedict. 1983. Gene for hereditary retinoblastoma assigned to human chromosome 13 by linkage to esterase D. *Science* **219**: 971–973.

Spector, D., H.E. Varmus, and J.M. Bishop. 1978. Nucleotide sequences related to the transforming gene of avian sarcoma virus are present in DNA of uninfected vertebrates. *Proc. Natl. Acad. Sci.* **75**: 4102–4106.

Srivastava, A., J.S. Norris, R.J. Schmooker-Reis, and S. Goldstein. 1985. c-H-*ras* 1 protooncogene amplification and overexpression during the limited replication lifespan of normal human fibroblasts. *J. Biol. Chem.* **260**: 6404–6409.

Srivastava, S., Z. Zou, K. Pirollo, W. Blattner, and E.H. Chang. 1990. Germ-line transmission of a mutated p53 gene in a cancer-prone family with Li-Fraumeni syndrome. *Nature* **348**: 747–749.

Srivastava, S., Y. Tong, K. Devadas, Z. Zou, V. Sykes, Y. Chen, W. Blattner, K. Pirollo, and E. Chang. 1992. Detection of both mutant and wild-type p53 proteins in normal skin fibroblasts and demonstration of a shared "second hit" on p53 in diverse tumours from a cancer-prone family with Li-Fraumeni syndrome. *Oncogene* **7**: 987–991.

Srivatsan, E.S., W.F. Benedict, and E.J. Stanbridge. 1986. Implication of chromosome 11 in the suppression of neoplastic expression in human cell hybrids. *Cancer Res.* **46**: 6174–6179.

Stanbridge, E.J. 1976. Suppression of malignancy in human cells. *Nature* **260**: 17–20.

———. 1990. Human tumor suppressor genes. *Annu. Rev. Genet.* **24**: 615–657.

Stanbridge, E.J. and J. Wilkinson. 1978. Analysis of malignancy in human cells: Malignant and transformed phenotypes are under separate genetic control. *Proc. Natl. Acad. Sci.* **75**: 1466–1469.

Stéhelin, D., R.V. Guntala, H.E. Varmus, and J.M. Bishop. 1976. Purification of DNA complementary to nucleotide sequences required for neoplastic transformation of fibroblasts by avian sarcoma viruses. *J. Mol. Biol.* **101**: 349–365.

Stéhelin, D., H.E. Varmus, J.M. Bishop, and P.K. Vogt. 1976. DNA related to the transforming gene(s) of avian sarcoma virus is present in normal avian DNA. *Nature* **260**: 170–173.

Steinmeyer, K. and W. Deppert. 1988. DNA binding properties of murine p53. *Oncogene* **3**: 501–507.

Stoler, A.B., F. Stenbach, and A. Balmain. 1993. The conversion of mouse skin squamous cell carcinomas to spindle cell carcinomas is a recessive event. *J. Cell Biol.* **122**: 1103–1117.

Su, L.-K., B. Vogelstein, and K.W. Kinzler. 1994. Association of the APC tumor suppression protein with catenins. *Science* **262**: 1734–1737.

Szpirer, C., M. Rivière, J. Szpirer, M. Genet, P. Drèze, M.Q. Islam, and G. Levan. 1990. Assignment of 12 loci to rat chromosome 5: Evidence that this chromosome is homologous to mouse chromosome 4 and to human chromosomes 9 and 11p arm. *Genomics* **6**: 679–684.

Temin, H.M. 1971. Mechanism of cell transformation by RNA tumor viruses. *Annu. Rev. Microbiol.* **25**: 609–648.

Tlsty, T.D., A. White, and J. Sanchez. 1992. Suppression of gene amplification in human cell hybrids. *Science* **255**: 1425–1427.

Toda, T., I. Uno, T. Ishikawa, S. Powers, T. Kataoka, D. Broek, S. Cameron, J. Broach, K. Matsumoto, and M. Wigler. 1985. In yeast, *RAS* proteins are controlling elements in adenylate cyclase. *Cell* **40**: 27–36.

Todaro, G.J. 1988. Autocrine growth in carcinogenesis. In *Theories of carcinogenesis* (ed. O.H. Iversen), pp. 61–80. Hemisphere, Washington, D.C.

Tolsma, S.S., J.D. Cohen, L.S. Ehrlich, and N.P. Bouck. 1993. Transformation of NIH 3T3 to anchorage independence by H-*ras* is accompanied by loss of suppressor activity. *Exp. Cell Res.* **205**: 232–239.

Trofatter, J.A., M.M. MacCollin, J.L. Rutter, J.R. Murrell, M.P. Duyao, D.M. Parry, R. Eldridge, N. Kley, A.G. Menon, K. Pulaski, V.H. Haase, C.M. Ambrose, D. Munroe, C. Bove, J.L. Haines R.L. Martuza, M.E. MacDonald, B.R. Seizinger, M.P. Short, A.J. Buckler, and J.F. Gusella. 1993. A novel moesin-, ezrin-, radixin-like gene is a candidate for the neurofibromatosis 2 tumor suppressor. *Cell* **72**: 791–800.

Trüeb, B., J.B. Lewis, and W.G. Carter. 1985. Translatable mRNA for GP140 (a subunit of type VI collagen) is absent in SV40 transformed fibroblasts. *J. Cell Biol.* **100**: 638–641.

Tsuchida, N., T. Ryder, and E. Ohtsubo. 1982. Nucleotide sequence of the oncogene encoding the p21 transforming protein of Kirsten murine sarcoma virus. *Science* **217**: 937–939.

Ullrich, A., L. Coussens, J.S. Hayflick, T.J. Dull, A. Gray, A.W. Tam, Y. Lee, Y. Yarden, T.A. Libermann, J. Schlessinger, J. Downward, E.L.V. Mayes, N. Whittle, M.D. Waterfield, and P.H. Seeburg. 1984. Human epidermal growth factor receptor cDNA sequence and aberrant expression of the amplified gene in A431 epidermoid carcinoma cells. *Nature* **309**: 418–425.

Vaheri, A., M. Kurkinen, V.-P. Lehto, E. Linder, and R. Timpl. 1978. Codistribution of pericellular matrix proteins in cultured fibroblasts and loss in transformation. Fibronectin and procollagen. *Proc. Natl. Acad. Sci.* **75**: 4944–4948.

van der Eb, A.J. and R. Bernards. 1984. Transformation and oncogenicity by adenoviruses. *Curr. Top. Microbiol. Immunol.* **110**: 23–51.

van der Elsen, P.J., A. Houweling, and A.J. van der Eb. 1983. Morphological transformation of human adenoviruses is determined to a large extent by gene products of region E1A. *Virology* **131**: 242–246.

Viskochil, D., A.M. Buchberg, G. Xu, R.M. Cawthorn, J. Stevens, R.K. Wolff, M. Culver, J.C. Carey, N.G. Copeland, N.A. Jenkins, R. White, and P. O'Connell. 1990. Deletions and a translocation interrupt a cloned gene at the neurofibromatosis type 1 locus. *Cell* **62**: 187–192.

Vousden, K.H. and C.J. Marshall. 1984. Three different *ras* genes in mouse tumours: Evidence for oncogene activation during progression of a mouse lymphocyte. *EMBO J.* **3**: 913–917.

Waterfield, M.D., G.J. Scrace, N. Whittle, P. Stroobant, A. Johnson, A. Wasteson, B. Westermark, C.-H. Heldin, J.S. Huang, and T.F. Deuel. 1983. Platelet-derived growth factor is structurally related to the putative transforming protein p28^{sis} of simian sarcoma virus. *Nature* **304**: 35–39.

Weinberg, R.A. 1989. The molecular basis of retinoblastomas. *Ciba Found. Symp.* **142**: 99–111.

Weinberger, C., C.C. Thompson, E.S. Ong, R. Lebo, D. Gruol, and R.M. Evans. 1986. The c-*erb*-A gene encodes a thyroid hormone receptor. *Nature* **324**: 641–646.

Whyte, P., K.J. Buchkovich, J.M. Horowitz, S.H. Friend, M. Raybuck, R.A. Weinberg, and E. Harlow. 1988. Association between an oncogene and an anti-oncogene. The adenovirus E1A proteins bind to the retinoblastoma gene product. *Nature* **334**: 124–129.

Wiener, F., G. Klein, and H. Harris. 1971. The analysis of malignancy by cell fusion. III. Hybrids between diploid fibroblasts and other tumour cells. *J. Cell Sci.* **8:** 681–692.

———. 1973. The analysis of malignancy by cell fusion. IV. Hybrids between tumour cells and a malignant L cell derivative. *J. Cell Sci.* **12:** 253–261.

———. 1974. The analysis of malignancy by cell fusion. V. Further evidence of the ability of normal diploid cells to suppress malignancy. *J. Cell Sci.* **15:** 177–183.

Willingham, M.C., I. Pastan, T.Y. Shih, and E.M. Scolnick. 1980. Localization of the *src* gene product of the Harvey strain of MSV to plasma membrane of transformed cells by electron microscopic immunochemistry. *Cell* **19:** 1005–1014.

Willott, E., M.S. Balda, A.S. Fanning, B. Jameson, C. Van Itallie, and J.M. Anderson. 1993. The tight junction protein ZO-1 is homologous to the *Drosophila* discs-large tumor suppressor protein of septate junctions. *Proc. Natl. Acad. Sci.* **90:** 7834–7838.

Wright, J.A., H.S. Smith, F.M. Watt, M.C. Hancock, D.L. Hudson, and G.R. Stark. 1990. DNA amplification is rare in normal human cells. *Proc. Natl. Acad. Sci.* **87:** 1791–1795.

Wu, X., J.H. Bayle, D. Olson, and A.J. Levine. 1993. The p53-*mdm*-2 autoregulatory feedback loop. *Genes Dev.* **7:** 1126–1132.

Xu, H.J., J. Sumegi, S.Z. Hu, A. Banerjee, E. Uzvolgyi, G. Klein, and W.F. Benedict. 1991. Intraocular tumor formation of RB reconstituted retinoblastoma cells. *Cancer Res.* **51:** 4481–4485.

Yang, Y.-C., H. Okayama, and P. Howley. 1985. Bovine papillomavirus contains multiple transforming genes. *Proc. Natl. Acad. Sci.* **82:** 1030–1034.

Yates, J.L., N. Warren, and B. Sugden. 1985. Stable replication of plasmids derived from Epstein-Barr virus in various mammalian cells. *Nature* **313:** 812–814.

Yin, Y., M.A. Tainsky, F.Z. Bischoff, L.C. Strong, and G.M. Wahl. 1992. Wild type p53 restores cell cycle control and inhibits gene amplification in cells with mutant p53 alleles. *Cell* **70:** 937–948.

Yoakum, G.H., J.F. Lechner, E.W. Gabrielson, B.E. Korba, L. Malan-Shibley, J.C. Willey, M.G. Valerio, A.M. Shamsuddin, B.F. Trump, and C.C. Harris. 1985. Transformation of human bronchial epithelial cells transfected by Harvey *ras* oncogene. *Science* **227:** 1174–1179.

Yunis, J.J. and N.K.C. Ramsay. 1978. Retinoblastoma and subband deletion of chromosome 13. *Am. J. Dis. Child.* **132:** 161–163.

Zenke, M., A. Muñoz, J. Sap, B. Vennström, and H. Beug. 1990. v-*erb*A oncogene activation entails the loss of hormone-dependent regulator activity of c-*erb*A. *Cell* **61:** 1035–1049.

Zenke, M., P. Kahn, C. Disela, B. Vennström, A. Leutz, K. Keegan, M.J. Hayman, H.-J. Choi, N. Yew, J.D. Engel, and H. Beug. 1988. v-*erb*A specifically suppresses transcription of the avian erythrocyte anion transporter (band 3) gene. *Cell* **52:** 107–119.

zur Hausen, H. 1991. Human papillomavirus in the pathogenesis of anogenital cancer. *Virology* **184:** 9–13.

Name Index

Subject Index